PHRASE STRUCTURE AND THE LEXICON

Studies in Natural Language and Linguistic Theory

VOLUME 33

The titles published in this series are listed at the end of this volume.

PHRASE STRUCTURE AND THE LEXICON

Edited by

JOHAN ROORYCK

Leiden University,
Leiden, The Netherlands

and

LAURIE ZARING

Macalester College, St. Paul,
Minnesota, U.S.A.

KLUWER ACADEMIC PUBLISHERS

DORDRECHT / BOSTON / LONDON

Library of Congress Cataloging-in-Publication Data

Phrase structure and the lexicon / edited by Johan Rooryck and Laurie Zaring.
p. cm. -- (Studies in natural language and linguistic theory ; v. 33)
Includes bibliographical references and index.
ISBN 0-7923-3745-X (hb : acid free paper)
1. Phrase structure grammar. 2. Lexicology. I. Rooryck, Johan. II. Zaring, Laurie Ann, 1954- . III. Series.
P158.3.P48 1995
415--dc20 95-37660

ISBN 0-7923-3745-X

Published by Kluwer Academic Publishers,
P.O. Box 17, 3300 AA Dordrecht, The Netherlands.

Kluwer Academic Publishers incorporates
the publishing programmes of
D. Reidel, Martinus Nijhoff, Dr W. Junk and MTP Press.

Sold and distributed in the U.S.A. and Canada
by Kluwer Academic Publishers,
101 Philip Drive, Norwell, MA 02061, U.S.A.

In all other countries, sold and distributed
by Kluwer Academic Publishers Group,
P.O. Box 322, 3300 AH Dordrecht, The Netherlands.

Printed on acid-free paper

Printed in the Netherlands

TABLE OF CONTENTS

LIST OF CONTRIBUTORS

Mark C. Baker
Department of Linguistics
McGill University
1001 Sherbrooke St. W.
Montreal, Quebec
Canada H3A 1G5
mbaker@langs.lan.mcgill.ca

William Croft
Department of Linguistics
University of Manchester
Oxford Road
Manchester M13 9PL
United Kingdom
w.croft@man.ac.uk

Anna-Maria Di Sciullo
Département de Linguistique
Université du Québec à Montréal
Case Postale 8888, Succursale
Centre-Ville
Montréal, Québec
Canada H3C 3P8
r36650@er.uqam.ca

Angelika Kratzer
Department of Linguistics
University of Massachusetts
Amherst, MA 01003
kratzer@cs.umass.edu

David Lebeaux
Department of Linguistics
Georgetown University
Washington, D.C. 20057

Johan Rooryck
Vakgroep Frans
Postbus 9515
Van Wijkplaats 2
RA 2300 Leiden
The Netherlands
rooryck@rullet.LeidenUniv.nl

Jerrold M. Sadock
Department of Linguistics
University of Chicago
Chicago, IL 60637
sadock@sapir.uchicago.edu

Margaret Speas
Department of Linguistics
University of Massachusetts
Amherst, MA 01003
pspeas@linguist.umass.edu

Dominique Sportiche
Department of Linguistics
University of California
Los Angeles, CA 90024-1543
sportich@cognet.ucla.edu

Tim Stowell
Department of Linguistics
University of California
Los Angeles, CA 90024-1543
iml7tim@mvs.oac.ucla.edu

Laurie Zaring
Linguistics Program
Macalester College
1600 Grand Ave.
St. Paul, MN 55105-1899
zaring@macalstr.edu

INTRODUCTION

Johan Rooryck and Laurie Zaring

0. BACKGROUND

The present volume has its origins a series of lectures examining the relation between phrase structure and the lexicon, which took place during the academic year 1992-1993 at Indiana University. Billed as the Indiana Lecture Series in Formal Syntax: Phrase Structure and the Lexicon, it featured thirteen speakers who were invited on a biweekly basis to lecture on their research in this area. Apart from the authors of the papers included in this volume, speakers for the lecture series also included Stephen Anderson, David Dowty, Richard Larson, and Beth Levin.

The lecture series was intended as a seminar and discussion forum for graduate students and faculty in the various language-oriented departments at Indiana University. The initiative for this lectures series grew out of the more informal Syntax Reading Group at Indiana University, which brought together the syntacticians of the various language-oriented departments. Besides the editors of this volume, who were active in the Department of French and Italian at the time, the lecture series project involved nine other linguists in seven departments: Clancy Clements (Spanish & Portuguese), Phil Connell (Speech & Hearing), Henry Smith (Germanic Studies), George Fowler (Slavic Languages & Literatures), Steve Franks (Linguistics/ Slavic Languages & Literatures), Louise McNally (Linguistics), Linda Schwartz (Linguistics), Alice ter Meulen (Linguistics/ Philosophy), Natsuko Tsujimura (East Asian Languages & Cultures). We would like to thank our colleagues and students for their unflagging energy, enthusiastic participation, and flawless cooperation in our joint enterprise.

One of our hopes for the lecture series was that it would provide a larger forum for the general Great Lakes area for linguists to come together to discuss syntactic theory. This hope was certainly realized, as the lecture series drew regular audiences not only from Indiana University but also from surrounding institutions such as Purdue University, Ohio State University, and the University of Illinois at Urbana-Champaign. The lecture series was made possible thanks to the generous support of the Multidisciplinary Seminars Fund of the Office of Academic Affairs and Dean of the Faculties at Indiana University.

1. OVERVIEW

The papers in this volume can be subdivided into three categories, each reflecting current and complementary concerns about the relation between phrase structure and the lexicon. These issues are traditionally important ones in various frameworks, and they become essential in a framework such as the Minimalist program, where the lexicon is largely reduced to configurational and computational properties of the grammar (Chomsky 1993, Hale & Keyser 1993). Topics addressed in this volume include the mapping between thematic information and phrase structure, the way in which the configurational character of functional categories determines interpretation in a theory of phrase structure, and methodological discussions about core assumptions of phrase structure itself. One of the essential themes shared by the first two issues is that projection and interpretation go hand in hand: a successful projection is an interpretable one.

In the last few years, there has been a radical shift in the way the relation between phrase structure and the lexicon is viewed in generative grammar. Until the 1980's, the prevalent view was that thematic roles or sets of roles were organized at different levels in 'grids' and 'Lexical Conceptual Structures'. Thematic roles were projected to an independent level of phrase structure (DS), and constrained by several mechanisms such as thematic hierarchies, the Projection Principle, and the Theta Criterion. Meaning and phrase structure were viewed as separate entities. In recent years, there has been a growing body of work arguing that, to a large extent, phrase structure itself encodes lexical information and determines interpretation in the thematic domain. Some of this work even reformulates the intuitions of Generative Semantics in a more constrained context.

In this vein, Anna-Maria Di Sciullo argues that subcategorization frames or theta-grids are insufficient to account for the properties of morphological selection. She shows that argument selection in word formation can be more successfully analyzed if selection is taken to be configurational in nature. More specifically, she proposes that morphological selection is X' selection: affixes select exclusively in terms of X' positions such as Specifier and Complement. As a result, selection is derived from independent properties of the grammar, and lexical information is expressed in terms of configurational properties.

Developing similar concerns in a different domain of the grammar, Mark Baker tackles problems raised by thematic hierarchies. Baker shows that inconsistencies between various thematic hierarchies proposed in the literature are due to the presence of Dative Shift alternations, and observes that unaccusative verbs do not exhibit these alternations. An explanation for this fact is derived from the interaction of principles of Binding theory with the projection of thematic roles in X' structure. On the basis of data from various languages, he argues that the correct hierarchy is Agent>Theme>Path. Developing his UTAH (Baker 1988), he proposes a set of universal mapping principles for thematic roles, where Path arguments map to the complement of

V, Theme/Patients to the lowest specifier of V', and Agents to a position outside the minimal VP. Again, thematic information is encoded in terms of configurational properties.

Addressing the issue of phrase structure in another domain, Margaret Speas investigates the status of null pronominal objects in Navajo. Following Rizzi (1986), she assumes that null pronouns must meet both a licensing and an identification condition. More specifically, she demonstrates that distributional restrictions on null pronominal objects in Navajo can be explained if it is assumed that null objects obey the identification condition expressed by the Generalized Control Rule of Huang (1984). Distinguishing three types of null objects, she argues that relevant licensing condition on two subtypes of null objects involves rich agreement. However, it appears that there are languages lacking rich agreement but with *pro* in object position. Speas accounts for these phenomena by a rule of economy of projection.

A second series of papers is concerned with the way in which functional categories derive aspects of sentential interpretation. Three issues in this research program are investigated here: external arguments as arguments of functional projections (Kratzer), the specificity interpretation of clitics (Sportiche), and the interpretation of tense (Stowell). In all three cases, phrase structure is put to use to derive interpretive effects.

Angelika Kratzer proposes that external arguments are not part of the verb. She argues that external arguments are mapped into phrase structure as parts of a functional projection corresponding to Voice (VoiceP), applying neo-Davidsonian argument association in the syntax. An analysis of gerunds is proposed in which the three different interpretations of gerunds (*of*$_{\text{ing}}$: *his rebuilding of the barn*, poss$_{\text{ing}}$: *his rebuilding the barn*, acc$_{\text{ing}}$: *we remember him rebuilding the barn*) result from the attachment of the *-ing* suffix to different categories, V, VP, and VoiceP. One of the interesting features of this analysis is that the notion 'external argument' can be dispensed with.

In 'The Phrase Structure of Tense', Tim Stowell attempts to derive the interpretation of tense from a set of functional projections. He develops a theory that seeks to reduce the interpretive effects of tense to independently motivated syntactic principles. Following Zagona (1990), TENSE is viewed as a dyadic predicate which takes two time-denoting arguments. [+PAST] T is a predicate with a temporal ordering similar to the preposition *after*, specifying a temporal ordering between S(peech) time and E(vent) time in sentences such as *John ate an apple* (S after E). The internal argument of T is a Z(eit)-phrase (ZP) where Z relates the VP to an E, much in the way D relates to NP by making it referential. The external argument of T is another ZP encoding S, which in embedded clauses has the properties of a PRO controlled by the ZP of the matrix clause. It is argued that Reichenbachian R(eference) time can be dispensed with.

Reconciling both the movement and base-generation approaches to clitics, Dominique Sportiche provides an analysis in which clitics are functional heads or clitic 'Voices' in the functional structure of the clause. In their specifier position, clitics license a moved *pro* which corresponds to the argument they designate. Two types of clitics are distinguished: clitics such as French *en* 'of-it' or *le* 'it/him', which give rise to specificity effects, and dative clitics such as French *lui* 'to-him/her' which do not exhibit such effects. The clitics entailing specificity are likened to *wh*-complementizers or negative heads, since specificity is viewed as a quantificational, operator-like property. This way of viewing things allows Sportiche to draw an interesting parallel between the licensing of [+specific] clitics and Germanic DP Scrambling, which also exhibits specificity effects; since Romance clitics are analyzed as clitic heads with an empty *pro* in specifier position, Germanic specific scrambled DPs may be accounted for as sitting in the specifier position of an empty clitic.

A third set of papers involve more general methodological discussions about core assumptions of phrase structure and its relation with the lexicon. Bill Croft's 'What's a Head?' is a methodological reflection on the criteria, observations, and intuitions that underlie the notion of 'head of a phrase' in various linguistic traditions. Within the perspective of functional and cognitive grammar, he uncovers interesting parallels with recent work in generative syntax. A semantic definition of head-hood is carefully developed, based on a notion of Primary Information-Bearing Unit (PIBU). Diachronic evidence from grammaticalization and categorial reanalysis are shown to be crucial for a proper understanding of head-hood.

In 'The Lexicon as Bridge between Phrase Structure Components', Jerry Sadock gives an incisive sketch of how context-free phrase structure grammar (PSG) can deal with natural language, thereby suggesting an alternative to a transformational view of syntax. In order to overcome the disadvantages of Generalized Phrase Structure Grammar formalisms, Sadock argues in favor of a grammar with distinct phrase structure grammars for syntax, semantics, and morphology, which are integrated via the lexicon. This framework is illustrated by its application to English complementation and West Greenlandic reflexive reference.

David Lebeaux's 'Determining the Kernel' addresses the question as to how children acquire D-structure on the basis of surface structure evidence after considerable syntactic movement has occurred. The question is raised as to what the basic phrase structure is. Lebeaux argues that children are able to determine which structures of a given set of sentences with different word orders (e.g., active, passive, object-focus) have no movement and constitute the 'kernel' of the grammar. Government-direction is set on the basis of this kernel of structures without movement: children do not admit sentences with traces into the kernel. With respect to head movement, kernel sentences involve bare lexical heads, but not combinations of lexical and functional heads, which have to be derived by movement. The methodological consequences of this analysis are worked out with respect to *wh*-movement, passive formation, and complementation.

The articles in this volume present various reflections on the nature of levels of representation and the basic elements and properties they involve in different domains of the grammar. They constitute an important contribution to the long-standing debate about the nature of phrase structure and its relation to the lexicon. It is the hope of the editors that this book will pave the way for a better understanding for these important issues.

REFERENCES

Baker, Mark: 1988, *Incorporation: a Theory of Grammatical Function Changing*, University of Chicago Press, Chicago.

Chomsky, Noam: 1993, 'A Minimalist Program for Linguistic Theory', in K. Hale and S. J. Keyser (eds.), *The View From Building 20*, MIT Press, Cambridge, MA, pp. 1-52.

Hale, Kenneth and Samuel J. Keyser: 1993, 'On Argument Structure and the Lexical Expression of Syntactic Relations', in K. Hale and S.J. Keyser (eds.), *The View From Building 20*, MIT Press, Cambridge, MA, pp. 53-110.

Huang, J.: 1991, 'Remarks on the Status of the Null Object', in Freiden, Robert (ed.), *Principles and Parameters in Comparative Grammar*, MIT Press, Cambridge, MA.

Rizzi, Luigi: 1986, 'Null Objects in Italian and the Theory of *pro*', *Linguistic Inquiry* **17**: 501-557.

Zagona, Karen: 1990, 'Times as Temporal Argument Structure', unpublished, University of Washington, Seattle.

ON THE STRUCTURAL POSITIONS OF THEMES AND GOALS*

Mark Baker

0. INTRODUCTION: THEMATIC HIERARCHIES

A central concern of linguistic theory is to account for how the arguments of a given lexical item are associated with positions in a syntactic structure. Many theorists hold that this mapping is mediated by a so-called thematic hierarchy. In Principles-and-Parameters style theories this typically works as follows. A verb selects arguments with certain thematic (θ-) roles. These θ-roles are ranked by the thematic hierarchy, and phrase structure is constructed according to the rankings. This mapping obeys a constraint like the one given in (1).

(1) If the θ-role of an argument X is higher than the θ-role of a second argument Y, then X c-commands Y at the level of D-structure.[1] (see Larson 1988, Speas 1990, Baker 1989, Grimshaw 1990).

Less structurally oriented theories get similar effects without the use of phrase structure by allowing certain principles to refer to the thematic hierarchy directly (Foley and Van Valin 1984, Kiparsky 1987, Bresnan and Kanerva 1989, Bresnan and Moshi 1990, etc.).

In spite of its rather wide acceptance, this body of work is threatened by well-known controversies about what exactly the thematic hierarchy is. All agree that agents rank higher than themes. However, there is no consensus on the ranking of goal and benefactive roles relative to themes and locations.[2] Suppressing certain finer-grained details, the different positions can be grouped into three major classes as summarized in (2).

(2) Thematic Hierarchies

a. Agent > benefactive/goal > theme > location
Kiparsky (1987) --(English idioms)
Bresnan and colleagues --various Bantu facts, indirectly
Machobane (1989) --various Bantu facts

(2) b. Agent > goal/experiencer/location > theme
Jackendoff (1972) --binding of English reflexives
Grimshaw (1990) --Light verbs in Japanese, psych verbs
Li (1990) --Chinese compounds
Foley and Van Valin (1984) --(various)

c. Agent > theme > goal/benefactive/location
Carrier-Duncan (1985) --Tagalog morphosyntax
Larson (1988) --(English idioms)
Baker (1989) --Serial verbs in Kwa, Creoles

The Kiparsky/Bresnan hierarchy in (2a) sharply distinguishes goals from locations, ranking goals higher than themes but locations lower. In contrast, the Jackendoff/Grimshaw hierarchy in (2b) combines goals and locations and ranks them both higher than themes. Finally, the Larson/Baker hierarchy in (2c) is like the Jackendoff/Grimshaw hierarchy in that it combines goals and locations; however it ranks them both lower than themes.

The difficulty in resolving this controversy is largely due to the presence of so-called Dative Shift alternations within and across languages. Thus, many three-place verbs in English can appear in either the NP-PP construction given in (3) or the double-NP construction in (4).

(3) a. John passed the ring to Mary.
b. Peter opened a beer for Max.

(4) a. John passed Mary the ring.
b. Peter opened Max a beer.

In sentences like (3), the theme clearly has prominence over the goal by a variety of syntactic tests, whereas in (4) the goal has prominence over the theme by those same tests (Larson 1988). In order to maintain a consistent thematic hierarchy, one must decide which of these constructions are basic, and which are derived. The picture is further complicated by the fact that some languages seem to have (3)-like constructions but not (4)-like ones (e.g., French); others seem to have (4)-like constructions but not (3)-like ones (e.g., Mohawk, some Bantu languages). Linguists have in practice assumed different thematic hierarchies in part because they have been concerned with different languages and different phenomena.

Significantly, this controversy occurs not only across theoretical frameworks, but also within theoretical frameworks, even when the role of the thematic hierarchy is held relatively constant. Thus within Principles-and-Parameters, Larson (1988) assumed that the NP-PP constructions are base-generated and NP-NP constructions are derived by NP-movement in English. However, this choice was not particularly principled, even given his assumptions. His analysis works just is well in reverse, where the NP-NP structure is base-generated and the NP-PP structure is derived by NP movement, as assumed in Aoun and Li (1989). Given the crosslinguistic differences alluded to above, one might even entertain the idea that languages differ on exactly this point, with theme-dominant constructions being basic in some languages (French) and goal-dominant constructions being basic in others (Sesotho and Mohawk, where 'Dative Shift' seems obligatory). Essentially this position is put forward by Dryer (1987) in a Relational Grammar framework; it is also mentioned by Larson (1988: 351, fn. 18).

This article contributes to the general discussion by pointing out a fact of considerable crosslinguistic generality that has largely escaped attention in the literature on Dative-Shift-like alternations: the fact that for the most part there is no similar Dative Shift alternation with unaccusative verbs. This fact is rather mysterious under most traditional accounts. It is particularly curious given that the restriction does not generalize to passive constructions. Nevertheless, a principled and adequately general explanation can be given using some recent developments in syntactic theory. In developing this explanation, I build an argument that (2c) is the correct thematic hierarchy. Indeed, we will see that this hierarchy is rather directly motivated even in languages like Sesotho and Mohawk, which otherwise seem to fit in more naturally with one of the other hierarchies.

1. A GAP IN THE PARADIGM OF DATIVE SHIFT

Since Burzio (1986), the standard assumption has been that unaccusative verbs have selectional properties which are the same as those of comparable transitive verbs. Indeed, the NP-PP sentences in (3) have straightforward unaccusative variants, as shown in (5).

(5) a. The ring passed t to Mary.
 b. The beer opened t for Max.

However, there are no unaccusative variants of the sentences in (4). In classical GB theory, such sentences would have the unremarkable-looking D-structure shown in (6).

(6) e [$_{VP}$ passed Mary the ring]

However, neither NP can be moved to derive an acceptable sentence from this source. If the theme NP moved, one would expect sentences like (7); if the goal NP moved, one would derive the sentences in (8).

(7) a. *The ring passed Mary t.
 b. *The beer opened Max t.

(8) a. *Mary passed t the ring.
b. *Max opened t a beer.
(OK only if *Mary* and *Max* are the agents)

Neither type of sentence is grammatical. As far as I know, there are no English verbs can be simultaneously a double-object verb and an unaccusative verb. The pattern is summarized in (9).[3]

(9)

English Vs		with agent	without agent
subcat frame	__NP PP	OK	OK
	__NP NP	OK	*

This gap becomes even more striking when one recalls that Dative Shift can interact with passive. Thus the sentences in (10) are acceptable, at least in some dialects.[4]

(10) a. Mary was passed t the ring.
b. Max was opened t a beer.

Under Burzio's assumptions, the underlying structure of unaccusatives like (8) is essentially identical to that of the passives in (10). Thus, it is hard to see why one should be good and the other bad.

The only reference I am aware of that considers roughly this range of data within a Chomskian framework is Everaert (1990). Everaert shows that essentially the same empirical generalization holds in Dutch and English, with sentences like (7) and (8) (which he calls inchoatives) being ungrammatical in both. His tentative account of sentences like (7) makes crucial use of the Jackendoff/Grimshaw thematic hierarchy in (2b). Thus, he takes 'inchoativization' to involve the lexical deletion of the external argument of a verb, followed by the externalization of the highest remaining argument on the thematic hierarchy. Since the goal is hypothesized to be higher than the theme, it becomes the external argument and hence the structural subject. (7) is thus ungrammatical because the goal is the external argument but is expressed in an internal position--a violation of Theta theory. By these assumptions, however, the sentences in (8) are expected to be fully grammatical, contrary to fact. These Everaert rules out by Case theory (1990:127): he claims that goal objects are inherently Case-marked, and as such cannot be moved to the subject position. This assumption is independently motivated by the fact that goal objects cannot move to subject position even in passive sentences in Dutch. Thus, (11a) and (11b) are taken to be parallel:

(11) a. *Hij werd __ het eten bezorgd (door mij). (cf. (10))
He was the food delivered by me.
"He was delivered the food by me."

b. *Hij onglipte __ de teugels. (cf. (8))
He slipped the reins.
"The reins slipped out of his hands."

However, Everaert's analysis does not generalize correctly beyond Dutch. In English there is little reason to say that the goal NP receives inherent Case; on the contrary, it may move into the subject position in passive sentences as shown in (10). Nevertheless, the unaccusatives in (8) are still ruled out. Thus, Everaert's suggestions are not adequate to properly distinguish passives and unaccusatives. Moreover, Everaert's theory holds that sentences like (7) are ruled out for fundamental Theta-theoretic reasons, while sentences like (8) are merely ruled out by Case theory. Assuming that the principles of Theta theory are more universal than those of Case assignment, we would predict that sentences like (8) should be possible in some languages, whereas sentences like (7) should be impossible in all languages. In fact, we will see below that the opposite is true. Thus, while Everaert's theory seems to appeal to the right ingredients for an explanation, the patterns do not come out correctly as they stand, particularly from a broad cross-linguistic perspective.

Nor do other generative frameworks hold the key to this problem. Perhaps the most likely place to find material on this topic would be the Relational Grammar literature, in the light of its extensive work on the possibilities and limits of grammatical relation-changing. In RG terms, the grammatical examples in (10) are derived by 3-to-2 advancement, followed by passive. Similarly, the impossible examples in (8) could be derived by 3-to-2 advancement, followed by unaccusative advancement. Such a derivation would not violate any known relational laws; indeed equivalent derivations have been proposed for certain psychological verbs (Donna Gerdts, personal communication). In order to rule out such a derivation, it seems that we must put a condition on 3-to-2 advancement (Dative Shift) such that it only applies in clauses that have a 1 (an underlying subject). This is a very peculiar-looking condition, and I take it to be more a statement of the problem than a solution to it. Thus, the ungrammaticality of the examples in (8) is as mysterious in classical RG terms as it is in classical GB terms.[5]

2. EVIDENCE FROM OTHER LANGUAGES

Significantly, the deviance of examples like (7) and (8) is not limited to English and Dutch. On the contrary, essentially the same effect can be seen in languages as geographically and typologically diverse as Mohawk, Japanese, and certain Bantu languages. This section briefly presents the relevant facts from Sesotho (Bantu), and Japanese; Mohawk facts will be introduced when they become relevant in section 3.

Sesotho[6] has no prepositions comparable to *to* or *for* in English. Hence there is no direct correlate of (3) in the language. Sesotho does however have applicative constructions that are very much like (4) in English; an example is given in (12).

(12) Banana ba-pheh-el-a 'me nama.
girls SP-cook-appl-fv mother meat
"The girls are cooking my mother meat."

Indeed, the applicative construction in Sesotho is much more productive than in English, perhaps because it is overtly marked by a morpheme on the verb. Benefactive applicatives can be formed from almost any transitive verb, as well as from unergative verbs:

(13) Bashanyana ba-hobel-l-a morena.
boys SP-dance-appl-fv chief
"The boys are dancing for the chief."

Nevertheless, benefactive applicative constructions cannot be formed from verbs that are unambiguously unaccusative. Again this is true regardless of whether the theme NP becomes the subject ((14)) or the benefactive NP becomes the subject ((15)).

(14) a. *Lintja li-hol-el-a nkhono.
dogs SP-grow-appl-fv grandma
"The dogs are growing for my grandma."

b. *Baeti ba-fihl-ets-e morena.
visitors SP-arrive-appl-fv chief
"The visitors have arrived for the chief."

(15) *Nkhono li-hol-el-a lintja.
grandma SP-grow-appl-fv dogs
"The dogs are growing for my grandma."

This restriction on applicatives was discovered in Machobane (1989); Alsina and Mchombo (1988) independently found the same paradigm in Chichewa.

Finally, consider the passive-applicative sentence in (16). This sentence is perfectly acceptable in Sesotho with the benefactive NP as the surface subject.

(16) 'Me o-pheh-ets-o-e nama
mother SP-cook-appl-pass-fv meat
"My mother has been cooked the meat."

Thus, the surprising contrast between unaccusatives like (8)/(15) and passives like (10)/(16) is found in both English and Sesotho.

Consider next Japanese.[7] (17) is a simple example of an agent-theme-goal verb:

(17) John-ga Mary-ni hon-o watashi-ta.
John-nom Mary-dat book-acc pass-pst
"John passed Mary a book."

Whether this should be taken as a Dative-Shifted sentence comparable to English (4) or a NP-PP structure comparable to (3) is a subtle question, given Japanese's relatively free word order and the presence of the particle *ni*, which could be analyzed as either a Case marker or a postposition. In fact, most Japanese specialists agree that (17) is like (4) in English in that the goal asymmetrically c-commands the theme (Hoji 1985); in this respect, (17) is comparable to a Dative-Shift structure. More controversial is the question of whether (17) is structurally ambiguous, having also an NP-PP structure in which the theme c-commands the goal. This seems to vary from speaker to speaker; see Zushi (1992) for relevant considerations and discussion.

Fortunately, the facts about morphologically related unaccusative verbs are clear. These are possible when the theme receives nominative Case:

(18) Hon-ga Mary-ni watar-ta.
book-nom Mary-dat pass-pst
"The book passed to Mary."

Moreover, the *ni*-phrase in this structure behaves unambiguously like a PP. For example, some Japanese speakers marginally allow quantifiers to be floated off of *ni*-phrases in transitive double-object sentences like (17). However, such speakers do not allow superficially similar quantifier float in sentences like (18). Thus, one finds minimal contrasts like the following:

(19) a. ?John-ga hon-o otoko-ni san-nin watashi-ta.
John-nom book-acc men-dat three-CL pass-pst
"John passed three men books."

b. *Hon-ga otoko-ni san-nin watar-ta.
book-nom men-dat three-CL pass-pst
"Books passed to three men."

This suggests that (18) is structurally parallel to the acceptable (5) in English. It also implies that there is no Japanese structure parallel to (7) in English; if there were, then the two sentences in (19) would have the same status.

On the other hand, unaccusative versions of sentences like (17) in which the goal is the nominative-marked surface subject are completely impossible:

(20) *Mary-ga hon-o watar-ta.
Mary-nom book-acc pass-pst
"The book passed to Mary." (lit. "Mary passed the book.")

Once again, there is a minimal contrast between (20) and passive constructions. In passives, it is perfectly acceptable for the goal phrase to become the nominative-marked subject:

(21) Mary-ga hon-o watas-are-ta.
Mary-nom book-acc pass-pass-pst
"Mary was passed the book."

Thus, some kind of Dative Shift seems possible in transitives and passives but not in unaccusatives—a generalization that holds true over these three otherwise quite different languages.

Machobane (1989) and Alsina and Mchombo (1988) both explain the ungrammaticality of examples like (14) and (15) in Bantu languages by way of a restriction on applicative formation in the lexicon. The specific condition that they propose makes crucial use of the thematic hierarchy in (2a):

(22) The external argument in an applicative construction must be higher on the thematic hierarchy than the argument introduced by the applicative suffix.

Since the subject of an unaccusative verb is a theme, and this is ranked lower than goal and benefactive in (2a), (22) forbids the applicative affix to add an argument with either of these roles to this type of verb. On the other hand, (22) allows a goal argument to be added to any verb with an agent role; it also allows one to add a lower role (such as a location) to an unaccusative verb. This proposal correctly describes the pattern in question. However, it is not clear whether these researchers want to analyze (22) as an ad hoc property of the grammar of (certain) Bantu languages or as a universal principle grounded in the fundamentals of Theta theory. If we take the first interpretation, then we miss the similarity between the Bantu facts and those of English, Dutch, and Japanese, none of which have (overt) applicative morphology. On the other hand, the proposal makes little sense as a universal, quasi-semantic claim. Surely, it is reasonable a priori to say that an event benefited someone even if that event was not caused or performed by a volitional actor. The grammatical English sentences in (5) are examples of this, as is the Japanese (18); we will see others below in Mohawk and even Sesotho. Thus, we want to derive the lack of these applicatives from principles of syntax, not from general semantic considerations.[8]

3. UNACCUSATIVES WITH THEME SUBJECTS

A full explanation of why there is no Dative Shift with unaccusative verbs involves two stages. First, one must rule out structures like (7) and (14), where the theme becomes the subject, and a bare NP goal remains a complement. Second, one must rule out structures like (8)/(15)/(20), in which the goal is the subject and the theme remains a complement. I consider the first set of examples first.

These sentences can plausibly be accounted for in terms of Case theory. Since Burzio (1986), it has generally been assumed that unaccusative verbs do not assign structural accusative Case. When the theme NP moves to the subject position it receives nominative Case from the tensed inflection. What then about the goal NP? The only remaining possibility is that it could receive inherent Case from the verb. However, inherent Case is tied directly to θ-role assignment; only NPs which bear a specific θ-role to a given head can receive inherent Case from that head (Chomsky 1986). Specifically, in double object constructions the theme can receive inherent Case from the verb, but the goal cannot. This is seen in the fact that theme NPs can get the inherent genitive case (realized as *of*) assigned by deverbal nominalizations, but goal NPs cannot:

(23) a. the gift of a book to John
b. *the gift of John (of) a book
(Chomsky 1986:194-95; cf. also Kayne 1984)

These assumptions also provide the basis for one way of explaining certain familiar asymmetries between the two NPs in a double object construction, as discussed in Baker (1988a, 1988b). Thus, we can rule out the unaccusative (24b) and the passive in (24a) in the same way: the goal phrase violates the Case filter in both.

(24) a. ?*The ring was passed Mary t.
b. *The ring passed Mary t. (= (7a))

Note that this analysis is almost the exact opposite of Everaert (1990), who assumed that the goal (not the theme) received inherent Case in double object constructions; hence Everaert ruled out (8) by the Case filter rather than (7).

This analysis makes an interesting prediction. It predicts that if the goal argument happens to be a nominal that for some reason does not need Case, then these sentences should become possible. This seems to be correct. Machobane (1989) points out that ungrammatical sentences like (14) in Sesotho can become grammatical when the benefactive argument is expressed as a pronominal clitic attached to the verb. Thus, there are minimal contrasts like (25).

(25) a. *Letebele leo le-hol-el-e rona.
Letelbele that SP-grow-appl-fv us
"May that Letebele (clan name) grow up for us!"

b. Letebele leo le-re-hol-el-e.
Letelbele that SP-us-grow-appl-fv
"May that Letebele (clan name) grow up for us!"

Everett (1987) argues that a category which is cliticized onto the verb does not need to receive Case in order to be visible for θ-role assignment; Baker (1988a) makes a similar argument based on noun incorporation and passive morphology. Hence, the Visibility Condition has been broadened from its original formulation in Chomsky (1981) into (26):

(26) In order for an argument to be visible for θ-role assignment at LF, it must either
(i) be assigned Case, or
(ii) have its head morphologically united with an X^0

The theme NP in (25b) gets nominative Case in the subject position, while the goal is visible apart from Case, due to cliticization. Therefore, the example is grammatical.

The analysis also predicts that applicatives of unaccusative verbs should be acceptable if there is a language-specific way of assigning structural Case inside the VP. This seems to be true in Mohawk.[9] Mohawk is like Sesotho in that it lacks any overt adposition or Case marker for goals. Mohawk is also like Sesotho in that it has a productive applicative construction; a simple example is given in (27).

(27) Wa-hi-nohare-'s-e' ne atya'tawi.
fact-1sS/MsO-wash-ben-punc NE shirt
'I washed the shirt for him.'

Such applicatives can be formed from unergative verbs as well as from a wide variety of transitive verbs. Strikingly unlike the situation in Sesotho, however, applicative morphology can also attach to many unaccusative verbs. Two examples are:

(28) a. Ukw-ate-nohare-'s-e' ne atya'tawi.
fact/1sO-srfl-wash-ben-punc NE shirt
"The shirt came clean for/on me.'

b. Wa-ho-wis-v-'s-e' ne Sak.
fact-MsO-glass-fall-ben-punc NE Sak
"The glass fell on Sak."

(The fact that the non-goal NP has been incorporated into the verb in (28b) gives independent evidence that the verb is unaccusative, given the theory of noun incorporation in Baker (1988a).) This indicates once again that the restriction in (22) cannot be a universal one, even for languages with true applicatives. Crucially, in these examples the benefactive NP triggers *object* agreement on the verb; if one puts subject agreement on the verb instead, the result is ungrammatical:

(29) a. *Wa'-k-ate-nohare-'s-e' ne atya'tawi.
fact-1sS-srfl-wash-ben-punc NE shirt
"The shirt came clean for/on me."

b. *Wa-ha-wis-v-'s-e' ne Sak.
fact-MsS-fall-ben-punc NE Sak
"The glass fell on Sak."

According to the theory of agreement developed in Baker (in press: chapter 5), this indicates that the benefactive NP is still inside the VP at the point in the derivation that feeds the PF component.

Sentences like (28) are made possible by two special properties of Mohawk. First, theme nominals can incorporate into the verb. This means that they do not need to receive nominative Case from Infl; rather, they pass the Visibility Condition in (26) by clause (ii). Second, the nominative Case associated with Infl can be assigned inside the VP in Mohawk. This seems to be a parametric option, available in some languages but not in others. For example, den Besten (1985) argues that this type of Case assignment is possible in German examples like (30).

(30) ...daß [$_S$ meinem Bruder [$_{VP}$ deine Musik nicht gefällt]].
that my brother-dat your music-nom not please
"...that my brother doesn't like your music."

Baker (in press) gives independent evidence that this is possible in Mohawk as well. Thus, the proper analysis of (28b) in Mohawk is sketched in (31).

(31) e Infl [$_{VP}$ glass$_i$-fall t$_i$ Sak]

nominative

In conclusion, we see that prepositionless theme-goal constructions in which the goal remains in the VP are actually acceptable in some languages. When such sentences are ruled out, they are ruled out for relatively superficial Case-theoretic reasons.

Before going on, one complication must be mentioned. More detailed comparative work reveals an important difference between the two structures compared in (24). Unaccusative sentences like (24b) are ruled out more or less universally, whereas passive sentences comparable to (24a) are sometimes judged acceptable by speakers. Thus, sentences like (32) are rejected by most American English speakers, but are accepted by some British speakers, depending on obscure lexical factors.[10]

(32) a. (*)The ring was given Mary.
     b. (*)A beer was opened Max.

Similarly, passives of applicatives in which the theme becomes the subject are acceptable in Sesotho:

(33) Nama e-pheh-ets-o-e 'me.
     meat SP-cook-appl-pass-fv mother
     "The meat has been cooked my mother."

Directly parallel sentences are not possible in the related Chichewa, however (Alsina and Mchombo 1988; Baker 1988b).[11] This lack of similarity raises some doubt as to whether a unified account of (24a) and (24b) is desirable. The problem is not as serious as it may seem, however; I return to it in section 5 after a more detailed analysis of the passive has been introduced.

4. UNACCUSATIVES WITH GOAL SUBJECTS

Next I move on to the task of explaining the ungrammaticality of unaccusative sentences in which the goal is the surface subject. This is more interesting for two reasons. First, the ungrammaticality of these sentences is more universal, holding without exception across the languages and dialects in my sample. Second, it is more surprising, because it is here that the parallelism between unaccusative verbs and passives fails completely, as shown again in (34).

(34) a. Mary was passed t a ring. (= (10a))
     b. *Mary passed t a ring. (= (8a))

This lack of parallelism implies that one cannot plausibly account for this pattern in terms of Case theory alone. In (34b) the benefactive NP *Mary* gets nominative Case from Infl, while *a ring* gets inherent Case from the verb. As the theme of the verb, *a ring* is fully qualified to receive such Case. Any simple-minded adjustments to these assumptions would incorrectly rule out the acceptable (34a) as well.

Since Case-theoretic problems would be solved if the benefactive NP could move to subject position in sentences like (34b), I conclude that such movement must be impossible. This result becomes understandable once one takes into account the theory of Dative Shift presented in Larson (1988), together with some innovations from Travis (1991). Larson argues that verbs can take only a single complement (cf. also Kayne 1984). This implies there must be a structural asymmetry between themes and goals: goals project as the complements of the verb, while themes are associated with a higher position, as specifier of the VP. Hence, the base structure of *John passed the ring to Mary* (3a) in English is something like (35).

(35)

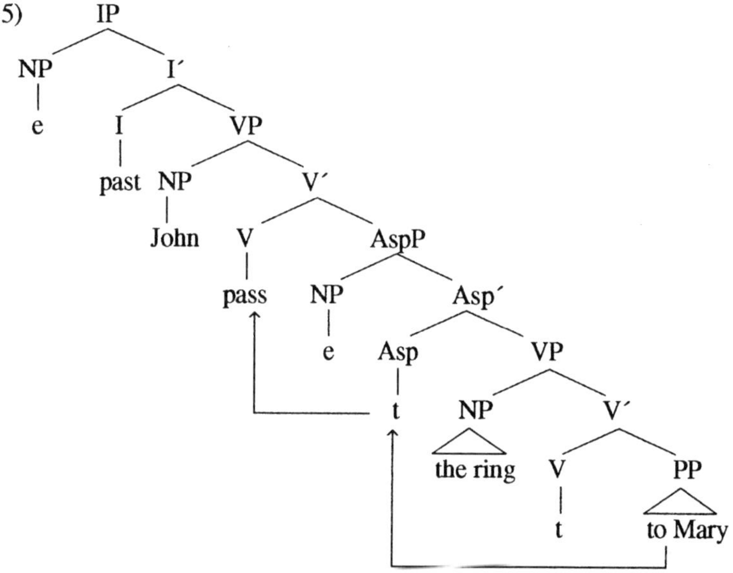

This structure correctly accounts for the fact that the theme NP acts like it c-commands the goal NP but not vice versa in sentences like (3).

Crucially, however, the c-command relationship is reversed in Dative-Shifted sentences like *John passed Mary the ring* (4a): here the goal phrase c-commands the theme phrase, but not vice-versa (Barss and Lasnik 1986). Larson accounts for this in terms of a passive-like NP movement. Following Travis (1991), I assume that the landing site of this movement is the specifier of an Aspect Phrase which immediately dominates the lower VP. Hence, the structure of (4a) is roughly (36).[12]

(36)

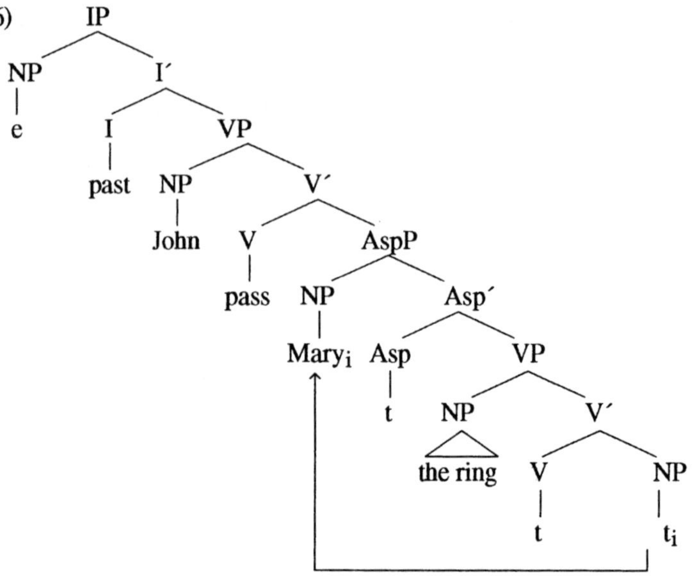

Furthermore, I assume that unergative verbs appear in exactly the same structures as transitive verbs, except that the specifier of the lower VP is left empty, because the verb takes no theme argument. (Alternatively, there might be a 'cognate object' generated in this position; compare Hale and Keyser 1993.) If an unergative verb appears with a goal or benefactive phrase, that phrase can either show up as a PP complement as in (35), or as an NP that moves to the specifier of AspP as in (36). This latter structure is the one associated with applicatives of unergative verbs, such as sentence (13) in Sesotho.

Consider now the structure of sentences with the unaccusative variant of *pass*. Here the underlying structure should be identical to that of the transitive variant, except that the higher VP shell is not generated, because there is no agent θ-role to assign. This does not disrupt the structure in (35) in any significant way; the theme *the ring* simply raises to the specifier of IP (possibly via the specifier of AspP) to receive Case, and nothing else changes. Thus, (37) is the analysis of *The ring passed to Mary* (5a):

(37)

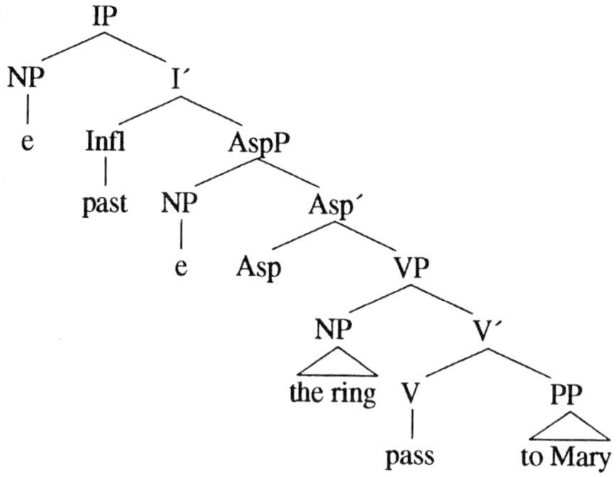

Consider, however, what a Dative Shift movement similar to (36) would look like if it started from an underlying structure like (37). If this were allowed, then the goal NP should be able to move on from the specifier of Aspect Phrase to the specifier of IP, generating ungrammatical sentences like *Mary passed the ring* (8a/34b):

(38)

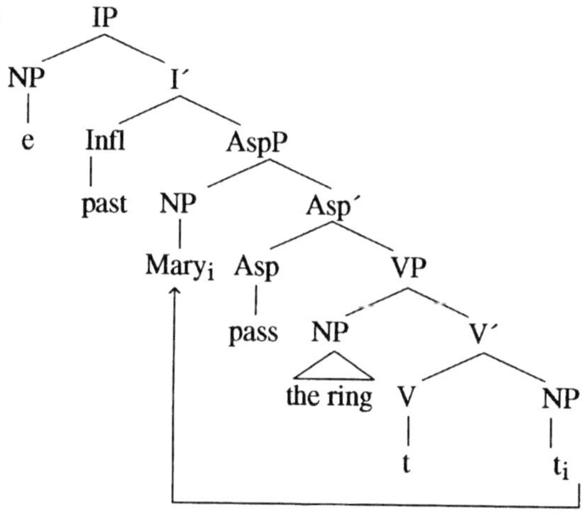

In purely geometrical terms, the illicit movement in (38) is identical to the grammatical movement in (36). There is, however, one crucial difference. In (38), the VP which the goal phrase moves out of is THEMATICALLY COMPLETE in the sense that all of the thematic roles determined by this version of *pass* are assigned within that VP. In (36) on the other hand, the VP which the goal phrase moves out of is not thematically complete in this sense: this version of *pass* takes an agent phrase that is not assigned until the higher VP shell. Suppose that this notion of thematic completeness is included in Chomsky's notion of a complete functional complex.[13] Then the desired distinction between (36) and (38) follows from known principles of UG plus the classical assumption from the Extended Standard Theory that NP traces are anaphors (Chomsky 1976; Chomsky 1981). The relevant notions of Binding theory can be characterized roughly as in (39), based on Chomsky (1986).

(39) a. A *complete functional complex* (CFC) is a category in which all the grammatical functions compatible with a head are present, and all the head's θ-roles are assigned.
b. The *governing category* of an anaphor X is the smallest CFC containing X, a governor of X, and a c-commanding NP distinct from X.
c. Anaphors (including NP trace) must be bound within their governing category.

According to these definitions, the NP-trace in (36) is bound within its governing category, but the NP-trace in (38) is not. Thus, (38) is ruled out as a kind of Specified Subject Condition violation. This is the core of my explanation of why unaccusative verbs cannot undergo Dative Shift crosslinguistically.

In this analysis it is the presence of the theme that prevents the goal from becoming the subject of the clause, because the theme NP counts as a kind of specified subject. This predicts that if the theme were somehow eliminated, movement of the goal should become possible. This is confirmed by the Sesotho contrast shown in (40).

(40) a. *Baeti ba-fihl-ets-e morena. (=(14b))
visitors SP-arrive-appl-fv chief
"The visitors have arrived for the chief."

b. Morena o-fihl-ets-o-e ke-baeti.
chief SP-arrive-appl-pass-fv by-visitors
"The visitors have arrived for the chief."

(40b) is the passive equivalent of the ungrammatical sentence in (40a); surprisingly, it is grammatical. Apparently, passive morphology in Sesotho has the unusual but not unprecedented property of being able to suppress the theme argument of an unaccusative verb.[14] Given this, the lower VP in a structure like (38) no longer qualifies as a complete functional complex, since it does not have a structural subject. Hence, the goal argument of the verb is not prevented from moving out of that VP, eventually reaching a position where it can receive nominative Case from Infl.

Note that in order for the analysis I have presented to work, certain quite precise assumptions must be made. To the degree the analysis is deemed successful, it counts as support for those assumptions, some of which bear on topics of recent interest within Principles and Parameters theory. First and most obviously, the analysis supports Larson's basic assumptions about the phrase structure of double object verbs. Larson's idea that theme NPs count as inner subjects in non-Dative Shifted structures had only rather abstract motivation. Here we have found evidence that such NPs may under certain circumstances count as subjects for Binding theory purposes, trapping goal phrases inside their c-command domain. On the other hand, it is not easy to see how a more traditional theory which had both themes and goals as complements of V could account for the fact that goals cannot reach the subject position when the verb is unaccusative.

Second, the analysis crucially assumes that goals project into a lower structural position than themes, in accordance with the Larson/Baker thematic hierarchy in (2c). If the goal were not generated lower than the theme, the theme could not prevent the goal from becoming a subject. Once again, my proposal is nearly the opposite of Everaert's (1990), because it rules out (8) by the thematic hierarchy rather than (7). While the two approaches appeal to very much the same range of concepts, I believe that mine is correct because it generalizes better to other language families. I take this conclusion about the thematic hierarchy to be the most important implication of the analysis, and single it out for further discussion in section 6.

Third, the analysis supports Travis' (1991) revision of Larson's theory over the original. Larson (1988) assumed that the landing site for the moved NP in Dative Shift constructions was the specifier position of the smallest VP. This position was freed up by a kind of suppression of the theme argument, which resulted in the theme's being generated in an adjunct position. However, there is no obvious reason why this suppression of the theme should not be just as possible with unaccusative verbs as with transitive ones. If it were, then the theme would not prevent the goal from moving to subject position in unaccusatives. Indeed, Larson's original approach would lose the striking contrast between (15) and (40b) in Sesotho, since the theme is supposedly suppressed or demoted in both. Travis (1991), on the other hand, argues that the landing site of Dative-Shift-like movements is the specifier of Aspect Phrase, a functional category outside of the smallest VP but inside the outer VP shell. This means that no suppression of the theme argument is necessary to allow Dative Shift in a transitive structure. This in turn implies that movement of the goal NP will be blocked if and only if the minimal VP counts as a CFC, as desired.

Fourth, it is worth emphasizing that this analysis confirms the classical Chomskian view that NP-traces are anaphors. This in turn supports the deeper claim of the EST/GB/P&P tradition that grammatical function changing is not a unique phenomenon, governed by a special section of linguistic theory; rather it shares important properties with other linguistic domains, such as antecedent-anaphor relationships and operator-variable relationships (Chomsky 1981). Recent work on 'super-raising' constructions has suggested that this property of NP-traces may be completely redundant: any construction which is ruled out by the binding theory is also ruled out by the antecedent-government condition of the ECP. However, we now see that this is not so: the crucial structure in (38) is ruled out by the Binding theory but *not* by standard formulations of the ECP, because the goal phrase is always governed by its theta-marker. If one switches to a framework built around Rizzi's (1990) Relativized Minimality condition instead, then one has the reverse problem. Both (36) and (38) involve NP movement of the goal over an A-position specifier. Thus neither is a 'shortest' movement in the intuitive, pretheoretic sense of the term, and both are in danger of being ruled out by a condition that requires shortest movement (Chomsky 1993). What seems to be required is that the notion of a CFC be built into the concept of shortest movement such that two positions are only equidistant (in the technical sense) if they are contained in the same CFC. This would be essentially an updated Minimalist formulation of the older claim that NP traces are anaphors.

Finally, this analysis seems to be incompatible with Belletti and Rizzi's (1988) influential theory of psychological verbs. On their account, the underlying structure of (the Italian equivalent of) a sentence like *The test worried/frightened/bothered Mary* is (41):

(41)

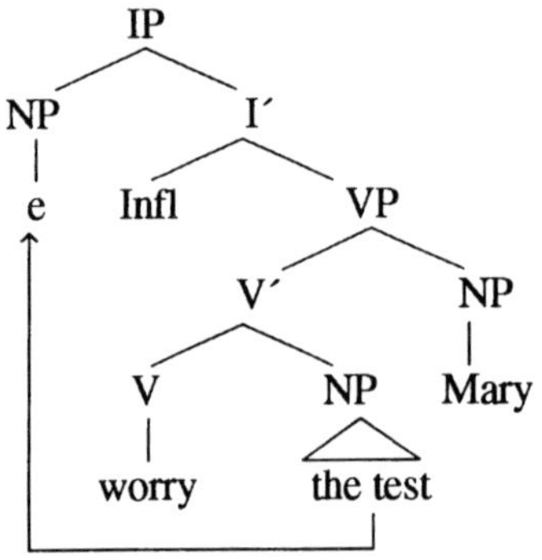

This structure is identical to (38) in all relevant respects. In particular, the NP *the test* moves out of a CFC; hence the derivation should be blocked for the same reasons that (38) is. We cannot rule out one and allow the other. Perhaps this contradiction is to be resolved by paying more careful attention to the details of Theta theory. With unaccusative verbs like *pass* it is relatively easy to identify the θ-roles by direct comparison with the transitive version of *pass*, which is a perfectly ordinary agent-theme-goal verb. In contrast, it is much less clear what the θ-roles of a verb like *worry* are. Belletti and Rizzi refer to *the test* as the theme of the verb, but it is not at all clear that this is a theme in the sense originally defined by Gruber and Jackendoff—i.e. the first argument of some kind of a *go* or *be* predicate at some level of representation. Meanwhile, Belletti and Rizzi refer to *Mary* as the bearer of the experiencer thematic role—a term which plays no role at all in the Gruber/Jackendoff conception of thematic roles. Perhaps the peculiar thing about psychological verbs is precisely this: that there is no unique best fit between them and the standard thematic roles, as proposed by Dowty (1991). This would make different mappings onto surface structure possible with out any appeal to NP movement. This in turn would imply that one must take a semantically-oriented approach to many of the facts that Belletti and Rizzi appeal to in motivating the analysis in (41), as argued in Pesetsky (1995). Thus, I tentatively conclude that psych verbs do not in fact shed much light on the questions of how themes and goals are projected or their possibilities for movement. Much more direct evidence comes from the inchoative verbs that been provided my primary focus.

5. PASSIVES AND DATIVE SHIFT

So far, we have only a partial explanation of the contrast in (34): I have explained why the unaccusative structure in (34b) is bad, but not why the passive structure in (34a) is good. Recall that this contrast is remarkably consistent across languages; the same difference is found in (15) vs. (16) in Sesotho, and in (20) vs. (21) in Japanese. Mohawk does not have a true verbal passive construction, but the same contrast can be found if Baker (in press) is correct in analyzing morphological reflexive constructions as being similar to passive constructions in syntactic structure (see Marantz 1984 for a general statement of this type of analysis). Thus, one finds minimal pairs like the one in (42), where the goal NP triggers subject agreement with a (passive-like) reflexive verb but not with an unaccusative one.

(42) a. Wa'-k-atate-nohare-'s-e' ne atya'tawi.
fact-1sS-refl-wash-ben-punc NE shirt
"I washed the shirt for myself."
(lit. "I was self-washed t the shirt.")

b. *Wa'-k-ate-nohare-'s-e' ne atya'tawi.
fact-1sS-srfl-wash-ben-punc NE shirt
"The shirt came clean for/on me." (lit. "I washed t the shirt.")

These facts strongly suggest that one cannot have a lexical account of passives. Such accounts typically treat passive verbs more or less as a special kind of unaccusative verb, derived in the lexicon by productive derivational morphology. This kind of approach can account for the many similarities between passives and unaccusatives pointed out in Burzio (1986) and other work. However, (34) shows an important and crosslinguistically valid difference between passives and unaccusatives that such an account cannot readily explain.

This contrast becomes understandable, however, once the theory presented here is combined with a syntactic theory of passive such as the one proposed in Baker, Johnson, and Roberts (1989). This theory claims that the passive morpheme is a distinct element in the syntax that receives the agent θ-role from the verb. Among other things, this forms the basis of an account of the implicit-argument effects found in passives. For concreteness, we may suppose that the passive morpheme is generated in the head of Aspect Phrase, and that it combines with the verb by way of verb raising. Then the syntactic structure of *Mary was passed the ring* (34a) would be (43).

(43)

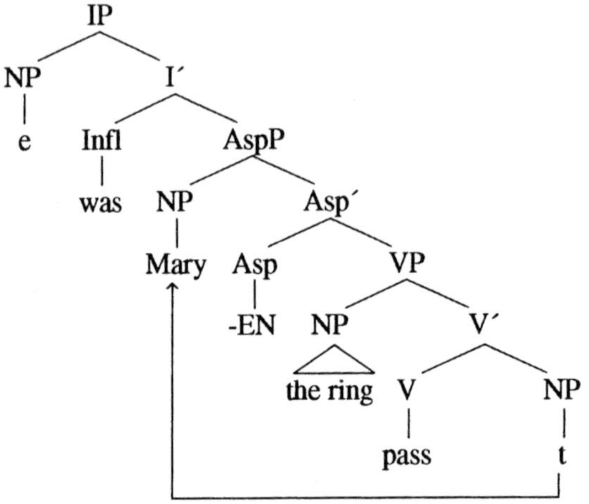

Here the lower VP does not count as a CFC because the verb's agent role is not assigned within it. Hence, the goal NP can move to the specifier of Aspect Phrase. On the other hand, the Aspect Phrase is not a governing category either, because it has no structural subject distinct from *Mary*. Hence, the goal NP can move on to the specifier of IP and receive nominative Case. Under these precise conditions, the specifier of Aspect Phrase functions as a kind of escape hatch permitting movement of the goal. This structure correctly accounts for the similarities between passives and unaccusatives, while allowing Dative Shift in passives only.

We are also now in a position to return to the residual problem left open in section 3. There it was pointed out that passive clauses with a bare goal in the VP and a theme subject are grammatical in some languages, even though similar unaccusative structures are not. This asymmetry arises in British English, Sesotho, and Japanese, although not in American English, Chichewa, or Mohawk. (44) gives a typical contrast of this type in Sesotho.

(44) a. *Lintja li-hol-el-a nkhono. UNACCUSATIVE VERB
dogs SP-grow-appl-fv grandma
"The dogs are growing for my grandma."

b. Nama e-pheh-ets-o-e 'me. PASSIVE VERB
meat SP-cook-appl-pass-fv mother
"The meat has been cooked my mother."

Implicit in my account of the deviance of sentences like (44a) was an appeal to Burzio's Generalization. The standard form of this principle is given in (45).

(45) A verb assigns (structural) accusative Case if and only if it assigns an external θ-role.

Since unaccusative verbs by definition assign no external θ-role, they can never assign structural Case. Hence, they can never Case-mark a bare NP goal, and sentences like (44a) violate the Case filter (unless there is some other source of Case, as in Mohawk).

Note, however, that under the analysis just reviewed passive constructions have the opposite status from unaccusatives with respect to (45). Passives *do* assign an external θ-role in the syntax—to the passive morpheme. Thus, (45) implies that passive verbs should be accusative Case assigners. In many languages, this makes little difference. The reason is that the passive morpheme counts as an argument of the verb, hence it often absorbs the structural Case feature of the verb (see Baker, Johnson, and Roberts 1989 for discussion). While the verb root is technically a structural Case assigner, this Case is discharged within the verb complex itself, so there is still no structural Case to assign to the goal NP. In this way, sentences like (44b) are ruled out as before in American English, Chichewa, and Mohawk. However, Baker (1988a) suggests that some languages—including presumably British English, Sesotho, and Japanese—allow their verbs to assign two (or more) structural Cases.[15] In this type of language, passive morphology may absorb one of the available Case features, but the verb still has at least one structural Case left over. This Case feature is thus neither absorbed by the passive morpheme nor 'turned off' by Burzio's Generalization. Since structural Case can be assigned to any NP regardless of its θ-role, it can license the goal in (44b). It follows that such sentences are grammatical in all and only languages with these Case properties.

In addition to filling a hole in the account, this analysis also gives further evidence for a major result of this section: that passives are not merely unaccusative verbs derived by productive lexical morphology. On the contrary, their syntactic structure is rather different.[16]

6. IMPLICATIONS FOR THE PROJECTION OF SYNTACTIC STRUCTURE

Finally, let us return to the issue of thematic hierarchies laid out in the introduction. There is was pointed out that transitive verbs give mixed evidence as to whether themes or goals should be ranked higher on the thematic hierarchy. In some languages and some constructions, themes seem to be more prominent than goals; in other languages and other constructions, goals seem to be more prominent than themes. It is not clear which constructions are basic and which are derived, or indeed whether they all can be basic in some situations.

Consider the facts about unaccusatives in this light. Here, I have claimed that there is little or no conflicting evidence: themes always have prominence over goals in the absence of an agent. Thus, the theme can occupy the subject position in the context of a goal. While Case theory pressures rule out some of the most obvious examples of this type in certain languages, the violation is relatively superficial and can often be avoided by some means or another: by making use of a goal preposition in English and Japanese, by assigning nominative Case inside VP in Mohawk, by cliticizing the goal in Sesotho. In contrast, the goal can never occupy the subject position in the context of a theme in any of the languages under consideration. Crucially, this generalization is true not only for English, where Dative Shift is optional, but even for languages like Sesotho and Mohawk, which otherwise seem to be 'goal-dominant' due to the absence of (overt) goal-prepositions.[17] Now if themes outrank goals in the absence of agents, presumably they also outrank goals in more complex constructions that include agents as well. Otherwise, one would be forced to assume some kind of context-sensitive thematic hierarchy, in which the relative values of theme and goal depend on the presence or absence of other material. As far as I know, this has never been proposed; indeed, it violates the spirit of a consistent thematic hierarchy. Thus, the Larson/Baker hierarchy of Agent > Theme > Location/Goal in (2c) is the correct one, finding relatively direct support even within languages that otherwise seem to call for one of the other hierarchies.

What then about transitive verbs, where one sees so much variation? Clearly there can be no solution purely in terms of a thematic hierarchy. Rather, the solution adopted here (following Larson) is that goals sometimes become prominent over themes because of NP movement. This is possible only with transitive verbs because the extra structure generated in order to assign the agent role in Larson's theory also creates a legitimate landing site for this type of NP movement. A more articulated representation thus makes possible a more complicated derivation.

In closing, I would like to point out two general reasons why I consider this result a promising one that points to a more elegant and constrained theory of the argument structure-phrase structure association. The Kiparsky/Bresnan hierarchy in (2a) requires at least four levels of ranking, given that it distinguishes goals and locations. In contrast, the Larson/Baker hierarchy requires only three primitive levels of ranking.[18] Interestingly, X′ theory traditionally defines exactly three types of positions with respect to a head: complement of the head, specifier of the head, and positions outside of the projection of the head.[19] If the role of the thematic hierarchy is to associate semantic arguments of a head with syntactic positions, and there are three such positions available, it makes sense that the hierarchy should distinguish exactly three categories. Thus, I propose (46) as universal mapping principles, thereby giving content to the Uniformity of Theta Role Assignment Hypothesis (UTAH) of Baker (1988a) (see also Baker (in press)).

(46) a. Path arguments (including goals, benefactives) map onto complement of V.
b. Theme/patient arguments map onto the (lowest) specifier of V′.
c. Agent/actor arguments map onto a position outside the (minimal) VP.

If these principles are correct, then the thematic hierarchy can be dropped from syntactic theory altogether. The thematic hierarchy limits the positions of arguments in phrase structure relative to one another; these relative orderings can be seen as direct corollaries of the absolute structural positions of arguments defined by (46).

The second advantage of the Larson/Baker hierarchy is that it does not force one to distinguish the PPs in sentences like (47) thematically.

(47) a. John threw the ball to Bill
b. John threw the ball (all the way) to the fence.
c. John threw the ball toward the fence.
d. John threw the ball into the dugout.

The PPs in (47b,c,d) are locational paths on anyone's theory. It seems artificial to say that the one in (47a) is not a locational path as well. Of course, (47a) differs from (47b,c) in that it may (or even must) undergo Dative Shift in some languages; this is part of the motivation for distinguishing them in the Kiparsky/Bresnan hierarchy. My claim, however, is that this is not a thematic distinction at all. Rather it is due to other factors. For example, goal/benefactive prepositions are often redundant semantically, hence deletable, whereas other locative prepositions generally are not (Larson 1988; Baker 1992). Second, goal/benefactive prepositions typically take animate NP objects, while other locative prepositions do not. Animate NPs differ in their Case theoretic properties from inanimate NPs in many languages; this can encourage or even force Dative Shift movement. However, I believe that encoding these other factors in the thematic hierarchy is inappropriate. It muddles things that are both more elegant and more explanatory when kept separate.[20]

NOTES

* This work is a revised and expanded version of a paper given at NELS 23, Indiana University, and the 6th Conference on Grammatical Relations. The original research it is based on was supported by the Social Sciences and Humanities Research Council of Canada, grant #410-90-0308, and by FCAR of Quebec, grant #91-ER-057. The article was finished while the author was a fellow at the Center for Advanced Study in the Behavioral Sciences, supported by NSF grant SES-9022192. I am thankful for these sources of support. I also wish to thank M. Zushi, L. Travis and D. Pesetsky for their help discussing these issues. Finally, I thank 'Malillo Machobane for help with the Sesotho data, Masanori Nakamura, and Kikuyo Ohkado for help with the Japanese data,

and Carolee Jacobs for help with the Mohawk data. Glosses for the languages discussed follow the glossing conventions of the cited sources.

1 This is how this statement is phrased in the references cited. However, the reference to the level of D-structure is not crucial. If, following Chomsky (1993), this level is removed from the theory, the same principle can easily be restated as a condition on the Merge operation that builds phrase structure, or (allowing for chains) as a condition on LF.

2 Some researchers distinguish goal, benefactive and recipient θ-roles. For purposes of this article, I do not make such a distinction, but rather refer to all of them as goals. This is partly an expository choice and partly a theoretically motivated one, given that I see (46) as a unified principle. More generally, I adopt a coarse-grained thematic theory, also not distinguishing patients from themes or agents from actors and causers.

3 Of course, no generalization about English goes unchallenged. Pesetsky (personal communication) points out (iii) as a possible counter-example:

(i) I got a book to Mary.
(ii) I got Mary a book.
(iii) Mary got a book.
(iv) *A book was gotten by Mary.

(iii) seems to be of the same type as (8). The ungrammaticality of (iv) apparently confirms this, since unaccusative verbs cannot be passivized (see Baker, Johnson, and Roberts 1989 and references cited there). However, a closer look suggests that different senses of the verb *get* are confounded here. Semantically, (ii) is not the Dative-Shifted version of (i), but rather of a sentence like *I got a book for Mary*. Indeed, (i) does not seem to undergo Dative Shift at all. However, (iii) seems to be semantically related to (i) rather than (ii). The fact that (iii) cannot be an unaccusative version of (ii) is explained by the theory I will present. What is not explained on anyone's account is the grammatical reading of (iii), and its possible relationship to (i). Rather than pursuing this single example, I content myself with pointing out that *get* in English has unique properties and occurs with a variety of other argument structures which may or may not be related to this problem.

Another class of verbs which may be counterexamples includes *inherit*, and *receive*. If possessors are a subclass of goals, as in a Gruber/Jackendoff style thematic analysis, then the sentences in (v) have goal subjects and theme objects. In this respect they are comparable to (8).

(v) a. Mary inherited the ring.
b. Max received a beer.

However, these verbs can be passivized, with the supposed 'goal' realized as the object of a *by*-phrase:

(vi) a. The ring was inherited by Mary.
b. The first beer was received by Max. (marginal for some speakers)

This shows that the subjects in (v) must be true external arguments of the verbs, rather than derived subjects. While they are certainly not canonical agents, they do arguably have more proto-agent properties than anything else in the clause; this would allow them to be treated as agents within a prototype theory of thematic roles like that developed in Dowty (1991). This may also explain why these verbs do not undergo causative/inchoative alternations, as shown in (vii):

(vii) a. *Susan inherited Mary the diamond ring.
b. *John received Max a beer.

Paul Postal (personal communication) points out one further class of verbs that may be relevant. This is exemplified by the verb *reach* in sentences like *The letter reached John on Thursday*. This arguably has a theme subject and a goal object, and hence is thematically similar to the sentences in (7). Baker (in press) includes some discussion of these fascinating verbs crosslinguistically; there I argue that such verbs do have theme subjects, but their objects are not goals but rather reference objects—the same theta role borne by the object of a locative preposition. If this is correct, then they are not directly relevant to the issue at hand.

4 There is considerable idiolectal variation among speakers of English as to which verbs allow Dative Shift and which verbs allow passive from a Dative Shift source. For many speakers, examples corresponding to the preposition *for* are more limited than those corresponding to the preposition *to*. Here I assume a fairly liberal dialect (that of the author) to facilitate comparison with other languages. These concerns about productivity do not seem to arise in the other languages considered in this article.

5 The RG literature does have various observations that 3 can advance to 2 only if the clause is transitive—i.e. if the clause has both a 1 and a 2. However, these are stated as language particular conditions, and must be because Dative Shift is possible with unergative verbs in some languages, as we shall see.

The Lexical Functional Grammar literature touches on a similar paradigm in the context of applicative verbs in Bantu languages. This is discussed in the next section. Similarly, the Lexical Functional Grammar literature touches on a similar paradigm in the context of applicative verbs in Bantu languages. This is discussed in the next section.

6 The Sesotho data comes from Machobane (1989; personal communication). The abbreviations used in the Sesotho glosses are: appl, applicative; fv, final vowel (a mood marker); pass, passive; SP, subject prefix.

7 Japanese data comes primarily from Zushi (1992; personal communication). Abbreviations used in the Japanese glosses include: acc, accusative; cl, classifier; dat, Dative; nom, nominative; pst, past.

8 It is important to point out that (22) captures a slightly wider range of facts than those reviewed here. For example, Alsina and Mchombo (1988) show that instrumental applicatives cannot be formed on unaccusative verbs, either—a generalization that they also derive from (22). This restriction probably does follow from quasi-semantic theta-theoretic considerations, however. Observationally, it seems to be true that instruments cannot appear with pure unaccusative verbs across languages, regardless of how the instrument is expressed (cf. ?**The door opened with a key*, where a marginal middle interpretation must be ignored). This makes sense if instruments are analyzed not as a primitive thematic role but as a kind of intermediate agent-patient, along the lines of Jackendoff (1987). Then it is semantically deviant to have a secondary agent without having (at least an implicit) primary agent. See note 20 for discussion of the third case that Machobane, Alsina, and Mchombo take to be relevant to (22).

9 Mohawk data comes from the author's field notes, collected at Kahnawake, Quebec between 1989 and 1993. See Baker (in press) for discussion. Abbreviations used in the Mohawk examples are: ben, benefactive; fact, factual mood; punc, punctual aspect; refl, reflexive; srfl, semireflexive; 1sS, first singular subject prefix; MsO, masculine singular object prefix; 1sO, first singular object prefix; MsS, masculine singular subject prefix. *Ne* is a very common particle whose exact meaning is unclear.

10 For example, the verb typically must be a canonical Dative-Shift verb such as *give* or *send*, and the goal must be short—a pronoun or simple proper name. In fact, the

specific sentences quoted may not be acceptable for any speaker, given that most British speakers I have asked are conservative Dative-Shifters who are already rather uncomfortable with the sentences in (4) and (10).

11 However, some dialects of Chichewa do allow the equivalent of (33), judging by Trithart (1977). There are some strange restrictions on (33) even in Sesotho; for example (33) cannot have an agent in a *by*-phrase, which is otherwise possible in the language. To complete the picture, sentences like (32) and (33) are possible in Japanese, but not in Mohawk.

12 Here I put aside tricky and controversial questions concerning the presence of the preposition *to* in (35) and its absence in (36). For current purposes, we can follow Larson in assuming that *to* is merely a Case marker absorbed in the passive-like process that derives (36). In fact, I believe that *to* is a head involved in θ-marking in these structures, and that part of the difference between (35) and (36) is that the former has an overt P while the latter has a null P (Baker 1992). However, this issue is somewhat orthogonal to the point at hand and reviewing it would take us far afield.

13 Larson (1988) also makes this assumption for overt anaphors such as *herself* and *each other*.

14 This property has been documented for passives in languages such as Lithuanian and Turkish. See Baker (1988a) for references and a possible analysis.

15 Importantly, this property can be independently motivated for the Bantu languages in question by other facts about three-argument verbs, as shown in Baker (1988a). See also Bresnan and Moshi (1990) for a somewhat different analysis of the contrast between Sesotho-like languages and Chichewa-like languages, as well as a very systematic presentation of the range of evidence relevant to this question.

16 It should be noted that this analysis uses Burzio's Generalization as an actual principle of grammar. Crucially, the facts do not follow in any obvious way from more functional/intuitive statements of Burzio's Generalization, such as "a construction has only as many structural Cases as it needs to license the arguments of its semantic head". Crucially (44a) has fewer Cases than it needs, due to (45). If correct, this may suggest that Case theory cannot be reduced simply to a theory of argument structure.

17 In the terminology of Dryer (1987), Mohawk and Sesotho are primary object languages.

18 Certain other thematic roles can be defined in terms of the basic ones. For example instrument can plausibly be analyzed as an intermediate agent/theme, along the lines of Jackendoff (1987); see also note 8. From this, its typical position as lower than a pure agent and higher than a pure theme can be derived. Zushi (1992) makes a similar argument for a certain class of source phrases in Japanese.

19 As far as I can see, the form but not the substance of this proposal is affected by Chomsky's recent (1994) proposal to eliminate stipulated bar-levels in the theory of phrase structure. In particular, his theory still draws a three-way distinction between complements of a head, specifiers of a head, and positions outside the projection of a head, although the first two notions are defined more indirectly, because there is no such a thing as V′. How exactly to integrate the UTAH with Chomsky's most recent proposals merits more careful consideration than I can give here, however.

20 One specific case in point relevant to the concerns of this paper is the contrast in (i), discussed by both Machobane (1989) and Alsina and Mchombo (1988):

(i) a. *Ngoana o-kul-el-a Lineo. SESOTHO
child SP-be.ill-appl-fv Lineo
"The child is ill on Lineo." (Lineo is adversely affected)

b. Ntate o-kul-el-a sepetlele.
father SP-be.ill-appl-fv hospital
"My father is ill in the hospital."

They interpret this contrast in the context of their condition (22) as evidence that goals are higher on the thematic hierarchy than themes, while locations are lower. However, the current theory invites an analysis of this in which the distinction is Case theoretic rather than Theta theoretic in nature. In (ia) the affected object *Lineo* violates the Case filter as discussed in section 3. In (ib), on the other hand, the location *sepetlele* does not need to receive Case, because it is morphologically oblique; indeed, such phrases in Sesotho behave like PPs in a variety of ways (see Baker (1992) for discussion). Given this, no distinction in terms of the thematic hierarchy is necessary for these data.

REFERENCES

Alsina, Alex and Sam Mchombo: 1988, 'Lexical Mapping In the Chichewa Applicative Construction', paper given at the 19th Annual African Linguistics Conference, Boston University, April 1988.

Aoun, Joseph and Audrey Li: 1989, 'Scope and Constituency', *Linguistic Inquiry* **20**, 141-172.

Baker, Mark: 1988a, *Incorporation: a Theory of Grammatical Function Changing*, University of Chicago Press, Chicago.

———: 1988b, 'Theta Theory and the Syntax of Applicatives in Chichewa', *Natural Language and Linguistic Theory* **6**, 353-389.

———: 1989, 'Object Sharing and Projection in Serial Verb Constructions', *Linguistic Inquiry* **20**, 513-553.

———: 1992, 'Thematic Conditions on Syntactic Structures: Evidence From Locative Applicatives', in I. M. Roca (ed.), *Thematic Structure: Its Role in Grammar*, Foris, Berlin, pp. 23-46.

———: in press, *The Polysynthesis Parameter*, Oxford University Press, New York.

Baker, Mark, Kyle Johnson, and Ian Roberts: 1989, 'Passive Arguments Raised', *Linguistic Inquiry* **20**, 219-251.

Barss, Andrew and Howard Lasnik: 1986, 'A Note on Anaphora and Double Objects', *Linguistic Inquiry* **17**, 347-354.

Belletti, Adriana, and Luigi Rizzi: 1988, 'Psych-verbs and θ-theory', *Natural Language and Linguistic Theory* **6**, 291-352.

Besten, Hans den: 1985, 'The Ergative Hypothesis and Free Word Order in Dutch and German', *Studies in German Grammar*, Foris, Dordrecht.

Bresnan, Joan and Joni Kanerva: 1989, 'Locative Inversion in Chichewa: A Case Study of Factorization in Grammar', *Linguistic Inquiry* **20**, 1-50.

Bresnan, Joan and Lioba Moshi: 1990, 'Object Asymmetries in Comparative Bantu Syntax', *Linguistic Inquiry* **21**, 147-185.

Burzio, Luigi: 1986, *Italian Syntax: A Government-Binding Approach*, Reidel, Dordrecht.

Carrier-Duncan, Jill: 1985, 'Linking of Thematic Roles in Derivational Word Formation', *Linguistic Inquiry* **16**, 1-34.

Chomsky, Noam: 1976, 'Conditions on Rules of Grammar', *Linguistic Analysis* **2**, 303-351.

———: 1981, *Lectures on Government and Binding*, Foris, Dordrecht.

———: 1986, *Knowledge of Language: Its Nature, Origin, and Use*, Praeger, New York.

———: 1993, 'A Minimalist Program for Linguistic Theory', in K. Hale and S. J. Keyser (eds.), *The View From Building 20*, MIT Press, Cambridge, MA, pp. 1-52.

———: 1994, 'Bare Phrase Structure', unpublished, MIT.

Dowty, David: 1991, 'Thematic Proto-roles and Argument Selection', *Language* **67**, 547-619.
Dryer, Matthew: 1987, 'On Primary Objects, Secondary Objects, and Antidative', *Language* **62**, 808-845.
Everaert, Martin: 1990, 'NP-movement 'Across' Secondary Objects' in *Grammar in Progress*, Foris, Dordrecht, pp. 125-136.
Everett, Daniel: 1987, 'Pirahã clitic doubling', *Natural Language and Linguistic Theory* **5**, 245-276.
Foley, William and Robert Van Valin: 1984, *Functional Syntax and Universal Grammar*, Cambridge University Press, Cambridge.
Grimshaw, Jane: 1990, *Argument Structure*, MIT Press, Cambridge, MA.
Hale, Kenneth, and S. J. Keyser: 1993, 'On Argument Structure and the Lexical Expression of Syntactic Relations', in K. Hale and S.J. Keyser (eds.), *The View From Building 20*, MIT Press, Cambridge, MA, pp. 53-110.
Hoji, H.: 1985, *Logical Form Constraints and Configurational Structures in Japanese*, unpublished Ph.D. dissertation, University of Washington.
Jackendoff, Ray: 1972, *Semantic Interpretation in Generative Grammar*, MIT Press, Cambridge, MA.
———: 1987, 'The Status of Thematic Relations in Linguistic Theory', *Linguistic Inquiry* **18**, 369-412.
Kayne, Richard: 1984, *Connectedness and Binary Branching*, Foris, Dordrecht.
Kiparsky, Paul: 1987, *Morphology and Grammatical Relations*, unpublished, Stanford University.
Larson, Richard: 1988, 'On the Double Object Construction', *Linguistic Inquiry* **19**, 335-392.
Li, Yafei: 1990, 'On V-V Compounds in Chinese', *Natural Language and Linguistic Theory* **8**, 177-208.
Machobane, 'Malillo: 1989, *Some Restrictions on the Sesotho Transitivizing Morphemes*, unpublished Ph.D. dissertation, McGill University.
Marantz, Alec: 1984, *On the Nature of Grammatical Relations*, MIT Press, Cambridge, MA.
Pesetsky, David: 1995, *Zero Syntax: Experiencers and Cascades*, MIT Press, Cambridge, MA.
Rizzi, Luigi: 1990, *Relativized Minimality*, MIT Press, Cambridge, MA.
Speas, Margaret: 1990, *Phrase Structure in Natural Language*, Kluwer, Dordrecht.
Travis, Lisa: 1991, 'Inner Aspect and the Structure of VP', paper presented at NELS 22, University of Delaware.
Trithart, M.: 1977, *Relational Grammar and Chichewa Subjectivization*, unpublished Ph.D. dissertation, UCLA.
Zushi, Mihoko: 1992, 'The Syntax of Dative Constructions in Japanese', unpublished, McGill University.

WHAT'S A HEAD?*

William Croft

0. INTRODUCTION

In this paper, I will critically examine the notion of head in grammatical theory, focusing on the debate between Zwicky (1985) and Hudson (1987), but also discussing recent proposals regarding functional heads in the generative literature. The notion of head is a fairly recent one, originating in more or less its modern form (as far as I know) in Sweet (1891). Specifically, the notion of head is a generalization over the concepts of agreement, government and modification in traditional grammar. In fact, Zwicky extends the notion of head to include grammatical relations such as that between the auxiliar and the main verb and the complementizer and its complement (in English). In its most general form, headhood represents the hypothesis that there is a general characterization of the 'dominant' member of any asymmetric dependency relation in grammar.

The importance of headhood among generative linguists dates from the introduction of X-bar theory in Chomsky (1970), in which the phrase structure node labels N(oun) and N(oun) P(hrase) are no longer accidental homonyms but are systematically related, so that the latter is a projection (specifically, the maximal projection) of the former category. In effect, this makes the noun the head of the noun phrase and its sisters (at various levels in the phrase structure tree) its dependents, or more precisely dependents of the constituent to which they are sisters.[1] The analysis of phrase structure since then has required the establishment of which elements are heads (that is, which categories have projections). This has become a topic of great interest because of claims that many categories other than the usual N, V, A, P can function as heads (Chomsky 1986, 1991; Abney 1987; Pollock 1989; and many recent papers) and that in fact these other categories are the heads of the syntactic units once called NP and S (whose status as a projection of V has been problematic anyway). These issues will come to the forefront later in this paper.

Zwicky provides a thorough enumeration of criteria for headhood, which is briefly surveyed in §2 below. He argues that most of the criteria for headhood that he discusses are in fact irrelevant, but he argues for a syntactic definition of headhood. Hudson, on the other hand, argues for a semantic definition of headhood, but (with one exception) argues that all of the syntactic phenomena are relevant to his semantic conception. Using a wider range of constructions and cross-linguistic data, I will argue in §3 that Zwicky is correct in discarding most of the proposed criteria for headhood; but in §4 I argue that Hudson is right in seeking a semantic definition for the concept. I then examine the semantic concept of headhood in Cognitive Grammar (Langacker 1987, 1991) and argue that although it is correct as far as it goes, it does not allow us to decide between lexical heads and functional heads (§5). A modification of Langacker's semantic definition, combined with an appeal to diachronic linguistic data in grammaticalization and reanalysis, leads to a definition that in fact restores the more traditional notion that the lexical head is indeed the head of its phrase (§6). Finally, in §7 I turn to the problem of heads in morphology, and argue that there are good semantic reasons why syntactic headhood is not easily extendible to morphology, and propose instead a definition of the root-affix distinction in the same spirit.

An important methodological subtheme runs through this paper. In fact, I consider this subtheme more important than the main theme, the semantic analysis of headhood proposed herein. The analysis of headhood presented here may prove in the long run to be empirically inadequate or conceptually unsatisfying; but the methodological subtheme is relevant to any analysis of headhood, or for that matter, any other grammatical phenomenon. The subtheme is, how do we give substance to our intuitions about the identity of a basic grammatical concept, such as headhood? What grounds do we have for choosing some syntactic criterion for that concept and discarding others? If we propose a semantic (or pragmatic or discourse-functional) basis for a grammatical concept, how do we know that we have captured the intuition that was intended by the original coiners of the term or the unquestioned but undefined informal use in the field? For example, I will argue here that a certain semantic property of syntactic constituents and lexical items accounts for certain cross-linguistic synchronic and diachronic facts of grammar. This, I hope, is empirically correct; but is it headhood? The position that one takes on these questions partially determines what sort of grammatical theory one ends up with: 'formalist', 'functionalist', etc. (for additional discussion, see Croft 1990a: 1-18, 27-39, 150-54, 246-59; Croft 1991: 1-32; Croft 1993: 18-20). I will be arguing for a specific approach, which has led me to a functional-typological analysis. By explicitly discussing these issues here, I hope to bring these methodological issues to the forefront, and linguists of any theoretical persuasion can judge for themselves the methodological arguments as well as the specific analysis of headhood that I propose.

1. CRITERIA FOR HEADHOOD

Zwicky (1985, henceforth Z) examines a series of grammatical criteria as candidates for determining headhood and applies them to the following English constituent combinations (Z, p. 4):

(i) Det + N
(ii) V + NP
(iii) Aux + VP
(iv) P + NP
(v) NP + VP
(vi) Comp + S

To illustrate his criteria, I will use here only the example of V + NP. This combination probably has the most widely accepted dependency analysis of the six constructions Zwicky discusses (namely, the verb is the head and the object NP is the dependent). In fact, all of the criteria (where applicable) generally point to that conclusion (problematic cases will be reserved for the next section).

(a) *Agreement* ("determination of concord", Z, p. 8-9): the dependent triggers agreement with the head. This is not applicable in English for V + NP, but instead can be found in languages with object agreement, such as Yimas (Foley 1991: 203), in which cases the NP generally determines the concordial properties of the V:

(1)	wanwa	wa-	ka-	tar-	wapi
	knife.IX.SG	IX.SG.O-	1SG.A-	CAUS-	sharp
	"I sharpened the knife."				

The Class IX noun *wanwa* 'knife' determines the choice of the Class IX object prefix *wa-*.

(b) *Obligatory constituent* (Z, p. 13). Zwicky characterizes this as an operational criterion which has nevertheless been treated as definitional in the literature. The head should be the obligatory constituent in the unit; the following example suggests that V is the head because it is obligatory whereas the NP is not.

(2) a. Janet ate lunch.
b. Janet ate.
c. *Janet lunch.

(c) *Distributional equivalent.* Zwicky describes this putative criterion for headhood as "the one constituent that belongs to a category with roughly the same distribution as the construct as a whole" (Z, p. 11). Of course, much depends on how strictly one interprets the word 'roughly' in Zwicky's definition. We can use (2a-c) again to illustrate that V has a similar distribution to VP, while NP does not.

(d) *Subcategorizand* (Z, p. 5-6). According to this criterion, the element in a constituent that requires a subcategorization frame is the head. This item must be lexical in Zwicky's model of syntax (see §2.3 for an alternative view), since the subcategorization frame is listed in the lexicon. In the V + NP case, we have the archetypal use of subcategorization in syntax, and the V is the subcategorizand:

(3) a. Tina hit the ball/*hit. [*hit* NP]
b. *Tina slept the ball/slept. [*sleep* _]

(e) *Governor* (Z, p. 7-8). According to this criterion, the head is the constituent that governs the grammatical form of its sister constituent(s). Zwicky argues that this is distinct from subcategorization. Subcategorization defines presence/absence of the sister of a particular syntactic type and has a semantic interpretation rule associated with it; government defines the form of a (usually subcategorized-for) constituent and that form does not enter into semantic interpretation. Zwicky distinguishes two types of government. In the first type, the morphological form is determined by virtue of the construction itself. In the second type, the lexical class of the head determines the form of the dependent. English V + NP illustrates the first type: the pronominal objective form is required by virtue of the fact that the pronoun is the object NP. The second type is illustrated in a language with a richer case system than English, Russian:[2]

(4) a. čitat' gazetu (*ACC*)
read magazine
"to read a/the magazine"

b. pravit' mašinoj (*INSTR*)
drive car
"drive a car"

c. mešat' rabote (*DAT*)
interfere work
"to interfere with the work"

Here the complement NP does not have its form purely by virtue of its being a complement NP (except for a default-case analysis of the accusative object in (4a)), but the verb determines the case form of the complement NP.

(f) *Morphosyntactic locus* (Z, p. 6-7). The element in the constituent which bears the morphosyntactic marks linking that constituent with higher-level constituents is the head. Zwicky intends this not as necessarily overt inflectional marks on the head of the constituent, but abstract syntactic properties that must be attributed to the putative head constituent in syntactic analysis. This can be illustrated in our example in that morphosyntactic properties dictated by constituents into which V + NP is embedded, such as tense and finiteness, are located on the V, not the NP, of the V + NP:

(5) a. I barbecued the steak.
b. *I barbecue the steaked.

These are the six potential grammatical criteria for headhood that Zwicky discusses, and I believe he has exhausted the list of most widely proposed criteria. In addition to these, Zwicky discusses one semantic criterion, which I will turn to in §4.

2. SYNTACTIC CRITERIA AND SYNTACTIC ARGUMENTATION

Part of the dispute between Zwicky and Hudson on headhood is whether the six grammatical criteria should converge on the same constituent or not. Zwicky argues they do not, Hudson argues that they do (after discarding one, agreement). But a more fundamental question (my subtheme's first appearance) is: why *should* they converge? One cannot simply collect as many grammatical constructions as possible which seem to converge on roughly the same distribution in a particular language and say that this phenomenon demonstrates the existence, importance, universality or whatever of a category such as head. Unfortunately, this approach to syntactic argumentation is very common in the literature. One serious problem with this approach is that it is usually applied in the analysis of a single language, and sometimes only with a subset of the relevant phenomena. It may be true that the six grammatical criteria for headhood converge for the six English constructions that Zwicky discusses (though in fact they do not), but it may not be true for many other English constructions, or for the equivalents of those six constructions in other languages.

There has to be a reason for the criteria to converge on a single grammatical concept. More accurately, there has to be a reason why the syntactic criteria selected to define a grammatical concept are *relevant* to the definition of that concept. One highly plausible place to look for that reason is the semantic, pragmatic or discourse function of the grammatical construction or process that is used as a criterion for headhood. If the functions of the constructions that are used as criteria for headhood (for instance) aren't related, or aren't relevant to headhood, then one would not expect them to converge, because their distribution will probably be defined on different functional criteria. In this section, I will review all of the grammatical criteria discussed by Zwicky except morphosyntactic locus (see §4), and argue that their function, clear or vague as it may be, has little to do with headhood and, not surprisingly, their distribution diverges. I will thus be following Zwicky's line of reasoning, but I will bring in other constructions of English that Zwicky does not discuss, and other constructions in other languages, which strengthen Zwicky's arguments.

I must also add that one need not believe in functional characterizations of the distribution of syntactic constructions to take this methodological point seriously. There must be *some* theoretical reason for particular syntactic tests or criteria to be relevant to the grammatical entity they are tests/criteria for, no matter what syntactic theory is being used.[3] The grammatical entity being tested is, after all, a theoretical construct. It need not be a functional one, though in my mind function provides a natural explanation for why criteria do in fact diverge.

This point can be illustrated by another problem with most of these criteria: how applicable they are to the full range of asymmetric dependency relations that the notion 'head' is supposed to cover. For example, applying the notion of subcategorization or government to Aux + VP or Comp + S is stretching both of these grammatical criteria beyond standard usage. A related issue is, what if some members of the category fit the criterion and others do not? For example, *this/that* are distributional equivalents of NP, since they can occur as pronouns in *This is beautiful*; but *the* and *a* are not distributional equivalents of NP, since they cannot: **The/a is beautiful*. Should one say that determiners pass the distributional equivalents test, because some of them do, or that they fail the test, because some of them do not? This is relevant because the theoretical claim that is being made with the concept of head is that this concept is general to all asymmetric dependency relations in grammar. This means that the criteria used to define heads should be relatively easily applicable to all such relations—another way in which the criteria must be theoretically relevant to the grammatical construct being studied.

I now turn to the specific criteria that Zwicky discusses.

2.1. *Agreement*

Although Hudson argues that almost all of Zwicky's criteria for headhood do converge, he agrees with Zwicky that one grammatical criterion for headhood, agreement, should be discarded. This is because another generalization holds for agreement: agreement morphemes agree (more precisely covary) with NPs (Lehmann 1981). In the case of verbs and adpositions, the NP is the argument of the predicate (functor); so the verb/adposition agrees with the dependent (in the usual analyses). With modifiers, the NP is the constituent containing the modifier; so agreement is with the head. (This analysis is somewhat more controversial, but Lehmann makes a persuasive case for it.) The fact that agreement is not useful for determining headhood is clearly demonstrated with a construction that neither Zwicky nor Hudson discuss, genitives. In some languages, the genitive modifier agrees with the head noun, as in Serbo-Croatian (Matthew Gordon, p.c.):

(6)	sestr	-ina	knjiga
	sister	-POSS:FSG	book:FSG
	"[the] sister's book"		

In other languages, the head noun agrees with the genitive modifier, as in Mam (England 1983):

(7) t- kamb' meeb'a
3SG.POSS- prize orphan
"[the] orphan's prize"

This is due to the fact that the genitive modifier is an NP, and it is a modifier within a larger NP. So either NP can trigger agreement, and cross-linguistically either one does.

This generalization can be phrased in functional, that is semantic terms, by noting that NPs are referring expressions. Zwicky subsumes all NPs as semantic arguments (Z, p. 3) without comment. This depends, however, on how one handles dummy or pleonastic NPs. Langacker (1991, §8.3.3), for example, argues that such NPs have reference, albeit maximally general reference. If one is not inclined to accept such arguments, then one can remain with the generalization that agreement is with the syntactic category NP. There is no connection to headhood, in either a syntactic or semantic characterization thereof.

2.2. *Obligatoriness and distributional equivalence.*

Hudson notes that these two criteria are related; I believe he is correct. However, they do not provide good criteria for headhood, as is clear from cross-linguistic variation.

Consider another construction that neither Zwicky nor Hudson discuss, Adj + N. In English, the noun is the obligatory constituent: one cannot say **the big*. The nearest construction to this involves the use of the pro-form *one*, which functions as the head of this collocation: *the big ones*. In other languages, such as Quechua, however, the noun is no more syntactically obligatory than the adjective (Schachter 1985: 17):

(8) a. hatun -kuna -ta
big -PL -ACC
"the big ones [object]"

b. alkalde -kuna -ta
mayor -PL -ACC
"the mayor [object]"

The adjective is also thereby the distributional equivalent of the noun phrase in such languages.

Another example in which cross-linguistic variation plays havoc with distributional equivalence for reasons not having to do with headhood is the Det + N example discussed above. There it was pointed out that in English, some determiners (e.g., *that*) are distributional equivalents, while others (e.g., *the*) are not: *that book/that* vs. *the book* vs. **the*. The reason for this, however, is that the distributional analog of the demonstrative pronoun for *the* is *he/she/it*, and it just happens that in English there is a suppletive relationship between the determiner and the third person pronoun. In other languages, however, this is not the case and 'the' is in fact a distributional equivalent for NP; the example here is from Luganda (Ashton et al. 1954: 41):

(9) a. eki- kwaso eky- o
CL.SG- pin CL.SG- the
"the pin"

b. eky- o
CL.SG- the
"it, the one"

But in still other languages, attributive demonstratives are not the distributional equivalent of NP; attributive and pronominal demonstratives are consistently different in form. Japanese represents this language type:

(10) Attributive: kono hito / *kono
"this man" "this"
Pronominal: kore / *kore hito
"this" "this man"

A slightly different explanation accounts for the differences in behavior for the combinations NP + VP, V + NP. The optionality of the object illustrated for English *eat* in (2b) is not general for all transitive verbs in English, and involves some distinct semantic properties that suggest that there are in fact two different verbs, *eat* [tr.] and *eat* [intr.]. If we are interested in distributional equivalence for NP + VP and V + NP in general, we must look at other languages. When we do so, we find distributional equivalence for the VP and V respectively depends on whether the language has null subject/object anaphora (*pro*-drop) or not. In English in general, there is no null subject/object anaphora (see Fillmore 1986 for various special types of null anaphora in English). In other languages such as Japanese, Chinese and Rennellese, from which the following example is taken (Elbert & Momberg 1965), null anaphora is quite general and also quite common:

(11) aano tutuku i mu'a Hangemangama
and.then spill in front H.
"And then [he] spilled [earth] in front of Hangemangama."

While the evidence from a null object anaphora language such as Rennellese suggests that the V is the head of V + NP by the distributional equivalence and obligatoriness criteria, an NP can be the distributional equivalent if the language uses NPs in predicate nominal constructions without the addition of copulas or verbal inflections, as in Russian:

(12) a. ona čitala knigu
she read book
"She was reading a book."

b. Ona spala
she sleep.PST
"She was sleeping."

c. Ona student
she student
"She was a student."

With the combination Aux + V discussed by Zwicky and Hudson, the obligatoriness/distributional equivalence of Aux depends on whether the language has so-called VP deletion, as in English (Z, p. 13), or lacks it, as in French (Z, p. 14):

(13) You haven't been to Rumania, but I have _.

(14) a. *Tu n' es pas allé en Roumanie, mais moi je suis _.
you neg are not gone in R. but me I am
"You haven't been to Rumania, but I have."

b. Tu n'es pas allé en Roumanie, mais moi j'y suis allé.
but me I there am gone
mais moi si.
but me yes
"You haven't been to Rumania, but I have (been there)."

None of these grammatical facts—whether there are distinct attributive and pronominal forms for any or all determiner s or other modifiers; whether there is general null anaphora for subjects and/or objects; whether a copula is required for predicate nominals; whether VP deletion exists in the language or not—has any obvious connection to headhood, either some intuitive semantic notion or any specific formal notion. This conclusion is essentially in agreement with Zwicky, although I have provided a wider range of evidence that should make even clearer that he is right to discard these criteria.

Another example of cross-linguistic variation has to do with the possibility of both constituents being obligatory. For example, in Palauan, every NP (and in fact also every VP) must be accompanied by a particle that might be described as a determiner (Josephs 1975):

(15) a ngẹlẹkek a mẹdakt a dẹrumk
DET my.child DET afraid DET thunder
"My child is afraid of thunder."

And in Papago (and also Warlpiri), every finite clause contains an Aux as well as a verb (since both languages have quite free word order, it is not obvious whether Aux combines with VP or V, or perhaps not with either); the example here is from Papago (Zepeda 1983):

(16) 'I:da 'o'odham 'o ñeok
this person AUX speak
"This person is/was speaking."

These are the clearest cases of multiple obligatory constituents for these constructions that I am aware of (see also §5).

Finally, we can make some general observations regarding obligatoriness for V + NP and any Mod + N combination. The appearance of [V NP] and [V] structures (in a language without null object anaphora) is really an effect of different subcategorizations of verbs, not of some independent criterion of optionality of dependents (for subcategorization, see the next section). For Mod + N combinations, the Mod is optional because it is not subcategorized for, since modifiers are adjuncts. This latter phenomenon is not (directly, at least) related to headhood because complements are generally dependents even though they are not adjuncts.

2.3. *Subcategorization, government and construction grammar*

This brings us to subcategorization and government. These criteria appear on the face of it to be more likely candidates for defining syntactic headhood (though we have not discussed semantic criteria yet). At least with the prototypical case, verbs and their complements, they strongly correlate with our intuitions. Zwicky argues that these are syntactically significant concepts, but they are to be related to the notion of semantic functor, not head as he wishes to define it (Z, p. 3, 9-10). While I agree that semantic functor is not the place to look for the concept of headhood (see §3 below), I believe there are some syntactic difficulties with treating subcategorization and government as reflections of semantic functor. This is based on a different sort of syntactic analysis than the one that Zwicky employs, which does away with the directionality that supports the head-dependent or even functor-argument asymmetry.

The argument in this section runs as follows. The extent to which there is an asymmetric syntactic relationship analogous to a semantic functor-argument relationship depends on the extent to which the syntactic relationship between a lexical item and its subcategorization or pattern of government is a function in the mathematical sense. That is, it depends on whether and to what degree there is a unique subcategorization/ government pattern for each lexical item. If so, then it is reasonable to assume that the functor determines the subcategorization. If not, then it is difficult to maintain this claim. I will argue that there is not, and in fact the subcategorization/government pattern has a syntactic and semantic life of its own, a view that takes center stage in syntactic models that go under the name of construction grammar. Although this argument may seem a digression at this point—we could just as well accept Zwicky's argument, since it is sufficient to demonstrate that subcategorization and government are not directly relevant to headhood—the notion of a grammatical construction as an independent syntactic-semantic entity will be employed in the remaining sections of this paper, so this argument can be treated as a brief introduction to the concept and its potential usefulness for grammatical description.

As mentioned in §1, Zwicky defines subcategorization as present when an element (necessarily lexical) specifies *what* sister constituents it can have; government, on the other hand, indicates what *form* those constituents are found in, e.g., accusative vs. instrumental case of objects. He argues that there are also semantic interpretation rules associated with subcategorizations.

However, the usual characterization of subcategorization in generative syntax assumes there is a particular directionality, so that the subcategorizand determines the subcategorization that it 'requires'. This is questionable to the extent that the subcategorization is not a function in the mathematical sense, i.e., that there is a unique subcategorization for each lexical 'head'. This is not generally the case, particularly in English. Many verbs can be used with or without an object—that is, they may occur in either the [_] subcategorization frame or the [_ NP] frame. Many ditransitive verbs take one of two subcategorization frames: [_ NP NP] or [_ NP *to* NP], as Zwicky himself notes. Levin (1993) describes a large number of argument structure alternations in English ('argument structures' are generally defined as subcategorization frames linked to particular thematic roles). It appears from her inventory that most verbs in English allow multiple argument structures.

In order to maintain the mathematical function relationship between a verb and its subcategorization frame, one could postulate two distinct verbs, each one taking a single subcategorization frame, thereby preserving the function-like character of the word-subcategorization relationship. However, there are also subtle semantic differences depending on which subcategorization frame is used with a particular verb, which can be argued to be contributed by the subcategorization frame itself (cf. Rice 1987 for transitivity, Goldberg 1989 for ditransitives and Goldberg 1992 for several other constructions relating to verbal subcategorization frames). Another example of more than one subcategorization per verb with a difference in meaning between the subcategorizations is the well-known locative alternation (Anderson 1971):

(17) [_ NP LocPrep NP]:
  a. Mary sprayed paint on the wall.
  b. They loaded hay on the truck.

(18) [_ NP *with* NP]:
  a. Mary sprayed the wall with paint.
  b. They loaded the truck with hay.

As has been noted by Anderson and others, the direct object is interpreted as more completely affected by the action than the oblique complement, and this appears to be an effect of direct object status in these argument structures, not the verb meaning.

The interactions between verbs and subcategorization frames are quite complex and are currently the focus of a great deal of interest in formal and nonformal syntactic theory (see Levin 1993 for references). No matter how they are to be analyzed, they cannot be simply interpreted as the choice of the verb determining the choice of the frame. One could just as easily argue that the subcategorization frames exist as independent syntactic entities and select which verbs can enter them, to the extent that the relationship between verb and frame is idiosyncratic. It would probably be more accurate to suppose that there is a meeting of two entities in the syntax: a lexical verb and the subcategorization frame (which can be renamed a grammatical construction), which jointly determine the syntactic and semantic properties of the resulting construction.[4] If this analysis is accepted, then there is no obvious directionality: the combinability of verbs and their complement arrays is a matter of semantic compatibility, or more likely a many-to-many relation that is dictated by neither the verb alone nor the subcategorization construction alone.

A similar argument applies to government. Zwicky argues that with government, there is directionality because it is the form of the governed complement that is chosen, while there is no such mark found on the governing constituent itself (e.g., the verb governing a case-marked object in German or Russian, or an auxiliar governing a nonfinite verb form in English). Again, this argument is weakened to the extent that the shape of the governed element is not uniquely determined by the lexical class of the head, and instead varies, possibly systematically, in relation to the head. For example, the relationship between the English auxiliaries *have* and *be* and the nonfinite verb forms they govern (*to* infinitive, bare infinitive, present participle, passive participle) is a many-to-many relation once again, and there is no clear semantic predictability in either direction, although there are relationships that suggest that the semantics of both the auxiliary and the verb form are involved. The choice of the case of objects in Russian or other languages is often dependent on semantic interpretation.

Worse from the point of view of the traditional government analysis, the governed alternations are productive in some languages. For example, the Warlpiri ABS-DAT alternations for patient arguments follows a pattern of degree of affectedness and is quite general (Hale 1982). Also, the argument based on the definition of government can be turned on its head in some cases. In a number of languages, the transitivity of the verb is overtly marked on the verb. One could argue that the presence of an object triggers a formal property of the verb, namely its transitivity marking. The complexity and range of possibilities of the relationship between a verb and its pattern of government is analogous to that between a verb and its subcategorization frame. Government too can be analyzed by having constructions as independently stored grammatical entities along with lexical items. Government merely specifies more precise structural information about the constructions, e.g., [Verb $NP_{Instrumental}$]; and to the extent that prepositions in English subcategorization frames correspond to government of case in languages with extensive NP case morphology, the two phenomena are in fact identical.

This is the approach taken by various cognitive linguistic theories, including Lakoff's (1987) and Fillmore and Kay's (1993) Construction Grammar and Langacker 's (1987) Cognitive Grammar. In these approaches, grammatical constructions such as the passive, the transitive, the so-called Dative Shift construction and so on are stored as grammatical entities in very much the same way as lexical items are. They share other properties with lexical items also. For example, they are polysemous. The locative alternation construction [V NP *with* NP] is just one of several uses of this construction:

(19) a. Mary sprayed the wall with paint.
b. Masha kicked the ball with her foot.
c. Misha presented her with the ring.
d. Misha played the sonata with sensitivity.

In this approach, even the most general syntactic rule is a construction: [NP VP], [Det Nom], [Adj N], etc. They differ only from idiomatic expressions and lexical items in their high level of generality or schematicity (which, incidentally, is what makes them quite productive).[5] In fact, the same construction exists at different levels of schematicity: e.g., [V NP *with* NP] is subsumed under [V NP PP], which is in turn subsumed under the maximally schematic [VP]. (This leads to the employment of psychological theories of categorization, including prototype theory, in formal syntactic analysis in these theories.) Finally, in this view, syntactic processing does not involve the assembly of words into syntactic units by means of rules, but of categorization of word combinations as instantiations of constructions. That is, in this view of grammatical organization, a listener does not assemble [spray], [the wall] and [with paint] into a VP by means of a rule VP → V NP PP; that is, a listener categorizes the phrase [spray the wall with paint] as an instance of the construction [V NP *with* NP] or more generally [V NP PP].[6]

This is a summary of the most important points of construction grammar's or cognitive grammar's model of grammatical organization, some of which will be relevant to the argument in the following sections. Although the footnotes of this section have emphasized continuities between construction grammar and generative or formal models of syntax and semantics, the construction grammar view leads to some rather dramatic changes which nevertheless simplify the structure of the grammar. For example, as we have seen here, construction grammar eliminates subcategorization and government as grammatical phenomena and replaces them by the more general interplay between construction schemas and the lexical items that instantiate elements in those schemas. In doing so, however, there is no a priori relationship between constructional schemas and the items that instantiate elements in those schemas, and hence no a priori way to identify one of those elements as the head.

3. THE MORPHOSYNTACTIC LOCUS

At this point I have simply eliminated from consideration a number of criteria that Zwicky and Hudson have discussed regarding the notion of a syntactic head. So far, what I have done is in the spirit of Zwicky's rather than Hudson's analysis. I have argued that various syntactic criteria that have been suggested to be relevant to headhood in fact are not. I have provided more extensive syntactic and typological evidence than Zwicky has, which further supports his points, even though I have couched some of my arguments in terms of a different model of syntactic organization (construction grammar) than Zwicky uses. Agreement or concord is keyed to a different function, having to do with NPs/referring expression; in this I follow both Zwicky and Hudson. Distributional equivalence and obligatoriness, to the extent that they exhibit regularity, are independent of the intuitive notion of head, at any rate; this is in agreement with Zwicky though against Hudson. Finally, I have argued that subcategorization and government are also the result of a different kind of phenomenon, the interplay of stored grammatical constructions with the lexical items that instantiate elements of those constructions. While this argument is couched in a model of syntactic organization that is different from that presupposed by Zwicky, Zwicky too argues that subcategorization and government are independent phenomena from the one that he wants to call headhood (for him, they are associated with the semantic functor).

This leaves the one morphosyntactic criterion that Zwicky does consider to be an indicator of headhood, the morphosyntactic locus of grammatical inflection. Zwicky's chief interest is in what is called percolation, a principle that morphosyntactic features of the head match the morphosyntactic features of the constituent that it is the head of. These features are generally inflectional features, such as gender, number, tense, etc. But this definition of headhood seems circular. Since the purpose of percolation is (as the name implies) to percolate features from one level to another, it is not surprising that the head is the element at the lower level bearing those features. Zwicky seems to feel some of this circularity, by suggesting that morphosyntactic locus is the primitive concept (Z, p. 3, 10), and concludes, "unless there is very good reason for doing otherwise, the morphosyntactic locus should be identified as the head in syntactic percolation" (Z, p. 10).

The question I want to raise now refers back to my methodological subtheme. One can accept that there is a syntactic property that is possessed by certain elements of a constituent and is defined by percolation of syntactic features. But is that the head? Is that the concept which appears to be so central to the analysis of syntactic structure in so many twentieth-century theories of grammar? I believe that as useful a concept as morphosyntactic locus may turn out to be, it is not the concept we should call the head of a constituent—or rather, it is a symptom, not an explanation, of headhood. Of course, my reasons for believing this are not strictly of an empirical sort; they are more of a theory-internal nature. First, the notion of head is intended to be a generalization over all asymmetrical dependency relations; hence, its application to all such relations should be straightforward. (This does not necessarily mean that the *result* of applying the criterion should be straightforward.) Second, it should be a criterion that is applicable across languages without being dependent on language-specific grammatical properties. I believe this is necessary for all grammatical categories that are claimed to be central to syntactic structure in general. Finally, the criterion should be founded on some sort of pretheoretical intuition that the criterion can be argued to reasonably capture.

I am not certain that morphosyntactic locus has the breadth of applicability or language-independence that the notion head seems to have, nor is it obviously based on some basic pretheoretic intuition about the nature of syntactic structure. The inflectional repertory of some languages is very limited, possibly nonexistent in some languages. The morphosyntactic locus can be rather variable also. For example, in languages with particle-like auxiliaries such as Lakhota, the morphosyntactic locus is the verb. In languages with verb-like auxiliaries such as most European languages, the morphosyntactic locus is the auxiliar. In some languages, such as some southern Bantu languages, both auxiliary and verb are inflected, so both appear to be the morphosyntactic locus. In languages such as Papago, the auxiliary carries certain inflections and the verb carries other, different inflections. Such variability is not in principle evidence against using this criterion for a putatively universal notion such as head.[7] Much typological research indicates that any language universal has to be a universal of limits on variation, not a simple absolute universals of the form 'all languages do X'. But this variation appears to call for some sort of explanation. In fact, I believe that morphosyntactic locus *is* related to headhood; but it seems that there must be some deeper phenomenon that the morphosyntactic locus is a manifestation of, which can be tapped more directly in comparing different constructions in the same language and in other languages. In particular, I believe that such a definition is semantic; it is hinted at in the earlier literature, and is explicitly discussed by Zwicky and Hudson, though both take it in different—I believe incorrect—directions.

4. A SEMANTIC DEFINITION OF 'HEAD': FIRST ATTEMPT

As was mentioned in §1, headhood lacks the millennia-old grammatical or philosophical tradition that is found with concepts such as noun, verb, subject and object and fixes our pretheoretic intuitions about such concepts to a great extent. The notion of head as a generalization over the traditional concepts of government, agreement and modification appears to be a relatively recent one. I begin by citing some basic texts that are drawn upon repeatedly in discussions of headhood.

An early antecedent (brought to my attention by Leon Stassen) are the medieval Modistæ. They took a largely binary view of the structure of a constituent (*constructio*) and described a generalized asymmetrical relation that is found across a wide range of constituents, usually described as *dependens* and *terminans* (Covington 1984: 48). The relations covered by these terms, and the choice of *terminans*, seems baffling on grammatical grounds, but Covington argues that essentially the *terminans* is an argument and the *dependens* is a predicate (functor; Covington 1984: 49-51); this is clear from the examples from Thomas of Erfurt given by Covington (ibid., 49). While the Modistæ undoubtedly describe a generalized asymmetrical dependency relation, it is quite distinct from that called head by more recent grammarians and should be most closely identified with the semantic function-argument relation.

The first reference to heads by name that I am aware of is Sweet (1891: 16):

> The most general relation between words in sentences from a logical point of view is that of adjunct-word and head-word...*book (books)* is an adjunct-word in *book-seller, bookselling, sale of books, he sells books, he sold his books,* the corresponding head-words being *seller, selling, sale, sells, sold.*

Sweet unfortunately does not define what a head-word is in general; the head-adjunct distinction is taken as self-evident. Likewise, most of the dependency grammarians focus on an abstract characterization of the asymmetric relation, calling the head the controller (Matthews 1981). These terms evoke the syntactic asymmetry rather than any pretheoretical characterization of the 'dominant' element. More specifically, they do not provide any clue as to how to determine independently which element is the head, except through the morphosyntactic criteria which I have argued to be largely irrelevant to the question.

Zwicky (Z, p. 2) cites a passage from Jespersen (1924: 96), which appears to describe the same position as Sweet's, though he does not use the word 'head':

> In any composite denomination of a thing or person..., we always find that there is one word of supreme importance to which the others are joined as subordinates. This chief word is defined (qualified, modified) by another word, which in turn may be defined (qualified, modified) by a third word, etc. We are thus led to establish different 'ranks' of words according to their mutual relations as defined or defining. In the combination *extremely hot weather* the last word *weather*, which is evidently the chief idea, may be called primary; *hot*, which defines *weather*, secondary, and *extremely*, which defines *hot*, tertiary.

As with Sweet, Jespersen focuses on the asymmetric relation, but not the property that determines which is the 'dominant' one in the relationship. However, he gives a hint in his example: "*weather*, which is evidently the chief idea...".

The oft-cited passage of Bloomfield, the starting-point of structuralist and generative theories of headhood, is as follows (Bloomfield 1933: 195):

> If all of the syntactic constructions which go to make up a phrase are endocentric, then the phrase will contain among its ultimate constituents some word (or several words, members of a co-ordination) whose form-class is the same as that of the phrase. This word is the *center* of the phrase. In the phrase *all this fresh milk*, the word *milk* is the center, and in the phrase *all this fresh bread and sweet butter*, the words *bread* and *butter* are the centers.

Bloomfield was a strict behaviorist by the time he wrote this passage, and so uses the criterion of distributional equivalence ("same form-class"), which we have argued is not relevant to headhood. But in addition to using the term 'head' (in another passage on the same page), Bloomfield here uses the term 'center', which is reminiscent of Jespersen's concept of the 'chief idea'.

This is the intuition that I believe headhood is about. Zwicky interprets Jespersen's concept of 'chief idea' as follows: "Like Jespersen in the quotation above, we could take the head/modifier distinction to be at root semantic: in a combination X + Y, X is the 'semantic head' if, speaking very crudely, X + Y describes a kind of the thing described by X" (Z, p. 4). Hudson says of this interpretation, "However crude it may be, I find this description very insightful, and I think it corresponds closely to the intuition that underlies many of the dependency analyses with which I am familiar" (Hudson 1987: 113).

Zwicky's interpretation of Jespersen is the right beginning point for a definition of head, I believe, and it appears to capture in rough form the intuitive notion that Sweet, Jespersen and Bloomfield allude to. Zwicky however promptly interprets 'being the same kind of' as a semantic argument (Z, p. 4). Hudson notices this and argues against Zwicky (Hudson 1987: 113-116)—but instead argues that the head must be interpreted as the semantic functor. Despite the initial conception of a semantic definition of headhood, Zwicky and Hudson proceed to go in opposite directions in defining this notion, and both of those directions are incorrect, or rather, lead to anomalous conclusions.

Zwicky tries to impose the functor-argument relation on his set of six construction types, and argues that some heads (in some intuitive sense, or at least with respect to the morphosyntactic locus) are functors and others are arguments. Hudson disputes Zwicky's functor-argument characterizations, demonstrating that the intuitions behind functor-argument are not at all clear beyond the standard examples. But even the standard examples clearly indicate that neither functor nor argument can be the proper semantic characterization of head. In V + NP, the verb is generally taken to be the functor and the NP the argument; this is the example that Hudson begins with in criticizing Zwicky. But in the standard Mod + Head constructions, particularly Adj + N, Adv + V, Adv + Adj, and Adv + S, none of which are in the set of six constructions that Zwicky (or Hudson) discusses, the Mod is generally considered to be the functor and the Head is the argument; but intuitions are equally clear that the Head describes the same kind of thing that the Mod + Head unit does (e.g., a *blue book* is a kind of book, not a kind of blue).

In fact, this is the basic problem in trying to unify modification and government/agreement to a more general concept of headhood: in modification, the semantic argument is the head, while in government/agreement, the semantic functor is the head. 'Being the same kind of' is a different semantic property from being functor or argument. Although formal semantics, from predicate logic to Montague grammar, have given pride of place to the predicate/functor-argument distinction (thus following the Modistæ), it is not the only semantic distinction relevant to syntactic structure. Recognizing this fact, we can now return to Zwicky's 'crude' characterization and move to a more fruitful semantic characterization of headhood.

I begin, however, by reversing Zwicky's characterization: *in a combination X+ Y, X is the semantic head if X describes a kind of the thing described by X + Y*. In other words, we have reversed the direction of determination of headhood from 'word to construction' to 'construction to word'. We begin with construction X + Y and determine what it denotes semantically. Then we look among its constituents, and discover what constituent, if any, has a denotation that best matches the denotation of X + Y. If a match is good enough, then we call it the head of the construction; if no match is good enough, then we say the construction is headless.

By reversing Zwicky's definition in this way, we make it clear that headhood is a property of a construction; it is a property of a particular word only by virtue of the construction it occurs in. This is critical in unifying the characterization of modification and government/agreement. In both *the broken vase* and *The vase broke*, *vase* is the semantic argument and (the relevant form of) *break* is the semantic functor. It is only by virtue of the Adj + N construction and the NP + VP construction that *vase* is head in the former but dependent in the latter. More precisely, it is only by virtue of the fact that the Adj + N construction denotes a thing and the NP + VP construction denotes a state of affairs that the vase is the head in the former and the dependent in the latter. In this way, we see some element as a head by virtue of its role in the construction X + Y, not that X + Y inherits some feature of a component element X.

Another advantage of reversing Zwicky's characterization of a semantic head is that the existence of two noncanonical possibilities is made explicit. First, a construction may have more than one head; this is possible if the denotation of the whole happens to coincide with the denotation of more than one of its parts, not an a priori impossible situation. Second, and more important for my argument, headedness may be a matter of degree, that is, the degree to which some element's denotation matches the denotation of the whole in semantic type. This match may not be perfect. This latter possibility is excluded if the denotation of a construction X + Y is something inherited from a (unique) component element X.

This is exactly the notion in Langacker 's Cognitive Grammar that he calls a PROFILE DETERMINANT (Langacker 1987, §8.2.1). Langacker's term PROFILE refers to the frame-semantic model of semantic structure (see Fillmore 1975, 1977, 1982, 1985), which he largely adopts. In frame semantics, the meaning of any linguistic element consists of two components. The first is the profile, which roughly corresponds to the traditional denotation of an element. The second is the base (Langacker) or frame (Fillmore), which is the set of background assumptions and concepts necessary for understanding the meaning of the profiled concept. The base/frame corresponds roughly to the presuppositions of a concept (see Searle 1979 as well as Fillmore and Langacker for arguments for the necessity of the base/frame in defining the meaning of a linguistic unit). The term 'determinant' is a little misleading, since it makes it sound as if a component element determines what is the profile of the construction as a whole, the characterization of the head-construction relation which I have just argued against.[8] To use Langacker's examples, in *that football under the table, football* is the profile determinant, but in the assertion *That football is under the table, football* is not the profile determinant. Headhood is nothing inherent about the syntactic status of the noun *football*; instead, it is a property of the constructions [Dem N PP] and [NP be PP]. I have indicated the property of profile determinacy by boldfacing the constructional element that Langacker takes to be the profile determinant in each case (these are Langacker's choices, incidentally, and will be examined critically below.)

Let us turn to a few constructions to see how the criterion works in general, before getting down to some problematic cases. Consider the Quechua headless nominal in example (8) above. This is headless because the whole denotes some (contextually understood) sort of object; it does not denote a property, although the property denoted by the adjective is specified for that thing. But there is no other constituent that denotes a thing, so we call it headless. Now consider pronouns, a special type of NP. They have a head, namely the pronoun itself; we can safely say that the denotation of the whole is in fact identical to the denotation of the relevant part. Finally, compare appositive structures such as *my brother the geophysicist*; here the denotation of the whole is identical not to just one but both of the component NPs. Langacker, in discussing similar examples (Langacker 1987: 291), suggests that we reserve the term 'head'/'profile determinant' to constructions in which there is a single element which possesses the relevant property as against other elements in the same construction. This would restrict usage of the term to prototypical noun phrases such as *the big turkey near the back*. Nevertheless, in general the notion of profile determinant, as a modification of Zwicky's interpretation of Jespersen's hint, appears to give us the intuitively right results.

A trickier case are coordinate structures: *Matt and Rina*. The entity denoted by the whole is a pair of people; neither proper name denotes that composite entity, nor does the connective. So we are inclined to call this construction headless also. This is contrary to Bloomfield (though not to most dependency grammarians, or to Matthews 1981). Bloomfield's position can be interpreted in this context as one in which all that matters is that the combination *X and Y* denotes a thing, and so do each of X and Y; the fact that X and Y together denotes a paired thing whereas X and Y each denotes an individual thing does not matter to Bloomfield. However, a more strictly defined relation between what the whole construction denotes and what its head denotes is more useful, and ultimately more firmly testable.

Another possibility that must be entertained for coordinate structures is that the semantics of *and* is such that it denotes a composite entity. This analysis is in fact (arguably) Wierzbicka's analysis of *and* (Wierzbicka 1980). Such an analysis would make *and* the head (profile determinant) of the coordinate construction because its denotation most closely matches the denotation of the whole construction X *and* Y. Hence, decisions about headhood are going to hinge on the semantics of the elements of the construction and how they relate to the semantics of the whole. Once closer attention is paid to those elements, we will see that some obvious decisions about headhood are not so obvious any more, and (some of) the functional head analyses constructed in recent Chomskyan theory (beginning with Abney 1987 and Pollock 1989) largely on theory-internal syntactic grounds of elegance of phrase structure actually have some semantic motivation.

5. PROFILE DETERMINANTS AND THE DECOMPOSITION OF PRAGMATIC FUNCTIONS.

There are currently two proposals out on the table for what is the head in a prototypical noun phrase. The traditional view is that the 'head noun', *turkey*, is the head. But a more recent proposal is that the determiner , in this case *the*, is the head (Abney 1987). Neither proposal is universally accepted, though the latter is dominant in generative grammar. What does the profile determinant analysis say is the head?

Before looking at the semantic analysis, it is worth considering what the morphosyntactic locus suggests is the head. Cross-linguistically, the data are mixed. In many languages the morphosyntactic locus is the noun; it is inflected for number, gender, case, etc. But in other languages, the only manifestation of inflectional categories is on the determiner. For example, in Dyirbal (Dixon 1972), the determiner differs as to the noun class of the noun, but there is no indication of the noun class on the noun itself. In still other languages, such as English, both the determiner and the noun inflect, in English for the category of number—significantly, the adjective or numeral does not inflect for this category.

Of course, this evidence is relevant only if morphosyntactic locus is a good indicator of headhood. It is suspicious that the morphosyntactic locus of a noun phrase appears to be just those two elements that have been proposed for headhood. But we can only develop a semantic account of the profile determination of noun phrases if we have a semantic theory for nouns, determiners and noun phrases, that is, a semantic representation of their profiles. Once that is accomplished, we can compare the profile of the noun phrase to that of the noun and the determiner, and make some conclusion as to which (if either) best fits the description of a head.[9]

The chief semantic argument in favor of determiners rather than nouns as the heads of the noun phrases they determine is that noun phrases refer, but simple nouns do not. In noun phrases with nouns as heads (in the traditional view), that is, most noun phrases in English and in many other languages, a referring expression is not complete without a determiner. It is the determiner that appears to fix reference, not the head noun which simply categorizes the referent in question as belonging to a particular semantic class. It is the determiner that achieves the act of reference and therefore most closely denotes the same thing as the whole noun phrase, namely a thing whose identity is established and is situated in the domain of discourse and the speaker and hearer's mutual knowledge. This is the intuitive semantic motivation behind the DP analysis, which makes it seem a reasonable alternative to the lexical head analysis.

But the most accurate description of what happens in reference is that the whole noun phrase fixes reference. Reference cannot succeed without some categorization of the object in almost all cases. In fact, it is worth noting that pronouns cross-linguistically act like 'super-prototypical' nouns (Croft 1991, §3.3.1), for example displaying even more nominal inflectional categories than nouns do. (In English for example, there are nominative and oblique forms for most pronouns, a distinction absent in common nouns.) This evidence suggests that in fact, pronouns are the most unmarked nouns, because they carry out the act of reference entirely. Nevertheless, even pronouns are frequently categorized by gender, class or animacy, and always for person (or deixis, in the case of demonstrative pronouns). Many languages lack determiners, that is, articles, so most nonpronominal NPs in such languages consist solely of a noun. The formal semantic and discourse models of file change semantics (Heim 1983) and discourse representation theory (Kamp 1984) also involve the setting up of a discourse file for an entity which involves categorizing it as well as leaving it available for anaphoric reference.

The best analysis of referring expressions is that they involve a complex pragmatic function which can be decomposed into component pragmatic functions. Specifically, it consists of the following three functions: (i) typing an entity into a category, (ii) instantiating the type, and (iii) grounding that type in the speaker and hearer's currently active shared knowledge, or 'discourse space'. The terminology here follows Langacker (1991); however, analogous analyses can be found in other frameworks. I described these three components as minor propositional acts consisting of categorizing, selecting (instantiating) and situating (grounding), the latter in either physical space or in a mental discourse space (Croft 1990b). In formal semantic systems involving restrictive quantification or generalized quantifiers, the function of categorizing is found in the restriction of the quantifier, and instantiating/grounding is found in the quantifier itself. In Langacker 's analysis, typing or categorizing is achieved by the noun stem; instantiation involves the noun inflection (for number or countability), which can be accompanied by quantification; and grounding of the referent in the discourse space is accomplished by determiner s (in languages which have them).

If the tripartite pragmatic analysis outlined in the preceding paragraph is accepted, then the notion that reference is achieved by the determiner mistakes the (necessary) final step of the referring act for the whole process of reference.

Reference is not established by the determiner alone either; it must work in coordination with the rest of the noun phrase. In particular, there must be an instantiation of the type, since it is that instantiation (that is, the concept of that instantiation) which is situated in discourse space/has a discourse or cognitive file opened for it, etc. (Langacker 1991: 96). And an instantiation has to be identified and distinguished from other instantiations by its type. If the determiner can stand alone syntactically, then it is functioning as a pronoun, as in the Luganda example (9) above, that is, it is fulfilling all three components of the referring act at once. If a language lacks determiners, then the noun alone can fill all of the functions, that is, the noun alone can, and usually does, stand as an NP in such languages.

Now, if we ask, what is the head of a normal multiconstituent NP, we can see that at one level, the answer is 'both N and Det': the act of reference achieved by the NP as a whole involves contributions by both the N and the Det (in languages that have determiners). The cross-linguistic evidence, based on the morphosyntactic locus, is appropriately equivocal: sometimes Det, sometimes N, sometimes both are the morphosyntactic locus. Langacker's definition of determiners, that is, grounding elements applied to nominals, follows a two-headed analysis. For him, the determiner profiles a thing, just as the head noun does; the grounding of the NP in the mutual knowledge of speaker/hearer and the discourse context is part of the base of the determiner's meaning (Langacker 1991: 95). Of course, the denotation of a thing specified by a determiner such as *a* or *the* is completely schematic, while that of the noun is much more specific. But in terms of the definition of head as profile determinant, both the head noun and the determiner qualify as heads of the NP in Langacker's analysis, since they each profile the thing denoted by the whole NP.[10]

Exactly analogous arguments can be made for Aux and V (using V as the head of VP). As noted at the beginning of this section, cross-linguistically the morphosyntactic locus is sometimes Aux, sometimes V, sometimes both. A prototypical V combines the semantic class of an action with the pragmatic function of predication (for stative predications and the copulas they are often found with, see §6.5). The same three semantic/pragmatic functions must operate in predications as well. When an event is predicated, it too must be categorized, instantiated and then grounded. Categorization is performed by the lexical verb root, parallel with categorization by the lexical noun root. Instantiation involves aspect and Aktionsart; many researchers have noted the parallels between countability or individuation for objects and aspect and Aktionsart for events. Grounding involves situating the event with respect to the knowledge and beliefs of the speaker and hearer. In particular, it must be situated in the appropriate mental space (Fauconnier 1985), or if you prefer, set of possible worlds. This is true even for events in the real world, which itself is a mental space in Fauconnier's view. Situating an entity in a mental space is accomplished by tense and mood in particular, and that function is generally performed by auxiliaries in languages that have them.

The predication function can be decomposed into (i) the scanning of a scene, as being of a particular semantic type, (ii) its instantiation and (iii) the situating of that event in a mental space. Part (i) of the predication function is accomplished by the verb, and parts (ii) and (iii) by the auxiliary (if present), which indicates tense-mood-aspect, and so both contribute to the profile of the whole clause. If a clause has only a verb (as in the simple tenses of English), then it is performing all three components of the predication function at once. As mentioned above, the cross-linguistic pattern of the morphosyntactic locus also finds it not coincidentally located on the auxiliar or the verb or both, but not elsewhere in the clause. Another parallel with nominal structure that is probably not a coincidence is that there are many languages which lack tense, that is the obligatory marking of the grounding of the event, just as many languages lack articles (the obligatory marking of the grounding of the object). In such languages, a simple verb form can perform the entire complex function of predication without an accompanying auxiliary or tense marking.[11]

The analyses of reference and predication in this section, and their consequences for headhood defined as the profile determinant(s), are likely to be controversial. I find the consequences of them problematic, and will propose a refinement of the semantic definition in the next section. However, the methodological conclusion that should be drawn from this section is that care must be taken in characterizing the semantics (i.e., the profile) of the whole construction and of each of its parts, when deciding what the profile-determinant definition predicts to be the head (or heads) of a constituent. Differences in the semantic analyses of the whole and of the parts will lead to differences in what is predicted to be the head of a constituent. In general, I believe that the profile-determinant definition of a head (as being 'of the same kind as' the whole constituent) is itself not crude. Instead, it is the analyses of the semantic structures of the syntactic and lexical units to which this definition is applied that need to be refined.

6. HEADS AND PIBU'S

For some people, myself included, the two-headed model for phrases and clauses implied by the profile-determinant semantic definition of head is an unsatisfactory conclusion. The idea of a two-headed phrase sounds about as natural as a two-headed baby. Maybe we have to accept such things—two-headed phrases, that is. For example, I think we need to accept that in many sentence types in many languages, the evidence as to which NP is subject is equivocal—two NPs are good candidates for subjecthood by the usual criteria, including criteria that a functionally-oriented linguist like myself consider to be the right ones. So maybe we just have to accept that categories as central to the syntactic structure of sentences as noun phrases and clauses are simply two-headed beasts. In fact, this analogy is not a good one. For subjects, it is only a (hopefully) small percentage of clauses in which subject properties are spread across more than one NP. But in the analyses of phrases and clauses given above, most if not all phrases and clauses have their head properties spread across two component elements. But in fact, I do not believe that we must accept the conclusion of the preceding section. There is other cross-linguistic morphosyntactic evidence that strongly suggests that phrases and clauses are normal single-headed creatures, and that the true head is the traditional one—noun for noun phrases, and verb for clauses. But we must take a diachronic perspective in order to uncover and use this evidence.

The evidence comes from the phenomenon of grammaticalization and reanalysis. To put it succinctly, given our two candidates for headhood in syntactic structure based on synchronic semantic analysis, there is a clear asymmetry in their diachronic behavior. The functional categories (Det and Aux) grammaticalize, and get reduced in their grammatical behavior. The lexical heads do not. In fact, if the functional categories originate as the head of the construction, then in the process of grammaticalization the lexical heads are reanalyzed so that they are no longer in the subordinate structure they originally came from; and the functional categories end up losing their status as autonomous syntactic units, and becoming affixed to—of course—the lexical head.

This is the usual pattern for both determiners and auxiliaries. Determiners begin their lives as demonstratives (which in turn probably begin their lives as independent NPs appositive to the head noun—this might be the right analysis for demonstratives). They are transformed into articles, and often come to be affixed to the head noun. When that stage is accomplished, the noun-plus-determiner -affix becomes a single word carrying out the referring function, and it is indubitably the (syntactic) head. The affixed article may disappear, leading to an articleless NP in which the noun is the only strong candidate for headhood.

Auxiliaries often begin as main verbs, with the future main verb in a subordinate clause. The main auxiliar verb gets grammaticalized, and the constituent structure of the construction is reanalyzed from [V [VP]] to [Aux VP]. The Aux may eventually come to be affixed onto the verb in many languages.[12] In fact, there appears to be a more general phenomenon of verbal attraction in which various dependent elements including direct argument pronouns and even object nouns attach themselves to the verb (Heine & Reh 1984, §1.1.3.1).[13] The lexical verb emerges triumphant.

Why does this happen? What semantic property does the noun and the verb have that the determiner and the auxiliar lack? The noun and the verb are the PRIMARY INFORMATION-BEARING UNITS (PIBUs); in common parlance, content words. PIBUs have major informational content that functional categories do not have. That is the asymmetry involved between functional heads and lexical heads. I therefore propose that the semantic definition of headhood is *the profile determinant that is the primary information-bearing unit*, that is, the most contentful item that most closely denotes the same kind of thing that the whole constituent denotes. The morphosyntactic locus is an indicator of profile determinacy, as we saw in the preceding section, and grammaticalization and/or reanalysis is an indicator of headhood (that is, PIBU + profile determinacy), as I have argued so far in this section. If there are two candidates for profile determinant, the one that is not the PIBU will undergo grammaticalization and possibly be attracted and absorbed by the true (PIBU) head.

There is a simple semantic definition of a PIBU, or rather, what makes the PIBU more contentful than its potential competition. If the criterion of profile determination produces two candidates for headhood, the less schematic meaning is the PIBU; that is, the PIBU is the one with the narrower extension, in the formal semantic sense of that term. Consider again Langacker 's analysis of English determiner s in a phrase such as *the golfer.* In Langacker's analysis, both *the* and *golfer* profile a 'thing' (his technical term for what a noun denotes; the precise characterization is not relevant to the point being made here). However, *the* profiles a thing at a very high degree of generality (schematicity): the only restriction is that it is uniquely available to speaker and hearer in the discourse context. Even that information is in the base (frame) of *the*'s semantic representation, not the profile. *Golfer*, on the other hand, is a much more specific kind of thing, and so in formal semantic terms its extension is much more limited. Hence, by the schematicity criterion, *golfer* is the head. A similar argument can be constructed for Aux and V, assuming that Aux and V both profile the process, Aux profiling the process as grounded in a mental space or discourse space, analogous to Det's profiling of the noun.

I now turn to some specific examples of how this definition of head accounts for synchronic and diachronic data, especially grammaticalization and reanalysis.

6.1 *Determiners and auxiliaries*

I have argued that reanalysis occurs concomitant with the grammaticalization of determiners and auxiliaries. This presupposes that in fact the situation was different in an earlier stage of the grammaticalization process, and that what I am calling the PIBU in fact was not the head, even under the semantic definition proposed here. This is certainly the case with auxiliaries, at least those auxiliaries that originated as main verbs. At the point when they were main verbs, there were two significant semantic differences from their later, nonhead, status. First, their meanings were more contentful. Second, they were the sole profile determinants of their clause. In an utterance like *I want to go home* and *She went to buy groceries*, it can be readily argued that what the sentence as a whole profiles is an instance of desire in the first case and motion in the second. In more grammaticalized versions such as *I will go home* and *She's gonna buy groceries*, however, the clause profiles the process described by the main verb. The former main verbs have changed meaning, that is, they have changed their profile so that the process is profiled and the auxiliaries merely ground (situate) that process in the future. At that point, both auxiliar and verb profile the process, the verb is the PIBU, and reanalysis has taken place.

The historical scenario with determiners is similar. The chief historical source of determiners are demonstratives. If the demonstrative source is originally a pronoun, then it would be in apposition to the noun phrase and would profile the same thing as the noun phrase. The demonstrative pronoun of course generally has more semantic information than a typical determiner, that is, deictic information and possibly some classifying information, and so is a better candidate for PIBU than an article. As the demonstrative becomes a determiner and is more tightly integrated into the noun phrase, then its profile competes with that of the noun, which is clearly the PIBU and hence leads the reanalysis of the determiner as a modifier. Unfortunately, I do not have well-attested examples of the earliest stages of this hypothetical process.

At this point we have assumed that profile determination is a necessary condition for headhood, and PIBU status is a secondary condition, which need only be invoked when there is more than one profile determinant in the clause. In other words, the semantic definition of headhood that I have proposed is not a prototype definition. However, we will now examine situations in which profile determination is not as clear-cut, and PIBU status appears to play a decisive role in syntactic reanalysis. I modified Zwicky's definition of 'of the same kind as' so that the element of the constituent whose profile most closely matched that of the constituent as a whole was a candidate for headhood. Up to this point, I have assumed largely perfect matches, although I did suggest that the pragmatic function profiled by an NP as a whole was distributed across the head noun and the determiner . Now I will consider some less straightforward instances. It must be repeated that part of what makes the instances to be discussed here less straightforward is that the decision as to what contribution to the profile of the whole constituent that each element makes depends on the analysis of the profile of each constituent, which is not uncontroversial in many cases.

6.2. *Numerals and quantifiers*

Let us begin with a well-known example of syntactic reanalysis found with numerals and quantifiers. Quantifiers and numerals frequently start out their lives as the heads of their constructions in a clear syntactic sense: the nouns that categorize the objects being quantified are in genitive subordinate phrases. But equally frequently a syntactic reanalysis occurs, so that the noun is no longer a genitive dependent of the numeral or quantifier, but instead the head of a noun phrase with the numeral as a modifier. The reanalysis can be described as [Num [N-gen]] > [Num N], using boldface for the profile determinant. This syntactic reanalysis appears to be unidirectional. In many cases, the synchronic situation is such that lower numerals have the syntactic behavior of adjectives, and so resemble modifiers, and higher numerals have the syntactic behavior of nouns, and so resemble the heads of noun phrases (Greenberg 1978: 285, Universal 47).

Langacker (1991: 83-84) argues that a numeral such as *three* has a slightly different profile if it is an adjective (and hence a modifier) or a noun (and thus a head). Roughly, Langacker 's semantic analysis is as follows. The (plural) noun combined with a numeral profiles a replicate mass, that is, a replicate entity of the type. Roughly, in Langacker's analysis the adjectival *three* means 'this replicate mass is of cardinality three'. The content of the numeral is the cardinality of the replication (or set(s), if you prefer), which he represents as a one-to-one correspondence with a number scale. A particular numeral such as *three* profiles a point on the number scale, in the same way as an adjective such as *red* indicates a point (more precisely, a region around a focal point), on the color scale. But an adjective is relational—in standard formal semantic terms, it takes an argument, namely the replicate mass. (Langacker calls this argument the trajector.) The trajector argument is in profile also, as is standard in cognitive grammar, and just as argument positions are part of the semantic representation of a predicate in formal semantics. The effect of this is that much of the contentful portion of the profile is the entity itself; only the point on the number scale is in profile besides the trajector. Langacker analyzes *three* as in *three (of them)*—an example of a genitive phrase headed by a numeral, the construction before reanalysis—as profiling the replicate mass alone. Thus, the whole profile for the nominal form is what becomes the trajector in the adjectival form under reanalysis. The point on the number scale is part of the base in the nominal form, but comes to be part of the profile of the adjectival form.

Langacker's analysis of what constitutes the profile in the nominal and the adjectival numeral forms provides an explanation for the reanalysis. In the nominal form, the numeral profiles the same kind of entity that the noun profiles, namely a thing in Langacker's terms. The whole construction also profiles a (grounded instance of) a thing. The noun, however, has a more specific meaning, and hence is the PIBU; so syntactic reanalysis is likely to occur, rendering it the head. The syntactic reanalysis involves two things: disposing of the genitive dependent relation and altering the profile of the numeral so that it is now an adjective, i.e., it is relational and the point on the number scale is profiled. The relation between the numeral and the replicate mass denoted by the noun is of course what the genitive encodes. The genitive is also held to have a meaning in cognitive grammar, but it is a highly general meaning covering the relation between two things (see Taylor 1989 and Langacker 1991, §4.3.2). The syntactic reanalysis reflects a reassignment of the relational aspect of the meaning of the whole expression from the genitive, which disappears, to the numeral, which now takes on the relational profile and the morphosyntactic properties of an adjective. The definition of headhood presented here provides the causal impetus for this syntactic change.

An example of an in-between stage of this process is found with measure expressions in English. They have the syntactic form of [N [of N]], which suggests that the first noun is the head (as indicated); but their behavior indicates that the genitive 'dependent' is functioning as the head:

(20) a. Tim drank a cup of coffee.
b. *Tim broke a cup of coffee.

The object argument of *drink*, i.e., what the object denotes, is a potable liquid. The phrase *a cup of coffee* denotes that liquid. The constituent that denotes that liquid, and hence the head in our semantic definition, is *coffee*, which syntactically is in a subordinate genitive here, or appears to be. But the fact that this construction has been reanalyzed as a Qnt + N construction can be seen by the badness of (20b). Contrast with the following, in which *cup* is indubitably the head of the compound:

(21) a. Tim broke a coffee cup.
b. *Tim drank a coffee cup.

Actually, *cup* in (20a) has changed meaning to denote a measure instead of a physical object. This change of meaning is critical in the syntactic change. The measure—like the quantifier—profiles the specific instantiation of the liquid. Since *coffee* in this context also profiles the (instantiation of the) liquid, the two profiles overlap in a way that the profiles of container and contained do not. The liquid as well as the measure is a profile determinant, and it is the PIBU. In fact the genitive is now reduced to *a cuppa coffee,* demonstrating that the preposition has lost its syntactic identity and no longer can be thought of as governing the following noun.

Examples like these have also been discussed by Sweet (1891: 44-46). In discussing *the majority of Englishmen*, he argues that the "logical head-word" is *Englishmen*, although the "grammatical head-word" is *majority*. Likewise, Sweet argues that in the predicative adjective *are tall* and the auxiliar construction *shall have seen, tall* and *seen* are the logical head-words, while *are* and *shall* are the grammatical head-words. He describes the logical head-words as "prominent and logically important" ideas in the utterance. He concludes by coining the term 'nucleus' to indicate the logical head-word. Sweet's 'logical head-word' or 'nucleus' is the PIBU, and we have added in the diachronic dimension to show that 'logical' headhood leads to a reanalysis of 'grammatical' headhood.

6.3. *Adpositions*

The next case that we will examine is one of the most problematic: adpositions. Here there is general agreement that adpositions are the heads of their phrases. However, there is some uncertainty as to how to handle them in the recent literature on functional heads: Abney (1987: 63) notes that adpositions seem to "straddle the line" between functional and lexical categories, and Ouhalla (1991: 202) states that "the status of prepositions with respect to the division worked out here is not clear" (Haspelmath to appear: 3). The diachronic facts here are again unequivocal: adpositions grammaticalize and eventually may come to be fused with the noun as case markers; in other words, they attach to their heads. In the analysis I have presented here, then, the noun is—ultimately—the head.

The qualification 'ultimately' is the important term here. We must consider the two extreme ends of the continuum of adpositions. The diachronic source of adpositions are most commonly (serial) verbs with meanings such as 'take' or 'use' for the instrumental relation or (relational) nouns with meanings such as 'face' for the benefactive relation, or body-part terms for various spatial relations (in addition, directional adverbs are a prominent source in Indo-European languages). In nominal or verbal adposition sources, the NP is clearly a dependent, a genitive dependent of the noun in the first case and an object dependent of the verb in the second case.

In the process of grammaticalization, the profile of the adpositional phrase/case-marked NP changes, but there is a twist here, not found with the numeral/quantifier example. Clearly, when the adposition-to-be is syntactically a verb or noun, its profile includes the content of that verb or noun, and the NP complement is only a part of that profile by virtue of its being a participant in the verbal event or the entity to which the relational noun is related. However, as grammaticalization progresses, two things happen. First, the meaning of the adposition gets more general. This makes it a less likely candidate for PIBU. Second, that meaning overlaps more and more with the meaning of the verb. This is clearest with adpositional phrases or oblique case NPs that are governed by the verb. In a sentence such as *Put the book back on the bookshelf*, the profile of the verb *put* includes the destination of the object *book*. This component of *put*'s profile overlaps considerably with the limited range of preposition meanings that are permissible in the locative PP complement of *put* (roughly, they must indicate a location which is the final location of the direct object). In this example, the preposition still provides more semantic content for that aspect of the action than the verb—compare *Put the picture over the couch.* But the content of the object NP and the NP governed by the preposition highly determine that locative relationship anyway. If we turn to nonspatial relations, the overlap is more complete. In *I agree with you*, the preposition *with* still possesses a meaning but its contribution to the verbal profile is minimal; *agree* already contains the symmetrical meaning of *with* and in fact chooses that meaning of *with* in contrast to the many other meanings that that preposition possesses. The next step is found in case marking for the core subject/object participants; such case markers generally have at most a highly abstract meaning, and the verb contributes the more specific meaning. The (case-marked) noun is clearly the head of its phrase, its dependents agreeing with it if such morphology is available in the language.

The difference in the evolution of adpositional phrases and the evolution of quantifier phrases is that the profile of the quantifier term shifts towards that of the noun which usurps its syntactic head status; but the profile of the adposition shifts towards that of the verb that governs it, leaving the noun it governed the head of its phrase by default, so to speak. This is the reason why the adposition looks very much like a syntactic head until very late stages of grammaticalization: it is unclear what the profile of the PP is, as the adposition's profile gets absorbed by the verb and the NP's inherent properties come to dictate more of its relation to the verb.

6.4. *Numeral classifiers*

An example of syntactic reanalysis not found in European languages occurs with numeral classifiers. The numeral classifier construction, with very few exceptions, has the syntactic structure [[Num Clfr] [N]] (order varies from language to language, of course). This structure appears to be an appositive one, that is, both [Num Clfr] and [N] are profile determinants. This is obvious from the commonest etymology of numeral classifiers, namely nouns; at some point in the past, [Num Clfr] was simply a [Num N] noun phrase. When a numeral classifier system is lost, as in some Micronesian languages, the classifier system breaks down; generally one classifier spreads at the expense of others. In the final stages of loss of classifiers, it is most common for the classifier (or what is left of it) to attach to the numeral, not to the noun whose profile it shares. Numerals have the profile described above, with a trajector (argument) that is the (multiplex) instantiation of the object. As the numeral classifier loses its semantic content, its profile overlaps with that of the numeral, and it is phonologically absorbed with it. Although its meaning also overlaps with that of the noun—all along, in fact—the classifier's syntactic association with the numeral presumably leads to its eventual absorption by the numeral rather than the noun. In the end, however, as with the numeral example discussed above, the noun is both the profile determinant and the PIBU, and becomes the head of the reanalyzed numeral construction.

6.5. *Copulas*

Another example of grammaticalization that leads to reanalysis is the merging of copulas with predicative nouns and adjectives, leading to inflected nominal and adjectival predications, or a special predicative nominal/adjectival form distinct from the form of nouns and adjectives found in NPs. A copula occurring with a predicative noun or adjective appears to be the profile determinant, because the overall clause profiles the classification of the subject as belonging to the category of the predicate nominal, or possessing the property of the predicate nominal. However, the copula verb itself is of minimal semantic content, adding only a predicative function (what Langacker analyzes as a 'temporal profile') to a maximally schematic categorization. It can be argued that the profile of the whole clause is determined partly by the copula and partly by the predicate noun/adjective—categorization of the subject entity as being of the type profiled by the predicate noun, or ascription of the property profiled by the predicate adjective. A plausible diachronic analysis is that the predicate noun/adjective itself comes to profile the predicating act; the profile of the predicate noun/adjective thus comes to overlap with that of the copula; but the former is the PIBU and therefore absorbs the latter, becoming an inflected predicate form by itself.[14]

6.6. *PIBUs in other syntactic processes*

In discussing these examples, I have assumed that being the profile determinant is a necessary condition for headhood, and the PIBU only enters into the picture when there are two profile determinants. This in turn causes a syntactic reanalysis because there is a shift in meaning of the determiner , auxiliar, quantifier expression, adposition or classifier such that its profile changes, overlapping with another candidate for profile determinant that is a PIBU (in the case of determiners, auxiliaries and quantifiers) or overlapping semantically another element which then absorbs its meaning, leading to its fusion with another word (in the case of adpositions and classifiers). While the details of the diachronic process differ significantly in each case, there is a commonality to all of them: a shift in semantic profile leads to another element with higher information content becoming candidate for profile determinant and hence syntactic headhood, and syntactic reanalysis occurs to make that possible.

But can the syntactic processes of grammaticalization and reanalysis occur without the shift in profile? A paper by Myhill (1988) suggests that something like grammaticalization, if not reanalysis, does seem to be driven by PIBU status alone. Myhill argues that the 'most informationally important' element of the sentence, which he calls the 'nucleus' (reminiscent of Sweet; Myhill 1988:261) and is the same as our PIBU, syntactically attracts elements of lower PIBU. This phenomenon he calls clustering, and gives the following examples:

High-PIBU nucleus	*Low-PIBU element attracted to nucleus (> bound form)*
Verb	pronoun (> agreement marker)
Verb	low-salience NP (> incorporated N)
Verb	auxiliary (> tense-aspect-mood affix)
Foregrounded verb	continuing topic NP
Foregrounded verb	coordinating conjunction (> narrative verb form)
Process verb	result or "framing" (Talmy 1991) particle (> affix)
Presentative NP	existential verb
Predicative NP	copula (> bound predicator)
Focused NP	equational verb in cleft (> focus NP form)
Emphasized element	pronoun

Figure 1. Properties of clustering (after Myhill 1988)

It appears that the phenomenon of attraction of a low-PIBU profile determinant, such as the determiner , auxiliar, or adposition/case marker, to its high-PIBU partner, may be part of a more general process of attraction of low-PIBU elements to high-PIBU ones regardless of profile determinacy. Nevertheless, the syntactic reanalyses described in this section specifically pertain to a shift in headhood, of which attraction and fusion of a low-PIBU profile determinant is just a single part.

An old paper by Langacker (1974) discusses a similar phenomenon and provided the inspiration for this analysis. Langacker argued that the movement transformations posited by generative grammar at that time, particularly generative semantics, had the function of moving more contentful information, which generally was found deeply embedded in deep structures, to the (surface-structure) main clause. Such deep structures for instance posited auxiliaries and tense markers as deep-structure predicates, so the main verb was found deeply nested in the deep structure. This is often a reflection of the historical origin of the auxiliar and affixal forms. Transformations in effect replicated the grammaticalization process described in §6.1, albeit in a slightly different form (they raised the arguments of the main verb to the matrix clause and then combined the verb with its auxiliaries and/or tense markings). The functional motivation for the transformations is the same, and to the extent that the transformations mimic historical processes of syntactic reanalysis, Langacker 's hypothesis conforms with the one advanced here: PIBU status is central to the organization of syntactic structure.

7. HEADS IN MORPHOLOGY?

It is commonly assumed in syntactic approaches to morphology, and also by certain semantic models, including cognitive grammar (e.g., Langacker 1991: 76), that the notion of headhood can be applied within a word as well as outside of it. Some have questioned the validity of this move (e.g., Bauer 1990), and heads do not have an obvious place in word-based approaches to morphology such as Bybee (1985) and Anderson (1992). I am generally in sympathy with the views of the latter regarding the (non-)role of heads in morphology. The process of grammaticalization and reanalysis described in §6 represent the lexical merging of the split profile determinants of the NP and S described in §5. It seems best to describe the whole word as the head of its syntactic constituent.

It is not entirely clear what aspects of morphological structure should be comparable to what goes on in syntactic structure. The most salient aspect of morphological organization (at least in those cases where morphemes are easily segmentable) is the distinction between root and affix. I argue here that the semantic notion of PIBU, but not the notion of profile determinant, is relevant to morphological organization at the word level with respect to the root-affix distinction; the problems encountered with attempts to apply the notion of head below the word level can be attributed to this fact.

The root-affix distinction is generally defined in phonological terms. Langacker provides a definition of an affix as a dependent morpheme and a root as an autonomous morpheme, a definition ultimately based on the structuralist notion of an affix as a bound morpheme and the root as a free one. However, in a language with obligatory inflection of root forms, in particular a language with obligatory inflection and no zero-expressed inflectional categories, the root in the intuitive sense is just as dependent as the inflection. Yet there is rarely any doubt as to which form is the root and which is the affix in such languages. The root is the PIBU.

In the preceding section, I argued that the grammatical fusion of determiners (and their meaning and inflectional categories) with the head noun and that of auxiliaries with the main verb led to the unification of both profile determinants within a single word. Within such a word, some have argued that the inflection is the head. Zwicky's criterion of morphosyntactic locus is not obviously applicable, since it is the inflectional affix itself whose headhood is in question.[15] The same arguments with respect to a semantic definition of headhood presented in sections 5-6 apply here also: both inflection and root contribute to the profile determinant of the whole; but the root is the PIBU.

This conclusion is rather different from that found in Haspelmath (1992), following Williams (1981) and others. Haspelmath argues that the head-dependent relations of syntax are continued into the morphology, and specifically the functional heads of syntax are continued into the inflectional morphology. I have argued for a different analysis of heads in syntax. I agree that what is found in the morphology is a continuation of the syntax to some extent, and that the syntax-morphology distinction is gradient. However, gradience need not imply continuity; that is, a phenomenon relevant to syntax such as headhood may not be continued all the way into the depths of the word, although the boundary between syntax and morphology is unclear. Instead, what matters is how the relevant semantic criteria operate in syntax and morphology; and I argue here that profile determinacy and PIBU behave rather differently in the morphology, and that headhood in particular is not helpful in defining morphological structure, in particular the root-affix structure of words. For example, as Haspelmath notes, in head-marking languages, affixes are etymologically dependents, namely pronominal arguments, while in dependent-marking languages, affixes are ultimately etymologically heads, namely former auxiliaries, adpositions, etc. The head-dependent distinction, to the extent that it is applicable to morphemes, does not account for the root-affix structure; and that is because PIBU status, not profile determinacy, is the most relevant semantic property for this structure.[16]

The properties of profile determinacy and PIBU part with each other in morphology in many derivational forms. For example, in agent nominalizations, the root (verbal or nominal) is the PIBU, but the agent-nominalizing affix is the profile determinant. It is believed that agent nominalizations (and other derivational affixes; Haspelmath 1992: 71) often originate from compounds, not unlike English *mailman, garbageman*, etc. In a compound, by definition, both morphemes are roots. The English agent compounds are clearly endocentric and *-man* is the head (because it is the profile determinant). But *-man* (by this point in its diachronic development) is not the PIBU.

In order to demonstrate this, we must extend the definition of PIBU to apply to cases in which the two candidate elements do not share profiles. When they do share profiles, it is relatively straightforward to determine which is more specific in meaning because its extension (in the formal semantic sense) is smaller. When they do not share profiles, one can employ the concept of paradigmatic contrast to determine which is the PIBU: whichever form is in paradigmatic contrast with more elements is the PIBU. With the agent nominalization example in the preceding paragraph, the root satisfies this test: there is a large number of contrasting verbal and nominal forms that can take agentive affixes, but the agentive affixes are in at most a paradigmatic contrast with a small number of other nominalizing affixes (patient, instrument, location, action nominalizations).

This criterion is used in grammaticalization theory, where it is called paradigmaticization (Lehmann 1981, 1985). Essentially, the semantic change by which a root comes to be used only in contrast to a small number of other forms in paradigmatic contrast is the loss of information content, which we take to be a defining characteristic of affix status.

Even if one accepts the notion that the affix is the profile determinant in inflection as well as in derivation, the functional account of headhood given here explains why the syntactic notion of headhood is difficult to apply below the word level. I have argued that the syntactic notion of headhood requires both profile determinacy and PIBU status. Above the word level, these two semantic properties coincide; if they do not, diachronic reanalysis eventually rights the alignment of the two. Below the word level, however, the nonalignment of profile determinacy (if inflectional and derivational affixes are analyzed as profile determinants) and PIBU status is the rule, not the exception, and morphological processes do not come into play to right the alignment of the two (except for complete fusion of stem and derivational affix). Above the word level, profile determinacy and PIBU status work together to define the (lexical) head. Below the word level, they do not work together; instead, the primary morphological division, between root and affix, is jointly determined by PIBU status and boundedness of the morpheme.

Earlier in this section, I argued that when both root and affix are bound forms, that is, neither can occur without the other, the semantic property of PIBU status identifies which is the root. There are also instances of the converse phenomenon: two morphemes have similar PIBU status, and cross-linguistically one is sometimes found as a root, sometimes the other, where 'root' is defined as 'free form'. For example, personal pronouns and case relations both form fairly compact semantic paradigms with a small number of contrasts. In other words, both personal pronouns and case relations have relatively low PIBU. Consider the meaning 'to her'. In some languages, such as Djabugay, the root is the pronoun 's/he' to which is affixed a case suffix meaning 'to': *gulu-nda* 's/he-DAT'. In other languages, such as Mam, the root is the preposition or relational noun meaning 'to', to which is attached a personal affix meaning 's/he': *t-ee* '3SG-to'. Another cross-linguistically common example of this phenomenon are personal pronouns and auxiliaries: each generally forms a relatively small paradigm and thus have an equally low PIBU status. In a language such as English, the contracted auxiliar cliticizes onto the subject pronoun, which is a free form; in other languages such as Papago (Zepeda 1983), the auxiliary is a free form to which subject pronominal endings are affixed.

The definitional properties of root presented here have a different ontological status from the definitional properties of head presented in §6. Profile determinacy is a necessary condition for headhood but not a sufficient one: a constituent may have more than one profile determinant, but in the theory presented here, there are not (necessarily) two heads.[17] PIBU status is a sufficient condition for headhood only jointly with profile determinacy: if the PIBU is not a profile determinant, it is not the head. For root, however, PIBU status and unbound (free) distributional status are singly sufficient: either one defines the root if the other condition is absent. If no morphemes in a word occur alone, the PIBU is the root. If both forms are roughly equal in PIBU status, then the free form is the root. If both are free and roughly equal in PIBU status, then we have two roots, that is, a compound. Profile determinacy is not relevant to root status; it can be applied to compounding and to a lesser extent to derivation, but its applicability to inflection is questionable. If it is applicable, then it is almost always divergent from the PIBU morpheme. These differences clarify what word-internal structure and syntactic structure have in common and how they differ, in a typological and diachronic perspective.

8. CONCLUSION

The semantic definition of headhood given here is in the spirit of Sweet's nucleus, Bloomfield's center, and Jespersen's chief idea. An analytical decision regarding a syntactic property such as headhood must be made on a principled basis—that is, there must be some reason that the syntactic criteria we employ are relevant. An examination of the full range of relevant syntactic constructions across a wide range of languages will generally reveal which syntactic phenomena have a chance of being criterial for the theoretical concept in question. In the case of heads, a broader empirical base confirmed Zwicky's decision to exclude all the syntactic criteria except for morphosyntactic locus.

Nevertheless, (surface) morphosyntactic locus is still problematic; at least, it does not give us an unequivocal universal category of head. But one can try to identify functional (semantic, pragmatic, or discourse) properties that are reflected by syntactic phenomena such as morphosyntactic locus. An advantage of (well-chosen) functional criteria is that they allow for cross-linguistic comparability and the possibility of a genuinely universal characterization of the phenomenon. The definition of headhood offered here is a universal one, and is universally applicable, once sufficient care is taken in the semantic analysis of the syntactic constructions (and, I might add, my decisions may not turn out to be correct). The semantic properties of syntactic headhood have distinct reflexes in cross-linguistic syntactic patterns. Profile determinacy taken alone determines the pattern of (surface) morphosyntactic locus, the only syntactic criterion that Zwicky considers relevant to headhood. Profile determinacy together with PIBU status controls the directionality of syntactic reanalysis, and provides an unequivocal universal category in syntactic structure to which the name 'head' seems quite appropriate.

The definition of headhood offered here also accommodates the fact that changes in syntactic headhood are caused by changes in the semantic properties of linguistic elements, which leads to a lag in syntactic change and hence the headlike behavior of (semantically) less headlike elements in the synchronic states of particular constructions in particular languages. The semantic generalization described here is intended to be interpreted diachronically. The exceptional character of particular synchronic configurations is not an arbitrary fact about an autonomous syntax but a consequence of the nature of historical processes and the tension between syntactic structure and the semantic structure that results from such processes. Language is a dynamic system of signs—symbolic units containing both form and function—not a static system of forms; and examination of typological and diachronic data confirms that view. The forces that determine the diachronic processes are part of a speaker's linguistic competence. After all, "languages don't change; speakers change language" (Croft 1990: 257). These forces are manifested by variation and innovation in synchrony, that can become language change in the long term. This view of a synchronic grammar is quite different from the static entity found in the structuralist and generative tradition for which change is an external event, not an internal dynamic. This alternative view can be stated quite succinctly. Synchrony is diachrony in the short term.

NOTES

* An earlier version of this paper was presented at the Indiana University Lecture Series on Formal Syntax and at a colloquium at the University of Michigan in December 1992. At the time this paper was written, I was not able to obtain a number of relevant books and articles, both recent and past, that I wished to consult for this paper (I note in particular Corbett et al. 1993); my apologies to those whose work touches directly on the topics covered here yet have not been cited. I dedicate this paper to the students of the Linguistics Program at the University of Michigan.

1 Until the last decade or so, discussions of the competing virtues of constituency and dependency focused on the fact that constituent structures allowed one to represent relationships between individual lexical items and syntactic units larger than lexical items, while dependency grammars indicated only relations between lexical items (see Hudson 1984). However, this restriction is not a necessary property of dependency grammars. Dependency grammars allowing for relations to hold between phrasal constituents are possible; in fact feature structures (e.g., Shieber 1986) indicate precisely that.

2 It does not matter that the first lexical verb class, those taking accusative objects, can be defined as the default type and the accusative as the default object NP case; that would then be the first type of government for the default class.

3 One might respond that there might be syntactic correlations that are not predicted by one's theory (either a formal or a functional theory), and so using only theoretically-defined tests would cause one to overlook those correlations. But in fact we need not be blind to such correlations. These correlations are empirical facts to be discovered, and verified by cross-linguistic comparison (which will reveal many such correlations to be accidental, or more complicated)—and then become interesting problems to be solved. But they should not be treated as definitional for a particular grammatical concept.

4 While this may appear to be a radical departure from formal theories of syntax and semantics, in fact it is not. Formal theories in the Montague grammar tradition involve a

matching of syntactic rule (including the rules forming constructions) to a semantic rule (the rule of semantic interpretation for that construction); this point is made by Dowty (1991:609) in another context. It is, however, quite divergent from recent Chomskyan models of syntax, in which the notion of construction is expressly rejected.

5 Again, this may seem counter to most views of generative syntax; but it is not that far from some approaches. But in a recent talk, Jackendoff (1992), a generative grammarian, comes very close to this position, though without extending it to the core syntactic constructions.

6 Yet again, this view of natural language processing may seem radically different from those derived from generative syntax; but again, it is not. In natural language processing systems based on phrase structure rules as are found in generative syntactic models, parsing involves an attempt to match the right hand side of a phrase structure rule with the input—which is virtually the same as categorizing the input as an instance of a construction, since a construction can be equated with the right hand side of a phrase structure rule.

7 Actually, Zwicky intends morphosyntactic locus to refer not to the actual locus of inflection in a particular construction in a particular language, but an abstract 'potential inflectional locus' (Z, p. 6) which is the bearer of abstract syntactic features which may or may not be realized. Zwicky presumably would reduce some of the cross-linguistic variability in Aux + V inflections described in this paragraph to a more abstract representation of feature percolation. But then one must bring in further arguments as to which constituent the features truly percolate to. Not having seen such arguments, I cannot comment further on such an analysis; it may be that those further arguments will draw on the same intuitions that I am about to use for my definition of headhood.

8 Langacker (p.c.; see also my review of his examples below) agrees that headhood is a property of constructions, not of words in a construction.

9 There has of course been an extensive amount of work on determiners in the formal semantic literature. Much of this work cannot be used to support the semantic analysis of headhood being pursued here, unfortunately, because of the way determiners are represented in the categorial grammar used by many formal semanticists. In a categorial grammar, semantic types (categories) are defined purely in terms of their combinatorics, so that for example a type or category defined as <X, Y> is a category that combines with a category of type Y to yield a category of type X. In this analysis, the only headed constructions would be those involving a category of type <X, X>. In fact, it is usually only modifiers such as adjectives and certain adverbs that are analyzed as such, hence all other constructions (including NPs and determiners) are headless if we interpret 'same kind of' as 'same categorial type as'. I believe that in fact the notion 'kind of X' should not be reduced to the categorial concept of semantic type, and that 'kind of X' is necessary and useful for describing at least some aspects of syntactic structure. Nevertheless, insights regarding the semantics of determiners found in the formal semantic literature can and should be captured in frame-semantic definitions of them.

10 Langacker's analysis of the meaning (profile and base) can be fruitfully compared to analyses in which the determiner is a function mapping the denotation of the noun (i.e., an instantiation of a type) to the particular instance in the speaker/hearer's knowledge. The argument of the function is the denotation of the noun, and in Langacker's analysis it is the profile of the determiner; the function itself is in the base.

11 This is not Langacker's analysis of the clause, however. For him, as for orthodox Chomskyan theory, the auxiliary is the clausal head (Langacker 1991, chapter 5). It is interesting to note that both Chomsky and Langacker readily admit that the auxiliary (or its decomposed remains, in the latest versions of Chomsky's theory) is the head of the verb phrase or clause, while neither has explicitly endorsed the claim that the Determiner is the (exclusive) head of the noun phrase.

12 Not in all cases, however. In English, the auxiliary in its contracted form cliticizes onto the subject NP. In Mosan languages, it has been argued (Anderson 1985) that the

auxiliary cliticizes onto the first constituent. If the auxiliary cliticizes onto unstressed pronouns, the pronoun-auxiliary 'clitic complex' can itself attach to the verb, as is argued to have happened in Nahuatl by Steele in the abstract to a talk at the Linguistic Society of America meetings in the 1970s, and possibly also has happened in Athapaskan languages and some non-Pama-Nyungan languages. In general, as Steele (1975) observed, auxiliaries have a predilection for positions defined by the clause (first, second and last) as well as positions defined by the lexical head (the verb). It is interesting to note that there appears to be an analogous phenomenon with determiners, which can occur in NP-second position in some languages (e.g., Bulgarian), as well as initial and final position, and in a position contiguous to the noun (observations based on an unpublished survey of 35 languages I performed in 1988; Chris Lyons, p.c., also confirms the tendency for second-position determiners).

13 I would predict that 'attraction' to other head categories, particularly the noun in a noun phrase, should also be found to occur.

14 Another possible diachronic analysis is that the two forms simply fuse morphologically and jointly provide the profile of the whole clause as a single word. The former analysis is preferable in a situation when the predicate noun/adjective develops the inflections at the same time as regular verbs do: the verb forms are acquiring a predicational profile, so it is reasonable to assume that the nonverbal predications are doing so also.

15 One could argue that it is trivially applicable, in that the inflectional affix itself is the morphosyntactic locus. I am not certain this makes sense, and the semantic considerations discussed so far point in another direction.

16 This is not to mention the problems for syntax-based morphology found in nonconcatenative morphology (Haspelmath 1992: 81-82; Anderson 1992; Spencer 1993).

17 I consider appositive structures to be genuinely two-headed; the types of constructions I am alluding to in the main text are the ones in which there is a division of pragmatic labor in reference and predication among elements of an NP or S respectively.

REFERENCES

Abney, Stephen P.: 1987, *The English Noun Phrase in its Sentential Aspect*, unpublished Ph.D. dissertation, MIT.

Anderson, Stephen R.: 1971, 'On the Role of Deep Structure in Semantic Interpretation', *Foundations of Language* **7**, 387-396.

———: 1985, 'Inflectional Morphology', in T. Shopen (ed.), *Language Typology and Syntactic Description, Vol. 3: Grammatical Categories and the Lexicon*, Cambridge University Press, Cambridge, pp. 150-201.

———: 1992, *A-morphous Morphology*, Cambridge University Press, Cambridge.

Bauer, Laurie: 1990. 'Be-heading the Word', *Journal of Linguistics* **26**, 1-31.

Bloomfield, Leonard: 1933, *Language*, Holt, Rinehart and Winston, New York.

Bybee, Joan L.: 1985, *Morphology: An Inquiry into the Relation between Meaning and Form*, John Benjamins, Amsterdam.

Chomsky, Noam. 1970. 'Remarks on Nominalization', in R. Jacobs and P. Rosenbaum (eds.), *Readings in English Transformational Grammar*, Ginn, Waltham, MA, pp. 184-221.

———: 1986. *Barriers*, MIT Press, Cambridge, MA.

———: 1991. 'Some Notes on the Economy of Derivation and Representation', in R. Freidin (ed.), *Principles and Parameters in Comparative Grammar*, MIT Press, Cambridge, MA pp. 417-54.

Corbett, Greville, Norman Fraser and Scott McGlashan: 1993, *Heads in Grammatical Theory*, Cambridge University Press, Cambridge.

Covington, Michael A.: 1984, *Syntactic Theory in the High Middle Ages: Modistic Models of Sentence Structure*, Cambridge University Press, Cambridge.

Croft, William: 1990a, *Typology and universals*, Cambridge University Press, Cambridge.
———: 1990b. 'A Conceptual Framework for Grammatical Categories (or, A Taxonomy of Propositional Acts)', *Journal of Semantics* **7**, 245-79.
———: 1991, *Syntactic Categories and Grammatical Relations: The Cognitive Organization of Information*, University of Chicago Press, Chicago.
———: 1993, 'Functional-Typological Theory in its Historical and Intellectual Context', *Sprachtypologie und Universalienforschung* **46**, 15-26.
Dixon, R. M. W.: 1972, *The Dyirbal Language of North Queensland*, Cambridge University Press, Cambridge.
Dowty, David: 1991, 'Thematic Proto-roles and Argument Selection', *Language* **71**, 547-619.
Elbert, Samuel H. and T. Momberg: 1965, *From the Two Canoes*, Danish National Museum, Copenhagen.
England, Nora C.: 1983, *A Grammar of Mam, a Mayan Language*, University of Texas Press, Austin.
Fauconnier, Gilles: 1985, *Mental Spaces*. Cambridge University Press, Cambridge.
Fillmore, Charles J.: 1975, 'An alternative to checklist theories of meaning', in C. Cogen et al. (eds.), *Proceedings of the First Annual Meeting of the Berkeley Linguistics Society*, Berkeley, Berkeley Linguistics Society, pp. 123-131.
———: 1977, 'Scenes-and-frames semantics', in A. Zampolli (ed.), *Linguistic Structures Processing* (Fundamental Studies in Computer Science, 5), North-Holland, Amsterdam, pp. 55-81.
———: 1982, 'Frame Semantics', in The Linguistic Society of Korea (ed.), *Linguistics in the Morning Calm*, Hanshin, Seoul, pp. 111-137.
———: 1985, 'Frames and the Semantics of Understanding', *Quaderni di Semantica* **6**, 222-54.
———: 1986, 'Pragmatically-controlled Zero Anaphora', in V. Nikiforidou et al. (eds.), *Proceedings of the Twelfth Annual Meeting of the Berkeley Linguistics Society*, Berkeley, Berkeley Linguistics Society, pp. 95-107.
——— and Paul Kay: 1993, *Construction Grammar Coursebook, Chapters 1 through 11 (Reading Materials for Ling. X20)* unpublished, University of California, Berkeley.
Foley, William: 1991, *The Yimas Language of New Guinea*, Stanford University Press, Stanford.
Goldberg, Adele E.: 1989, 'A unified account of the semantics of the English ditransitive', in K. Hall, M. Meacham and R. Shapiro (eds.), *Proceedings of the Fifteenth Annual Meeting of the Berkeley Linguistics Society*, Berkeley, Berkeley Linguistics Society, pp. 79-90.
———: 1992, *Argument Structure Constructions*, unpublished Ph.D. dissertation, University of California, Berkeley.
Greenberg, Joseph H.: 1978, 'Generalizations about Numeral Systems', in J. Greenberg, C. Ferguson and E. Moravcsik (eds.), *Universals of Human Language, Vol. 3: Word Structure*, Stanford, Stanford University Press, pp. 249-95.
Hale, Kenneth: 1982, 'Some Essential Features of Warlpiri Verbal Clauses', in S. Swartz, p. (ed.), *Papers in Warlpiri grammar in memory of Lothar Jagst*, SIL-AAB Work Papers, Canberra, pp. 217-315.
Haspelmath, Martin: 1992, 'Grammaticization Theory and Heads in Morphology', in M. Aronoff (ed.), *Morphology Now*, State University of New York Press, Albany, pp. 69-82 and 194-98.
———: to appear, 'Functional Categories, X-bar Theory, and Grammaticalization Theory', to appear in *Sprachtypologie und Universalienforschung*.
Heim, Irene: 1983, 'File Change Semantics and the Familiarity Theory of Definiteness', in R. Bäuerle, C. Schwartz, p. & A. von Stechow (eds.), *Meaning, Use and Interpretation of Language*, Walter de Gruyter, Berlin, pp. 164-189.

Heine, Bernd and Mechthild Reh: 1984, *Grammaticalization and Reanalysis in African Languages*, Helmut Buske Verlag, Hamburg.

Hudson, Richard: 1984, *Word Grammar*, Basil Blackwell, Oxford.

——: 1987, 'Zwicky on heads', *Journal of Linguistics* **23**, 109-32.

Jackendoff, Ray: 1992, 'If idioms aren't in the lexicon, then where are they?' Invited talk, Eastern States Conference on Linguistics, Buffalo, New York.

Jespersen, Otto: 1924, *The Philosophy of Grammar*, Norton, New York.

Josephs, Lewis S.: 1975, *Palauan Reference Grammar*, The University Press of Hawaii, Honolulu.

Kamp, Hans: 1984, 'A Theory of Truth and Semantic Representation', in J. Groenendijk, T. Janssen and M. Stokhof (eds.), *Truth, interpretation and information*, Foris, Dordrecht, pp. 1-41.

Lakoff, George: 1987, *Women, Fire and Dangerous Things: What Categories Reveal about the Mind*, University of Chicago Press, Chicago.

Langacker, Ronald W.: 1974, 'Movement Rules in Functional Perspective', *Language* **50**, 630-664.

——: 1987, *Foundations of Cognitive Grammar, Vol. I: Theoretical Prerequisites*, Stanford University Press, Stanford.

——: 1991, *Foundations of Cognitive Grammar, Vol. II: Descriptive Application*, Stanford University Press, Stanford.

Lehmann, Christian: 1981, *Thoughts on Grammaticalization: A Programmatic Sketch, Vol. I.* (Arbeiten des Kölner Universalien-Projekts, 48.), Institut für Sprachwissenschaft, Köln.

——: 1985, 'Grammaticalization: Synchronic Variation and Diachronic Change', *Lingua e Stile* **20**, 303-318.

Levin, Beth C.: 1993, *English Verb Classes,* University of Chicago Press, Chicago.

Matthews, Peter H.: 1981, *Syntax*, Cambridge University Press, Cambridge.

Myhill, John: 1988, 'Categoriality and Clustering', *Studies in Language* **12**, 261-297.

Ouhalla, Jamal: 1991, *Functional Categories and Parametric Variation,* Routledge, London.

Pollock, Jean-Yves: 1989, 'Verb Movement, Universal Grammar and the Structure of IP', *Linguistic Inquiry* **20**, 365-424.

Rice, Sally A.: 1987, *Towards a Cognitive Model of Transitivity*, unpublished Ph.D. dissertation, University of California, San Diego.

Schachter, Paul: 1985, 'Parts-of-speech Systems', in T. Shopen (ed.), *Language Typology and Syntactic Description, Vol. 1: Clause Structure*, Cambridge University Press, Cambridge, pp. 3-61.

Searle, John: 1979, 'Literal Meaning', in *Expression and Meaning*, Cambridge University Press, Cambridge, pp. 117-136.

Shieber, Stuart: 1986, *An Introduction to Unification-Based Approaches to Grammar* (CSLI Lecture Notes, 4.), Center for the Study of Language and Information, Stanford.

Spencer, Andrew: 1993, Review of Rochelle Lieber, *Deconstructing Morphology*, *Language* **69**, 580-87.

Steele, Susan: 1975, 'On Some Facts that Affect and Effect Word Order, in C. Li (ed.), *Word Order and Word Order Change*, University of Texas Press, Austin, pp. 197-268.

Sweet, Henry: 1891, *A New English Grammar, Logical and Historical, Part I,* Clarendon Press, Oxford.

Talmy, Leonard: 1991, Path to Realization: A Typology of Event Integration, *Buffalo Working Papers in Linguistics* **91-01**, 147-87.

Taylor, John R.: 1989, 'Possessive Genitives in English', *Linguistics* **27**, 663-686.

Wierzbicka, Anna: 1980, *Lingua Mentalis: The Semantics of Natural Language*, Academic Press, New York.

Williams, Edwin: 1981, 'On the Notions 'Lexically Related' and 'Head of a Word', *Linguistic Inquiry* **12**, 245-74.
Zepeda, Ofelia: 1983, *A Papago Grammar*, University of Arizona Press, Tucson.
Zwicky, Arnold M.: 1985, 'Heads', *Journal of Linguistics* **21**, 1-29.

X' SELECTION*

Anna-Maria Di Sciullo

0. INTRODUCTION

Current theories on argument structure and derivational morphology assume subcategorization frames or theta-grids for encoding the selectional properties of derivational affixes. We show that taken individually, these representations constitute partial generalizations and that taken as a whole, they fail to account for the basic nature of morphological selection.

We argue on the basis of English and French word-formation that morphological selection is basically configurational in nature: it is specified in terms of X' categories. This hypothesis, the X' Selection Hypothesis, is a natural one within frameworks where X' structures encode the grammatical properties of linguistic expressions.

The consequences of our hypothesis are the following. Argument structure asymmetries in derivational morphology can be accounted for, apparent lexical gaps can be reduced and the form of lexical information can be simplified. Furthermore, morpho-syntactic-semantic parallels can be captured and the relation between phrase structure and the lexicon can be clarified further.

This paper is organized as follows. In the first section we discuss the shortcomings of subcategorization frames and theta-grids for derivational affixes. In the second section, we formulate our hypothesis for encoding selectional properties. In the third section we discuss one consequence of our proposal. In the last section we propose a way to derive selection from independent properties of the grammar.

1. SELECTION

1.1. *Subcategorization frames*

Since Chomsky (1965), categorial selection has taken the form of strict-subcategorization frames in lexical entries. Strict-subcategorization specifies the categorial nature of the complement of a lexical head. It also plays a role in the rule of lexical insertion given that it restricts the insertion of items in D-structure positions.

(1) a. shine: [_]
b. hit: [_NP]
c. put: [_NP PP]
d. wonder: [_CP]

Strict-subcategorization is also assumed in derivational morphology, as in Aronoff (1976), Selkirk (1982), Borer (1990), Lieber (1992), Anderson (1992), among others. A morphological subcategorization frame provides a complex of information in the lexical entry of a derivational affix. It specifies the categorial nature of the subcategorized item, its linear position with respect to the affix, as well as the dominance relation involved: the affix and the subcategorized item are sisters. For example, the nominal affix *-er* subcategorizes for a verb which precedes it, the verbal affix *-ize* subcategorizes for an adjective which also precedes it, and so on. Subcategorization frames such as (2) are assumed to be part of the lexicon. They restrict word-formation rules, as in Aronoff (1976), they limit lexical insertion into morphological structures such as the ones in (3), as in Lieber (1992).

(2) a.-er: [V_]
b.-ize: [A_]
c.-able: [V_]

(3)
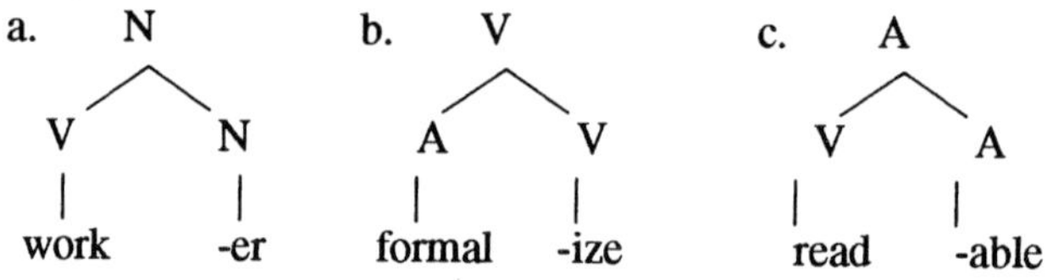

Putting aside the difference in linear order between syntactic and morphological subcategorization in languages where there is an asymmetry in the position of the head in syntactic vs. morphological structures, as in Germanic and Romance languages, strict-subcategorization plays a similar role in the syntax and in the morphology. Morphological subcategorization is generally taken to be a head-to-head relation, as it is the case for syntactic subcategorization, where a lexical head, say a verb, selects an XP complement, the head of which has given properties. Thus, *wonder* selects a CP complement the head of which is a complementizer introducing indirect questions, such as *if* but not *that*.

(4) wonder: [_CP]

(5)

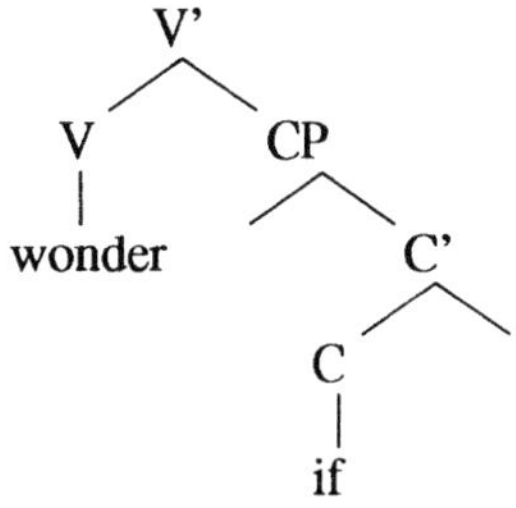

Formulating selection as a head-to-head relation seems desirable at first sight, as it would preserve simplicity and locality of lexical insertion at base structure. However, there are empirical as well as theoretical problems with head-to-head selection. We point out three problems in what follows focusing on morphological subcategorization.

A first problem with this view is that morphological subcategorization does not account for the asymmetries of selection imposed by certain derivational affixes on the argument structure of their stems.

For example, it is generally the case that the nominal suffix *-er* in English does not combine with an ergative verb (cf. Rappaport and Levin 1988), or with a verb that takes a small clause (SC) complement. The suffix does however generally combine with verbs that project a subjectposition within the VP (external argument).

(6)	a.	*a departer	(depart DP)
	b.	*an arriver	(arrive DP)
	c.	*a faller	(fall DP)

(7)	a.	*a beer	(be SC)
	b.	*a considerer	(consider SC)
	c.	*a seer	(see SC)

(8)	a.	a dreamer	(DP dream)
	b.	an eater	(DP eat DP)
	c.	a thinker	(DP think CP)

Configurational approaches to argument structure (cf. Burzio 1986, Kuroda 1986, Fukui and Speas 1986, Sportiche 1988, Speas 1990, Hale and Keyser 1992, Chomsky 1993, Di Sciullo 1993 and Gruber in press, to name a few) provide a way to express the restrictions imposed by a derivational affix on the projection it combines with. In a configurational approach to argument structure, ergative verbs and verbs that take a SC complement are similar with respect to the form of their argument structure: they do not project a subject position within the VP. Thus, the restriction imposed by the nominal affix *-er* on the projection it combines with can be stated straightforwardly.

On the other hand, if morphological selection is a head-to-head relation, the facts in (6)-(8) cannot be accounted for in a unified way, given that neither the complement position nor the VP internal subject position of the selected head are visible to the affix.

A second problem with morphological subcategorization is that it does not account for the fact that certain derivational affixes may select for stems which project more than one argument structure, given that again only heads are visible. For example, it is impossible to predict that the nominal suffix *-er* may combine with unergative verbs as well as with transitive verbs, provided that they are not PP transitive verbs.

(9)	a.	a shiner	(DP shine)
	b.	a barker	(DP bark)
	c.	a snorer	(DP snore)

(10)	a.	a cutter	(DP cut DP)
	b.	a hitter	(DP hit DP)
	c.	a reader	(DP read DP/CP)

(11)	a.	*an agreer	(DP agree with DP)
	b.	*an accesser	(DP access to DP)
	c.	*a looker	(DP look at DP)

Here again, head-to-head selection for derivational affixes does not account directly for these facts given that only heads are visible.

A third problem with morphological subcategorization is that it cannot account for the case where the selectional requirements of a given affix are satisfied by other elements in the structure it is part of and not by the stem it attaches to. This is the case in compounds such as (12). While an ergative verb may not generally combine with the nominal suffix *-er*, it may do so in a compound including an adverbial.

(12) a. an easy-faller
b. an early-departer
c. a late-arriver

The verbal stem in (12) is ergative. This is evidenced in (13) by the fact that its participial form can appear pre-nominally, as it is generally the case for ergative verbs in English (cf. Hoekstra 1992). Thus, the nominal suffix may combine with ergative verbs in compounds such as (12) and it may not otherwise, when the derived nominal is not part of a compound, as in (6) above, and when it is part of a deverbal compound, as in (14).

(13) a. a fallen leaf
b. a departed father
c. an arrived letter

(14) a. *a leaf-faller
b. *a father-departer
c. *a letter-arriver

Morphological subcategorization, viewed as a head-to-head relation, does not account for this fact. Even if subcategorization were to be refined with head features such as [+ergative] and [-ergative], it would still be insufficient to account for the existence of the compounds such as the ones in (12).

One way to account for these compounds while preserving the restrictions imposed by *-er* on its complement domain is to assume that the adverb in the compounds licenses a subject position within the VP. This position would satisfy the selectional requirements imposed by the affix on its complement domain. Basically, this requirement is that there must be a projected subject position within VP in the complement domain of the affix, whether there is an argumental complement position projected or not within this VP. These selectional properties can be expressed given the X' Selection hypothesis we formulate below.

To sum up, the facts presented above indicate that morphological subcategorization is inadequate. It predicts the existence of items which are not part of a given language (**a departer*), it does not define accurately the set of possible derived items (*a hitter*, **a considerer*), it does not account for the fact that certain derived words are only admissible in certain structures (**a departer*, *an early-departer*).[1]

1.2. *Theta-grids*

A theta-grid provides the semantic information in the lexical entry of a derivational affix (cf. Roeper 1987, Grimshaw 1990). Defining semantic selection in terms of a list of theta-roles (Agent, Theme, Goal, etc.) is also based on the idea that selection is a head-to-head relation, given that a theta-grid is a property of a head.

Let us point out two problems with the claim that the semantic selection imposed by a derivational affix on its stem is encoded in terms of theta-grids. First, theta-grids do not account in a unified way for the fact that derivational affixes may select predicates with different theta-grids. In effect, a given derivational affix, say the adjectival suffix *-able*, but also the nominal suffixes *-tion* and *-er*, may select a predicate whose theta-grid includes an agent, as in (16), or an experiencer, as in (17). Thus, assuming the theta-grid approach, the semantic selection of a derivational affix cannot be reduced to a unique theta-grid, since both (17a) and (17b) are selected by the affixes. The theta-grid approach to the semantic selection of derivational affixes cannot capture the fact that agents and experiencers have a property in common: they are projected in the subject position within the VP. This property is not expressed in individual theta-grids, which are lists of theta-roles selected by given heads.

(15) a. These goods are exportable.
b. the production of the opera
c. the destroyer of the city

(16) a. This person is detestable.
b. the detestation of the hero
c. Faust's admirer

(17) a. [Agent, Theme]
b. [Experiencer, Theme]

The limits of a theta-grid account for semantic selection can also be observed considering the selection of roles projected in complement position within the VP. For example, the prefixes considered above may also select a projection which may or not include a Goal argument. Thus, alongside structures such as (15) and (16), structures such as (18) are also possible. The additional theta-grid in (19) would also be part of the lexical entry of the affixes considered above. In fact, a descriptive account for these facts would require a disjunctive lexical specification, such as the one in (20), for these affixes. This is an undesirable move, assuming that complex lexical entries, including specifications such as (20), fail to express the generalizations mentioned above on the configurational nature of selection.

(18) a. This object is transformable.
b. The transformation of the metal.
c. The transformer of the system.

(19) [Agent, Theme, Goal]

(20) { [Agent, Theme]
[Experiencer, Theme]
[Agent, Theme, Goal] }

Secondly, further shortcomings of the theta-grid approach to semantic selection can be seen by considering the fact that certain derivational affixes do not seem to select any particular theta-grid. This is the case of the nominal affix *-ing*, which is considered to be a very productive affix in English, as it may combine with most verbs to yield derived nominals, as in (21).

(21) a. the killing of the lamb
b. the dreaming of the guardian
c. the falling of John

In a theta-grid approach to selection, an affix that would not select any theta-grid in particular would presumably have an empty theta-grid in its lexical entry, as in (22). This could be the case for the nominal affix as well as for the adjectival affix *-ful*, which combine with most transitive verbs, while reducing their theta-grids, as in (23).

(22) [ ]

(23) a. The children are playful.
b. This drug is harmful.
c. They are useful.

There are, however, restrictions that override the theta-grid approach to selection including empty theta-grids, as the examples in (24) illustrate.

(24) a. *the resembling of Paul to John
b. *the knowing of grammar
c. *the descending of the child
d. *They are hitful.
e. *The students are likeful.
f. *They are eatful.

Thus, the absence of specification in the theta-grid of certain derivational affixes does not cover the facts and other factors must be invoked. In the case of the productive suffix *-ing*, the existence of nominals with the same function (e.g., *resemblance*, *knowledge*, *descent*) would block the formation of the *-ing* nominals. In the case of the adjectival suffix *-ful*, one would have to appeal to the fact that the suffix is not productive in English.

This indicates that theta-grids constitute partial generalizations with respect to the semantic selection. They do not offer an explanation for the existence of these restrictions. Disjunctive lexical representations can be avoided in a modular system where semantic selection reduces to configurational selection and which allows selection to vary within the limits imposed by the configuration, as we will suggest below.

We will thus reject the theta-grid approach to semantic selection and formulate an hypothesis which is compatible with current approaches to theta-structure, such as Hale and Keyser (1992) and Gruber (in press), where theta-roles are not primitives but derived from X' positions. The next section spells out our hypothesis and presents empirical evidence supporting it.

2. X' STRUCTURE

We formulate an hypothesis for encoding the selectional properties of heads that does not face the problems associated with subcategorization frames and theta-grids. In the following paragraphs we present our assumptions and our proposal, as well as three arguments supporting it.

2.1. *Word-internal X' positions*

Assuming that the grammar provides the X' configuration in (25) on universal grounds (cf. Chomsky (1993, 1994)), we propose that a derivational affix, as any other head, projects an X' structure.

(25)
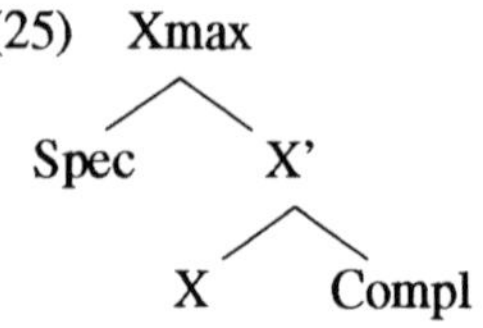

We thus take a derivational affix to have an X' domain where a complement (Compl) position is asymmetrically c-commanded by a specifier (Spec) position. Moreover, we will take the complement domain (cf. Chomsky 1993) of a derivational affix to be an X' structure, where a Spec position asymmetrically c-commands a Compl position.

(26)
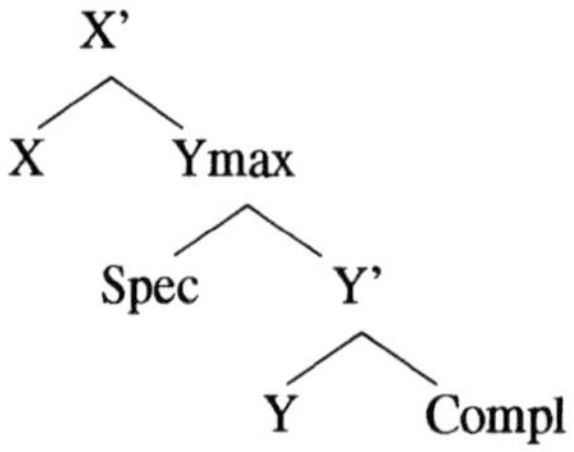

We assume a strict version of X' structure where unspecified Compl and Spec positions are projected by default, and where there is only one Spec and only one Compl position per head, as well as only one head per X' projection.

Given that word-formation affects argument structure, viz., some affixes (*-able*, *-ive*) modify the distribution of the arguments of their stems while others (*-er*, *-ee*) saturate arguments of their stems, and assuming that argument structure is encoded in terms of X' structure, we will take the Spec and the Compl positions to be either argument (A) or nonargument (~A) positions.[2] Given that the X' schemata is unspecified, we will assume that the Spec and Compl positions are ~A positions by default, A positions being marked positions. We posit that a word-internal ~A position is always subject to linking (coindexation) to an A position, while an A position may be linked to a ~A position or remain unlinked. We posit further that an A position is saturated (cf. Higginbotham (1985), Di Sciullo and Williams (1987)) word-internally only if its head is linked by a ~A head, such as a suffix in derived words or a predicative head in a compound. An A position that is not saturated word-internally can be projected as an oblique complement of the word.

We will see that our theory accounts in a unified way for the selectional properties of derivational affixes. We consider first the structure projected by the derivational affix itself, represented by the projection of X in (27), then the internal structure of its complement domain, represented by the projection of Y in (27).

(27)

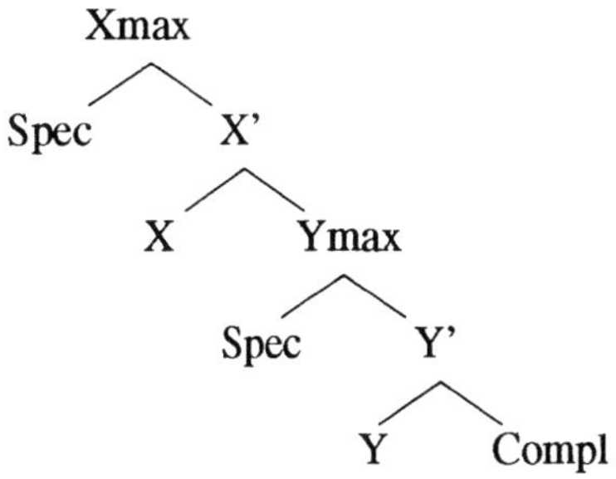

On the basis of the fact that a derivational affix may combine with a set of configurations (cf. (7), (8), (10)), we claim that only a sub-part of its complement domain determines its selection, as discussed below.

2.2. *The lexical entry*

Our proposal is couched in a modular view of the grammar which includes no construction-specific rules and where a lexical entry includes the minimal information that must be learned. This information must be obtained at the interfaces between the grammar and the performance systems, Phonetic Form (PF) and Logical Form (LF), for a linguistic expression to be interpretable.

We thus propose that a lexical entry L specifies the LF and the PF properties of an item which are not derivable from other properties of the grammar. Let us assume the general form in (28).

(28) L: <LF, PF>

The linear order as well as the phonological properties of a derivational affix are part of its PF specifications, and its argument structure properties are part of its LF specifications.

We will take the PF features (phonological and the morphological features) to be underspecified (cf. Archangeli 1984 and Farkas 1990) and extend underspecification to the LF features. In our theory, a lexical entry does not contain default value features; these are provided independently by the grammar. Thus, for a feature value to be specified in the lexicon, it must not be a default value feature.

Central to our topic here is that neither subcategorization frames nor theta-grids are part of the lexical entry, since the information they convey can be derived, a point to which we come back. This is desirable in a model such as Di Sciullo and Williams (1987) theory, where lexical insertion does not occur at D-Structure or in the Minimalist framework (cf. Chomsky 1993, 1994) where there is no D-Structure level and no rule of lexical insertion based on subcategorization frames as well as no Projection Principle based on the thematic properties of lexical items.

2.3. *X' Selection*

In order to capture the selectional restrictions of a derivational affix, we propose that an affix selects in terms of X' positions, as part of its LF specifications. We take morphological subcategorization not to be a head-to-head relation, but to be defined in terms of Spec and Compl positions in the X' domain of the affix. Thus, assuming that the grammar provides on universal grounds unspecified X' configurations, we propose that a derivational affix has an X' domain where its selectional restrictions are encoded in terms of X' positions. Let us assume the working hypothesis in (29).

(29) X' Selection Hypothesis
A head selects an X' position.

(30)

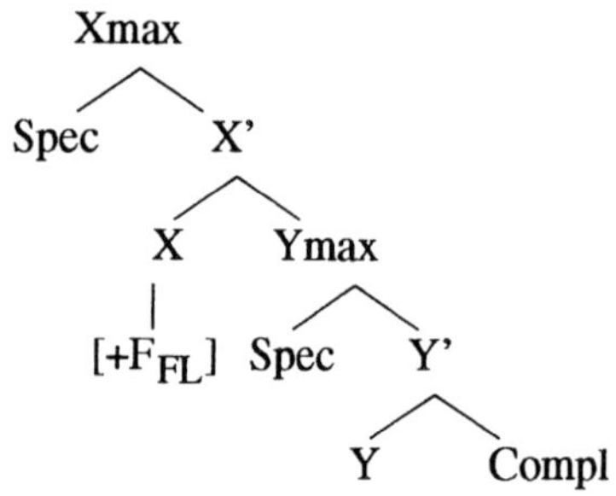

Morphological subcategorization has traditionally been stated in terms of head-to-head relations in the X^0 domain of a derivational affix on the basis of the structure depicted in (31). We claim that morphological subcategorization is a partial generalization and that it follows from X' selection, given independent properties of the grammar.

(31)

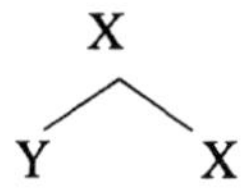

If our hypothesis is correct, we expect to find differences amongst affixes with respect to the projection of A positions. We also expect to find differences amongst affixes with respect to the presence of A positions in the complement domain of the affixes. Furthermore, we expect to find differences between affixes of the same category. These predictions are borne out, as we will see on the basis of English and French data. Let us first illustrate these differences with the structures in (32), where the category in bold indicates an A position. In (32a), the verbal head projects an A Spec position; in (32b,c) the adjectival and nominal heads project ~A Spec positions. A and ~A positions are also part of the complement domain of the affixes. In (32a') only the Compl is an A position, in (32b') the Spec and the Compl are both A positions and in (32c') the Spec is an A position.

(32)

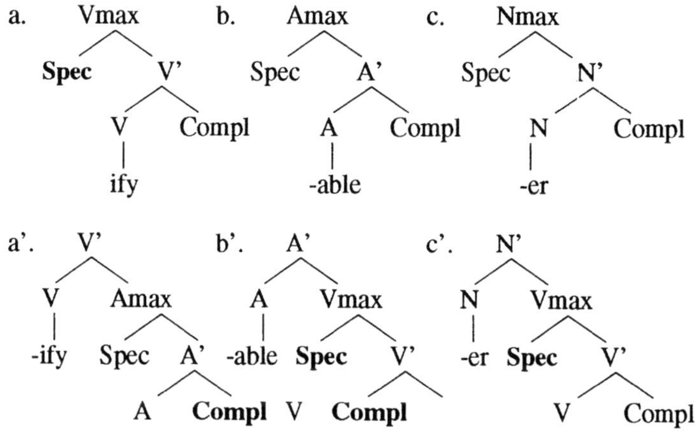

The following paragraphs provide arguments in favor of our proposal. We justify the need for a Spec position in the X' projection of derivational affixes to account for the argument structure properties of derived items. We justify further our proposal in showing that it reduces lexical gaps and that it captures generalizations that disjunctive lexical specifications cannot express.

2.4. *Justifications*

2.4.1. *Argument structure*

Assuming a configurational representation of argument structure based on strict X' projections (cf. Gruber (in press)), a derivational affix must project a Spec position in order to account for the differences amongst affixes with respect to argument structure as well as to account for the argument structure properties of the derived item it is a part of.

The Spec position is needed to express the argument structure properties of the derivational affixes themselves. These properties differ whether the affix is verbal, nominal or adjectival. Since derivational affixes are heads, their properties, including argument structure, determine the properties of the derived form, as discussed in Williams (1981) and in Di Sciullo and Williams (1987). In D&W's theory, this is stated in terms of the law of Function Composition. According to Function Composition, the external argument of the head is the external argument of the derived form and the arguments of the non-head are its internal arguments. In the theory we present here, there is no need for Function Composition. The effects of this law follow from independent configurational properties of derivational affixes, as discussed below.

If our hypothesis is correct, we expect that the presence of an A or ~A Spec position to be determinant for category-changing affixes in that it allows correct distinctions to be made with respect to argument structure properties. This is indeed what we find, as we will see.

For example, the verbal affixes *-ify*/*-ize* in English combine with nouns and adjectives to yield denominal and deadjectival verbs, as illustrated in the following examples.

(33) a. simple, simplify; certain, certify, solid, solidify,....
b. glory, glorify; class, classify,...
c. standard, standardize; immune, immunize,...
d. union, unionize; form, formalize; computer, computerize,....

Central to our point is the fact that the derived verbs are causative/inchoative verbs. The subject of the derived verbs is agentive and the object is an entity that undergoes a change of state. The Agent role may only be projected by the verbal affix since bare nouns or adjectives do not project an Agent. If the verbal affix projects the causative/inchoative structure, it follows that denominal and deadjectival verbs are transitive verbs. This is what we find, as the following examples illustrate.

(34) a. They simplified the theory.
b. *They simplified.
c. They unionized the workers.
d. *They unionized.

The fact that the verbal affixes are causative/inchoative is reinterpreted in X' theoretic terms in our theory, where they are lexically specified for the projection of an A Spec position, as in (35). We come back to the lexical specification of the verbal affixes *-ify* and *-ize* below.

(35) **<Spec>**

Thus, the argument structure properties of derived verbs in English bring empirical support to our claim that derivational affixes project a Spec position. In the case of the verbal affixes *-ify* and *-ize*, the Spec is an A Spec.

The argument structure properties of deverbal adjectives also support our claim, as we will see immediately. The adjectival suffix *-able* affects the argument structure of the verbal projection it combines with. Stated in terms of subject/object categories, the object of that verbal projection is the subject of the *-able* adjective used predicatively. This is illustrated in the examples in (36).

(36) a. Anybody can read this paper.
b. This paper is readable (by anybody).
c. Nobody can open this box.
d. This box is not openable (by anybody).

Our theory provides a straightforward account for this fact, via ~A Spec positions. The adjectival affix *-able* projects a ~A Spec position, which must be linked to another position within the structure, given it is a ~A position. In this specific case, it must be linked to the Compl position of the verbal projection the adjectival affix combines with. The adjectival affix does not project an A Spec, otherwise we would expect *-able* adjectives to be transitive, contrary to fact, as evidenced in (37). Thus, the specifier of the adjectival affix can only be a ~A position.

(37) a. This paper is readable. / a readable paper
b. This is readable (*of the paper).
c. This box is not openable. / an unopenable box.
d. This is unopenable (*of the box).

In our theory, we assume the strong form of X' structure, according to which the asymmetrical relation between the Spec and the Compl positions of a head is always obtained even though the position may not necessarily be an A position. Thus, in the case at hand, the adjectival suffix does project a Spec position, albeit a ~A Spec position. This position is linked to the A Compl position of the verbal projection it combines with, as depicted in (38), the semantic content of which originates in the A Compl position.

(38)

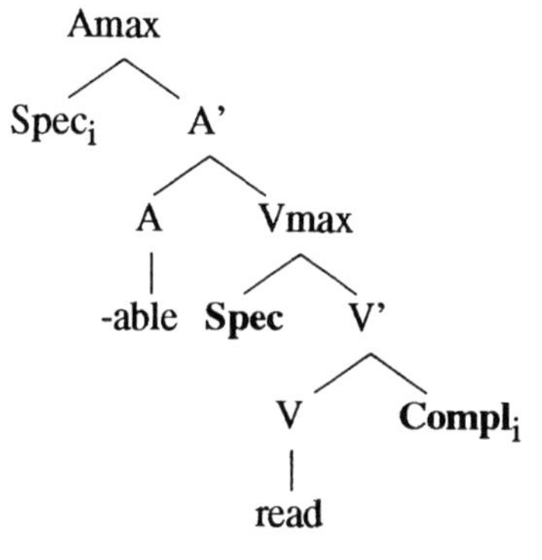

The properties of *-ive* deverbal adjectives also motivate the need for ~A Spec positions in the projection of derivational affixes. Again, stated in terms of subject/object positions, the examples in (39) illustrate the fact that the subject of *-ive* adjectival predicates is the subject of the verbal projection it combines with.

(39) a. The guards impress the crowd.
b. The guards are impressive.
c. Enemies destroy the city.
d. Enemies are destructive.

Stated in X' terms, the adjectival suffix *-ive* projects a ~A Spec position. Given our theory, a ~A position must be linked. In the case at hand, the ~A Spec position of the adjectival affix is linked to the A Spec position of the verbal projection it combines with, as in (40).

(40)

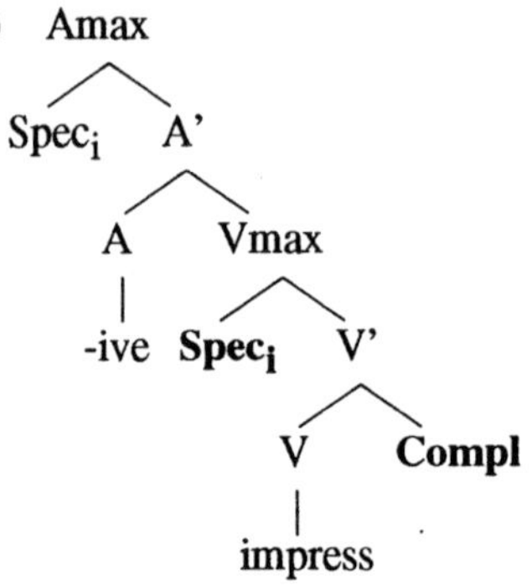

The adjectival suffix does not project an A-Spec since the derived adjective is not transitive. However, the complement of the verbal projection the affix combines with may be projected as an oblique complement (adjunct), as illustrated in (41).

(41) a. The guards are impressive (*of/to the crowd).
b. Enemies are destructive (*of/to the city).

Thus the argument structure properties of adjectival affixes and consequently the argument structure properties of the derived adjectives they head follow from the presence of a ~A-Spec in the projection of the adjectival affix. The presence of this ~A position ensures that the adjectival affixes do not 'add' an argument to the verbal projection they combine with. This ~A position must be linked to an A position. While *-ive* requires this position to be linked to the Spec of the verbal projection it combines with, *-able* requires this position to be linked to the Compl position of the verbal projection it combines with. Given these linking relations, the argument structure properties of the derived adjective follow. Thus, *-able* as well as *-ive* adjectives are intransitive adjectives. The argument position of *-able* adjectives is the A Compl (internal argument) of the verbal projection it combines with, while the argument position of *-ive* adjectives is the A Spec (external argument) of the verbal projection it combines with.

Further evidence for a Spec position in the projection of a derivational affix comes from the argument structure properties of deverbal nouns. Nominal affixes combine with verbs and also determine the argument structure of the resulting deverbal noun. This is the case for the nominal affixes *-er* and *-ee* in English. The examples in (42) illustrate the facts. The complement of an *-er* deverbal noun is the object of the verbal projection the nominal affix combines with, whereas in the case of an *-ee* deverbal noun it is the subject. Furthermore, these deverbal nouns may not license adjuncts related to argument positions.

(42) a. John employs Paul.
b. the employer of Paul (*by John)
c. the employee of John's (*of Paul)

These facts are accounted for as follows in our theory. The nominal suffixes *-er* and *-ee* project a ~A Spec that is related to an A position of the verbal projection it combines with, namely the Spec position of the verbal projection in the case of *-er* and the Compl position in the case of *-ee*, as depicted in the following trees.

(43) a.

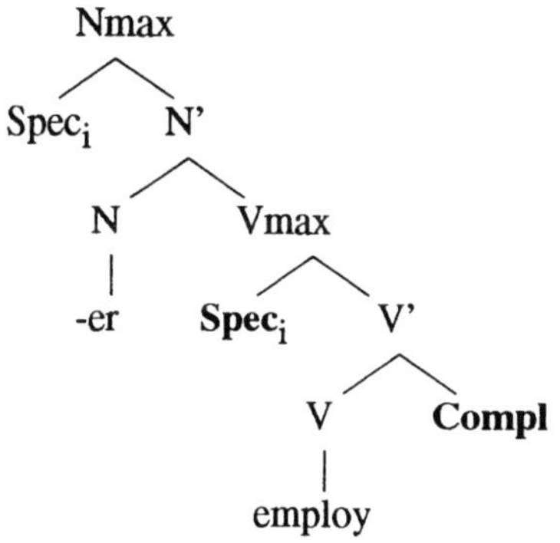

b.

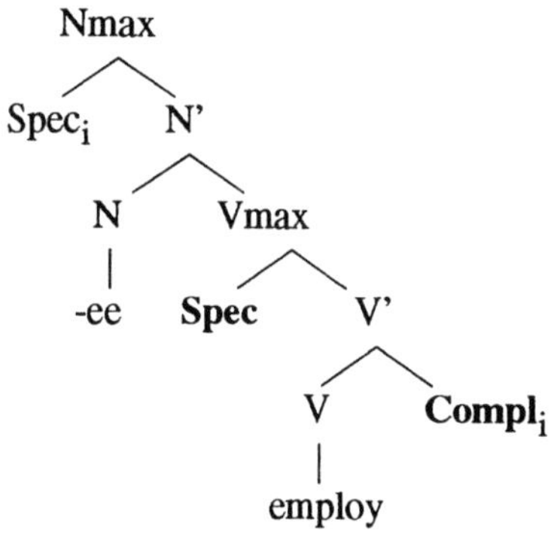

These positions cannot be projected as adjuncts because they are ~A-linked by suffixal heads which have quantifier-like properties, as we discuss below. The Spec of the verbal projection that combines with *-er* is linked by *-er* and the Compl of the verbal projection that combines with *-ee* is linked by *-ee*.. We will come back to this point below. Let us note for now that the nominal affixes *-er* and *-ee* differ from the nominal suffix *-tion* and *-ing* in this respect. Compare (42) and (44).

(44) a. the production of movies by Spielberg
b. the producing of movies by Spielberg

Thus, the first argument in favor of a specifier position in the projection of derivational affixes is that it contributes to an account of the argument structure properties of the derived forms. Without this position it would not be possible to account in a simple and unified way for the difference in transitivity between derived verbs on the one hand and derived adjectives and nouns on the other.

2.4.2. *Lexical gaps*

A second argument in favor of a Spec position in the projection of a derivational affix is that such a position contributes to an explanation of the restrictions observed in derivation that are often referred to as 'lexical gaps'. One such restriction can be observed with the verbal suffixes *-ify* and *-ize*. These affixes may not combine with transitive predicates, either transitive nouns or adjectives, as illustrated in the following examples.

(45) a. She is proud of him.
b. He made Mary proud.
c. *He proudified Mary.

(46) a. Paul is the father of John.
b. She turned Paul into a father.
c. *She fatherized Paul.

This follows in our theory including a strict version of X' structure where there is only one Spec per head. Transitive nouns and adjectives project their own A Spec position and thus they may not combine with the verbal affixes that project their own A Spec position. On the other hand, the verbal suffixes *-ify* and *-ize* combine with a nominal or an adjectival projection lacking an A Spec position, such as intransitive nouns and adjectives.

(47) a. He solidified the product.
b. They certified the results.
c. He unionized the workers.
d. They computerized the data.

These restrictions are not accounted for by categorial selection, assuming the specifications in (48), from Lieber (1992: 55), for these affixes, where only categorial features are specified.

(48) a. -ize: $[\{N,A\}\underline{\quad}]_V$
b. -ify: $[\{N,A\}\underline{\quad}]_V$

A theta-grid approach along the lines of Roeper (1987) cannot be advocated here because the verbal affixes *-ify* and *-ize* do not fit in the proposed system which is designed to account for the properties of either matching (*-able*), inheriting (*-ing*) or blocking (*-ful*) affixes.[3]

On the other hand, stated in terms of X' categories, LF restrictions imposed by affixes on the projection they combine with narrow down the set of interpretable derived verbs. In our theory, the LF restriction reduces to the requirement that the nominal or adjectival projection that combines with the verbal suffixes project a ~A Spec position. This restriction is derived from the strict version of X' structure that we assume here, where there is only one Spec per head.

While the verbal suffixes (*-ize*, *-ify*) project an A Spec as a lexical specification, nominal (*-er*, *-ee*, *-tion*, *-ing*) and adjectival affixes (*-able*, *-ive*) project a ~A Spec by default, assuming that affixes that are not specified for projecting an A Spec project a ~A Spec. We are thus reduced to the lexical specification in (35) above for the set of derivational affixes that we have considered so far. Thus, not only does our theory reduce what are generally considered lexical idiosyncrasies or lexical gaps, it also leads to the reduction of the lexical specifications in the grammar.

Let us now turn to the restrictions imposed by a derivational affix on its complement domain. In our theory, the complement domain of a derivational affix is an X' projection where a Spec position asymmetrically c-commands a Compl position. Here again, the Spec position may be an A or a ~A position. The representations in (30) above express the restrictions imposed by derivational affixes on their complement domain, again under the assumption that the argument structure properties of lexical heads are expressed in terms of X' structure. The central difference between the verbal, adjectival and nominal affixes that we considered is that while the verbal affixes (*-ify*) do not have an A Spec in their complement domain, the adjectival (*-able*) and the nominal (*-er*) do have such a position as well as an A Compl position. The following paragraphs bring empirical support to this claim.

The verbal affix *-ify* combines with ergative adjectives, such as *certain*, which is an ergative adjective according to Cinque (1990), and not with transitive ones, such as *proud*, as illustrated below. This restriction is represented in (32a) above.

(49) a. This is certain.
b. They certified this.
c. He is proud.
d. *They proudified him.

The adjectival suffix *-able* combines with a transitive verb, as in (50a,b). It does not combine with ergative verbs, as in (50c,d) as well as unergative verbs, as in (50e,f), even though (50g) is possible. This restriction is expressed in (32b) above.

(50) a. This dress is washable.
b. This person is loveable.
c. *This vase is fallable.
d. *The train is arrivable.
e. *The sun is shinable.
f. *He is snorable.
g. Cut flowers are perishable.

The nominal suffix *-er* generally combines with unergative verbs, as in (51a), as well as transitive verbs, as in (51b), but not with ergative verbs, as illustrated in (51c). The representation in (32c) above represents this fact.

(51) a. He is a swimmer/boxer/dreamer/worker,...
b. He is a killer/an eater/a hitter/producer,....
c. *He is a faller/an arriver/a departer,....

The selectional restrictions imposed by the nominal affix on the verbal projection it combines with is expressed in a unified way in our theory. The affix attaches to verbal projections including an A Spec position. This is a configurational property of unergative verbs as well as transitive verbs which exhibit an asymmetry between the Spec and the Compl position. This requirement also covers the semantic selection imposed by the nominal affix on the verbal projection it combines with. The nominal affix *-er* does not combine with verbs that are symmetrical statives, such as *resemble/*resembler*, but it does combine with asymmetrical stative verbs, as in *lover/lover* and *hate/hater*, as exemplified in (52). Furthermore, it does combine with culminating transitions (using Pustejovsky's 1988 terminology) that are unergative verbs, as in *lose/loser* and *win/winner*, but not if they are ergative verbs as in *die/*dier* and *arrive/*arriver*, as illustrated in the examples in (53).[4]

(52) a. John resembles Paul. ⟶ Paul resembles John.
b. *He is a resembler.
c. John hates Mary. ⟷̸ Mary hates Paul.
d. He is a hater.

(53) a. John wins.
b. He is a winner.
c. Mary arrived.
d. *She is an arriver.

The facts indicate that asymmetrical X' positions play a role in derivational morphology. The properties of the nominal affix *-er* indicate that the semantic selection of a derivational affix is parasitic on configurational properties: the asymmetrical relation imposed by the affix on the argument structure of its complement overrides the selection set in terms of aspectual classes. On the other hand, if argument structure has conceptual and aspectual dimensions also encoded in terms of X' structure, as discussed in Di Sciullo (1993), the fact that *-er* may combine with statives projecting an asymmetrical aspectual structure can be accounted for.

If selectional restrictions in derivational morphology were not encoded in terms of X' categories, it would be impossible to account in a simple way for the facts presented here. In particular, these restrictions are not covered by morphological subcategorization, which is restricted to the categorial features of heads. Let us stress further that morphological subcategorization cannot be saved if we extend the categorial features to the transitive/intransitive distinction or to the unergative/ergative/transitive distinction without appealing to disjunctive specifications.

The projection of an A or a ~A Spec position in the complement domain of a derivational affix captures the restrictions in a unified way. We proposed that a ~A Spec position must be projected in the complement domain of a verbal affix, while an A Spec position must be projected in the complement domain of an adjectival or nominal affix for affixation to be obtained.

2.4.3. *Disjunctive selection*

A third argument in favor of our hypothesis is that it accounts in a simple way for cases that otherwise would require a disjunction in categorial selection but not in semantic selection. The generalization, we claim, can be captured in terms of the projection of an A Spec position.

We will illustrate this point by considering the properties of the French verbal affixes *-e-* and *-i-* (*-er* and *-ir-* in the infinitival form) in denominal and deadjectival verb formation. The examples in (54a) illustrate *-e-* verb formation from a nominal base, and the examples in (54b) illustrate *-i-* verb formation from an adjectival base.

(54) a. code, coder — programme, programmer
'code', 'to code' — 'program', 'to program'

dessin, dessiner — beurre, beurrer
'drawing', 'to draw' — 'butter', 'to butter'

b. pâle, pâlir — rouge, rougir
'pale', 'to become pale' — 'red', 'to redden';

gros, grossir — vieux, vieillir
'fat', 'to gain weight' — 'old', 'to age'

It is generally the case that the affix *-e-* combines with a nominal projection, while the suffix *-i-* combines with an adjectival projection (cf. Di Sciullo in press a, b; Houle 1993). A morphological subcategorization frame approach to denominal and deadjectival verb formation would require the two lexical specifications in (55) to describe the restrictions. However, the lexical specifications in (55) do not constitute an explanation as well since they present only partial descriptions.

(55) a. -e- : [N__]
b. -i- : [A__]

In fact, there are cases where the c-selection does not differentiate *-e*-and *-i-* verbs in French verb formation. This is illustrated in (56). In (56a) both verbal suffixes combine with the same base; in (56b) *-i-* combines with a noun and *-e-* combines with an adjective, contrary to the general case specified in (55). To cover all the cases of disjunction in categorial selection, a specification as in (57) would be required.

(56) a. [$_N$terre], [$_V$[[a[$_N$terre]] e$_V$]r],[$_V$[[a[$_N$terre]] i$_V$]r]
'land', 'to overwhelm', 'to land'

b. [$_N$fin], [$_V$[$_N$fin]i$_V$]r], *finer
'end', 'to end'
[$_A$saoul], [$_V$[$_A$saoul]e$_V$]r], *saoulir
'drunk', 'to get drunk'

(57) a. -e- : [{N, A}__]
b. -i- : [{A, N}__]

However, if the categorial selection of these verbal affixes may vary, the argument structure properties of the derived verbs is constant. Thus, a derived *-i-* verb is inchoative, denoting a change of state, even when it combines with a noun, as in *fin/finir*; while a derived *-e-* verb is causative/inchoative, even when it combines with an adjective, as in *saoul/saouler*. As expected, this semantic difference manifests itself in the difference in transitivity between derived *-e-* and *-i-* verbs, as illustrated in the examples in (58). The examples in (58a,b) illustrate the fact that *-e-* verbs are transitive, whether their base form is nominal, as in (58a), or adjectival, as in (58b). The examples in (58c,d) illustrate the fact that *-i-* verbs are intransitive

(58) a. *Jean atterre. / Jean atterre Paul.
"John overwhelms." / "John overwhelms Paul."

b. *Jean saoule. / Jean saoule Paul.
"John makes drunk." / "John makes Paul drunk."

c. Le film finit. / *Jean finit le film.
"The movie ends." / "John ends the movie."

(58) d. Jean pâlit. / *Paul pâlit Pierre.
"John becomes pale."/ "Paul gets Pierre pale."

In our theory, the difference between the two verbal affixes resides crucially in the projection of an A or a ~A Spec position, as in the specifications in (59), where (59b) need not be stipulated since it is a default value for an X' position in our system.

(59) a. -e- : **<Spec>**
b. -i- : <Spec>

Extending Hale and Keyser's (1992) proposal for the analysis of English denominal verbs to the French case, we take *-e-* to be the morphological spell out of the abstract causative verb [CAU], and *-i-* to be the morphological spell out of the abstract inchoative verb [INC], as depicted in the structures in (60). In these structures, the verbal affixes take an X' complement and the noun or the adjective the affix combines with is embedded in its complement domain.

(60)

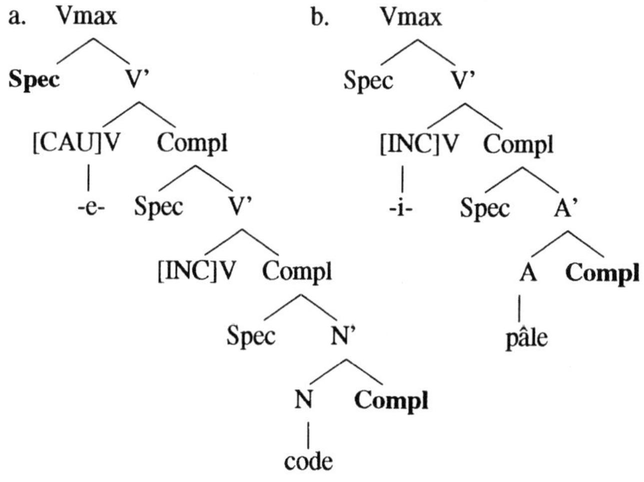

These structures express the argument structure properties of denominal and deadjectival verbs in French. They include two A positions (in bold) in the case of *-e-* verbs and only one argument position in the case of *-i-* verbs. Furthermore, the complement domain of *-e-* verbs includes a verbal projection, which is not present in the complement of *-i-* verbs. The verbal affix *-e-* includes an inchoative (verbal) projection in its complement domain, whereas no such projection is part of the complement domain of the verbal affix *-i-*. In the case of *-i-*, it is a stative (adjectival) projection which is projected in the complement domain of the affix. These selectional differences between affixes of the same category are expressed configurationally within our theory. They are not expressed by morphological subcategorization frames or theta grids.

The difference in transitivity between derived *-e-* and *-i-* verbs observed above follows from the fact that the causative affix *-e-* projects an A Spec position, while *-i-* projects a ~A Spec position. Given our theory, it also follows that derived *-e-* verbs project an A Spec position and derived *-i-* verbs do not. This result, in conjunction with the requirement that ~A positions must be linked, accounts for the difference in transitivity between the derived verbal structures.

The facts presented in this section cannot find a unitary explanation if morphological selection is couched in terms of subcategorization frames or theta-grids, even if we allow disjunctions to be part of morphological subcategorization frames or theta-grids.French

2.5. *Predictions*

Let us consider the general predictions made by the A/~A Spec position in derivational morphology. The difference between A and ~A Spec positions in the X' projection of derivational affixes allows for the following two predictions. The first prediction is that the projection of an A or a ~A Spec for a derived item follows from the A/~A Spec property of the affixal head it includes. Only derived items projecting an A Spec position include an affix that projects such a position. Likewise, only derived items that project a ~A Spec position include an affix projecting such a position.

Secondly, the difference between A and ~A Spec projections of a derivational affix predicts that derivational morphology affects argument structure. If a derivational affix projects an A Spec position, this position will be projected by the derived item but not by the item the affix combines with without violating the strict X' structure allowing only one Spec position per head. If a derivational affix projects a ~A Spec position, the distribution of the arguments of the category it combines with will be affected.

2.6. *Summary*

In this section, we justified the need for Spec and Compl positions in the X' projection of a derivational affix. We showed how the presence of this position accounted for the restrictions on derivation as well as making the correct prediction with respect to the argument structure of derived items. We spelled out the predictions made by the differences between A and ~A Spec positions in derivational morphology.

3. PARALLELS

Let us now consider one consequence of our hypothesis according to which a derivational affix projects an X' structure and takes a complement domain the head of which also projects an X' structure. One consequence of this hypothesis is that morpho-syntactic-semantic parallels can be captured in an elegant way. The following paragraphs present some evidence to this effect on the basis of English.

3.1. *Passive-like morphemes*

A first parallel that can be expressed is the one between *-able* adjectives and passive structures. The specifier of the whole construction originates in the complement position of the embedded VP. In the examples in (61a,c) the complement of the verbal stem *break* is projected in the specifier of AGRs. The adjectival affix and the passive morphology share similar properties, which on the one hand prevent the argumental specifier of the VP from being projected in the overt subject position and on the other forces the A Compl of the VP to be linked to a ~A Spec position, as in (62a) for *-able* and in (62b) for the past participle (pp) morpheme. Thus, the X' Selection Hypothesis captures the parallels in the distribution of arguments in *-able* adjectives and in passive structures.

(61) a. The glass has been broken.
b. a broken glass
c. The glass is breakable.
d. a breakable glass

(62)

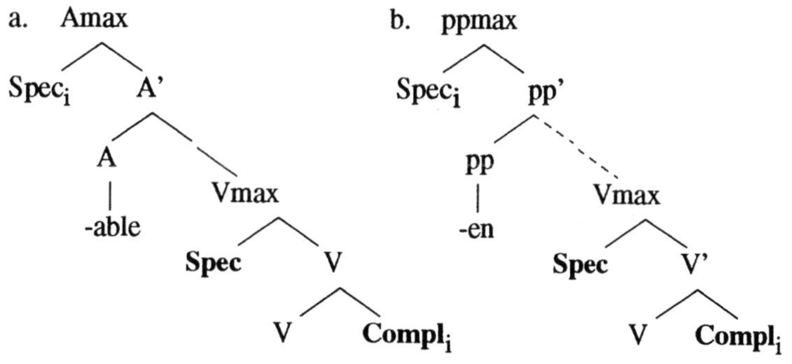

Furthermore, similar selectional restrictions are observed for both morphemes. Ergative and unergative verbs as well as verbs with a small clause complement do not passivize, just as they do not combine with *-able*.

(63) a. * The sun has been shined.
b. * The sun is shinable.
c. * The leaf has been fallen.
d. * The leaf is fallable.
e. * Four has been equalled.
f. * Four is equallable.

It is possible to account for this fact in terms of our hypothesis. Basically, the structure projected by an ergative or an unergative verb does not satisfy the configurational requirements imposed by either affix on the argument structure of its complement.

3.2. *Causative morphemes*

A second parallel that can be captured in terms of our hypothesis, is the one that relates structures headed on the one hand by lexical causatives, and on the other by causative affixes. This is exemplified below, where in (64) the construction is headed by the verb *make* and in (65) the deadjectival verbs are headed by the verbal affix *-ify*.

(64) a. He_i made $himself_i$ cut the bread.
b. $John_i$ made $himself_i$ cut the bread.
c. *He_i made him_i cut the bread.
d. *$John_i$ made $John_i$ cut the bread.

(65) a. It is certain that this will occur.
b. This is certain.
c. They certified this.
d. *It is proud that they did this.
e. They are proud of him.
f. *He proudified them.

In the lexical causative construction, linking is possible between elements that do not both have independent reference, where an anaphor, an element lacking independent reference, is linked to an R-expression or a pronominal as in (64a,b). Linking is excluded between elements with independent reference, as in (64c,d). Likewise morphological causative constructions are possible where they involve adjectives that do not project a specifier that may have independent reference. This is the case with *certain*, which may project an expletive in Spec (65a), but not with *proud*, which may not do so (65d).

Stated in our terms, the A Spec of a lexical or a morphological causative can be part of a chain including the Spec of the embedded VP if these positions differ formally. In (64a,b), the Spec of the embedded VP is an anaphor and the Spec of the lexical causative verb is an R-expression or a pronoun and the Spec positions can be part of a chain. In fact they must be given the principle A of the Binding Theory (cf. Chomsky 1981, 1986, 1994) according to which an anaphor must be bound in its local domain. On the other hand, the two A Spec positions in (64c,d) cannot be part of the same chain given that they are formally the same categories, R-expressions or pronouns. In fact they cannot be part of the same chain without violating Principle C of the Binding Theory, according to which R-expressions must be free, as well as Principle B, according to which a pronominal is free in its local domain.

Likewise, the A Spec of a causative affix is linked to the Spec of the projection it combines with if it is a ~A Spec. As we noted above, *-ify* may only combine with an adjective that does not project an A Spec, as it is the case with the ergative adjective *certain*, but not with a transitive one such as *proud*, as illustrated above.

The fact that the Spec positions in lexical and morphological causatives must be formally distinct can be captured straightforwardly within our theory, as represented in (66).

(66)

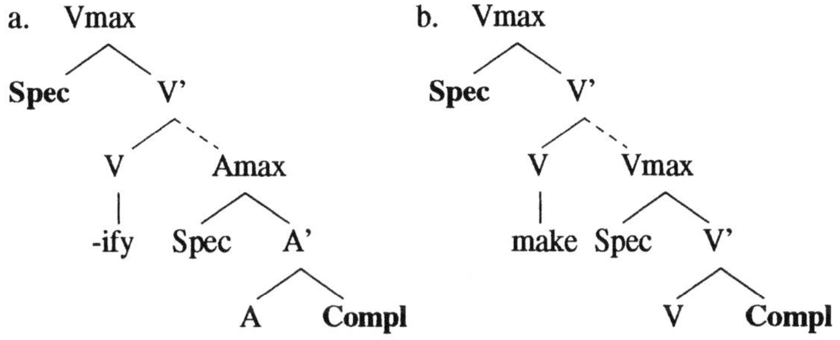

In a morphological causative construction (66a) the embedded Spec must be ~A to be part of a chain with the higher A Spec; in a lexical causative construction in (66b) the embedded Spec must be an element with no independent reference, an anaphor, to be part of a chain with the higher A Spec.

3.3. *Nominal morphemes*

A further parallel exists between *-er* and *-ee* nominals and quantified structures, which can also be expressed given our hypothesis. The restriction against vacuous quantification (cf. Chomsky (1986)) observed in phrasal structure also obtains in morphological structures. In the structures in (67a,b) each quantifier (*wh*) binds only one variable in its domain at LF. However, in (68a) two quantifiers (*wh*) bind the variable in Spec, VP at LF, and in (68b), two quantifiers (*wh*) bind the same variable in Compl, VP at LF.

(67) a. Who likes what?
b. What does who like?

(68) a. *Who does who like what?
b. *What does who likes what?

The structures in (69b,c) are also cases of vacuous quantification, since there is no variable to be bound by the *wh*-quantifier at LF.

(69) a. It seems that John is sick.
b. *What seems that John is sick.
c. *Something seems that John is sick.

The examples in (68) and (69) include verbs the argument structures of which do not project an external argument. However in phrasal structure, the subject position must be filled by an expletive, as in (68a) and (69a), in order to satisfy the Extended Projection Principle (cf. Chomsky (1981, 1986, 1994)). Central to our point is that this position may not be questioned or quantified, as the examples in (68b,c) and (69b,c) illustrate.

Similarly, *-er* nominal formation is excluded with raising verbs, as in (70); that is, with verbs that do not project an A Spec position in our theory.

(70) a. *a seemer.
b. *an appearer.
c. *a probabler

These facts, in conjunction with the interpretative parallels between *-er*, *-ee* nominals and quantified expressions, as in (71), suggest that the nominal affixes have quantifier-like properties.

(71) a. employer
one that employs: the x | x employs y

b. employee
one that is employed: the y | x employs y

The parallels between the nominal affixes and *wh*-structures can be expressed in our theory, where linking occurs word-internally. This is illustrated in (72) and (73), where linking affects the ~A Spec of the head of the construction and the A Spec or the A Compl of the embedded Vmax.

(72)
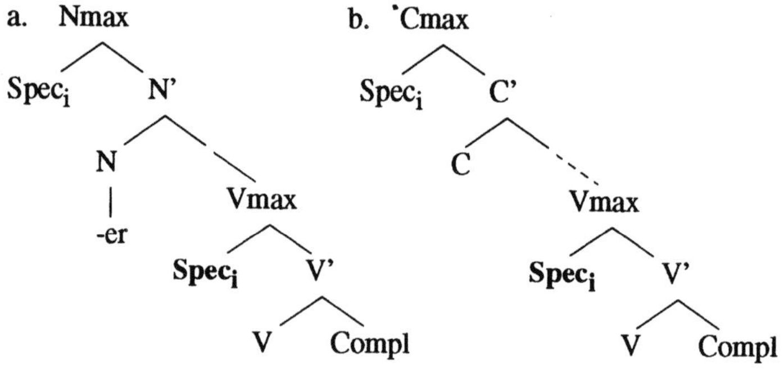

(73)

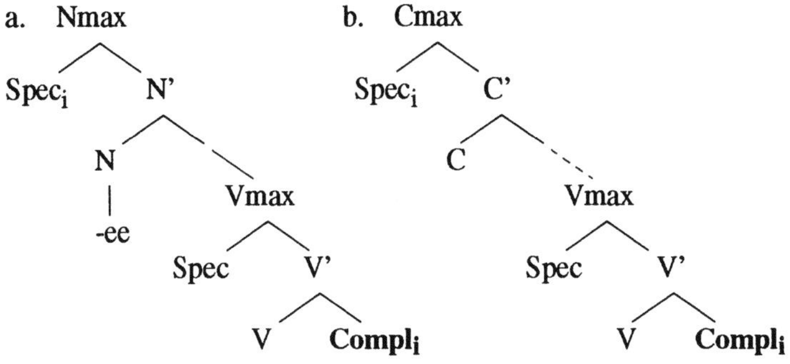

There are nonetheless differences between derived nominals and quantified structures. One of them is the fact that while ergative verbs are generally excluded in the complement domain of the nominal affixes *-er* and *-ee*, ergative verbs can be part of a quantified structure including a relative clause. This is illustrated in the following examples.

(74) a. one that arrives on time
b. Everyone arrives on time.

(75) a. *an arriver on time
b. *an arrivee on time

The difference in (74) and (75) follows from the fact that while morphological operations affect the A positions within the Vmax (the argument structure of a head), syntactic operations, if reduced to feature checking along the lines of Chomsky (1994), do not affect the A positions within the VP (the argument structure of a head).

4. DERIVING HEAD-TO-HEAD SELECTION

The selectional restrictions imposed by a derivational affix on its stem follow from X' selection in our theory. We propose that the selectional properties of derivational affixes are encoded in terms of X' categories, as in the lexical representations in (76), where the suffixes are specified for an A position, either a Spec or a Compl in their VP complement domain.

(76) a. -er : < **Spec** >
b. -ee : < **Compl** >
(76) c. -ive : < **Spec** >
d. able: < **Compl** >

In our theory, the nominal and adjectival affixes project an ~A Spec. The ~A Spec position is not part of the lexical entries since ~A is a default value. Given that a ~A position must be linked to an A position in the X' domain of a derivational affix, the ~A Spec projected by the nominal and adjectival affixes must be linked to the A positions marked in (76). The specifications in (76) cannot be derived from other properties of the grammar and thus must be part of the lexical entry. They are part of the LF lexical specifications for the derivational affixes, which we dissociated from their PF specifications. They provide a finer account of the restrictions imposed by an affix on its stem which, as we showed above, cannot be captured with head-to-head selection, including categorial selection and theta-grids. They instantiate our central hypothesis, the X' Selection Hypothesis, according to which selection is stated in terms of X' positions.

The fact that the nominal and the adjectival affixes have a verbal projection (VP) in their complement domain need not be stipulated. These affixes are category changing and they affect argument structure, the basic form of which is a VP. Furthermore, the fact that the nominal and adjectival affixes combine with verbal configurations and not with verbal categories is captured in our theory. Thus, given the lexical specification in (76a), the A Spec position in the complement domain of the nominal affix *-er* must be linked, and the nominal affix may only combine with verbs that project an A Spec position. That is, the stem must be a transitive or unergative verb, and not (generally) an ergative verb. This result cannot be obtained in a unified way by morphological subcategorization. Likewise, given the lexical specification in (76d), the A Compl position in the complement domain of the adjectival affix *-able* must be linked; thus the adjectival affix may combine with transitive verbs, but not generally with ergatives or unergatives. This result may only be obtained by extending the descriptive power of morphological subcategorization.

The question remains whether the specification in (35) above for the verbal affixes such as *-ize* and *-ify* needs to be stipulated at all. According to Ken Hale (p.c.), if verbs must project an external position for independent reasons, no stipulation is required. On the other hand, if they project an A Spec they cannot select an A Spec in their complement domain, but only an A Compl. This is in fact what we found. Moreover, the fact that the verbal affixes combine with adjectival and nominal categories may be seen as following from their category-changing property.

In this section, we suggested that the selectional properties of derivational affixes encoded in terms of head-to-head relations can be derived. This is a desirable result given a model of grammar such as here, subcategorization frames and theta-grids are no longer justified.

5. SUMMARY

In this paper, we proposed that the selectional properties of derivational affixes are stated in terms of X' positions. This hypothesis predicts the existence of argument structure asymmetries in the selectional properties of a derivational affix. Furthermore, the mapping between semantic selection and categorial selection can be simplified, given that semantic and categorial selection are encoded in a unique format. Moreover, parallels can be captured in a simple way. Finally, we proposed that morphological subcategorization derives from the linking properties of derivational affixes.

If lexical specifications are encoded in terms of X' positions, the relation between phrase structure and the lexicon is narrowed down. If, as we suggest, a lexical entry is a pair of PF and LF specifications, the form of lexical information is radically constrained.

NOTES

* Many thanks to the members of the Modularity Project at UQAM for discussion. Special thanks to Noam Chomsky, Ken Hale, Jeff Gruber, Tom Roeper, Johan Rooryck and Laurie Zaring for their comments and suggestions on earlier versions of this paper, as well as to the audience at the Syntax Reading Group at Indiana University where the X' Selection hypothesis was presented in April 1993. Any error is my own responsability. This study was supported in part by the Social Sciences and Humanities Research Council of Canada (grant number 411-92-0012).

1 There are of course other constraints which play a role in the cooccurrence relationships between derivational affixes and stems. Phonological conditions impose contextual restrictions such as the impossibility for an adjective ending with a nasal obstruent to take the verbal inchoative suffix *-en*, as in *open/*openen* and *warm/*warmen* as opposed to *red/redden* and *thick/thicken*. Other morphological conditions also play a role such as the fact that certain affixes, such as *-tion*, do not attach to a [-latinate] base, as in *hit/*hitation*, but only to a [+latinate] base, as in *destroy/destruction*. Furthermore, the relative productivity of a derivational affix and blocking also play a role in the cooccurrence restrictions (cf. Aronoff 1976, Scalise 1985, Anderson 1992). These constraints are however of a different nature than the constraint imposed by morphological subcategorization and we will not discuss them here.

2 An A position is argumental, as the object position of passives is. A ~A position is not argumental, e.g., the subject position of passives.

3 It is worth noting that a Lexical Conceptual Structure (LCS) approach to derivational affixes, viz., the decomposition of the meaning of lexical items into semantic primitives (cf. Booij 1992, Lieber 1992) does not capture the restrictions on verb formation either. For example, in the lexical specification in (i), proposed in Lieber (1992:119) for the verbal affix *-ize*, nothing restricts the argument structure properties of the *Base* (nominal or adjectival) that the verbal affix combines with.

(i) -ize: $[_{Event}$ CAUSE $([_{Thing}], [_{Event}$ BE (*LCS of the Base*)])]

The LCS in (i) does not express the restrictions imposed by the verbal affix on the projection it composes with, either a nominal or an adjectival projection, as stipulated in the morphological subcategorization frame (47a) above, also from Lieber (1992).

4 The representation in (i) from (Lieber 1992:136), including the morphological subcategorization and the LCS for the nominal affix *-er*, does not capture the restrictions that we observed.

(i) -er:]V___]N
LCS: x [LCS of the input V]

Neither the subcategorization frame nor the LCS specify the argument structure properties of the imput V.

REFERENCES

Anderson, Steven: 1992, *A-Morphous Morphology*, Cambridge University Press, Cambridge.

Archangeli, Diana: 1984, *Underspecification in Yawelmani Phonology and Morphology*, Ph.D. dissertation, MIT.

Aronoff, Mark: 1976, *Word-Formation in Generative Grammar*, MIT Press, Cambridge, MA.

Booij, Geert: 1992, 'Morphology, Semantics and Argument Structure', in I. Roca (ed.), *Thematic Structure. Its Role in Grammar*, Walter de Gruyter, Berlin.

Borer, Hagit: 1990, 'Derived Nominals and the Causative-Inchoative Alternation: Two Case Studies in Parallel Morphology', unpublished, University of California at Irvine.

Burzio, Luigi: 1986, Italian Syntax, Foris, Dordrecht.

Chomsky, Noam: 1994, 'Bare Phrase Structure', *MIT Occasional Papers in Linguistics* **2**.

———: 1993, 'A Minimalist Program for Linguistic Theory', *MIT Occasional Papers in Linguistics* **1**.

———: 1986, *Knowledge of Language: Its Nature, Origin and Use*, Praeger, New York.

———: 1981, *Lectures on Government and Binding*, Foris, Dordrecht.

Cinque, Guglielmo: 1990, 'Ergative Adjectives and the Lexicalist Hypothesis', *Natural Language and Linguistic Theory* **8**, 1-39.

Di Sciullo, Anna-Maria: (in press a), 'Prefixes and Suffixes,' in Claudia Parodi, Carlos Quicoli, Mario Saltarelli and Maria-Luisa Zubizarreta (eds.), *Romance Linguistic in Los Angeles: Selected Papers from the XXIV Linguistic Symposium on Romance Languages held at USC and UCLA*, Georgetown University Press, Washington, DC.

———: (in press b) 'On Word Structure and Conditions,' in Anna-Maria Di Sciullo (ed.) *Projections and Interface Conditions*, Oxford University Press, New York.

———: 1993, 'The Complement Domain of a Head at Morphological Form', *Probus* **5**, 95-125.

Di Sciullo, Anna-Maria and Edwin Williams: 1987, *On the Definition of Word*, MIT Press, Cambridge, MA.

Farkas, Donka: 1990, 'Two Cases of Underspecification in Morphology', *Linguistic Inquiry* **21**, 539-551.

Fukui, Naoki and Margaret Speas: 1986, 'Specifiers and Projections', *MIT Working Papers in Linguistics* **8**, 128-172.

Grimshaw, Jane: 1990, *Argument Structure*, MIT Press, Cambridge, MA.

Gruber, Jeff: (in press), 'Modularity in a Configurational Theta-Theory,', in Anna-Maria Di Sciullo (ed.), *Projections and Interface Conditions*, Oxford University Press, New York.

Hale , Ken and S. J. Keyser: 1992, 'The Syntactic Character of Thematic Structure', in I. Roca (ed.), *Thematic Structure. Its Role in Grammar*, Walter de Gruyter, Berlin, pp. 107-141.

Higginbotham, James: 1985, 'On Semantics', *Linguistic Inquiry* **16**, 547-594.

Houle, Jocelyne: 1993, 'Verbes déadjectivaux: morphèmes verbaux et structures d'arguments', in Anna-Maria Di Sciullo (ed.) *Les structures d'arguments*, Rapport de recherche CRSH, Université du Québec à Montréal, pp. 240-259.

Hoekstra, Teun: 1992, 'Aspect and Theta Theory', in I. Roca (ed.), *Thematic Structure. Its Role in Grammar*, Walter de Gruyter, Berlin.

Kuroda, Y. 1986, 'Whether we Agree or Not', unpublished, University of California at San Diego.

Law, Paul: 1990, 'Head, Arguments and Adjuncts in Derivational Morphology', *MIT Working Papers in Linguistics* **12**.

Lieber, Rochelle: 1992, *Deconstructing Morphology: Word-Formation in Syntactic Theory*, University of Chicago Press, Chicago.

Pustejovsky, James: 1988, 'The Geometry of Events', in Carol Tenny (ed.), *Studies in Generative Approaches to Aspect. MIT Lexicon Project Working Papers* **24**, 19-39.

Rappaport, Malka and Beth Levin: 1988, 'What to do with Theta-Roles?', in W. Wilkins, (ed.), *Syntax and Semantics* **21**, Academic Press, New York.

Roeper, Tom: 1987, 'Implicit Arguments and the Head-Complement Relation', *Linguistic Inquiry* **18**, 267-311.

Scalise, Sergio: 1985, *Generative Morphology*, Foris, Dordrecht.

Selkirk, Elisabeth: 1982, *The Syntax of Words*, MIT Press, Cambridge, MA.

Speas, Margaret: 1990, *Phrase Structure in Natural Language*, Kluwer, Dordrecht .

Sportiche, Dominique: 1988, 'A Theory of Floating Quantifiers', *Linguistic Inquiry* **19**, 425-449.

Williams, Edwin: 1981, 'Argument Structure and Morphology', *Linguistic Review* **1**, 81-114.

SEVERING THE EXTERNAL ARGUMENT FROM ITS VERB

Angelika Kratzer

0. MODES OF ARGUMENT ASSOCIATION

In his analysis of action sentences, Donald Davidson drew a clear distinction between arguments and adjuncts. Neglecting temporal relations, sentences like

(1) We bought your slippers in Marrakesh.

are analyzed as

(1') $\exists$e [buy (your slippers)(we)(e) & in(Marrakesh)(e)].

In (1'), *buy* is a three-place predicate. Apart from an Event Argument, it has an argument denoting the agent and another one denoting what was bought (the theme, in the terminology of Gruber 1965). That is, the subject and the object in (1) correspond to arguments of the main predicate in the logical representation (1'), while the locative argument *Marrakesh* is introduced by a secondary predicate (the preposition *in*). What (1') says, then, is that there is an event which is a buying of your slippers by us, and which takes place in Marrakesh.

Davidson's distinction between arguments and adjuncts was criticized by Castañeda right after Davidson's talk (Castañeda 1967), and has been abandoned in the work of Parsons. Both Castañeda and Parsons let agents and themes introduce independent predicates as well. For Parsons (not for Castañeda), the independent predicates are two-place predicates denoting thematic relations. On this proposal (inspired by Panini and Fillmore's case grammar, Fillmore 1968), (1) has the logical form (1''):

(1'') $\exists$e [buying(e) & Agent(we)(e) & Theme(your slippers)(e) & in(Marrakesh)(e)]

(1'') says that there is an event which is a buying, whose agent is us, whose theme are your slippers and which takes place in Marrakesh. Some terminology will be useful. (1') uses what Dowty (1989) call the 'ordered-argument' method for the association of agent and theme arguments with their verb. In (1'') we see what Dowty labels the 'neo-Davidsonian' method. On the neo-Davidsonian method, arguments are associated with their verbs via secondary predicates.

Davidson and Parson's theories are theories of logical form, where 'logical form' is not the same as the syntacticians' 'Logical Form', a level of syntactic representation (as in May 1977, 1985). Parsons' logical form is more like the linguists' semantic structure or conceptual structure.[1] Parsons' (1993) emphasizes that the theory presented in Parsons (1990) is a "proposal for the logical forms of sentences, unsupplemented by an account of how those forms originate by combining sentence parts." In other words, Parsons' theory is a theory of logical or conceptual structure that is not committed to particular claims about argument association in the syntax. It is possible to agree, for example, that English verbs are associated with their arguments by the ordered argument method. Here is an illustration of what such a quarrel would be about.[2]

The first position: Ordered argument association in the syntax and in conceptual structure

buy $\lambda x \lambda y \lambda e[\text{ buy}(x)(y)(e)]$

Figure 1

The second position: Ordered argument association in the syntax, neo-Davidsonian association in conceptual structure

buy $\lambda x \lambda y \lambda e[\text{ buying}(e) \ \& \ \text{Theme}(x)(e) \ \& \ \text{Agent}(y)(e)]$

Figure 2

Both proposals agree that the English verb *buy* is a three-place predicate. The Event Argument is the highest argument, the agent argument comes next, and the theme argument is at the bottom. Note that the hierarchy of arguments is part and parcel of a verb's meaning, and doesn't have to be stipulated. I think of verb meanings in the way semanticists in the Fregean tradition usually do.[3] They are functions. Following Schönfinkel (1924), we construe the (classical Davidsonian) denotation of *buy* as a function-valued function f which, if applied to an individual a, yields a function g which, if applied to an individual b, yields a function h which, if applied to an event c, yields truth if and only if c is an event of b's buying a. Fregean denotations of this kind make it possible to maintain the generalization that predicates and their arguments semantically combine by Functional Application.

What distinguishes the two views presented above is their assumptions about the counterpart of English *buy* in logical form or conceptual structure. For a classical Davidsonian it would be a three-place predicate as well. For a neo-Davidsonian, it would be a predicate with just one argument, the Event Argument. Implemented in this way, the neo-Davidsonian view would have no consequences for the syntactic theory of argument structure, and I would have very little to add to the issue beyond what you find in Parsons' work.

The enterprise that I am about to embark on is of a different nature. In this paper (and subsequent work, Kratzer (forthcoming)), I will show that some neo-Davidsonian argument association is present in the *syntax* of verbs. Not all of a verb's arguments are syntactically associated by the ordered argument method. Most importantly, I am going to argue that all external arguments in the sense of Williams(1981) are associated by the neo-Davidsonian method in the syntax. This view has radical consequences for the syntactic theory of argument structure. A verb like *buy* is now a predicate without an external argument. It does not have an agent argument anymore. Here is what its lexical entry looks like:

Severing the external argument from its verb

buy $\lambda x \lambda e$ [buy(x)(e)] or
$\lambda x \lambda e$ [buying(e) & Theme(x)(e)]

Figure 3

On this proposal, the English verb *buy* is a two-place predicate in the syntax (I want to stay uncommitted as to its status with respect to logical form or conceptual structure). The inner argument is the theme argument denoting what is being bought. The higher argument is the Davidson Event Argument. Since the agent argument is not an argument of *buy*, it has to be added via secondary predication. The challenge for the present proposal is to tell a good story about the addition of external arguments in natural languages. Why cannot all verbs add external arguments? What is it that makes external arguments obligatory with many verbs? What is it that determines the thematic role of external arguments? (Not all external arguments are agent arguments.) In this paper, I will not be able to address those important questions in any detail (see Kratzer (forthcoming)). All I intend to do here is present some arguments that show that the proposal I just made has initial plausibility.

1. EXTERNAL ARGUMENTS

Most contemporary theories of argument structure assume some kind of asymmetry between the agent argument and the theme argument of a verb like *buy*. More generally, most theories of argument structure give a special status to the external argument. For Williams (1981), the special status is indicated by underlining. Rappaport and Levin (1986) use angled brackets to distinguish external and internal arguments. For Grimshaw (1990), the external argument is defined as the most prominent argument with respect to both a thematic and an aspectual dimension. Marantz (1984) makes a proposal that comes closest to what I am arguing for here: for him, too, the external argument of a verb is not an argument of the verb. His lexical representations look as follows (neglecting a distinction between internal arguments that is not relevant to the present discussion):

(2)	buy	(theme)
	give	(theme, goal)
	steal	(theme, source)

In these representations (as in mine), information about the external argument is missing. According to Marantz, the object of a verb is an argument of the verb and is assigned a semantic role by the verb. Subjects are arguments and semantic role assignees of predicates (where 'predicates' is used in the sense of Williams (1980), referring to maximal projections like VPs or APs), and this is why the external argument does not appear in the lexical representation of verbs. Marantz is not explicit about how to execute his proposal. If a verb does not carry any information about the presence of an agent argument, how can the VP it projects acquire this information? Consider a VP that consists of the verb *buy* and the object NP *your slippers*. Assuming the usual interpretation mechanisms, semantic composition would proceed via Functional Application in the following fashion:

(3)

VP λe [buy(your slippers)(e)]

V $\lambda e \lambda x$ [buy(x)(e)] — **NP** your slippers

buy — **your slippers**

If this is how the meanings of VPs are composed, it is impossible for the VP to have an agent argument without the V having such an argument to begin with. In the example above, the VP ends up denoting a property of events that is true of any event if it is an event of buying your slippers. No agent argument has come into existence. Trying to maintain Marantz' account, we have to consider the possibility that a verb and its object are not semantically combined via Functional Application. We may associate a special composition rule with syntactic configurations that combine a V and an NP into a VP:

(4) **Input configuration** **Semantic interpretation**

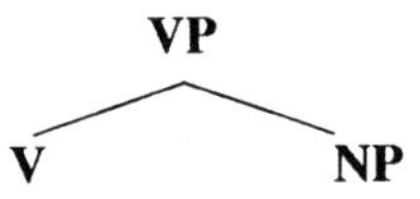

If V* is the denotation of V, and NP* is the denotation of NP, then $\lambda x \lambda e$ [Agent(x)(e) & V*(NP)(e)] is the denotation of VP.[4]

Applying this rule yields the right result for our example: an agent argument is added.

(5)

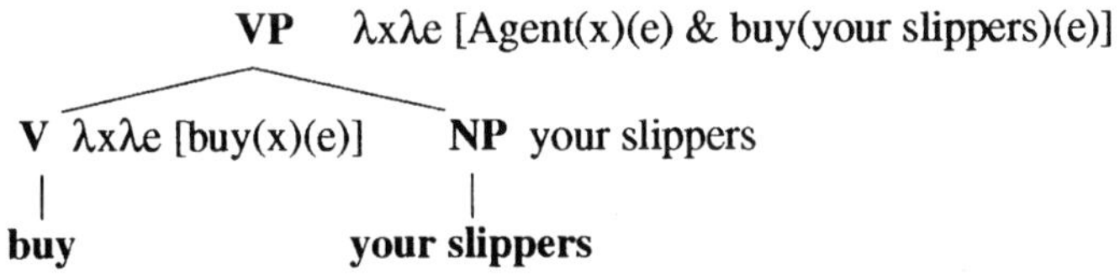

On this proposal, the agent argument is an argument of the VP without being an argument of the V, as desired. This execution of Marantz's proposal does not come for free, however. Its price is a semantic stipulation that would be a blemish for any serious theory of semantic composition.[5] We would be forced to give up the fundamental generalization that heads and their arguments semantically combine via Functional Application. Marantz's proposal, then, does not tell an optimal story about the introduction of the external argument.

Yet Marantz presents an important argument supporting the assumption that external arguments are not true arguments of their verbs. He observes that there are many instances where a particular kind of internal argument triggers a particular interpretation of the verb, and claims that there are few (if any) instances where an external argument does the same. Here are some of his examples (Marantz 1984):

(6) a. throw a baseball
b. throw support behind a candidate
c. throw a boxing match (i.e., take a dive)
d. throw a party
e. throw a fit

(7) a. take a book from the shelf
b. take a bus to New York
c. take a nap

(7) d. take an aspirin
e. take a letter in shorthand

(8) a. kill a cockroach
b. kill a conversation
c. kill an evening watching TV
d. kill a bottle (i.e., empty it)
e. kill an audience (i.e., wow them)

Marantz point out that these facts follow if external arguments are not true arguments of their verbs. Bresnan (1982) and Grimshaw (1990) reply that they can be equally well explained by any theory that has it that external arguments are semantically processed after internal arguments. Since most theories currently on the market are of this kind, Marantz's argument would lose much of its force if Bresnan and Grimshaw were right. While his generalization may very well follow from his assumptions, it couldn't be used to distinguish his theory from most of the others.

> In short, one could capture the subject/non-subject generalization without affecting the lexical representation of predicate argument structure, simply by giving the subject a distinguished role as final argument in the semantic composition of the sentence. (Bresnan 1982: 350)

> In any theta-marking calculation, the external argument is the last to enter in. Thus, in effect, calculations performed over the internal arguments are done without reference to the external arguments, but any a-structure calculation involving the external argument will of necessity involve the internal ones. The special properties of externals follow from their occupying the position of maximal prominence. (Grimshaw 1990: 35)

What is interesting and highly relevant about the data in (6) through (8) is that the phrases listed there do not involve completely frozen idiom chunks. Consider the expression *kill an evening*. This is not a real idiom, since we can have variations of the following kind:

(9) a. kill every evening (that way)
b. kill an afternoon (reading old Gazettes)
c. kill a lovely morning (paying overdue bills)

I can think of two ways of approaching these alternations. One possibility is that there is a number of homophonous verbs *kill*, all closely related in meaning. The range of variation for the object in (9) would then indicate that the *kill* that means 'waste' semantically selects a time interval for its internal argument; that is, it denotes a partial function that is only defined for time intervals. The other verbs *kill* have different semantic selection properties. If *kill* is paired with an object that does not denote a time interval, then the 'waste' reading cannot be chosen, since it would lead to uninterpretability. Hence the impression that properties of the internal argument influence the interpretation of the verb. If the phenomenon illustrated by (6) through (8) can be reduced to a very narrow kind of semantic selection, it should be able to show up with any one of a verb's arguments, since a verb can impose any kind of selectional restrictions on any of its arguments *regardless* of its hierarchical position and the order of semantic processing. By way of illustration, suppose that a two-place predicate denotes the (function valued) function f. If we want to impose a selectional restriction on its inner argument, we state that f is only defined for individuals that obey this restriction. If we want to impose a selectional restriction on the outer argument, we state that for any individual a in the domain of f, f(a) is only defined for individuals that satisfy the restriction. If external arguments are true arguments of their verbs, then we expect verbs to impose selectional restrictions on external arguments that are similar to the ones observed in (6) through (8). If they are not, no comparable selectional restrictions are expected. There would be no way of stating them as part of a verb's meaning.

Marantz does not think of the alternations in (6) through (8) in this way. He is of the opinion that one "would be hard pressed to argue that a different predicate implies a different (homophonous) verb in each case." (Marantz 1984: 25). Suppose that this is so. We would then have a single verb *kill* whose denotation is a function that does not treat all arguments in the same way. Assuming (just for the purpose of illustration) that *kill* has its traditional denotation (agent and theme argument, no Event Argument), its denotation would be a function f with the following properties: If its argument is an animate being a, f yields a function that assigns truth to any individual b if b kills a. If its argument is a time interval a, f yields a function that assigns truth to any individual b if b wastes a. If its argument is a conversation or discussion a, f delivers a function that assigns truth to any individual b if b dampens a. And so on. If this is the correct account of the phenomenon illustrated in (6) through (8), we would again expect that it should affect any argument of a verb, regardless of hierarchical position and order of semantic processing. Any argument of a verb could trigger a particular interpretation of the verb. Here is a fictitious example where the highest argument does so. Suppose that the (traditional) denotation of some two-place predicate is a function f that yields the following output for individuals a in its domain:

(10) If b is a time interval, then f(a)(b) = truth iff a exists during b.
If b is a place, then f(a)(b) = truth iff a is located at b.
If b is a person, then f(a)(b) = truth iff b is the legal owner of a.
. . . . etc. . . . .

It is not true, then, that one could capture the subject/non-subject generalization simply by giving the subject a distinguished role as final argument in the semantic composition of the sentence (contra Bresnan and

Grimshaw). There is no technical obstacle to having verb meanings like the function f if external arguments are true arguments of their verbs. If they are not, Marantz's generalization is expected, however. This means that Marantz's data are very suitable indeed for deciding between theories that assume that external arguments are true arguments of verbs from those that maintain that they are not.

2. THE SYNTAX AND SEMANTICS OF VOICE

If external arguments are not true arguments of their verbs, where do they come from? Suppose that quite generally, arguments are introduced by heads. This helps keep the theory of semantic composition as general and elegant as it should be. Consider now the following simple English sentences:

(11) **Elsa** wrote those poems with this pen.
(12) **Franz** read the poems on this sofa.
(13) **George** sold the sofa to my aunt.

On the story that I am in the midst of telling, we are assuming that in sentences (11) through (13), the agent argument is introduced by a non-overt head. What kind of a head? Is it lexical or functional?

Suppose it is a lexical head. We would then have a higher empty verb present in (11) through (13), maybe a silent *do*. A proposal along those lines has been made for Malagasy. Hung (1988) proposes that the agent argument of active sentences in Malagasy is introduced by a prefix *-an* that heads a higher VP in a layered structure of the following kind:[6]

(14) a.

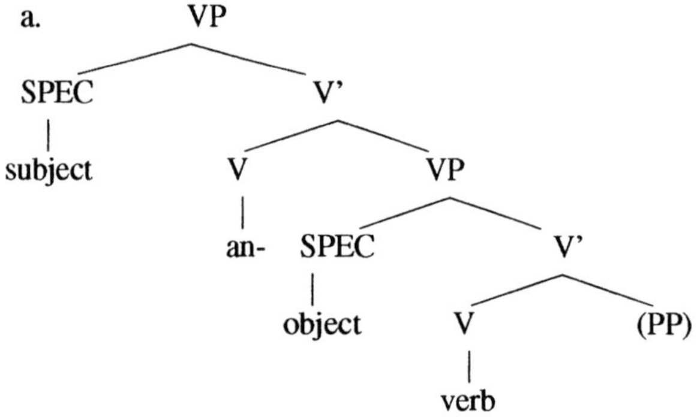

(14) b.

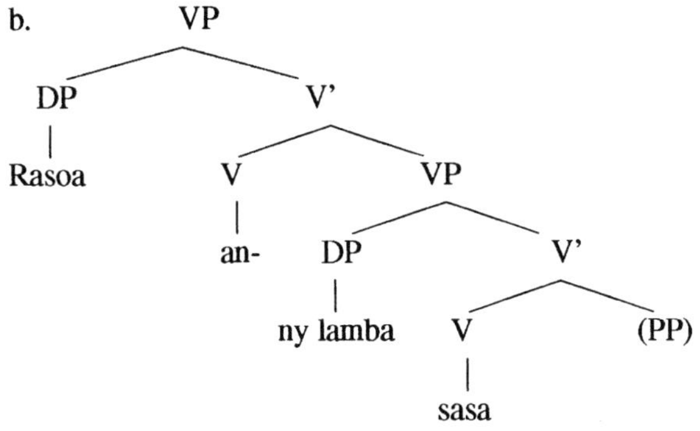

The layered VP structure was originally proposed in Larson (1988) to account for certain properties of the double object construction. In contrast to Larson, Hung assumes that the higher V-node is not empty, but hosts a lexical element that selects the agent argument. Movement of the lower verb to the higher V-position allows the agent affix to incorporate into the verb.[7] Further movement of *an*+verb into I and of the subject into SPEC of IP produces a sentence like (15).[8]

(15) M+an+sasa ny lamba (amin ny savony) Rasoa.
wash+active the clothes with the soap Rasoa
"Rasoa washes the clothes (with the soap)."

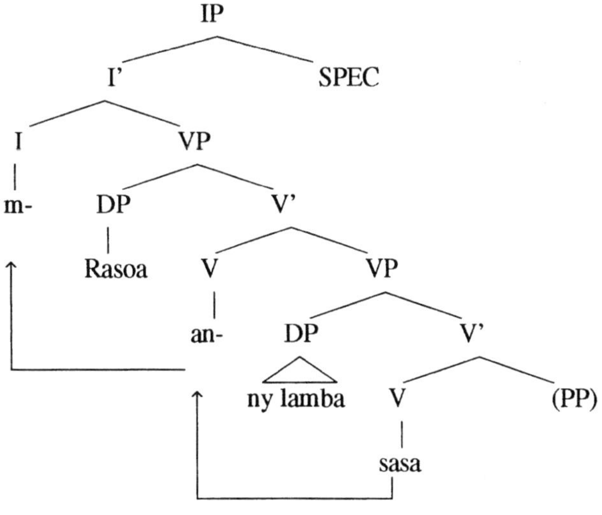

Hung reports that "while the root *sasa* is not a word in itself, it is recognized by speakers as being a root with the meaning 'being washed' or 'having the quality of being washed'. It therefore acts (along with an optional instrument) as a V' predicate of the theme *ny lamba.* The complete reading of the sentence is thus something like 'I caused the clothes to be washed (with soap)', or rather 'I did the (soap) washing of the clothes'." (Hung 1988: 12). Hung takes *an-* to be a light verb like *do* that has two functions. It adds the agent argument and it assigns Case to the object.[9]

Whether or not this proposal is right for Malagasy, I have a few qualms with adopting it for English. If external arguments are introduced by verbs, what is it that makes their introduction obligatory in sentences (11) through (13)? We may try out the idea that verbs like *write*, *read*, and *sell* have an empty incorporated preverb whose existence is forced by a morphological requirement. Without the preverb, then, these verbs would not be morphologically well-formed. We'll see below, however, that the head that introduces the external arguments is not always present (e.g., in gerunds). If it is a lexical head, its defective distribution comes as a surprise. It is not a familiar phenomenon. But if it is an inflectional head, it is expected that it must be present in some constructions, and absent in others. In particular, it must be present in finite constructions. This explains its obligatoriness in (11) through (13).

My second qualm with the proposal that external arguments are introduced by lexical heads has to do with Case assignment. Hung proposes that Malagasy *an-* is a sister of VP. In this position, it can assign structural Case via government to the object in the SPEC of VP position:

(16)

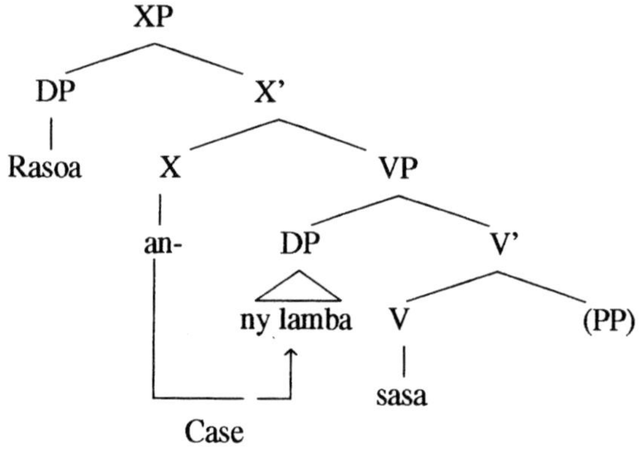

Most traditional and contemporary syntacticians rely on a notion of structural or grammatical Case that is distinguished from lexical Case. Structural Cases are nominative and accusative, lexical Cases are Cases like ablative, locative, and instrumental. The status of dative is and has been controversial.[10] What is structural Case? Consider the following characterization:

(17) Structural Case: Structural Case is Case that is assigned (checked) by inflectional (=functional) heads.

Some such assumption is made in much recent work. Chomsky (1991, 1992) proposes that structural Case for objects is not assigned (checked) by the verb, but by some functional head right above VP. If the head that introduces the external argument is not a lexical, but a functional element, we can maintain that it assigns (checks) accusative Case, while preserving the generalization that structural or grammatical Case is assigned (checked) by functional heads.

If external arguments are introduced by inflectional heads, we understand why in serial verb constructions verbs can share external, but not internal, arguments, as argued in Collins (1993). According to Collins (1993: 56, 91), "a serial verb construction is a succession of verbs and their complements (if any) with one subject and one tense value that are not separated by any overt maker of coordination or subordination." Here is an example of an Ewe serial verb construction with two transitive verbs:

(18) Kofi a *fo* Ama wu.
Kofi fut hit Ama kill
"Kofi will strike Ama dead."
(Collins 1993: 140)

In (18), the two verbs share the inflectional element *a*, and they share the agent argument *Kofi*. They do not share the direct object *Ama*, however. Collins presents clear evidence for the presence of an empty object NP within the projection of *wu*. If external arguments are introduced by a verb's inflection, verbs that share all of their inflection also share their external argument.

Assuming that the heads that introduce external arguments are functional heads, we are able to connect our analysis to proposals for English phrase structure such as Pesetsky (1989), Johnson (1991), and Bowers (1991, 1993). In making this connection, we can harvest many of the pleasant syntactic consequences of those proposals. Take Johnson (1991), for example. Johnson postulates an unidentified functional head μ that is a sister of VP, and to which the verb must adjoin.[11] He argues that object NPs must move to the specifier of VP, and that the force that drives this movement is the necessity for object NPs to be assigned structure Case from μ via government:

(19) Government (Johnson 1991)
A node α governs a node β iff α c-commands β, and at most one node dominates β, but not α.

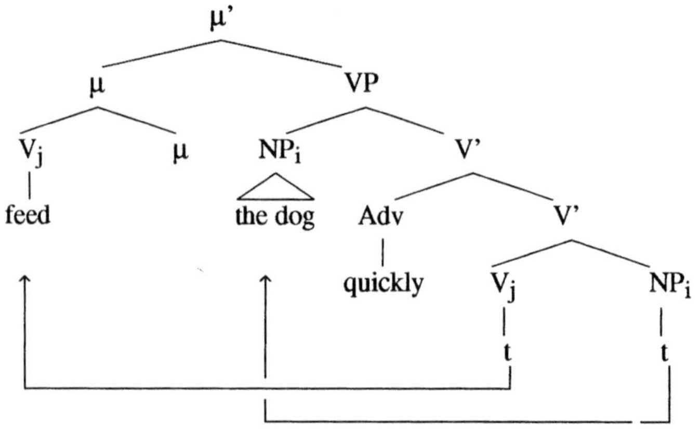

If NPs and only NPs move to the specifier of VP, it follows that they precede adverbs and other complements of the verb. This is illustrated by the following examples (from Johnson 1991):

(20) a. *Gary introduced to Sam Mittie.
b. *Gary told to leave Sam.
c. *Mikey visited quietly his parents.
d. *Chris hit quickly the dog.
e. Chris walked quickly down the street.
f. Mikey talked slowly to Gary.
g. Gary tried diligently to leave.

(20a-d) are ungrammatical since the object NP has not moved to the specifier of VP. (20e-g) show that only NPs must undergo this movement.

What I want to suggest is that Johnson's μ is a head that introduces the external argument in addition to assigning accusative Case. Having acquired semantic content, μ deserves a meaningful name. I will call it VOICE. This choice of name is not arbitrary. Kratzer (forthcoming) argues that Voice is truly at the heart of a theory of voice.

In the spirit of Bowers (1993), we may now assume that, quite generally, heads syntactically realize their arguments in their specifier position at D-structure: external arguments are arguments of Voice, and hence are base-generated in SPEC of VoiceP. Direct objects (of verbs) are arguments of V, and hence are base-generated in SPEC of VP.[12] They do not have to move there as assumed by Johnson. Yet we still derive the 'object first' generalization that he was interested in.

(21)

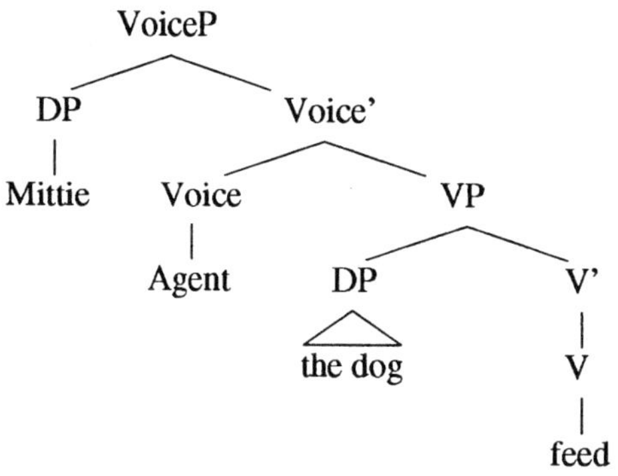

Let us now examine how the phrase structure tree in (21) is interpreted within an event semantics. I will introduce the semantic framework as we walk through an example computation.

(22) VoiceP: semantic interpretation

1. **feed*** = $\lambda x_e \lambda e_s$[feed(x)(e)]

2. **the dog*** = the dog

3. (**the dog feed**)* = λe_s[feed(the dog)(e)]
   From (1), (2) by Functional Application.

4. **Agent*** = $\lambda x_e \lambda e_s$[Agent(x)(e)]

5. (**Agent** (**the dog feed**))* =
   $\lambda x_e \lambda e_s$[Agent(x)(e) & feed(the dog)(e)]
   From (3), (4) by Event Identification.

6. **Mittie*** = Mittie

7. ((**Agent** (**the dog feed**)) **Mittie**)* =
   λe_s[Agent(Mittie)(e) & feed(the dog)(e)]
   From (5), (6) by Functional Application.

The calculation just given is a step by step derivation of the denotation of the tree in (21). The interpretation process assigns denotations to bracketed strings of lexical items in a type-driven fashion (Klein & Sag 1985). For any string α, α* is the denotation of α. Possible denotations are individuals, events, truth-values, and functions construed from those entities. They are given through expressions of an extensional type logic with three basic types: individuals (type e), events (type s), and truth-values (type t). The denotations of lexical items are provided in the lexicon. To calculate the denotations of complex expressions, we have a handful of composition principles that apply freely whenever they can.[13] In this particular example, the applicable composition principles are Functional Application and a principle I dubbed 'Event Identification'.[14] Event Identification is one of several admissible conjunction operations and can be stated as follows:

(23) Event Identification

f	g	->	h
<e,<s,t>>	<s,t>		<e,<s,t>>
			$\lambda x_e \lambda e_s$ [f(x)(e) & g(e)]

Event Identification makes it possible to chain together various conditions for the event described by a sentence. It takes a function f and a function g (order irrelevant) as input and yields a function h as output. Input functions f and output functions h are of type <e,<s,t>>. Input functions are of type <s,t>. If s is the type of events, e the type of individuals, and t the type of truth-values, then entities of type <s,t> are functions from events to truth-values, and entities of type <e,<s,t>> are functions that map individuals to functions from events to truth-values.[15] The lambda expression defines the output function h in terms of the input functions f and g. In the computation above (step 5), Event Identification achieves the following:

(24) Example of Event Identification

f	g	—>
<e,<s,t>>	<s,t>	
$\lambda x_e \lambda e_s$ [Agent(x)(e)]	λe_s [feed(the dog)(e)]	

h

<e,<s,t>>

$\lambda x_e \lambda e_s$ [Agent(x)(e) & feed(the dog)(e)]

If the addition of the external argument proceeds via the operation of Event Identification, we expect a connection between the Aktionsart of a verb and the thematic role of its external argument. What are Aktionsarten? I'd like to think of them as originating from selectional restrictions for the Event Argument, not an entirely orthodox use of the term, but a useful one.[16] Event Arguments may be restricted to actions, states, events proper, and so on. An action predicate like *wash the clothes*, then, expresses a partial function that is only defined for actions. A stative predicate like *own the clothes* expresses a partial function that is only defined for states. Actions and states are subkinds of events (or 'eventualities' in the terminology of Bach 1977). That is, they are both entities of type s. The operation of Event Identification is only defined if the two predicates that are being conjoined have compatible Aktionsarten. Here is an example:

(25) Mittie owns the dog.

In (25), the verb is stative, and the external argument denotes the person who is the holder of the state consisting in owning the dog. To compute the meaning of (25), we need a head adding the external argument, call it 'Holder' for convenience. we have then:

(26) **Holder*** = $\lambda x_e \lambda s_s$[holder(x)(e)]
own the dog* = λs_s[own(the dog)(s)]

In spelling out the denotations for *Holder* and *own*, I used the metalanguage variable *s* (for 'state', not to be confused with the semantic type s) to indicate a restriction to eventualities that are states. Since the Event Arguments of both predicates are restricted to states, Event Identification can proceed as before, with no clash so far. What we cannot do, however, is combine the holder function with the denotation of an action predicate or the agent function with the denotation of a stative predicate. Supposing that the set of actions and the set of states are disjoint, the operation of Event Identification comes out undefined in those cases. Given the two input functions, there is no output function of the required kind. This, then, explains why there is a connection between the Aktionsart of a verb and the thematic role of its external argument. The connection is forced by the operation of Event Identification.

How tight is the connection between Aktionsarten and external arguments? Can the kind of external argument always be predicted from the Aktionsart of the corresponding verb? The answer is not a straight 'yes'. A more complicated story has to be told. This is done in Kratzer (forthcoming), but here is a very simplified sketch of the main idea. Suppose there are two kinds of voice heads in English: active and non-active. Active voice heads add external arguments and assign (check) accusative Case. Non-active voice heads do not add external arguments and do not assign (check) accusative Case. They may have a minimal semantic denotation like λe_s[event proper(e)], selecting eventualities that are neither actions nor states. Suppose furthermore that the repertoire of (basic) active voice heads is very limited. Maybe there are just two of them, one adding an agent argument to an action verb, and the other one adding the holder argument to a stative verb. Basic voice markers could now be selected via Aktionsart: action verbs get agent arguments, stative verbs get holder arguments, all other verbs start out with non-active voice markers, and hence without an external argument. They *start out* that way, but they do not have to *stay* that way. If a language learner encounters a transitive verb that has an external argument that doesn't correspond to an active voice head in the basic repertoire, (s)he has to posit a non-active voice head, and build an external argument from a PP via preposition incorporation in Voice (which thereby becomes active). If the preposition originates in a PP within VP, this kind of syntactically derived subject shares some properties with unaccusative subjects. We thus derive the properties of experiencer verbs like *worry*.[17] Preposition incorporation into Voice, then, can create a syntactically derived external argument in the very same way as preposition incorporation into a verb can create a syntactically derived direct object (Baker 1988).

4. THE LOCATION OF VOICE

I have argued that external arguments are introduced by independent heads that I call 'Voice'. In the generativist tradition, voice heads have been proposed for a number of languages. Rivero (1990) postulates an inflectional head labeled 'Voice' right above VP for Greek and Albanian. Following Bowers (1990; see also Bowers 1991, 1993), Mitchell's (1991) analysis of Finnish Case relies on a functional projection ('Predicate Phrase') whose specifier position is the site where external arguments are base-generated.

Is there any strong motivation for placing the Voice head right above VP? Rivero presents two arguments in support of this assumption. If we assume with Roberts (1987) and Baker, Johnson and Roberts (1989) that passive inflection is a realization of the external argument of the verb, by which it is assigned Case and theta-marked, we expect some tight locality condition between Voice and verb, since theta-marking and Case assignment are local relations. My Voice heads are not arguments, and Kratzer (forthcoming) presents arguments against this assumption. Consequently, Rivero's first argument yields no support for the analysis presented here. Rivero's second argument comes from certain verb forms in Modern Greek and Albanian which she claims have an overt mediopassive affix that is adjacent to the verb root. This argument was challenged by Joseph and Smirniotopoulos (1993) for Modern Greek. Rivero parses the verb *plíθikan* 'they were washed/they washed themselves' as follows (gloss and spelling are from Joseph and Smirniotopoulos):

(27)	plí -	θ -	ik -	a -	n
	Root	Voice	Aspect	Tense	AGR

Joseph and Smirniotopoulos point out the *-ik-* is not exclusively an aspect marker, rather it "marks non-active voice, past tense, and perfective aspect all together" (p. 391). This is shown by the fact that *pliθún* is non-active and perfective but not past, *plínane* is past and perfective but active, and *plénondan* is non-active and past but not perfective. While I do not think that these data show that Modern Greek doesn't have independent heads for Voice, Aspect, and Tense, I agree with Joseph and Smirniotopoulos that no evidence has been given that it does. Modern Greek, then, doesn't help us with the question where voice heads are located with respect to other inflectional heads.

While I have argued that the external argument is not an argument of its verb, there is nothing in my proposal so far that would exclude voice heads that *also* carry temporal or aspectual information. That is, in the absence of evidence to the contrary, there is no semantic obstacle to having voice heads with denotations of the following kind:

(28) $\lambda x_e \lambda e_s$ [agent(x)(e) & past(e) & accomplishment(e)]

The question whether an affix like Modern Greek *-ik-* is the morphological spellout of one of several inflectional heads, then, cannot be answered by the semantics. It could go either way.

It will be useful to know about the constraints that the semantics imposes on possible locations for Voice. If the semantic connection between Voice and its verb is established by the operation of Event Identification, Voice can appear anywhere in the hierarchy of a verb's inflectional heads, as long as the Event Argument is not existentially quantified. Let me illustrate this point by returning to the computation of our English example.

(29)

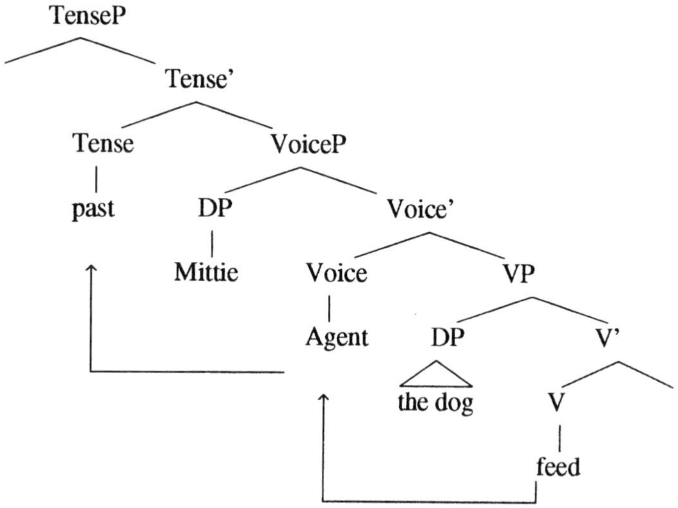

We saw that the VoiceP in this sentence receives the following denotation:

(30) ((**Agent (the dog feed) Mittie**))*
= λe_s[Agent(Mittie)(e) & feed(the dog)(e)]

This VoiceP, then, denotes a property of events, and not yet a truth-value, the canonical denotation for a sentence within an extensional semantics. One possibility for getting us to a truth-value is to build existential quantification into the semantics of some higher inflectional head (in the spirit of Higginbotham 1985). If this inflectional head turns out to be Tense, then one of the functions of Tense is to existentially quantify the Event Argument. Here is a possible denotation for a Tense head:

(31) **past** - * = $\lambda P_{<s,t>} \exists e_s$ [P(e) & past(e)]

The denotation of the TenseP in (29) is a truth-value, as can be seen from the following computation:

(32) **(past ((Agent (the dog feed)) Mittie)) ***
$= \lambda P_{<s,t>} \exists e_s$ [P(e) & past(e)] (λe_s [Agent(Mittie)(e) & feed(the dog)(e)])
$= \exists e_s$ [Agent(Mittie)(e) & feed(the dog)(e) & past(e)]
From (30), (31) by Functional Application and two instances of Lambda Conversion.

Once the Event Argument is existentially quantified, the operation of Event Identification becomes inapplicable. From this, we conclude that Voice cannot appear above whatever head existentially quantifies the Event Argument. If we have more than one inflectional head in addition to Voice (possibly all of Tense, Agr, Mood, and Aspect), we have to find out which head does the existential quantification. What we know already, however, is which possibilities for the location of Voice are permitted by the semantics of Voice. For the time being, let us tentatively assume that Voice is located directly above VP, but stay open to the possibility that it may turn out that there are intervening inflectional heads after all. In this case, the verb's object would have to move further up to receive accusative Case.

I have argued that the heads that introduce external arguments are inflectional elements that assign accusative Case. The following section will present more support for the existence of such heads.

5. GERUNDS AND PARTICIPLES: WINDOWS INTO THE HIERARCHY OF INFLECTIONAL HEADS

Gerunds and participles are hybrids that share properties with two syntactic categories. Over the years, a number of scholars have argued that different kinds of gerunds arise from nominalizing different segments of a verb's projection, and that this is what accounts for their hybrid nature.[18] Abney (1987), for example, proposes that the English nominalizing affix *-ing* can attach to Vs, VPs, or IPs, thereby giving rise to of_{ing}, $poss_{ing}$, and acc_{ing} gerunds:

(33) a. of_{ing}: His rebuilding of the barn took five months.

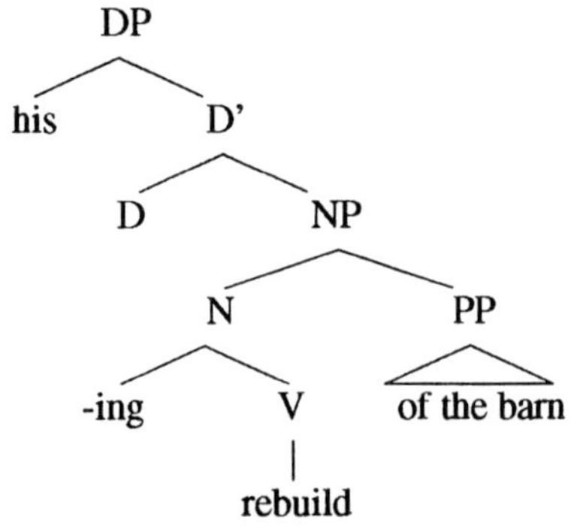

(33) b. poss_{ing}: We remember his rebuilding the barn.

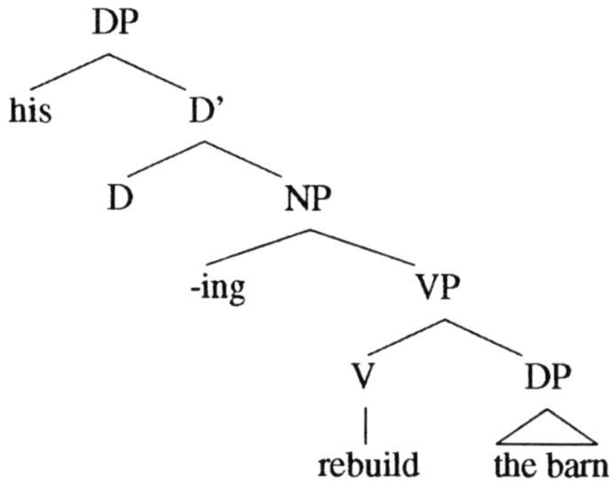

c. acc_{ing}: We remember him rebuilding the barn.

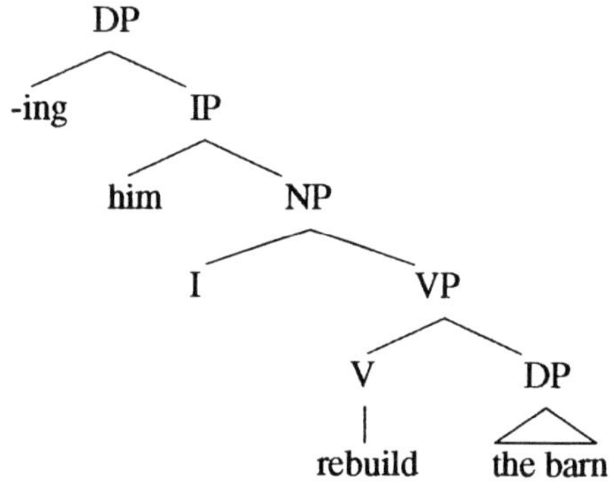

If we say that different kinds of gerunds are created by nominalizing different segments of verbal projections, we understand the term 'verbal projection' in an extended sense. Abney distinguishes s-projection (semantic projection) from c-projection (category projection). For him, the maximal c-projection of V, I, and C are VP, IP and CP respectively, and the maximal s-projection of V, I, and C is CP. Grimshaw (1991) uses the term 'extended projection' in very much the sense of Abney's s-projection. Assuming a more articulated sentence structure, the extended projection of verbs might include Tense Phrases, Aspect Phrases, Voice Phrases, Agreement Phrases and the like. Gerunds, then, are formed by nominalizing different segments of a verb's extended projection.

Jackendoff (1977) and Abney (1987) suggest that we might expect other affixes to behave like *-ing* in attaching to lexical or phrasal elements. Both authors think that the English passive participle morpheme *-en* is a case in question, and consider the possibility that *-en* is an affix that turns verbal projections into adjectives. If it attaches to a phrasal element, it attaches to a VP, and the result is a phrasal passive. If it attaches to a lexical element, it attaches to a V, and this yields a lexical passive. A very similar view is expressed in Borer (1984).

If different kinds of gerunds and participles result from affixation to different segments of extended verbal projections, we expect these hybrid structures to offer an ideal window into the hierarchy of inflectional heads. This becomes clear as soon as we incorporate Jackendoff's and Abney's insights into the present approach. Let us return to the English gerunds for the remainder of this section. Participles are discussed in Kratzer (forthcoming).

Assuming the theory presented so far, the fact that the direct object in an of_{ing} gerund cannot receive accusative Case has to be taken as a sign that the nominalized constituent doesn't contain Voice, and hence can be at most a VP. This is compatible with it being a V. Suppose it *is* as V. In example (33a), it would then be the verb *rebuild* that is nominalized. The interpretation of the gerund would proceed as follows: the denotation of the verb is inherited by the N-node (assuming that *-ing* adds at most aspectual information, a contribution that we can afford to ignore here).[19] This means that the denotation of the N-node is the function λxλe[rebuild(x)(e)]. The N-node, then, requires an argument denoting what is being built. This argument is realized by an NP, and since this NP is an object of a noun, it is Case-marked in the way objects of nouns are usually Case-marked. Since there is no Voice, there cannot be an agent argument. This last conclusion seems to be contradicted by the sentence in (33a). Doesn't the genitive pronoun *his* express the agent argument? That it doesn't is brought out more clearly by the following example:

(34) Maria's reading of *Pride and Prejudice* received better reviews than Anna's.

To be sure, (34) is compatible with Maria and Anna being the agents of their respective readings of *Pride and Prejudice.* Yet (34) does not have to be understood that way. Suppose the 180th anniversary of the publication of *Pride and Prejudice* is celebrated with readings in every public library. Maria attends a reading in Conway, Anna attends a reading in Ashfield. In this context, we may understand (34) as reporting that the reading of *Pride and Prejudice* that Maria attended received better reviews than the one Anna went to. The genitive NPs in (33a) and (34), then, express a general notion of relatedness of which the agent relation is but a special case. I conclude that in of_{ing} gerunds, the absence of accusative Case is accompanied by the absence of the verb's external argument. This is further confirmed by the following 'control' facts which are modeled after Wasow & Roeper (1972).

(35) Maria enjoyed a reading of *Pride and Prejudice*.

(36) The killing of her cat upset Maria.

In the absence of Voice, the denotation of *reading of Pride and Prejudice* denotes the function λe[reading(Pride and Prejudice)(e)]. The whole sentence, then, states that there was an event in which *Pride and Prejudice* was read and Maria enjoyed this event. This interpretation leaves it open whether Maria or somebody else did the reading. Similar considerations apply to (36). *Killing of her cat* denotes the function λe[killing(her cat)(e)]. Consequently, (36) means that there was a unique event in which Maria's cat was killed, and this event upset Maria. Again, the sentence is compatible with Maria or someone else killing the cat.

If it is VPs that are nominalized in of_{ing} gerunds, the semantic interpretation proceeds in essentially the same way, and the genitive NP and 'control' facts are predicted to be the same. The only difference is that the object of the verb is saturated in the local domain of the verb, rather than in the local domain of the noun. Since the nominalized constituent doesn't include Voice, the object still cannot receive accusative Case. There are some clear instances of VP gerunds in English. The following examples are from Jespersen (1940: 109).

(37) The shutting of the gates regularly at ten o'clock had rendered our residence very irksome to me.

(38) From the daily reading of the Bible aloud to his mother. . . .

(37) and (38) both contain adverbs (*regularly* and *aloud*). Since adverbs must modify verbs, we can conclude that what is nominalized is *at least* a VP. Moreover, the verb is unable to assign accusative Case. On the present approach, this is a sign that the nominalized constituent is *at most* a VP.

Given that direct objects in poss_{ing} and acc_{ing} gerunds are marked accusative, our approach forces us to depart from Abney and assume that neither construction is a nominalization of a VP. The constituent that is nominalized must at least include Voice. Otherwise, structural accusative could not be assigned. Suppose that only zero or maximal projections, but no intermediate projections can be nominalized. We can now infer that the nominalized constituent in poss_{ing} and acc_{ing} must at least include the maximal projection of Voice. Then it must include the agent argument. That it does is shown by the following examples:

(39) We remembered Maria's reading *Pride and Prejudice*.

(40) We remembered Maria reading *Pride and Prejudice*.

In (39) and (40), Maria can only be understood as the agent of the reading event. If the agent argument isn't overt in a poss_{ing} gerund, it is realized as PRO. If PRO must be controlled, it follows that poss_{ing} gerunds show obligatory control. This is illustrated by sentences (41) and (42) (again modeled after Wasow and Roeper 1972).

(41) Maria enjoyed reading *Pride and Prejudice*.

(42) Killing her cat upset Maria.

(41) implies that Maria herself read *Pride and Prejudice*. Moreover, (42) implies that Maria herself killed the cat. The control contrast between (35) and (36) on the one hand, and (41) and (42) on the other is accounted for if one and the same head assigns accusative Case and introduces the external argument.

The discussion of English gerunds confirmed our claim that external arguments are introduced by independent heads that are also responsible for the assignment of accusative Case. The relevant properties of the three kinds of gerunds follow now simply from the assumption that the nominalizing affix *-ing* can attach at least to V, VP and VoiceP. No other stipulations are necessary.

It may be instructive to compare the analysis of gerunds presented here with an otherwise fairly compatible analysis that is based on the assumption that external arguments are arguments of their verbs. Take Borer (1984), where the properties of the suffix *-ing* in of_{ing} gerunds are described as follows:

(43) a. It triggers a category change from V to N.
b. The ability to assign accusative is eliminated.
c. It obligatorily selects an agent theta-role.
d. An aspectual (progressive) reading is added.

Borer argues that the first three of those properties violate the Projection Principle of Chomsky (1981), which requires that all lexical features must be represented at every syntactic level. From this she concludes that the formation of of_{ing} gerunds takes place in the lexicon, and not in the syntax. Let us look at the four properties in turn. Property (a) is not a violation of the Projection Principle if we assume with Höhle (1976, 1982) and Williams (1981) that affixes may belong to syntactic categories and head words. The category change in gerunds, then, is not a change in features, but the result of attaching an affix that is an N. On the approach advocated here, the verb's ability to assign accusative Case is not eliminated in of_{ing} gerunds since it was never there to begin with. As for property (c), we have seen above that it is not a property that of_{ing} gerunds have. They do not have an obligatory agent argument. Again, this does not come as a surprise to us. If there never was an external argument, none has to be eliminated. These gerunds, then, do not violate the Projection Principle. While they may very well involve affixation of *-ing* to a lexical category (that is, V as opposed to VP), there is no reason to assume that this affixation is a process that takes place in the lexicon, that is, in a word-building component prior to the syntax.

In fact, the assumption that of_{ing} gerunds are built in the lexicon runs into at least two serious difficulties. The first one is that it would not explain why (even though the lexicon is assumed to be the place where lexical requirements can be violated) of_{ing} gerunds *must* preserve the internal arguments of the verb, as demonstrated by Lebeaux (1986) (see also Grimshaw 1990):

(44) a. The felled *(trees).
b. The felling *(of the trees).

(45) a. They destroyed *(the city).
b. The destroying *(of the city).

The second serious obstacle to the assumption that of_{ing} gerunds are formed in the lexicon is the fact that they may (at least optionally) be formed by attaching *-ing* to a phrasal constituent. The evidence comes from the presence of adverbs in Jespersen 's examples repeated from above:

(46) The shutting of the gates regularly at ten o'clock had rendered our residence very irksome to me.

(47) From the daily reading of the Bible aloud to his mother. . . .

I conclude that of_{ing} gerunds can be built in the syntax. On the approach defended here, this is possible without giving up the principle that lexical information is preserved at all syntactic levels of representation.

6. ABOLISHING THE NOTION 'EXTERNAL ARGUMENT'

The discussion in the previous sections makes it possible to do away with the notion of external argument (Williams 1981). This notion has no theoretical significance any longer. It does not figure in any theoretical statement. While I have continued to use Williams' term 'external argument' informally for arguments like the agent argument in active sentences, this term has now acquired a different meaning. Strictly speaking, the agent argument of a verb is not really one of its arguments anymore. Here is an illustration of the different kinds of arguments in the present framework:

(48) We bought your slippers in Marrakesh.

$\exists$e [bought(your slippers)$(e)_1$ & Agent(we)$(e)_2$ & in(Marrakesh)$(e)_3$]

a. (your slippers): internal argument of *bought*
b. $(e)_1$: Event Argument
c. (we): internal argument of *Agent*; informally, external argument of *bought*
d. $(e)_2$: Event Argument
e. (Marrakesh): internal argument of *in*
f. $(e)_3$: Event Argument

In Williams' theory, the external argument is simply a distinguished argument that is singled out by underlining. The main property of the external argument of a lexical item is that it has to be realized outside of the maximal projection of that item. This property must be stipulated since there is no necessary connection between underlining an argument and its having to be realized in a particular way. On the present proposal, we don't have to say anything special about the realization of external arguments. All we seem to need is a very general principle for the syntactic realization of *all* arguments (excluding the Event Argument, which doesn't have to be syntactically realized). Here is a version of the principle:[20]

(49) The Realization Principle
Arguments of a head must be realized within the projection of that head.

The possible locations for arguments are now determined by the possible locations of the heads they are arguments of. If external arguments are arguments of Voice, and if Voice is a head right above VP, we get the following configuration:

(50)

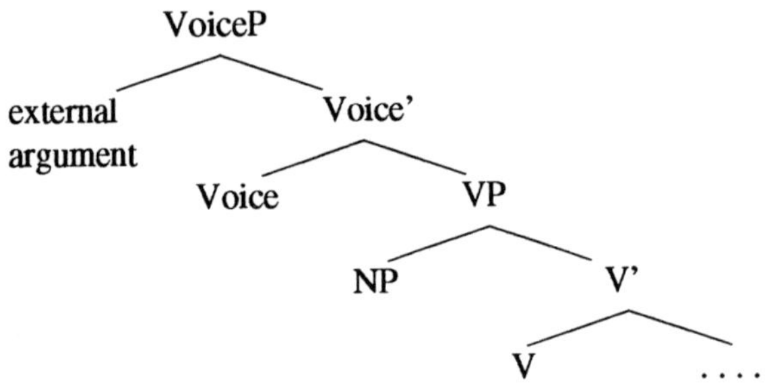

The fact that the external argument must be realized outside of VP follows from the Realization Principle and the fact that external arguments are introduced by inflectional heads.

Another peculiarity of external arguments is that they disappear under certain conditions, and they take accusative Case with them when they go away. Why is that? Many answers have been given. One is to deny that external arguments and accusative Case truly disappear. This is the basis for the analyses of passive in Jaeggli (1986), Roberts (1987), and Baker, Johnson and Roberts (1989). I think that these authors are right about the cases they discuss. Yet there are other cases where we have fully developed VPs without any evidence for the presence of even a hidden external argument. *Of*$_{ing}$ gerunds are an example. Adjectival passives are another example, as shown in Kratzer (forthcoming). If external arguments were true arguments of their verbs or VPs, we would have to stipulate that they are suppressed under certain conditions.[21] On the present approach, no such stipulation is necessary. If the external argument is introduced by an inflectional head that assigns accusative Case, a bare VP without inflection is expected to have neither external argument nor accusative Case. It could not be otherwise. Again, no special statement has to be made about external arguments. This notion has become superfluous.

NOTES

1 See Bierwisch (1983, 1989), Jackendoff (1983, 1990), Hale and Keyser (1987, 1992), Speas (1990), among others.

2 What follows is the beginning of my presentation at SALT II, Ohio State University, Columbus, May 1992. It is reassuring to see that Parsons (1993) independently presents his syntactic options in very much the same way.

3 See, for example, Lewis (1972), Montague (1984).

4 See Parsons (1985) for a similar rule introducing the external argument at the point where a VP combines with its subject.

5 Klein & Sag (1985), Fanselow (1985), Higginbotham (1985), Heim and Kratzer (forthcoming), von Stechow (1991), Portner (1992), Bittner (1994).

6 I am indebted to Lisa Travis for informing me about Hung's work.

7 Cf. Baker (1988).

8 A related proposal is made in Speas (1990) for English. Speas assumes with Hale and Keyser (1987) that agentive predicates have a higher verb *do* in their lexical conceptual structure. Consequently, they license the projection of an extra verbal head at D-Structure. The result are structures of the kind that Larson proposes for double object constructions. Hale and Keyser's proposal is not compatible with my earlier arguments that information about the presence of an agent argument should not be part of the verb's lexical representations at all.

9 Jan Voskuil informs me that the prefix *an-* in Malagasy is not necessarily linked to agentivity.

10 "Man teilt Kasus der idg. Sprachen ihrer ursprünglichen Natur nach ein in *lokale*, d.h. solche, die irgend ein räumliches Verhältnis zur Vorstellung bringen, und *grammatische*, d.h. solche, die eine rein grammatische Beziehung des Nomens zu einem anderen Satzteil ausdrücken; WUNDT spricht statt dessen von Kasus der äusseren und inneren Determination, MARTY unterscheidet relative und korrelative zu den grammatischen den Nom. und Akk. über Zugehörigkeit des Dativs aber zur einen oder zur andern Gruppe ist viel gestritten worden...." (Brugmann 1913: 428).

11 Johnson refers to work by Pesetsky (1989) and Jaeggli and Hyams (1989) for further discussion of this head.

12 The Event Argument is not syntactically realized at all. Indirect objects are introduced by additional heads.

13 See Fanselow (1985), Higginbotham (1985), Heim and Kratzer (forthcoming), Portner (1992), and Bittner (1994).

14 The term is reminiscent of Higginbotham's term 'Theta Identification'. See Higginbotham (1985).

15 In an intensional version, e would be the type of possible individuals, s the type of possible events, and t the type of propositions, where propositions are sets of possible worlds or situations. Note that the resulting intensional language is different from Montague's intensional logic, even though I am using the same type names. The kind of intensional language I have in mind is a λ-categorial language (Cresswell 1973), with an additional basic type for events.

16 My use of the term 'Aktionsart' corresponds very closely to the notion 'situation type' in Smith (1991). I would have to recognize actions as one of the linguistically most significant situation types, however.

17 See Belletti & Rizzi (1988), Grimshaw (1991), Pesetsky (1995), among others.

18 See, for example, Grimshaw & Selkirk (1976), Jackendoff (1977), Borer (1984, 1990, 1991), Baker (1988), Abney (1987), Zucchi (1988), Hazout (1990).

19 See Kratzer (forthcoming) for more discussion of this kind of inheritance rule.

20 See Larson (1988), Speas (1990), Bowers (1993) for similar principles.

21 See, for example, Zubizarreta (1985, 1987), Grimshaw (1990), Grimshaw and Mester (1988).

REFERENCES

Abney, Steven: 1987, *The English Noun Phrase in its Sentential Aspect*, unpublished Ph.D. dissertation, MIT.

Bach, Emmon: 1977, *Five Chapters on Natural Language Metaphysics*, unpublished, University of Massachusetts, Amherst.

Baker, Mark: 1985, 'Syntactic affixation and English gerunds', in Jeffrey Goldberg, Susannah MacKaye and Michael T. Wescoat (eds.), *West Coast Conference on Formal Linguistics 4*, Stanford Linguistics Association, pp. 1-11.

———: 1988, *Incorporation: A Theory of Grammatical Function Changing*, University of Chicago Press, Chicago.

Baker, Mark, Kyle Johnson and Ian Roberts: 1989, 'Passive Arguments Raised', *Linguistic Inquiry* **20**, 219-252.

Bierwisch, Manfred: 1983, 'Semantische und Konzeptuelle Repräsentation Lexikalischer Einheiten', in R. Ruzicka and W. Motsch (eds.), *Studia Grammatika* **22**, 61-99.

———: 1989, 'Event Nominalizations. Proposals and Problems', *Linguistische Studien*, Reihe A 194, Akademie Verlag, pp. 1-73.

Belletti, Adriana and Luigi Rizzi: 1988, 'Psych-verbs and Θ-theory', *Natural Language and Linguistic Theory* **6**, 291-352.

Bittner, Maria: 1994, 'Crosslinguistic Semantics', *Linguistics and Philosophy* **17**, 53-108.

Borer, Hagit: 1984, 'The Projection Principle and Rules of Morphology', in Charles Jones and Peter Sells (eds.), *The Proceedings of NELS 14*, GLSA, University of Massachusetts, Amherst, pp. 16-33.

———: 1990a, 'Derived Nominals and the Causative-Inchoative Alternation: Two Case Studies in Parallel Morphology', unpublished, University of California, Irvine.

———: 1990b, 'V+ing: It Walks like an Adjective, It Talks like an Adjective', *Linguistic Inquiry* **21**, 95-103.

———: 1991, 'The Causative-Inchoative Alternation: A Case Study in Parallel Morphology', *The Linguistic Review* **8**, 119-158.

Bowers, John: 1990, 'A Structural Theory of Predication', unpublished, Cornell University, Ithaca, NY.

———: 1991, 'The Syntax and Semantics of Nominals', in Steven Moore and Adam Zachary Wyner (eds.), *Proceedings from SALT 1. Cornell University Working Papers in Linguistics* **10**, 1-30.

———: 1993, 'The Syntax of Predication', *Linguistic Inquiry* **24**, 591-656.

Bresnan, Joan: 1982, 'The Passive in Lexical Theory', in Joan Bresnan (ed.), *The Mental Representation of Grammatical Relations*, MIT Press, Cambridge, MA.

Brugmann, Karl and Albert Thumb: 1913, *Griechische Grammatik. Lautlehre, Stammbildungs und Flexionslehre, Syntax, Handbuch der klassischen Altertums-Wissenschaft*, 4th ed., C. H. Beck'sche Verlagsbuchhandlung, Munich.

Castañeda, Hector-Neri: 1967, 'Comments on Donald Davidson's 'The Logical Form of Action Sentences'', in Nicholas Rescher (ed.), *The Logic of Decision and Action*, University of Pittsburgh Press, Pittsburgh, pp. 104-112.

Chomsky, Noam: 1981, *Lectures on Government and Binding*, Foris, Dordrecht.

———: 1991, 'Some Notes on Economy of Derivation and Representation', in Robert Freidin (ed.), *Principles and Parameters in Comparative Grammar*, MIT Press, Cambridge, MA.

———: 1992, 'A Minimalist Program for Linguistic Theory', *MIT Occasional Papers in Linguistics* **1**.

Collins, Christopher Thad: 1993, *Topics in Ewe Syntax*, unpublished Ph.D. dissertation, MIT.

Cresswell, Max J.: 1973, *Logics and Languages*, Methuen, London.

Davidson, Donald: 1967, 'The Logical Form of Action Sentences', in Nicholas Rescher (ed.), *The Logic of Decision and Action*, University of Pittsburgh Press, Pittsburgh, pp. 81-95.
Dowty, David: 1989, 'On the Semantic Content of the Notion of 'Thematic Role'', in Gennaro Chierchia, Barbara H. Partee and Raymond Turner (eds.), *Properties, Types and Meaning. Volume II: Semantic Issues*, Kluwer Academic Publishers, Dordrecht.
———: 1991, 'Thematic Proto-Roles and Argument Selection', *Language* **67**, 547-619.
Fanselow, Gisbert: 1991, *Minimale Syntax, Volume 32, Groninger Arbeiten zur germanistischen Linguistik*. Germanistisch Instituut, Reijksuniversiteit Groningen, Groningen.
Fillmore, Charles J.: 1968, 'The Case for Case', in Emmon Bach and Robert Harms (eds.), *Universals in Linguistic Theory*, Holt, Rinehart and Winston, New York, pp. 1-88.
Grimshaw, Jane: 1990, *Argument Structure*, MIT Press, Cambridge, MA.
———: 1991, 'Extended Projection', unpublished, Brandeis University.
Grimshaw, Jane and Armin Mester: 1988, 'Light Verbs and Q-Marking', *Linguistic Inquiry* **19**, 205-232.
Grimshaw, Jane and Elisabeth Selkirk: 1976, 'Infinitival Noun Phrases in Italian', unpublished, University of Massachusetts, Amherst.
Gruber, Jeffrey S.: 1965, *Studies in Lexical Relations*, unpublished Ph.D. dissertation, MIT.
Hale, Kenneth and Samuel J. Keyser: 1987, 'A View form the Middle', *Lexicon Project Working Papers*, **7**, Center for Cognitive Science, MIT.
———: 1992, 'On Argument Structure and the Lexical Expression of Syntactic Relations', unpublished, MIT.
Hazout, Ilan: 1990, *Verbal Nouns: Theta-Theoretic Studies in Hebrew and Arabic*, unpublished Ph.D. dissertation, University of Massachusetts, Amherst.
Heim, Irene and Angelika Kratzer: forthcoming, *Semantics in Generative Grammar*, Basil Blackwell, Oxford.
Higginbotham, James: 1985, 'On Semantics', *Linguistic Inquiry* **16**, 547-593.
Höhle, Tilman N.: 1976, 'Die Aktiv-Passiv Relation im Deutschen. Grundlagen einer lexikalistischen Syntaxtheorie', unpublished, Universität Köln.
———: 1982, 'Über Komposition und Derivation', *Zeitschrift für Sprachwissenschaft* **1**, 76-112.
Hung, Henrietta J.: 1988, 'The Structure of Derived Nouns and Verbs in Malagasy: A Syntactic Account', unpublished, McGill University.
Jackendoff, Ray: 1977, *X' Syntax: A Study of Phrase Structure*, MIT Press, Cambridge, MA.
———: 1983, *Semantics and Cognition*, MIT Press, Cambridge, MA.
———: 1990, *Semantic Structures*, MIT Press, Cambridge, MA.
Jaeggli, Osvaldo: 1986, 'Passive', *Linguistic Inquiry* **17**, 587-622.
Jaeggli, Osvaldo and Nina Hyams: 1989, 'On the Independence and Interdependence of Syntactic and Morphological Properties: English Aspectual *Come* and *Go*', unpublished, University of California, Los Angeles.
Jespersen, Otto: 1927, *A Modern English Grammar on Historical Principles*, Part III (Syntax), Ejnar Munksggard, Copenhagen.
———: 1940, *A Modern English Grammar on Historical Principles*, Part V (Syntax), Ejnar Munksggard, Copenhagen.
Johnson, Kyle: 1991, 'Object Positions', *Natural Language and Linguistic Theory* **9**, 577-636.
Joseph, Brian and Jane C. Smirniotopoulos: 1993, 'The Morphosyntax of the Modern Greek Verb as Morphology and not Syntax', *Linguistic Inquiry* **19**, 388-398.
Klein, Ewan and Ivan Sag: 1985, 'Type Driven Translation', *Linguistics and Philosophy* **8**, 163-201.

Kratzer, Angelika: forthcoming, *The Event Argument and the Semantics of Voice*, MIT Press, Cambridge, MA.

Larson, Richard K.: 1988, 'On the Double Object Construction', *Linguistic Inquiry* **19**, 335-391.

Lebeaux, David: 1984, 'Nominalizations, Argument Structure, and the Organization of the Grammar', unpublished, University of Massachusetts, Amherst.

———: 1986, 'The Interpretation of Derived Nominals', in A. M. Farley, P. T. Farley and K. E. McCullogh (eds.), *CLS 22: Papers from the General Session at the Twenty-Second Regional Meeting of the Chicago Linguistics Society*, University of Chicago, Chicago, pp. 231-247.

Lewis, David: 1972, 'General Semantics', in Donald Davidson and Gilbert Harman (eds.), *Semantics of Natural Language*, D. Reidel, Dordrecht, pp. 169-218.

Marantz, Alec: 1984, *On the Nature of Grammatical Relations*, MIT Press, Cambridge, MA.

May, Robert: 1977, *The Grammar of Quantification*, unpublished Ph.D. dissertation, MIT.

———: 1985, *Logical Form. Its Structure and Derivation*, MIT Press, Cambridge, MA.

Mitchell, Erika: 1991, 'Case and the Finnish Object', in Almeida J. Toribio and Wayne E. Harbert (eds.), *Cornell University Working Papers in Linguistics* **9**, 193-228.

Montague, Richard: 1974, *Formal Philosophy*, Yale University Press, New Haven, CT.

Parsons, Terence: 1980, 'Modifiers and Quantifiers in Natural Language', *Canadian Journal of Philosophy*, Suppl. Vol. **6**, 29-60.

———: 1985, 'Underlying Events in the Logical Analysis of English', in Ernest LePore and Brian McLaughlin (eds.), *Actions and Events: Perspectives on the Philosophy of Donald Davidson*, Basil Blackwell, Oxford.

———: 1990, *Events in the Semantics of English. A Study in Subatomic Semantics*, MIT Press, Cambridge, MA.

———: 1993, 'Thematic Relations and Arguments', unpublished, University of California, Irvine.

Pesetsky, David: 1989, 'Language-Particular Processes and the Earliness Principle', unpublished, MIT.

———: 1995, *Zero Syntax*, MIT Press, Cambridge, MA.

Portner, Paul: 1992, *Situation Theory and the Semantics of Propositional Expressions*, unpublished Ph.D. dissertation, University of Massachusetts, Amherst.

Rappaport, Malka and Beth Levin: 1986, 'What to Do with Theta-Roles', *Lexicon Project Working Papers* **11**, Center for Cognitive Science, MIT.

Rivero, Maria-Luisa: 1990, 'The Location of Non-Active Voice in Albanian and Modern Greek', *Linguistic Inquiry* **21**, 135-146.

———: 1992, 'Adverb Incorporation and the Syntax of Adverbs in Modern Greek', *Linguistics and Philosophy* **15**, 289-331.

Roberts, Ian G.: *The Representation of Implicit and Dethematized Subjects*, Foris, Dordrecht.

Roeper, Thomas and Muffy E. Siegel: 1978, 'A Lexical Transformation for Verbal Compounds', *Linguistic Inquiry* **9**, 199-260.

Schönfinkel, Moses: 1924, 'Über die Bausteine der mathematischen Logik', *Mathematische Annalen* **92**, 305-316.

Smith, Carlota S.: 1991, *The Parameter of Aspect*, Kluwer Academic Publishers, Dordrecht.

Speas, Margaret J.: 1990, *Phrase Structure in Natural Language*, Kluwer Academic Publishers, Dordrecht.

Stechow, Arnim von: 1991, 'Syntax und Semantik', in Arnim von Stechow and Dieter Wunderlich (eds.), *Semantik/Semantics. Ein internationales Handbuch der zeitgenössischen Forschung/An International Handbook of Contemporary Research*, de Gruyter, Berlin, pp. 90-148.

Williams, Edwin: 1980, 'Predication', *Linguistic Inquiry* **11**, 203-238.

———: 1981a, 'Argument Structure and Morphology', *The Linguistic Review* **1**, 81-114.
———: 1981b, 'On the Notions 'Lexically Related' and 'Head of a Word'', *Linguistic Inquiry* **12**, 245-274.
Zubizarreta, Maria Luisa: 1985, 'The Relation between Morphophonology and Morphosyntax: The Case of Romance Causatives', *Linguistic Inquiry* **16**, 247-289.
———: 1987, *Levels of Representation in the Lexicon and in the Syntax*, Foris, Dordrecht.
Zucchi, Alessandro: 1988, *The Language of Propositions and Events. Issues in the Syntax and Semantics of Nominalization*, unpublished Ph.D. dissertation, University of Massachusetts, Amherst.

DETERMINING THE KERNEL*

David Lebeaux

O. INTRODUCTION

I would like to start off this paper with an apology. While I am relatively sure that the way that I have set the problem here is the correct one, I am much less sure that my solution is correct. In this case, setting the problem is one half the battle. But the problem here is a gigantic one, and one which really should be tackled by the linguistics community as a whole, and particularly by linguists who speak exotic languages—who needn't necessarily be language acquisition specialists, since the problem here is really a problem of the "logical problem of language acquisition".

The problem is the following: how does the child arrive at D-structures in the face of extensive movement? Suppose that we take as an example the setting of the government direction parameter (the head parameter). To set the government direction parameter, the child must have a D-structure or its equivalent in terms of an S-structure (i.e. a structure with traces). But the child isn't given the actual S-structure which would allow the D-structure direction to be registered by its traces, but simply some sort of surface structure, without any traces. (I am speaking of a D-structure here, but even in a theory which has no D-structure, e.g. Chomsky (1992) the government direction parameter must be set, deciding to determine on which side of the verb to place the complements (not assuming Kayne 1994). How then does the child manage to project backwards to the D-structure? The basic problem is that the child must prevent movement constructions from either leading him or her to being perplexed as to the setting of parameters, or leading to the positive mis-settings of parameters: for example, the child must not be lead into thinking that the language that s/he is learning is a free word order language, when it isn't. This last conclusion would not be an arcane one at all, as will soon be apparent, given the great confusion of the surface order, and the great amount of movement. Thus the basic problem is the projection of D-structure from PF, with all sorts of data left out, where by PF I mean a surface structure, not an S-structure and not a phonological form.

We can suppose that some of the surface geometry is given by Pinker's (1984) semantic bootstrapping hypothesis. Thus consider a data set like that in (1), where the child is given a sentence like *John saw Mary*.

(1) Data Set 1:

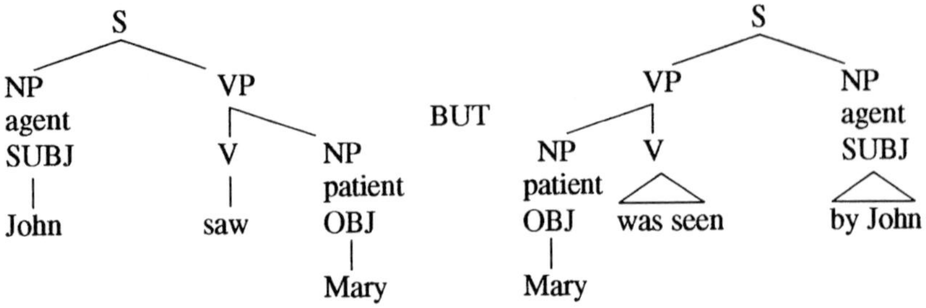

(2) Semantic Bootstrapping (Pinker 1984)

object ———> NP
action ———> V
John = object ———> NP
see = action ———> V
Mary = object ———> NP
John = actor ———> agent ———> SUBJ
Mary = acted upon ———>patient ——> OBJ
Subject ———> [NP, S]
Object ————> [NP, VP]

Let us assume with Pinker that the child is able to label the tree in such a way that *John* is labeled as a noun phrase by virtue of the fact that *John* is a physical object, and *Mary* is labeled as a noun-phrase by virtue of the fact that she is an object. The verb *see* is labeled as a verb by virtue of the fact that it denotes an action. Then, as in Pinker (1984), the child is able to label *John* as an agent and *Mary* as a patient by looking at the situation. By using the canonical linking of thematic roles to grammatical functions, s/he is able to label *John* as a subject and *Mary* as an object. Using then the canonical structural relations, going back to *Aspects* (Chomsky 1965), the child would know that *Mary* is a daughter of VP, and *John* is a daughter of IP or S, so the child would be able to build up a whole tree—given under data set (1), where the S —> NP VP, and both the noun phrases are appropriately labeled. I use the older terminology for convenience. This basic tree may now be used for sentences in which the subject is not an agent, and the object not a patient. For further discussion, see Pinker (1984) and Grimshaw (1981).

The problem with Pinker's solution is that while it works fine for canonical systems, it also gives the wrong solution for constructions with noncanonical linkings, for example passive sentences, if directly applied (as Pinker himself also realized). So consider now the tree on the right hand side of (1): *Mary was seen by John*. In this case, semantic bootstrapping would give *Mary* as a patient and *John* as an agent, hence *Mary* as an object and *John* as a subject, and hence *Mary was seen by John* would have *Mary* in the object position and *by John* in the subject position, as shown. In other words, the rewrite rules would be S —>

VP NP or S —>VP XP and VP —>NP V, and the child would conclude that s/he was facing an OVS language, at least optionally. Obviously, then, Pinker's procedure, while working brilliantly for a canonical sentence, *John saw Mary* (and being really so far the only explicit procedure in the literature that does work), must somehow be prevented from providing a patterning for *Mary was seen by John* which would ultimately end up overgenerating those structures of the language and thus getting the wrong government direction for the structures of the language.

I would like to disallow something immediately that Pinker probably would not, namely I would like to disallow a solution in terms of frequency. According to this solution, *Mary was seen by John* is simply much less frequent in the input than *John saw Mary*. I will not allow that as a possible explanation for the fact that the child doesn't come up with the wrong structure. I would like instead to come up with a purely formal explanation for the child not arriving at the wrong structure for *Mary was seen by John*, and thus I would like a purely formal answer for the question of how the child isn't fooled by movement constructions in the language.

Let us take a second data set, that given in (3).

(3) a. John saw Mary.
b. Who did John see?
c. Mary, John saw.

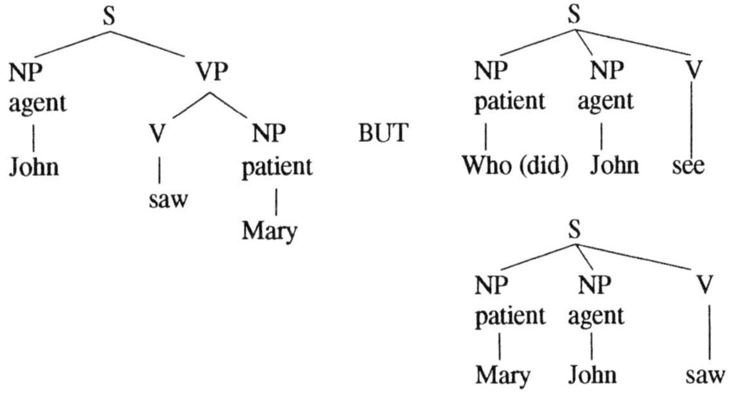

On the one hand, there is the correct PS tree: *John saw Mary*. Again, the right structure can be given for that by semantic bootstrapping. But there is also *Who did John see?* In this case, *who* would be registered as a patient, and *John* would be registered as the agent. If one tried to construct a VP, it would be impossible to do so without crossing branches, assuming that the patient is the sister of the verb. Thus the only possible solution given a routine like that of Pinker would be to flatten out the entire structure, with the patient and agent and the verb all being daughters of S. Obviously that is the wrong structure. The only other alternative is that movement is hypothesized for one of the structures, but how does the child know that movement has occurred, rather than the language being simply a free word order language? Furthermore, if s/he does know that movement has occurred, how does s/he know *what* has moved?

Thus semantic bootstrapping, working off of *Who did John see?*, would again give the wrong structure in the language. As before, we wish to disallow solutions in terms of frequency. Further, we wish to disallow a sort of over-particularistic (and unprincipled) solution, such as "questions sound different", and so are excluded from the input for that reason.

Similarly, the topicalized sentence *Mary, John saw* would have a flat structure given the semantic bootstrapping hypothesis, where the verb and both of the noun phrases would be direct daughters of the S. At best this gives very erroneous or multiple phrase markers, from which government direction can't be set. At worst, the child would actually come to the wrong conclusion, namely that English is a flat or free word order language (if such exist). It would not be possible to recover from this conclusion on the basis of positive evidence, because it would overgenerate the language.

Consider now a German example, given in (4).

(4) a. . . . dass Berthold Heinrich sah.
that B. H. saw
". . . that Berthold saw Heinrich."

b. Berthold sah Heinrich.
B. saw H.
"Berthold saw Heinrich."

(a)

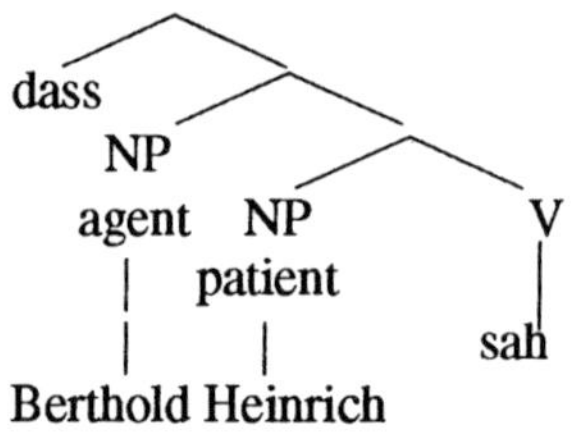

(b)

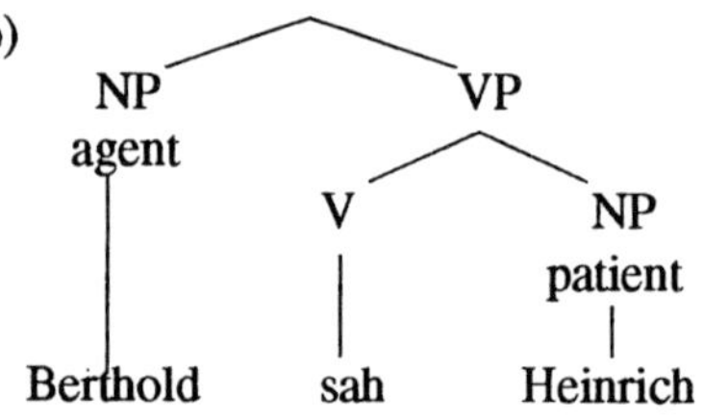

The child of course doesn't immediately know that a lot of movement has taken place in the second sentence under data set (4). Thus while for the first structure, s/he would come up with the correct branching structure, with the verb VP final, and *Berthold* in subject position (using the bootstrapping procedure), for the second sentence, *Berthold sah Heinrich*, s/he would get *Berthold sah*

Heinrich, with *Berthold* in subject position, and (using bootstrapping) the verb simply preceding the object. Thus two coherent geometries would be recovered, and there is no way that the child would know a priori that one of those geometries represents the correct D-structure. From the surface, at least, the government direction is indeterminate, and the child must be able to solve the problem of determining which one of the structures in (4) is the basic structure, before s/he could actually draw the appropriate tree and get the correct verb placement and governing direction. Thus the basic problem is this: parameter setting, and setting of government direction, depends on the D-structure order; but the child must first determine the D-structure. How is this done in the face of distorting movements? The advance to parameter-setting does nothing to resolve this problem, since once the D-structure tree structure is determined, the government direction parameter may be set trivially, by reading it off the tree— and thus it comes in with its aid after the problem has already been determined. It is the problem *before* the parameter-setting, the isolation of the correct tree structure, which is the crucial one.[1]

1. DETERMINING THE KERNEL

I would like to now outline two possible solutions to the problem of the isolation of D-structures (or construction moment structures), and thus to the government direction parameter (head parameter).[2] These are alternative solutions, and we must choose which one we wish to follow. One is the following: the child is able to determine the S-structure with traces, somehow, and then the traces determine the government direction and the other properties. The child needs a full set of sentences to determine the S-structures, and once s/he or she has all the traces, s/he simply uses them to determine government direction. The second approach, which is radically different, is the following: the child somehow manages to throw out all structures which have traces in them, or all parts of structures which have traces in them. Thus s/he ends up with a resultant set of sub-trees or structures which necessarily evince the D-structure order, because s/he has managed to throw out all those which have traces. S/he just has captured those which don't have traces in them. Let us call these *the kernel.* From this set, the governing direction can be set. It is this second approach that I have chosen to advocate here: namely, that the child is able to determine somehow which structures don't have movement in them (or which sub-structures in a structure), and throw out the rest. Then s/he uses just this subset of the structures to determine the government direction. We can call this solution *Determining the Kernel.*

Thus there will be a two-stage analysis in the acquisition sequence. In Stage I, the child would be faced with three sentences such as those given in (5): *John saw Mary*, *John was seen by Mary*, and *Who did John see?*. From these, the child would have to determine which one of these sentences was the basic one, namely, *John saw Mary*, and from that, s/he would be able to set the parameters, in this case the government direction parameter. That analysis would take place at something like nine months or a year, because that is presumably when the child learns the government direction of his or her language. Then in the actual learning of the passive, which is a different process, the child would be handed *John saw Mary* and *Mary was seen* and would project a trace. That is given in (5b).

(5) a. Stage I:

John saw Mary
John was seen by Mary
Who did John see

determine kernel ——————>

John saw Mary

set parameter ——————>

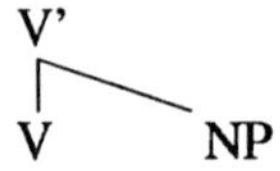

b. Stage II:

John saw Mary
Mary was seen

determine passive ——————>

Mary was seen t

Stage I analysis takes place at age 9 to 12 months (whenever government direction is set). I'll assume that Stage II analysis takes place much later, when the passive itself is learned, so at age 3 or 4. In other words, I will assume a two stage, or two pass, model: one which initially sets the government direction, and somehow is able simply ignore all passive sentences, and the other process, the actual learning of the passive, involves positing the trace. So by dividing up the problem into that of determining the kernel vs. actually projecting the traces, we make the proposal that there are actually two passes in the acquisition sequence. The second problem, the learning of the passive, is no doubt much the easier one, given that the active structure is already known. So now we are left with a different problem, the central one with which I will be concerned in this paper, and which I take to be the central problem of language acquisition theory: how does the child determine the kernel structures, i. e., the structures in which no movement has taken place, so that the parameters can be set? Note that this problem is a very difficult one, and recourse to the idea of setting parameters simply doesn't face up to it, in my opinion, since the child has to determine the data set from which the parameter is set. This *Determining the Kernel* may be the most difficult problem in the acquisition literature.

(6) Determining the Kernel:

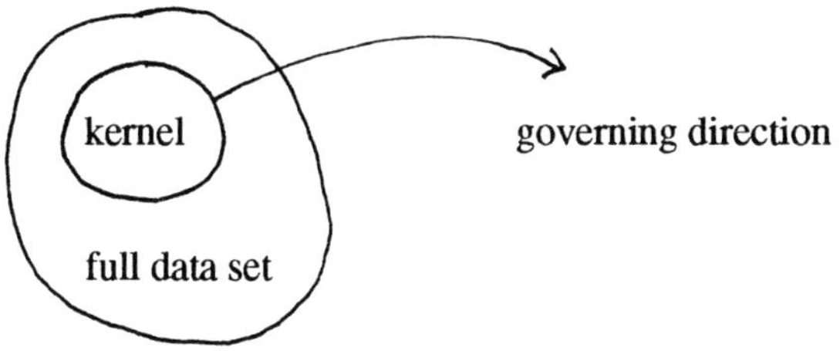

Things get even more complex, perhaps to the point of unresolvability, if one notices that movement is the usual thing: so, for example, in (7) the verb moves into inflectional position in French (Pollock 1989), and possibly in English at LF (according to Chomsky 1992), or in German the verb moves into inflection and then into a C position, and the subject moves from a subject position to a SPEC, CP position, in tensed sentences.

(7) a.

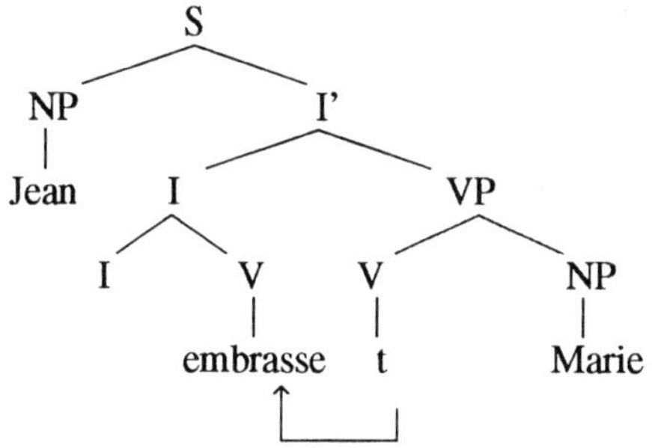

b.

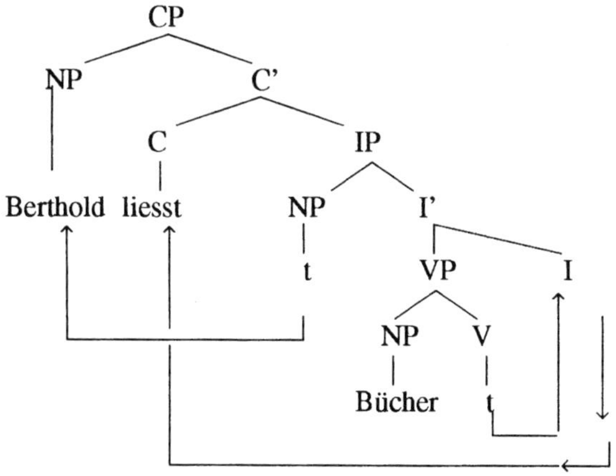

Thus movement is very much a normal thing, and the way of determining the kernel is not obvious. Of course, it might be argued that there aren't *any* substructures in which no movement has taken place; in that case, this line of attack is doomed to failure. But precisely how to determine the inverse of

Move-α, and the projection of traces in structures which have none, is by no means obvious either.

2. THE NOTION 'EXTRA FUNCTIONAL MATERIAL'

Let us consider then the different types of movement which could perplex us. First, there is movement of a head into a higher head, to give a complex higher head. In this case one would get a complex head via incorporation according to Baker (1988). This turns out to be crucial for the following analysis. Second is the possibility of a grammatical function changing rule, e.g. OBJ —>SUBJ. Third, there is *wh*-movement or focus movement of some sort, giving rise to a complex intonational pattern which we might think of as being associated with the COMP, and then being spread out over the whole structure. A fourth possibility is raising type constructions, which don't seem to have any marker at all. Finally, there is object shift or scrambling (e.g., in the Germanic languages), which I will not discuss here. I will now make a specific proposal, using the kernel approach, but make it somewhat tentatively, because I think that the problem itself is clearer than my proposal for solving it.

A kernel structure is a (sub)-structure in which movement has not taken place. The diagnostic of the kernel structure is the following: given some sort of subtree L(exical)P, LP is kernel if the closed class category F(unctional) associated with the head L is not filled; it is non-kernel if it is filled. Considering F + L together (a reason to do so will be given below), a kernel structure is one whose lexical head is minimal, in other words, one which is not marked by a c-commanding F:

(8)

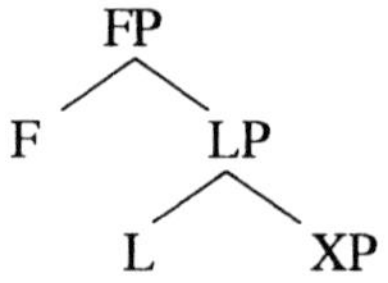

F: functional category
L: lexical category

If F is absent or bare, then movement has not taken place: LP is a kernel structure.
If F is filled, then movement has taken place within LP: LP is not kernel.

Take the English passive as the paradigm case of a nonkernel structure. It can be determined to be nonkernel by having a filled closed class functional category associated with the verb, namely, the *be+ed*. The structure of the passive is as in (9), where the LP is a VP, and the larger category is projected by the passive auxiliary itself.

(9) be hit by Bill

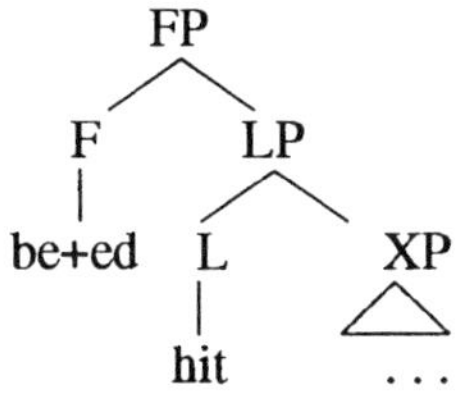

In this case, then, the *be+ed*, is a closed-class functional category of the AUX type which is associated with the lexical head. The presence of the passive is marked by the presence of the closed class category associated with the head. When that element, or some similar element, is not filled, it is evidence that the resulting structure is a kernel one. When the closed class functional head is filled, it is evidence that the structure is nonkernel, and so may be eliminated, without even locating the trace.

This is, then, the paradigm case of the difference between a kernel and a non-kernel structure. The child throws out a passive VP phrase since it is marked as nonkernel by the 'extra material', *be+ed.* As a result, there is no danger of inducing OVS order from this structure.

This type of approach fits in precisely with Baker's (1988) work with grammatical function changing rules. According to Baker, whenever there is a grammatical function changing rule, which is associated with Move-α, there is also incorporation. However, because there is incorporation, there is some sort of additional complexity on the head, and because there is additional complexity on the head, the subtree will be thrown out. This is especially obviously the case in languages other than English, where syntactic GF changing rules are marked morphologically in a more direct fashion on the surface.

Consider the case of the applicative, or the English Dative Shift. According to Baker, the applicative (and the dative) require the relevant P to incorporate into the V. The applicative is given directly in (10) below (from Baker 1988), while the English dative is shown in (11) (Larson's (1988) shell structure is irrelevant here, so I will simply ignore it).

(10) Chichewa

a. Mbidzi zi- na- perek-a msampha **kwa** nkhandwe
zebras SP-PAST-hand-ASP trap **to** fox
"The zebras handed the trap to the fox."

b. Mbidzi zi- na- perek-**er**- a nkhandwe msampha
zebras SP-PAST-hand- **to**-ASP fox trap
"The zebras handed the fox the trap."

(11) DS:

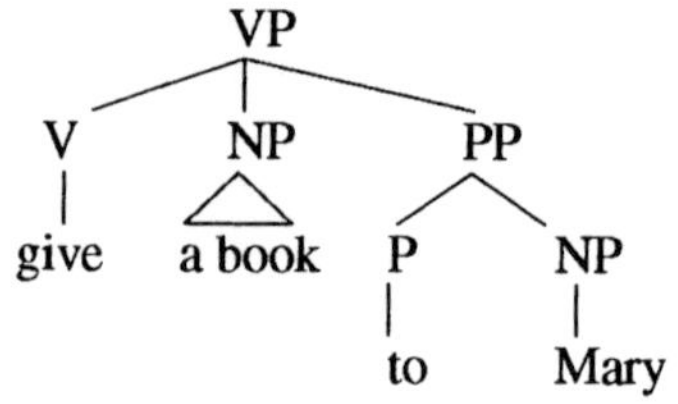

SS:

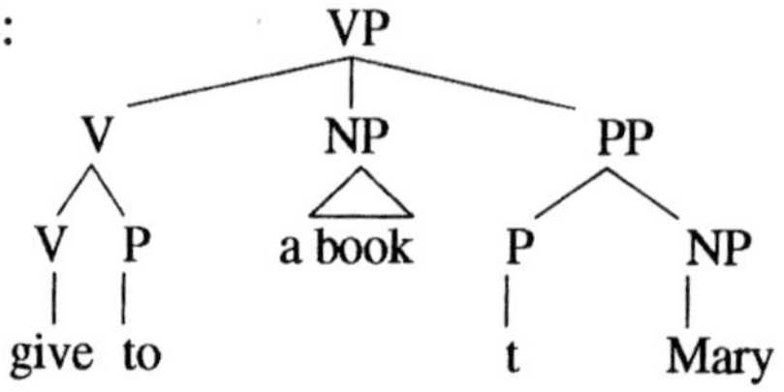

Later rules will require the adjacency of the *to*-phrase and the head.

Two comments are in order. First, in languages other than English, the applicative incorporation can be directly observed. In English, the incorporation must (unfortunately) be abstract. Second, the S-structure in (11) does indeed have a complex head, and thus might be expected to be nonkernel, and consequently eliminated from consideration. No location of the trace is necessary. However, the claim of (8) is somewhat more specific than that. It states that in the structure $[_{FP}\ [_{F'}\ F\ [_{LP}\ L\ \ XP]]]$, LP is nonkernel if F is filled. In (11) it is not the case that F is filled, but rather that F + L form a complex unit (by head movement). Let us therefore reanalyze Dative Shift not directly as incorporation but rather as movement to an operator position outside of the VP (this will be slightly changed to the V', assuming Larsonian shell structure). This S-structure then has a functional category on the periphery of the LP (the VP or V'). The *to* and the verb are later reanalyzed as a single unit.

(12) a. DS:

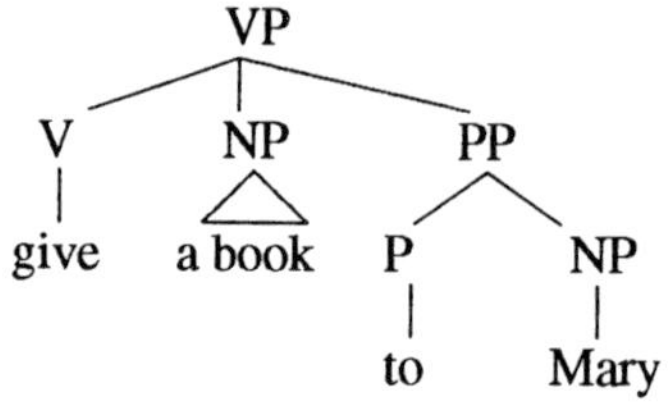

(12) b. Intermediate:

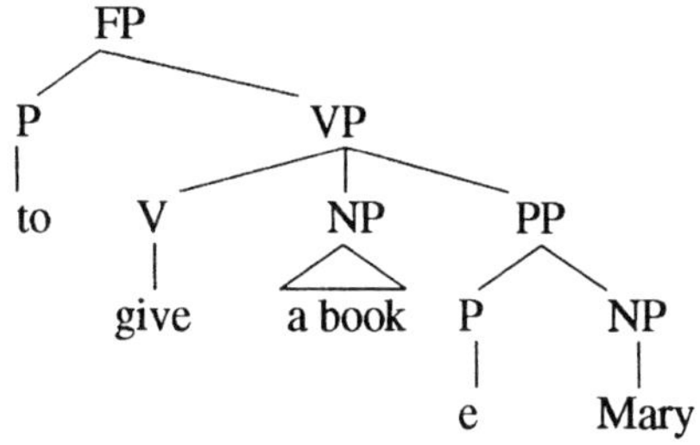

c. SS:

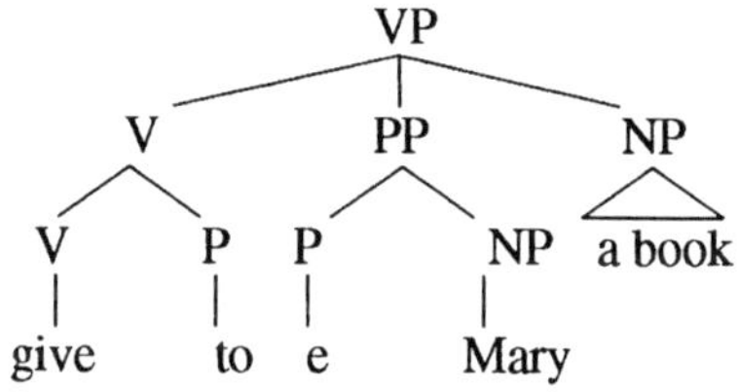

I suggest that a similar analysis may be given to clitics. The *to* (or clitic) first moves to an operator position associated with the maximal projection, and later is analyzed with the head (see also Uriagereka (1995) and Sportiche (this volume)).[3]

This covers two cases of NP-movement. An additional complication arises in the case of dative movement, since the *to* in English, unlike the incorporated applicative marked in Baker's languages, is not directly visible. Thus more must be said about how the child detects the complex [F + V]: it is not directly visible. One (rather unattractive) possibility is that the child notices that the NPs are switched and uses this information (backwards) to project a complex *give-to* head. Another more satisfying but speculative possibility is that the incorporation of a null preposition into a verbal head may actually have phonological effects. In particular, it could induce stress shift in bisyllabic forms. This would give rise to two forms like dónate-donáte. By Wexler's Uniqueness principle on phonological forms and lexical entries, the second of these forms is impossible. Therefore incorporation of *to* into bisyllabic Latinate forms is impossible.

Consider now *wh*-type movement, movement out of a clause into the SPEC, CP position.

(13)

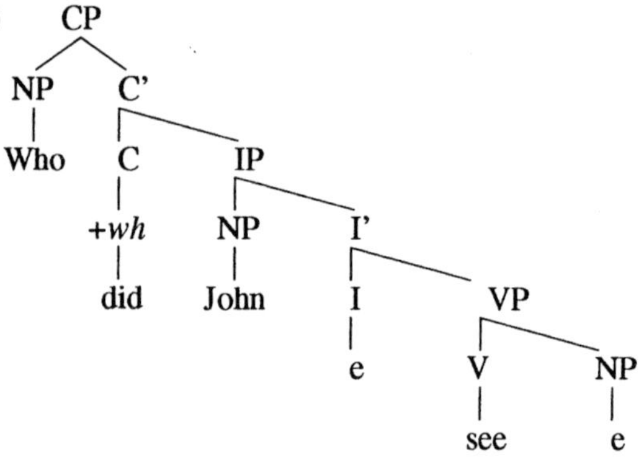

As a nonkernel structure, this must also be eliminated from consideration during the first pass of acquisition. Suppose that the IP is nonkernel. This means that the FP dominating the IP, which in this case is the CP, must contain extra (functional) material: in particular, the head of the FP, C, must contain extra material. In what sense is this true? There is one obvious place where this might be so: the question intonation. Suppose that the question intonation results from a question intonational morpheme being associated with the C; this, then, is the additional functional material that the question involves. The intonation is distributed over the whole sentence by the phonology, but it is extra material in the C slot, from the point of view of the syntax. The *wh*-question, i.e. A'-movement, then falls under the same rubric as A-movement.

Another question arises at this point. Is the additional *wh*-material in COMP extra in terms of the syntax as well? Note that in general it has long been assumed that features have a [+/-] character: i.e. that the COMP may be either [+*wh*] or [-*wh*]. But if we wish to retain the notion that the functional projection in the phrase marker in (8) (repeated below) has something *extra* in it, it is not clear that the [+] and [-] features will do the job.

(14)

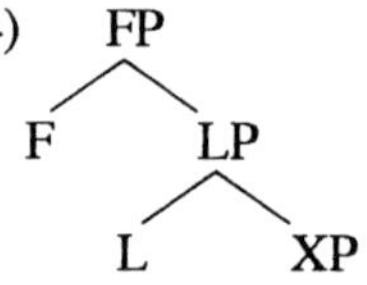

F: functional category
L: lexical category

If F is filled with extra material, then LP is nonkernel.
If F is bare or nonexistent, then LP is kernel.

Under the conventional view, F here would be [+*wh*] if IP is nonkernel, and [-*wh*] if IP is kernel; but in what sense does [+*wh*] have more material in it than [-*wh*]?

In order for the definition of kernel to function accurately, it would be better—in fact, necessary—to adopt a privative theory of features, i.e. a unipolar one. That is, rather than the distinction being [+/-], it is [+*wh*/Ø] ([+*wh*/null]). Then, the [+*wh*] feature at the CP level does in fact contain more material than the simple null. (This is obviously not the case with a [+/-] *wh* feature.) The possibility of the [-*wh*] feature being null conforms to a simple syntactic fact: that a verb subcategorizes for the tense of its complement just in case a *wh*-phrase is not present. In all cases where a *wh*-phrase is present, the embedded sentence may be tensed or not; when the *wh*-phrase is not present, it varies from verb to verb:

(15) a. John didn't know what PRO to do.
what he should do.
what he had done.

b. John tried PRO to leave.
*John tried that he leave.

c. *John muttered PRO to see Mary at 10.
John muttered that he saw Mary at 10.

While this fact is well-known, its ramifications have never been clearly addressed. Where there is a *wh*-phrase present, and hence a [+*wh*] feature, then the tense of the embedded clause varies freely. If there is *wh*-element, and hence no [+*wh*] feature, the tense is subcategorized for. This, however, suggests that the [+*wh*] feature blocks the subcategorization for tense, and that the (putative) [-*wh*] feature does not block. This in turn suggests that in the [-*wh*] feature case, the feature heading the clause is transparent. The simplest way to capture this is to posit no [-*wh*] feature at all, but literally null. This then means that in the so-called [-*wh*] case there is no CP projection at all, but just a headed IP, giving the matrix verb the possibility of looking directly into the embedded clause, and subcategorizing for its head, the I. If there is no CP, then the IP embedded clause must look like (16), with the *that* adjoined.

(16)

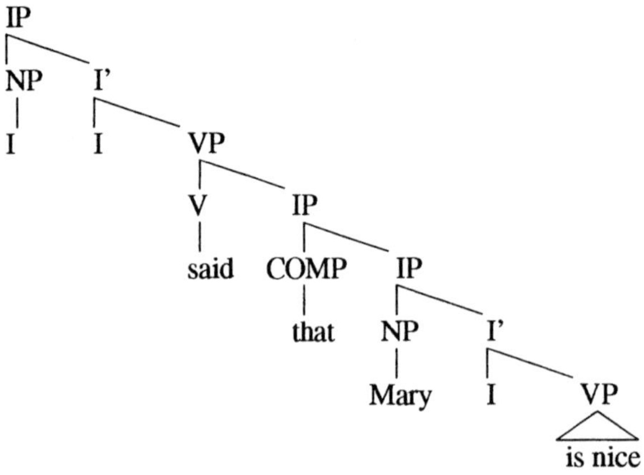

A structure like that in (16), while radical from the point of view of current syntax, would allow the matrix verb to directly subcategorize for the embedded tense. This is necessary for the unipolar theory of features to be maintained in its strongest form, which is in turn necessary if the child is to be able to determine the kernel through the mechanism of extra functional material. A potential argument for this structure is given by the fact that the lower IP cannot be null.

(17) a. I saw someone, but I don't know who $[_{IP}$ e].
b. Mary's books are nicer than John's $[_{NP}$ e].
c. *I said that Bill was nice, and Joan said that $[_{IP}$ e].

The adjoined structure immediately explains the data set in (17).[4] This (radical) syntactic analysis, then, goes hand-in-hand with the central acquisition point that a notion of extra functional material is needed and necessary.

To summarize then, I have argued that for NP-movement, exemplified by Dative Shift and Passive, on the one hand, and *wh*-movement on the other, the movement of the NP is signaled by extra material on, or the presence of, a functional head, where this functional head is associated with a lexical head. In the LP headed by this lexical head, the movement is found. This F is in effect a marker that movement has taken place, and thus evidence that the structure is a nonkernel structure. It therefore is eliminated from consideration in the child's analysis (for example, for determination of government direction).

3. THE PF CONJECTURE

The above analysis has suggested that the child looks at a structure such as that in (18) on the right hand side (repeated from (8)) to determine that movement has taken place. This is a rather large stored structure. Is it necessary for the child to consider the whole thing?

(18) General Case (nonkernel)

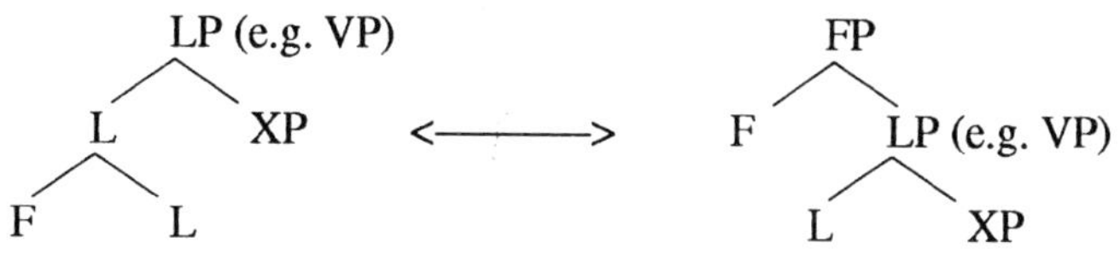

PF **DS**

Paradigm:

F1 + L
F1 + F3 + L
F2 + F4 + L

I now make a conjecture which I will call *The PF Conjecture*. While the D-structure (or some intermediate structure) has the character on the right in (18), the PF has the character on the left. In Passive, for example, the *be+ed* and the stem are grouped together. In (18), while the functional category is sister to the LP at all the syntactic levels DS-SS-LF, at PF the functional category is just a sister to the L. As a result, the geometries of the PF and the D-structure are quite different. The D-structure is right branching, the functional category taking LP as a complement, whereas the PF has the F and the L grouped together in one lexical item, as in (18). (I shall defend this in more detail later.) This forms *The PF Conjecture*.

(19) *PF Conjecture*
If F selects for LP at D-structure, then F is a sister or specifier of L at PF.

This simple syntactic difference means that there will be a radically different type of evidence for the child to scan over at PF. Rather than having to look at the whole tree [$_{FP}$ F [$_{LP}$ L XP]], the child may simply have to look at the complex of the head. If this is a simple L, then the structure is simple and kernel. If it is a [F L] complex, then the subtree associated with it is nonkernel. Therefore, there will be a paradigm for the child to look at which will have the lexical item plus different functional categories, as s/he is looking over the full set of input—F1 + L, F3 + L, and so forth, as shown in (18). In the kernel case, there will not be any Fs. This is shown in (20).

(20) Kernel Case

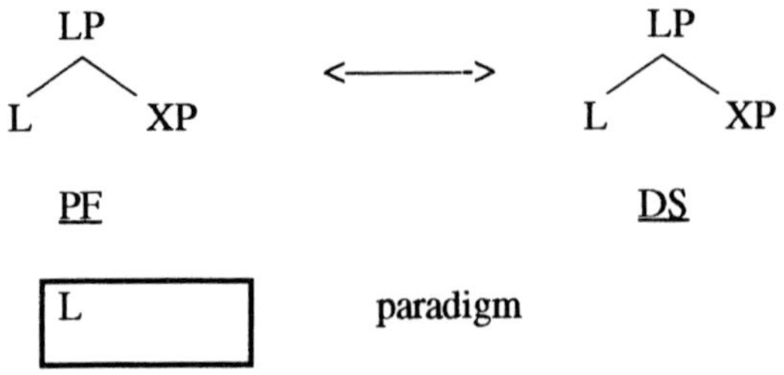

This means that the child will be able to detect F as part of the L in the PF representation (c.f., the paradigm in (18)). Consider how this would work in the case of the English passive. Here, the kernel is of course headed by the verbal stem [+V], while the nonkernel is marked by a function element on the periphery, *be+ed* (21a, b).

(21) a. $[_{VP}$ hit Mary]
b. $[_{VP}$ be+ed [hit by Mary]]
c. PF: [[be+ed + hit] by Mary]

However, the child need not parse the entire VP and its peripheral element *be+ed*, because *be+ed* is structured with the head, as in (21c). This is the PF Conjecture. The passive subtree may thus be thrown out, and will not confuse the child. The situation is actually slightly more complex than this, as shown in (22). By semantic bootstrapping and the PF constraint, the child will treat the first element as the object, and group *was* with *hit*, as in (22). The V is thus parsed as $[_v$ V F], a 'heavy' verb, at PF. This heavy verb at PF is taken to represent the syntactic structure $[_{FP}$ F $[_{VP}$ V XP], where the F is at the periphery, at D-structure. It is this D-structure, a nonkernel structure since it contains an extra F, which is the reason that the structure is eliminated from the kernel.

(22) Semantic Bootstrapping and PF Conjecture: NOT KERNEL

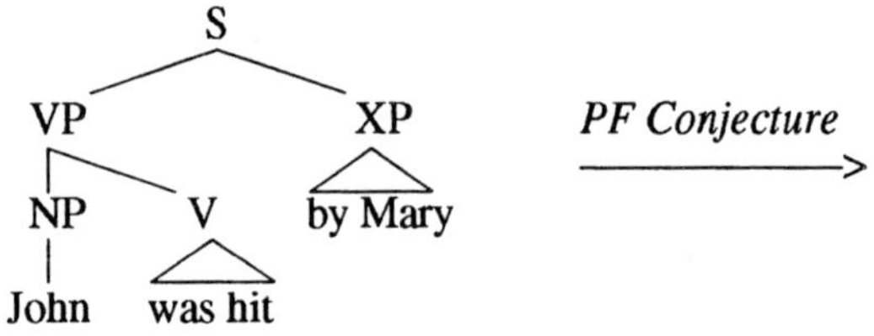

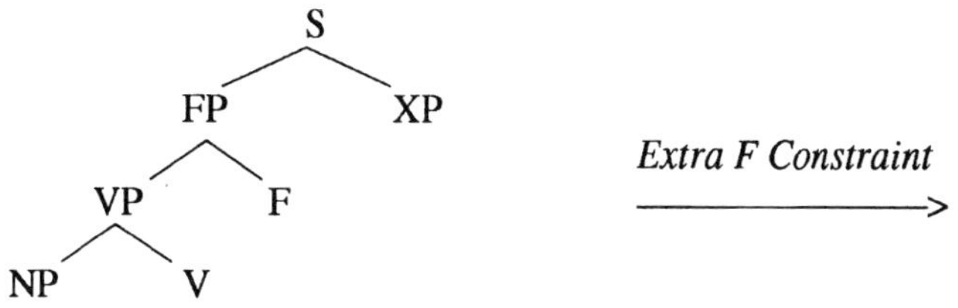

The *was* is initially grouped with *hit* at PF, since that is what the PF looks like. *John* is placed as an object of the verb, by semantic bootstrapping. But the PF in which *was* and *hit* are joined together corresponds to a D-structure in which the F is adjoined to the VP. This is the 'determining the kernel' structure, and is thrown out because the F is extra material.

For the kernel structure, D-structure will be an LP dominating an L and XP, and this will also be the PF, with the paradigm of the head being simply a bare L, as in (20). This is the case when the child is faced with a kernel structure: it is something whose head is minimal in the paradigm. On the other hand, in the nonkernel structures, the F selects for LP at D-structure, as in (18). This however corresponds to a PF in which the F is grouped with the L as a sister (and perhaps a specifier at PF). The F and L form a complex unit at PF. Thus every structure which has a D-structure (and LF) structure of [F [L XP]], has a PF of [[F+L] XP]. This makes the extra material very locally determinable.

In English questions with standard intonation marking, the nonkernel, by hypothesis, has standard intonation marking plus the question marking, associated with the COMP. This is a heavy F, and the structure is excluded. In GF changing rules, the standard form is just the basic verb, while the nonkernel form is that verb and the incorporated element (e.g., a preposition). The child sets up a paradigm of verbs, locally storing them. The incorporated verb is heavy in this paradigm [V + F], and corresponds to a [$_{FP}$ F [$_{VP}$ V COMP]] structure, so the resultant structure is excluded. Thus, in each of these cases there is a real difference between the kernel form and the nonkernel form. In the nonkernel form, where movement has taken place, that movement, even if it is not movement of the verb itself, is registered on the verb. More directly, movement of the nonhead associated with the head is registered on the head, making that head more complex.

We now arrive at the following minimal structures involved with the head at PF. The presence of a kernel head at PF (a minimal head) is associated with a lack of an immediately dominating F projection at D-structure, and the lack of such projections is associated with a lack of movement. This theory has two properties. First, it is morphologically driven, in the sense that it is the [L F] pair that is focused on by the child, in the child's paradigm. Second, it does not differentiate between 'good' and 'bad' functional categories. I wish now to complicate the first point, and discuss in more detail the second.

Consider first the matter of good and bad Fs. I have suggested above that the structure [$_{FP}$ F [$_{LP}$ L XP]] is dangerous for the child in the sense that F signals the possibility of a nonkernel structure. This is certainly the case with

[+*wh*], *be+ed*, and incorporated *to*, the discussed structures. However, it might be argued that these are bad functional categories to have on the periphery of an LP, ones that specifically signal nonkernel structures. Aren't there good functional categories as well, such as INFL on the periphery of a VP ($[_{IP}$ I $[_{VP}$ V ...]]), or Det on the periphery of a NP (assuming the DP hypothesis: $[_{DP}$ the $[_{NP}$ N ...]]). In fact, it might (rightfully) be argued that the entire tree of the form $[_{FP}$ F $[_{LP}$ ...]], for some functional category or other, is bad, so that I will be throwing out the entire data base by throwing out structures of the form $[_{FP}$ F $[_{LP}$ L ...]].

This is a very difficult question to address, and my answer will be only partial. The most obvious type of solution would be to look for some mark on the bad functional categories which sets them off from the good ones. But there is no such mark, certainly not available at the age of nine months. A different sort of solution would look for a correlate, for example movement, in the case of the bad functional categories; but that was exactly the problem to be solved.

A promising line of attack is the following. The bad functional categories all have the property of being optional and non-null. For example *be+ed* is an optional subcategorizer-of or operator-on the VP, *to* is an optional operator (in this analysis), and [+*wh*] is optional in main clauses. On the other hand, INFL, say TNS, is obligatory in its [+finite] or [-finite] guise (to be consistent, I should analyze [-finite] as null), and DET is (let us say) always required. This means that these functional categories are obligatory. The $[_{FP}$ F $[_{FP}$ F $[_{FP}$ F $[_{LP}$ L....]]]] structure, i.e., an LP surrounded by Fs preceding it, will therefore have the following character: one F will be obligatory [INFL], and the others optional. Here, F1 is always repeated.

(23) Structure of the Paradigm (PF):

F4 + F2 + F1 + L
F1 + L
F3 + F1 + L
.
.
.

The minimal element in the paradigm will therefore be L + F1, and all other elements will be thrown out. This will correctly diagnose the structure of IP, for example. In the listing in (24), only (24c) will be minimal.

(24) a. will have seen (=PRES will have+en see)
b. would see (=PAST will see)
c. saw (=PAST see)
d. was seen (=be+ed PAST see)

Note that the verb plus all the functional projections associated with it are counted as a single word, a verb. They form a complex verb, as shown in (23) above. Another way of putting it is that they are stored as a single unit in a paradigm.

By looking at the morphological paradigm the child can determine the minimal element, and thus the obligatory element. Thus, s/he can see that only (24c) has the single obligatory element. Alongside this morphological means of determining the minimal element, there is also a quite straightforward syntactic means. Suppose that UG had the following stipulation:

(25) UG: INFL is always present in the phrase marker.

Suppose that the constraint on $[_{FP}$ F $[_{LP}$ L...]] being thrown out (being analyzed as nonkernel) holds only if F is non-obligatory. Then the simplest structure would be retained, and all the others excluded. This is perhaps even preferable to the morphological means.

Consider again the general case in light of the syntactic means, where X, Y, and Z are possible complements:

(26)

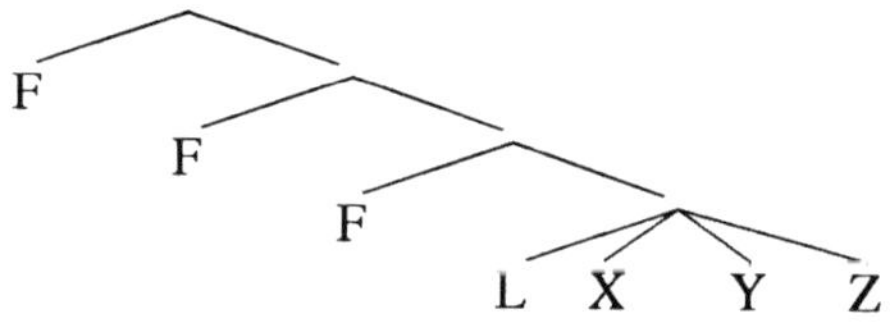

To recapitulate, we have said above that functional categories on the periphery of the lexical head are potentially dangerous, as signaling nonkernel structures. How could the child tell that there were no functional categories on the periphery of the L head? The morphological route consists simply of looking for such material directly, as above. The syntactic means, on the other hand, calls for *looking in subcategorized contexts.*

Suppose that the structure in (26) has above it some subcategorizing V. Suppose that this V, rather than subcategorizing for an FP, subcategorizes for an LP, as a matter of Universal Grammar. Then the child is assured automatically of satisfying the constraint of no peripheral functional categories, since the upper head, for example a V, would subcategorize directly for a constituent with no functional categories on its periphery.

(27) Subcategorized context (no peripheral functional categories):

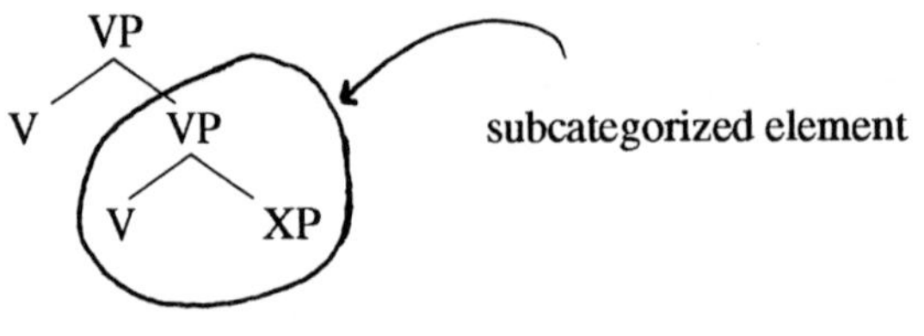

(27) gives one such example, where a head V subcategorizes for a bare VP, with no functional categories in its periphery.

Thus within this LP (by hypothesis), there is no movement, since it is not signaled on the periphery of the LP. This is much in accord with The Penthouse Principle of Ross (1967), and the general observation that obfuscating movement is to be found principally in root contexts (Emonds 1976). The child has the possibility in particular subcategorized contexts to tell that there is no peripheral functional morpheme, precisely because the peripheral functional morpheme is not subcategorized for.

Let us consider a primary case where this might come into play, namely, an instance of head movement. Consider the German example:

(28) a. dass Berthold Heinrich sah
that B. H. saw
"....that Berthold saw Heinrich"

b. Berthold sah Heinrich
B. saw H.
"Berthold saw Heinrich."

(29) a. [Einen Beruf zu haben] ist notig.
a career to have is necessary
"To have a career is necessary."

b. Ich versuchte [ein Buch zu lesen]
I tried a book to read
"I tried to read a book."

Here, the child must determine the governing direction parameter in (28) and (29), but the data is ambiguous: (28a) suggests that the verb governs to the left, while (28b) suggests that it governs to the right. How does the child tell which is the kernel structure?

There seems to be one decisive difference: the kernel case is infinitival while the nonkernel case is finite. Let us suppose then, that this is the crucial difference and the child determines the basic governing direction from the infinitival form. Since the child has no a priori knowledge that s/he is facing German (or a Germanic language), it is necessary that this be universally so, i.e., that the child determines basic governing direction from the infinitival form, eliminating all noninfinitival forms as (potentially) dangerously nonkernel:

(30) UG: The child determines the basic governing direction from the infinitival form.

This is a fairly large bullet to bite, but I see little alternative but to bite it, given the approach advocated here.

How does the stipulation in (30) fit in with the general theory advanced here? First, and principally, the infinitival form must be that which is bare of the peripheral functional categories which signal potentially nonkernel forms. Therefore, we are led again to a feature set which is not [+/- finite] (i.e., bipolar), but rather [+ finite/null]. It is only in this latter case that we can say some functional projection is unequivocally present (or missing). This leads us to say that the infinitival projections in (28) or (29) are bare, and finite projections are not. This is another bullet to bite, and seems to suggest a Bresnan (1982) type analysis of infinitival complements: one in which the VP is directly subcategorized for (and INFL is absent). For the sake of concreteness, I record that here.

(31)

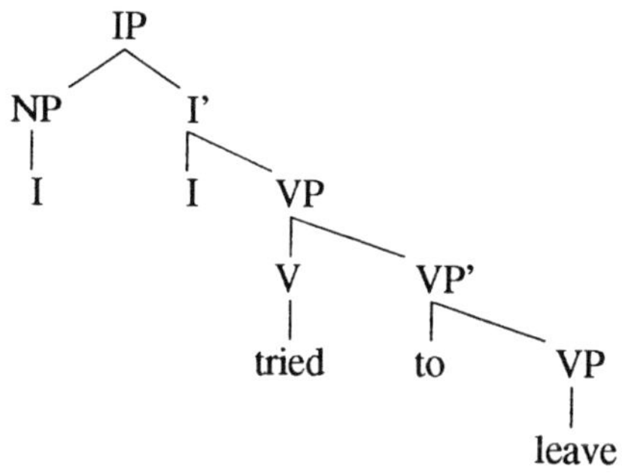

However uncomfortable this conclusion may be, the logic of the analysis demands it. Note that the obfuscating head movement of the lower verb is now barred because there is no head for it to move into (and no head to signal movement in the lower projection). This gives the phrase marker an accordion-like character, where some functional projections may be present or absent.

The second point to note is that the presence of bare structures can be determined not only by the analysis of the head itself (it is a stem, rather than an inflected form), but by the presence of the subcategorizing form: it subcategorizes for a bare complement (i.e., one lacking functional projections).

We now arrive at the following conclusion: the lack of an F can be determined in any of *three* ways: morphologically, syntactically, and semantically. These are summarized as in (32):

(32) **Morphologically**: the L associated with the F is morphologically simplex in a paradigm.
Syntactically: another element, the governing element, shows it to be syntactically simplex by *not* subcategorizing for the associated functional category.
Semantically: it is semantically simplex or dependent.

I will not elaborate much on the semantic criterion here, but simply note that according to Stowell (1982), an infinitival complement has a particular unrealized reading as to tense. If that is so, then the child may be bootstrapped into knowledge of the kernel structure in this, a third way, by noting that its semantics are unrealized, or otherwise simple. There are thus three convergent ways to tell that the kernel structure has been reached. Generalizing (32), then, we arrive at conclusion that the syntactic way to set parameters is by looking at *governed* domains, though not necessarily embedded inside the clause. The reason that one needs to look in governed domains is that some functional category, such as [+finite], will be subcategorized as *not* present, i.e., the null option will be chosen by the subcategorizing verb. This can be seen in the German case, repeated below, which maintains the correct governing direction (in the embedded sentence).

(33) Ich versuchte [ein Buch zu lesen]
I tried a book to read
"I tried to read a book."

6. PHONOLOGICAL PHRASING AND TELEGRAPHIC SPEECH

I want to close the discussion with a rather long section on what the PF might look like, and how this fits into the general scheme outlined here. A crucial generalization has been made in work on the syntax-phonology interface by Kaisse (1985) and Nespor and Vogel (1986). Kaisse notes that governing auxiliaries cliticize onto V, and governing determiners cliticize onto N, in terms of phonological phrasing. Thus *was eating the pie* is bracketed [was eating] [the pie], and *the picture of Mary* is bracketed [the picture] [of Mary]. Similarly, Nespor and Vogel note that closed class elements on the nonrecursive side of the head are part of the same phonological phrase as the head. This means that the abstract D-structure in (34a) is given a PF of (34b), where the peripheral functional categories have been grouped with the head.

(34) a. Abstract DS

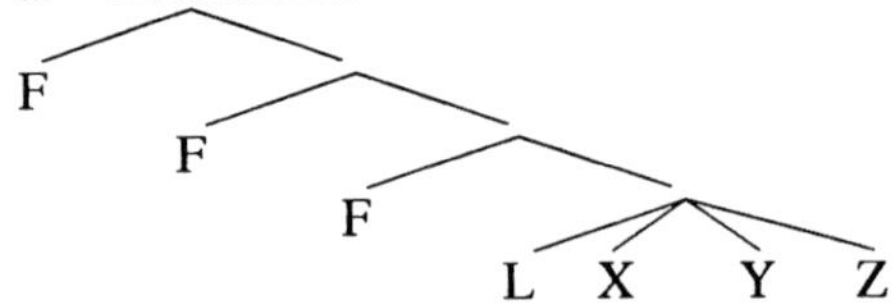

(34) b. PF

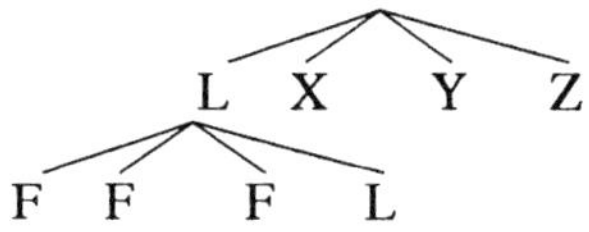

The different phonological phrases are given in (35), where the same thing holds.

(35) a. John **may have seen** Mary

b. John **may have given** Mary a book

c. John **may have given Mary** a book

d. Mary **was eaten** by a shark

e. **the picture** of Mary

Similarly, consider (36). While the old Ross (1967) structure of the noun phrase doesn't seem to hold at S-structure, it does in fact seem to be relevant to the PF. The PF structure, the phonological bracketing, seems to be precisely that in (36b). Similarly, in (37), while the new fashioned right branching structure of the auxiliary does very well as a rendition of what the auxiliary would look like when we consider D-structures and S-structures, it must cede something to the structure in (37b), the old *Syntactic Structures* analysis, which is the appropriate one for the phonological form or PF (as just shown by (35)).

(36) a. D Structure

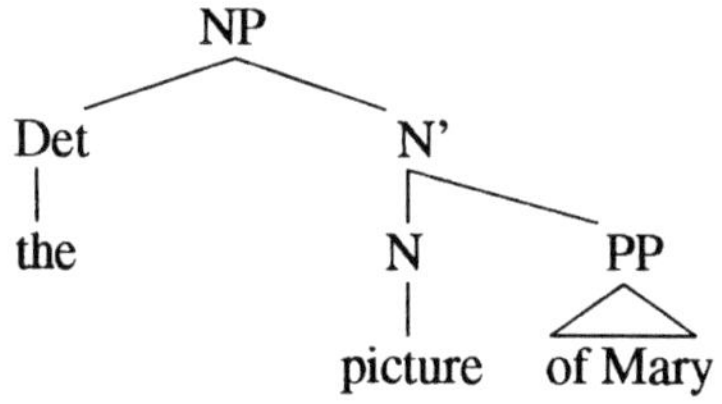

b. PF and Ross (1967) structure

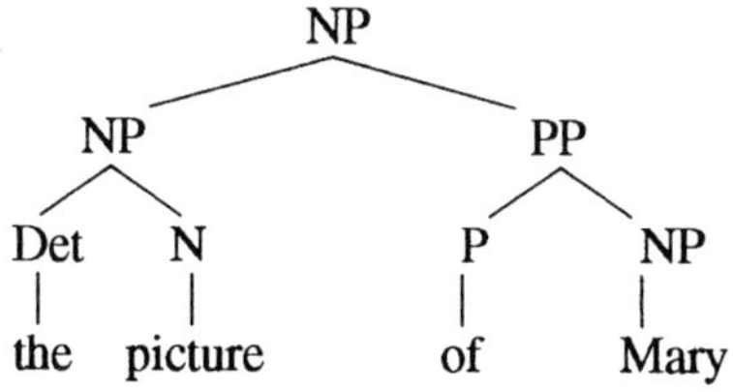

(37) a. General current right branching analysis

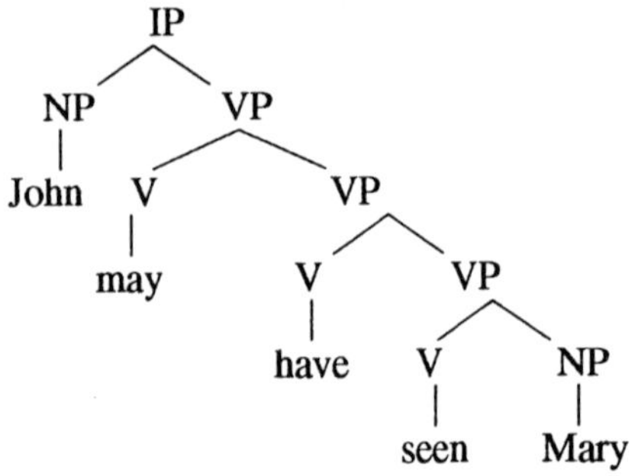

b. Approximate *Syntactic Structures* and PF

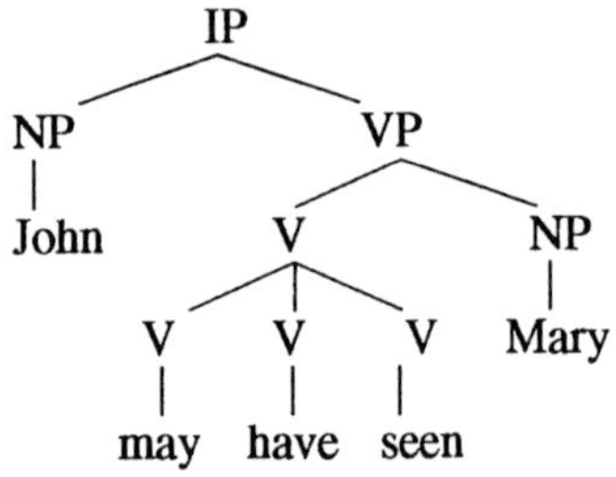

It appears then that there is a generalization about the types of structures that we are faced with, at D-structure and S-structure on the one hand, vs. PF on the other. The D-structure looks universally analytic and right branching, like that in (37a), while the PF has the functional categories grouped with the head, as given in (37b). These structures are exactly what would be expected if the child stores paradigms of the functional heads together with the verbal head or the lexical head, and uses them to determine the minimal category.

Of course, more general questions arise: how is this sort of PF derived? What would be the purpose of having such radically different branching structures (for PF vs. D-structure-LF)? I address the first question in work in progress, and while the considerations in the previous paragraph perhaps give a learnability inroad into the second question, it would be well if this could be supported by some structural-grammatical reason for why a PF should look this way, although it is beyond the scope of the present paper to do so.[5]

Let us now consider the following. Suppose that two phrase markers, Phrase Marker 1 and Phrase Marker 2 are *alignable* if by removing elements from both, and letting the terminals of Phrase Marker 1 or Phrase Marker 2 re-project, the two converge on the same phrase marker. That is, elements are taken away from PM 1, and the same, or different, elements are taken away from PM 2, and the two now form the same phrase marker. Now consider the maximal alignment of PM 1 and PM 2, the phrase marker which is constructed by taking the fewest elements away from each. Consider (38), the PF and D-structure of the same phrase marker, according to the foregoing.

(38) a. DS

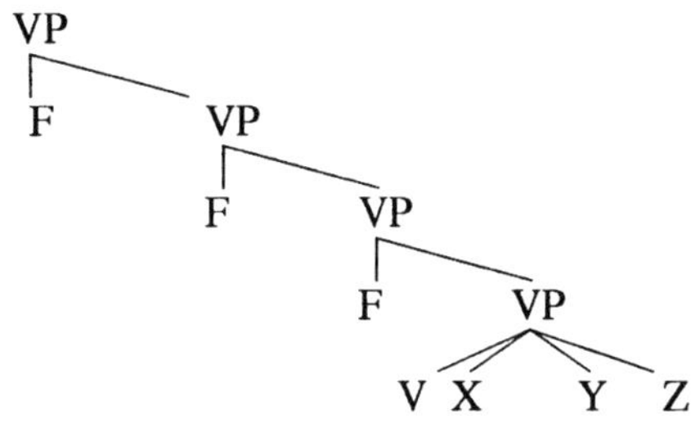

b. PF

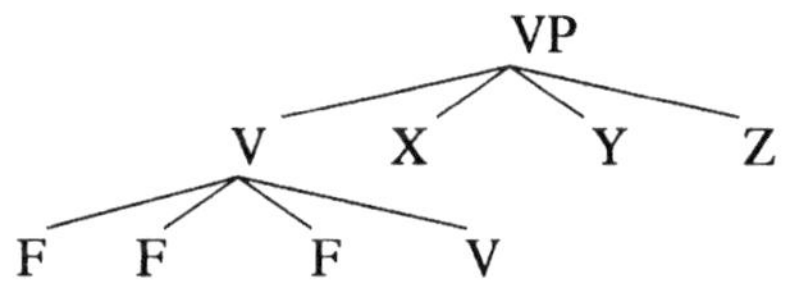

What is the maximal alignment of these two phrase markers? What one must do is to remove categories from each one of them until we get down to some phrase marker which is exactly the same for the two of them. There is only one way to do that: by removing all the functional elements. These are in a different position in the two phrase markers. Thus we are left with (39), the maximal alignment.

(39) Maximal alignment of (38a, b)

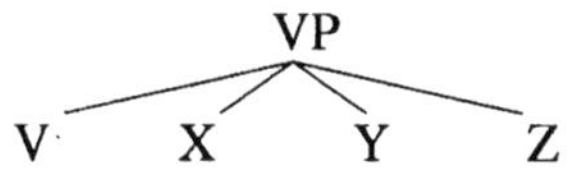

In the example *John may have seen Mary*, the maximal alignment of the two structures is given in (40). One structure, the DS-SS-LF, will be right branching. This is given in (40a). The structure at PF, on the other hand, will have *may have seen* as a constituent—this is the phonological phrasing. The alignment of those two is given in (40c): *John see Mary*. Notice that all the F elements are filtered out in the discrepancy between levels of representation.

(40) a. John [may [have [seen Mary]]]
b. John [[may have seen] Mary]
c. Maximal alignment: John [see Mary]

Similarly, in (41a) and (b), if one removes the discrepant elements, those creating distinct trees, we are left with the function element *the* filtered out, i.e. with *picture of Mary*.

(41) a.

b.

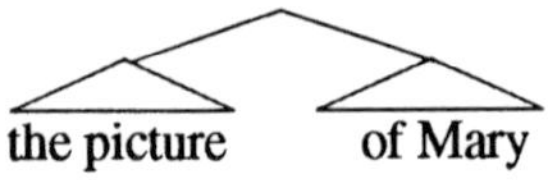

c.

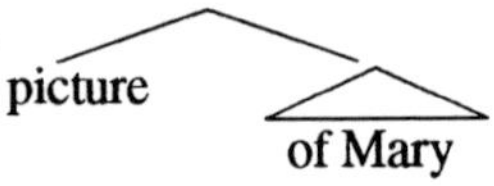

Note that all F elements are filtered out in the discrepancy between the levels of representation. It is as if the greatest common denominator between contrasting representations is created: this is the maximal alignment. This leads to the conjecture in (42):

(42) UG: Telegraphic speech is the maximal alignment of two structures, one which is given at PF, and the other is given at D-structure, which is determined by UG.

The D-structure determines the scope ordering of auxiliaries and such. Thus, the child is given one structure by Universal Grammar, and another structure by PF. These two structures are not coherent, and the child does not have movement in the early stages. So what does the child do? S/He eliminates the discrepant elements between the two, and arrives at the resultant, which is what I am calling the maximal alignment. That maximal alignment is telegraphic speech.

To summarize, I have argued for the following ideas. First, children in initial stages of acquisition determine the base form not by projecting a tree with all its traces, but rather by throwing out all subtrees which have movement in them. The remainder, *the kernel,* necessarily evinces the base form, and is used to set parameters, e.g., the government direction parameter. Second, the element that signals the nonkernel form is a piece of extra functional material, F, on the periphery of an LP. The child therefore *determines the kernel* by avoiding such forms for setting parameters. Third, for this extra material to be conceived as truly extra, a [+/null] theory of features must be posited. Fourth, the extra material is grouped with the lexical head at the level of PF. That is, a syntactic bracketing like [F [L XP YP]] has a phonological bracketing of [[F + L] XP YP]. This means that all the child has to do is to look over the paradigm of the lexical head to see if it contains extra material. Fifth, along with detecting extra functional material by looking at the complex of the head, it is possible to note the presence of an F, or the lack of it, by looking at subcategorized contexts. Thus, if a verb subcategorizes for an LP directly, there is no peripheral F, and the LP must be kernel. Finally, telegraphic speech is the maximal alignment of two structures, the PF in which the F is grouped with the head ([[F + L] XP YP]), and D-structure and S-structure, in which the functional category is peripheral to the lexical projection ([F [L XP YP]]).

APPENDIX

In this appendix, dissatisfied somewhat with the above, I would like to return again to the question of A'-, A-, and head movement, and the question of subcategorization.

In the text, I have not actually differentiated between A-, A'-, and head movement in terms of the peripheral functional category: all require it if nonkernel, as it is the signal of a nonkernel structure. The types of examples that were given above are repeated below:

(1) A-movement (e.g. passive): [[be + ed] [hit Bill]]
(2) A'-movement (e.g. *wh*-movement): [+*wh* [John hit who]]
(3) Head movement (e.g. V to I): Heinrich [+finite [Bücher lesen]]

It seems likely however, that the head movement case is different; and in some respects, opposite, from the other two. While A- and A'-movement are signaled by functional morphemes at the periphery, head movement involves the functional morpheme *itself*, with movement to it. For example, consider the German finite construction:

(4) Heinrich liesst Bücher t

H. reads books
"Heinrich reads books."

The idea that the functional element is dangerous in head movement constructions comes not so much from the fact that it is a marker or operator (in the passive and [+*wh*] constructions), but rather that it is an attractor of movement, as abstractly shown below.

(5)

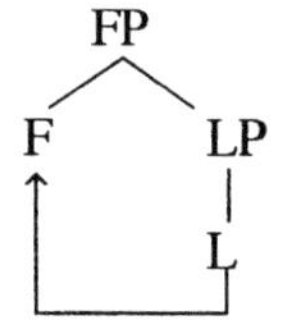

Is it worthwhile to posit that the child only looks at constructions in which the F is not present? The answer is equivocal, contra the assertion in the body of the text. I maintained above that a subcategorizing head not subcategorizing for F is crucial. This gives rise to the following situation, where the higher L immediately subcategorizes for the lower one, with no intervening F.

(6)
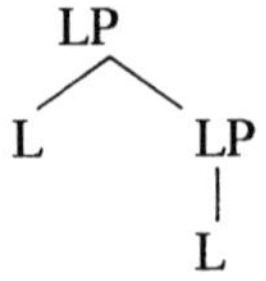

For the answer in the text to be relevant, the structure in (6) must require that the lower LP—the potential kernel structure—not have any instance of head movement. And indeed we have eliminated head movement of the lower L to the intermediate F, since it is no longer present. But have we barred head movement in general? Clearly not, since the lower L could be moved into the higher L instead.

(7)
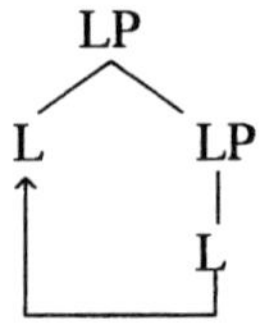

Thus the ban on peripheral functional categories does not really do what it is intended to.

This reservation is valid, but there is still one line of reasoning that might allow us to maintain the analysis. The movement of L to F is not the movement of any old head to a higher head, but specifically that of V to a finite element (in the German movement case). Suppose that this coherence between heads is not arbitrary, but rather itself is a part of Universal Grammar; i.e., there is some requirement between V and [+ finite] which requires that the former move into the latter. In this case, the removal of the F head, while abstractly laying open the possibility of the V moving into the higher head, does not in practice do so. This would be because the V is not missing any arbitrary feature, but specifically the feature associated with the [+ finite] node. This reasoning would seem to be in line with that of Chomsky's (1992) Minimalist Program where movement is triggered by the lack of some feature.[6]

There is one other feature of head movement constructions which is quite interesting, and suggests that, logically at least, they pattern the opposite of A- and A'- constructions. Consider again the pattern in (5), repeated below.

(8)

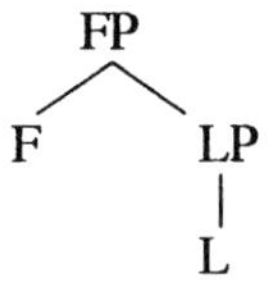

What would prevent movement of the L? Absence of the F would not, since the L could move into a higher L. What would prevent movement, rather, would be the presence of F, *where that F is filled.* In that case head movement of L into F would be blocked (F is already lexically filled), and movement to a higher head would also be blocked, by the ECP.

Thus the presence of an F could actually be constructive—signaling a kernel construction—for head movement constructions. This case is by no means academic, but occurs when the German (or English) modal position is filled. The verb stays at the end.

(9) No movement of V to I because I is already filled

Heinrich [mag [Bücher lesen]]
H. may books read
"Heinrich may read books."

More generally, the absence (or presence) of head movement can be determined by what we might call a domino theory of head movement. Suppose that the child wishes to determine the relative order of C, I, and V.

(10) C, I ,V order: one possibility

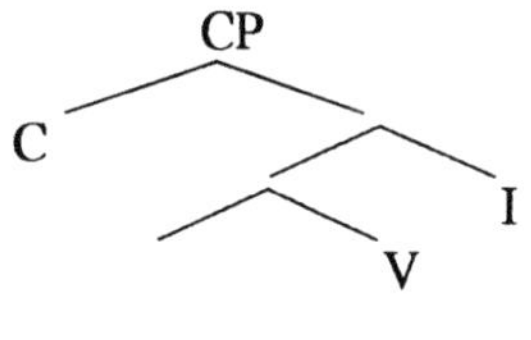

How can the child tell that V has not moved? Simply, as above. If I is filled then V cannot move into I; nor can it move into C, by the ECP. Consequently, V must be in its D-structure position. How can the child tell the ordering of all three? Again the ordering of I will just be confusing (potentially nonkernel) if C is unfilled. If C is filled (e.g., by *dass*), then I would not be able to move into it. Thus the base position of V can be determined by looking at structures with lexically filled Is; the base position of I can be determined by looking at structures with lexically filled Cs. This is a sort of domino theory because the presence of a filled head means that its c-command*ed* head must be in its base position.

Is this how the child actually proceeds with respect to heads? It seems unlikely, though possible. To determine the base position of the V (the first visibly generated category of the three) the child would first have to sort out the modal verbs (the lexical elements of I), and look specifically at constructions which contained both M and V. Thus the base position of modals, and their categoricity would have to be learned prior to the base position of Vs. This seems possible but unlikely. Similarly, to determine the base position of M/INFL, the child would have to examine structures with filled Cs. Only in such structures could the position of I with respect to C be determined. Pairs of such structures V-I (I filled), and C-I (C filled) would be sufficient to determine the positions of the heads, and in particular V. But this would mean that the functional categories would have to be learned first, counter to the outputted data. I will simply set aside the issue for now.

There is a second concern from the basic analysis presented earlier that I wish to further investigate here. It was pointed out that the absence of a (dangerous) functional category could be determined in one of two ways: directly (i.e. morphologically), and by looking at a higher subcategorizing head. In the latter case, the absence of the functional category would be determined by the subcategorizing head not subcategorizing for the F category, for example, in the subcategorization of a verb like *try*.

(11) Ich versuchte [ein Buch zu lesen]
I tried a book to read
"I tried to read a book."

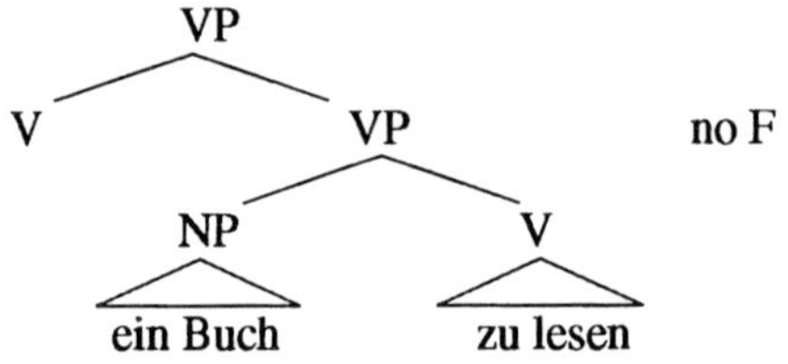

In this case, since there is no F (recall that the feature set is [+/null], not [+/-], there is no F to move into, and the structure isn't dangerous; thus it is kernel. What this requires is that some head obligatorily not subcategorize for a given functional morpheme.

While subcategorization works for this example, it is not clear that it generalizes well, and it may be that it operates differently for the cases of head movement, A'- movement, and A-movement. Consider the case of Dative Shift and Applicative constructions. Here, by hypothesis, *to* moves to an operator position, and then is construed with the verb at PF: this movement allows the permutation of the two NPs.

(12)

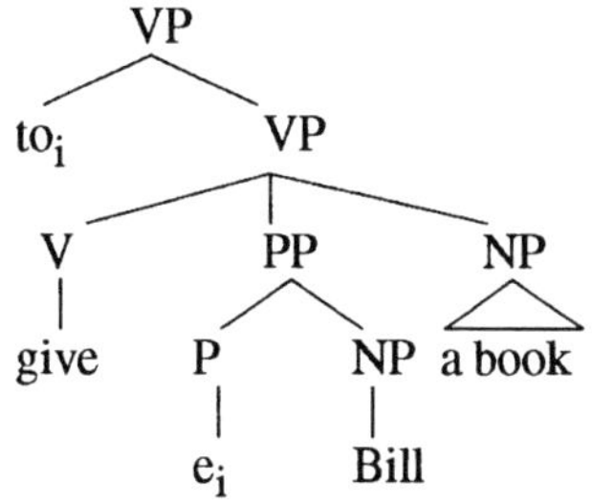

Or consider the case of a *be+ed*, preceding the VP:

(13) [be + ed [hit Bill]]

In neither of these cases is the functional morpheme precisely subcategorized for; or, more exactly, in neither of these cases is there some higher c-commanding head which would rigorously exclude *to* or *be+ed* on the periphery, and thus guarantee that the structure is kernel. That is, the presence of *to*, and of *be+ed* is at most optionally subcategorized by modals and perfective and progressive auxiliaries which dominate it. This means that *be+ed* always may occur, and never need not. This makes it fundamentally different from the case of the nonfinite marking on the embedded clause in *try [to leave]*, where the infinite form is required by some subcategorizing head.

An interesting question then arises: is there any principled syntactic difference between those heads which are subcategorized for as excluded by some subcategorizing head (e.g. [+ finite], [+*wh*]), and those which cannot be rigorously excluded by a subcategorizer (e.g. passive)? In the latter case, the child would be forced to use the direct method of detection, looking at the complex [F+L] while in the former case, only the subcategorizer would have to be looked at.

I believe that the data that I have here are too few to answer the question. At first, it appears that the following chart may be relevant.

(13)

type of movement	**signaling morpheme not subcategorized** (kernel detected by subcategorizer)
head movement	yes (e.g. finite/null)
A'-movement	yes (e.g. +*wh*, null)
A-movement	no (e.g. passive)

Here, INFL (or PROG or PERF) cannot exclude passive, and hence the subcategorizing element cannot determine the kernel. While it may appear from the examples above that A-movement is cut apart from the other two, there are also cases of A'-movement in which no subcategorizer seems to rigorously exclude the signaling morpheme (and hence the possibility of movement must be detected directed). Consider focus:

(14) a. Bill, I like.
b. I said that Bill, I like.

This presumably is either adjunction to IP, or movement to a focus phrase inside CP. Suppose that it is the latter. How are focus movement phrases excluded as nonkernel? Suppose that there is a [+FOC] feature as head of the phrase; the phrase is universally specified as [+FOC/null]; and the [+FOC] feature instantiates itself as a particular type of intonation, focus intonation.

How then is the [+FOC] phrase, a nonkernel phrase, detected? Logically, this would either directly or by subcategorization. It is clear how the direct detection would work, namely by the intonation itself. What about subcategorization? In this case, unlike with a *wh*-dependency, the presence or absence of the [+FOC] phrase doesn't appear to be subcategorized for or not: focus is optional.

(15) a. I said that I like Bill.
b. I said that Bill, I like.

Thus this A'- dependency appears to be closer to the A- dependencies noted above: detected directly rather than by looking at the subcategorizing head. This then would throw into doubt the generality of (13) above, distinguishing A-movement from the other two.

NOTES

* This paper was originally given as talks at Indiana University, GLOW parasession on language acquisition, the University of Geneva, and the University of Gröningen. Much of the research was conducted at NIAS (the Netherlands Institute of Advanced Studies), and I would like to thank both the Director of the Institute, Dr. Van de Kaa, and the members of group, led by Teun Hoekstra and Harry van der Hulst. Thanks to Tom Roeper, Steve Franks, Teun Hoekstra, and Christina Schmitt for helpful comments. Special thanks to Steve Franks, Laurie Zaring, and Johan Rooryck for a very special welcome at Indiana University, and the chance to contribute to this volume. All problems and difficulties—and there are many—are mine.

1 The situation is thus a little like that faced by Samuel Johnson, in the writing of his English Dictionary, and his patron, a Lord. The story that goes that through the long years of penury in writing the dictionary, Johnson suffered with no assistance from his patron. Yet he persisted. Finally, when he was finished, the patron offered him thanks and heartfelt congratulations.

2 Rather than using the latest Minimalist structures, including subject raising and the movement of the object to Spec, Agr O, I will use slightly archaic structures. Hopefully, this does not change the structure of the problem.

3 The actual formation of the dative, given the Larsonian shell structure would involve the adjunction of the *to* to a small V', or the inner VP shell:

4 A newer explanation given is that the deletion is possible just in case the head category agrees with the SPEC (Lobeck 1990).

5 I should also point out a potential criticism to the position above that a verbal head is construed along with its functional modifiers as a single unit at PF. This is that while in English, the functional categories are adjacent to the verb, in other languages, e.g. German and Dutch, these need not be string adjacent, and thus of course will not form

part of the same phonological phrase. This was pointed out to me by Eric Reuland. Rather than giving up the approach entirely, I would prefer to define an abstract PF for these languages, in which indeed the functional peripheral categories are grouped with the verbal head. That is, the child still forms paradigms, and PF groupings of the form F-F-F-F-V in these languages, even though the functional categories are not string adjacent. These are abstract(ly formed) paradigms for these languages.

6 I nonetheless find this possibility uncomfortable, for two reasons. First, does the verb in general need a [+finite] feature? If so, how is the derivation prevented from crashing when the verb is not finite—there is no [+finite] feature to pick up. If not, i.e. finiteness need not be picked up by the verb, what forces movement of the verb in the finite case? Recall that Greed allows only self-saving movement. This reservation notwithstanding, it seems quite possible that there is a formal association in the grammar between the L and the immediately c-commanding F element: a relation which would make movement to the F possible, but movement to some higher L impossible.

REFERENCES

Baker, Mark: 1988, *Incorporation*, University of Chicago Press, Chicago.
Bresnan, Joan: 1982, 'Control and Complementation', in Joan Bresnan (ed.), *The Mental Representation of Grammatical Relations*, MIT Press, Cambridge, MA.
Chomsky, Noam: 1957, *Syntactic Structures*, Mouton, The Hague.
———: 1965, *Aspects of the Theory of Syntax*, MIT Press, Cambridge, MA.
———: 1981, *Lectures on Government and Binding*, Foris, Dordrecht.
———: 1992, 'A Minimalist Program for Linguistic Theory', *MIT Occasional Papers in Linguistics* **1**.
Emonds, Joseph: 1976, *A Transformational Approach to English Syntax*, Academic Press, San Diego.
Grimshaw, Jane: 1981, 'Form, Function, and the Language Acquisition Device', in C. L. Baker and J. McCarthy (eds.), *The Logical Problem of Language Acquisition*, MIT Press, Cambridge, MA.
Kaisse, Ellen: 1985, *Connected Speech: The Interaction of Syntax and Phonology*, Academic Press, San Diego.
Kayne, Richard: 1994, *The Antisymmetry of Syntax*, MIT Press, Cambridge, MA.
Larson, Richard: 1988, 'On the Double Object Construction', *Linguistic Inquiry* **3**, 335-391.
Lebeaux, David: 1988, *Language Acquisition and the Form of the Grammar*, unpublished Ph.D. dissertation, University of Massachusetts, Amherst.
Lobeck, Anne: 1990, 'Functional Heads as Proper Governors', in J. Carter, R.-M. Déchaine, B. Philip, and T. Sherer (eds.), *Proceedings of the North East Linguistic Society 20*, Graduate Linguistic Student Association, University of Massachusetts, Amherst, MA.
Nespor, M. and I. Vogel: 1986, *Prosodic Phonology*, Foris, Dordrecht.
Pinker, S.: 1984, *Language Learnability and Language Development*, Harvard University Press, Cambridge, MA.
Pollock, J.-Y: 1989, 'Verb Movement, Universal Grammar, and the Structure of IP', *Linguistic Inquiry* **20**, 365-424.
Ross, J. R.: 1967, *Constraints on Variables in Syntax*, unpublished Ph.D. dissertation, MIT.
Sportiche, Dominique: 1995, 'Clitic Constructions', in Johan Rooryck and Laurie Zaring (eds.), *Phrase Structure and the Lexicon*, Kluwer, Dordrecht.
Stowell, Tim: 1982, 'The Tense of Infinitives', *Linguistic Inquiry* **13**, 561-570.
Uriagereka, Juan: 1995, 'Aspects of the Syntax of Clitic Placement in Western Romance', *Linguistic Inquiry* **26**, 79-124.

THE LEXICON AS BRIDGE BETWEEN PHRASE STRUCTURE COMPONENTS

Jerrold M. Sadock

0. PHRASE STRUCTURE GRAMMAR

Context-free phrase structure grammar (henceforth PSG) is capable of describing infinite languages consisting of finite strings drawn from a finite vocabulary and associating with each string of the target language a division into immediate constituents that can be represented as a labeled tree. This much, it would seem, is the least that we can expect of any grammar that would pretend to adequacy as a scheme for describing languages of the kind spoken by human beings. PSG has several advantages over competing systems of grammatical description. In particular:

- PSG is a conceptually simple formalism. Because PSG describes only a single level of analysis, movement rules and the constraints on them and triggers for them are eliminated. The ramifications of a postulated PSG rule are ordinarily immediately obvious and immediately testable against fact.
- PSG is completely formalizable. A finite set of rules and a finite vocabulary fully defines a PSG. The formal properties of such systems can be studied, and in fact there is a considerable formal literature on the subject. (See, for example Partee, et al. 1990 and the references it contains.). There are numerous interesting results concerning the classes of string sets and the classes of tree sets that PSGs are capable of specifying.
- PSG is computationally tractable. Quite efficient algorithms exist for parsing expressions in terms of PSGs. Though the parsing time of the best of these is still an exponential function of the length of the string, it is less disastrously so than for other formal grammar types.

No wonder, then, that PSG or its equivalent figures in one way or another in most viable theories of grammar.

1. THE ADEQUACY OF PSG

For most of the 1960's and 1970's, the prevailing view (following Chomsky 1957) was that PSGs were incapable in principle of handling the full range of sentences of natural languages, but even if they were able, technically speaking, to specify the correct sets, they could do so only with difficulty, artificiality, and lack of generality. On this basis, PSG, despite its obvious advantages, was rejected in favor of the much more powerful and mathematically uncertain theory of transformational grammar. As Chomsky wistfully put it in a preface to a textbook on mathematical linguistics (Gross and Lentin 1970):

> The schema for grammatical description that seems empirically motivated by the facts of particular languages specifies a class of systems that are for the moment, much too complex for fruitful and far-reaching mathematical investigation; furthermore, it must be borne in mind that any proposals that can be made today concerning this universal schema are both highly tentative and also somewhat loose in important respects. At the same time, there have been interesting and suggestive studies of much more restricted schemata for grammatical description—the theory of so-called 'context-free languages' is the primary example—but these systems are surely empirically inadequate.

Most of the perceived problems with PSG as a model of language center around the fact that a single structure such as PSG provides fails to capture a number of important principles of the organization of language. Natural languages seem to be organized into competing structures such as TG offers in the form of D(eep)S(tructure), S(urface)S(tructure), P(honological)F(orm) and L(ogical)F(orm). Thus ordinary surface structure does not seem a very good model of the meaning relations in natural-language sentences (pace work in Montague Grammar (e.g. Dowty, et al. 1981)), morphological features of the structure of expressions are sometimes at odds with apparent syntactic structure, and finally, various stylistic features of expressions perturb the government relations that play a role in Case assignment, agreement, and so forth. To remedy these apparent insufficiencies, Chomsky suggested enriching PSG with a transformational component that maps the trees that are output of a PSG to other trees. While the result is certainly powerful enough to remedy the empirical failings, it does so at the cost of losing the clarity, formality, and mathematical handiness of PSG.

2. THE REEMERGENCE OF PSG

In a move of astonishing intellectual independence, Gazdar (see, for example, Gazdar et al. 1985) challenged the transformational view, and in a series of papers, he and a group of followers demonstrated that most of the supposed proofs of the literal inadequacy of PSG were fallacious, and that by copious use of various abbreviatory devices, there seemed to be a hope of constructing elegant and general grammars within the restricted framework. As research in this model continued, though, the bright promise of the new theory of G(eneralized) P(hrase) S(tructure) G(rammar) began to dull.

The last major work in GPSG was the rather ponderous overview of the theory, Gazdar et al. (1985). To its credit, this work is as formal as it needs to be, leaving few if any definitions up in the air. This laudable rigor has its downside, however: the resulting theory is cumbersome and intricate, especially as regards the relation of syntax to meaning. Furthermore, the theory is incomplete in that it lacks a fully formal morphology. Few researchers seemed to find this the paradigm of their dreams, and GPSG rapidly faded from the scene after the publication of Gazdar et al. (1985).

3. MULTIPLE PSG

There is a way of hewing largely to PSG while overcoming its major disadvantages. Suppose we take a grammar to consist of several phrase structure grammars including one for the (surface) syntax, one for the semantics, and one for the morphology, as originally suggested in Sadock (1985). This model, called Autolexical syntax (ALS), provides the multiple representations as in TG that seem necessary to describe language naturally while retaining all of the computational advantages of PSG (since it consists of PSGs). Perhaps surprisingly, it offers greater descriptive power than any individual PSG. While the formal properties of multiple PSGs are just beginning to be uncovered (Latta 1993), it has been known since Scheinberg (1960) that the languages that lie at the intersection of those specified by PSGs include languages that cannot be parsed by any single PSG.

In multiple PSG, and particularly in ALS, the independent grammars are integrated principally through the agency of the lexicon, a list of the basic expressions of the language with explicit indications of the role that they play in the several autonomous modules.

A distinct advantage of multiple PSG as opposed to TG is that the various competing descriptions of composition of an expression are realistic. Only genuine morphological information is to be found in the morphological representations and only genuine semantic information in the semantic structures. In TG, at least as it is commonly practiced nowadays, the levels DS, LF, and even SS are quite abstract and unavailable to intuition. Thus in works in the Minimalist framework, DS has become a level in which certain essentially semantic elements, some purely morphological elements, and a number of rather abstract syntactic elements are uncomfortable bedfellows.

Treating each of the fundamental modules of grammar as an independent PSG has a further attraction: it allows for the simplification of each. The complexities of language that lead Chomsky to postulate the vastly more flexible scheme of transformational grammar can often be handled as the interaction of individually simple components with competing demands. I will illustrate this below with a brief discussion of two phenomena that would require quite complex accounts at a single level but turn out to receive very straightforward descriptions in terms of independently justifiable autonomous levels of description.

4. ENGLISH COMPLEMENTATION

One of the major accomplishments of early TG was Rosenbaum's (1967) theory of the classes of English complement-taking verbs. Put rather crudely, what Rosenbaum suggested was that the deep structures in which the various types of verbs are found are reasonable approximations of semantic representation. These deep structures were then transformed through a complicated series of transformational rules, some obligatory, and some optional.

Rosenbaum's idea can be adapted in an obvious way in the multimodular theory. The different classes will have partly different combinatoric properties in syntax and semantics. In particular, the two kinds of Raising verbs and the two types of Equi verbs (i.e. control verbs) will have one of two types of syntax, subcategorizing either a VP alone, or an NP and a VP, and one of three types of semantics, being either functions from propositions to propositions (i.e., intransitive operators, IOPs), or functions from propositions to functions from entity expressions to propositions (transitive operators, or TOPs), or functions from propositions to functions from entity expressions to functions from entity expressions to propositions (ditransitive operators, or DTOPs), all standard sorts of semantic objects in the logical literature. This typology is displayed in the following chart.

Figure 1. A Verb Typology

Semantic type / Syntactic type	IOP	TOP	DTOP
[__ VP]	a. *seem*	b. *try*	c. --
[__ NP VP]	d. --	e. *believe*	f. *persuade*

Some of the phenomena that motivate the classical distinction among types of complement-taking verbs fall directly out of this simple theory involving independent syntactic and semantic combinatorics. The type (b) 'Obligatory Equi' verbs like *try* never have an expressed complement subject: **John tried (for) Bill to leave*. This follows directly from their syntactic subcategorization properties, which disallow an NP in this position. There is no need to make these verbs "positive absolute exceptions" (Lakoff 1970) or for an ad hoc assumption that they are verbs of "obligatory control" (Chomsky 1981), or anything else. We simply observe that such verbs have the syntax we see them display.

The type (f) 'Object-Controlled Equi' verbs like *persuade* cannot have expletive or idiom-chunk direct objects. This follows from the fact that expletives and idiom chunks lack the semantic status of arguments. Since verbs of this type combine semantically with propositions to form the semantic counterparts of transitive verb phrases, there must be two full-fledged semantic arguments outside of the inner proposition. **John persuaded there to be a riot* is ungrammatical (strictly speaking, unsemantical) because there is only one NP in the verb's clause to count as an argument. It is unsemantical for much the same reason that **John gave there a book* is: *there* lacks the semantic status of an argument.

Types (a) and (e), i.e. Raising verbs, allow semantically empty NPs in the position to which an NP is raised (to cast it in the terms of classical transformational grammar). Since these verbs have an NP in a syntactic position that corresponds to no semantic position, the subject of Raising-to-Subject verbs, and the object of Raising-to-Object verbs will be allowed to be semantically empty, or part of an idiom, just in case that sort of meaning has semantics appropriate to combining with the meaning of the VP complement to form a proposition.

Many of the verbs in classes above alternate between taking infinitive complements and *that*-clause complements. This is a function of the fact that all of the verbs in question are operators, i.e., functions from propositions to some other category. Since *that*-clauses ordinarily express propositions, it is not surprising that many of these verbs can take clausal complements as well.

With *that*-clauses, the verbs in question do not take a direct object if the form with the infinitive does, and they take an expletiveexpletive subject if the form with the infinitive has no direct object. These facts follow from the semantics of the verbs. With a meaningful subject and a clausal complement, a verb like *seem* would occur with too many semantic arguments to form a well-formed expression. *Ann seems that Bill has left* is syntactically well formed, but unsemantical since its only semantic argument is filled by the meaning of the complement S.

I believe that straightforward explanations like this lurk in disguised form behind the combination of the Theta Criterion and Case requirements of syntactic theories following Chomsky (1981). The Theta Criterion is nothing more, it seems to me, than the requirement that semantic structure be well formed and the Case Filter simply the requirement that superficial syntax be well formed. In a multimodular system, wellformedness is given directly in terms of the PSGs of the various levels. There is no need for auxiliary statements like the Theta Criterion or Case Filter in such a system of grammar. There cannot be either more or fewer arguments at any level of description than the PSG rules of that level provide for.

Furthermore, Theta Theory and Case Theory are fraught with well known difficulties and so far, at least, have defied full formalization. In terms of independent PSGs for syntax and semantics, all that is required for making the properties of the verbs above fully explicit is a syntactic grammar such as (1), a semantic grammar such as (2), and a lexicon like that in (3) that serves as a bridge between the two grammars.

(1) Syntax
(i) S --> NP VP
(ii) VP --> V[1] VP
(1) (iii) VP --> V[2] NP VP
(iv) VP --> V[3] S

(2) Semantics
(i) PROP --> ARG IV
(ii) IV --> ARG TV
(iii) PROP --> IOP PROP
(iv) IV --> TOP PROP
(v) TV --> DTOP PROP

(3) Lexicon
(i) *try*:
syntax = V[1]
semantics = TOP

(ii) *seem*:
syntax = V[1] or V[3]
semantics = IOP

(iii) *believe*:
syntax = V[2] or V[3]
semantics = TOP

(iv) *it* (expletive):
syntax = NP
semantics = nil

There is obviously much more to English than what I am able to present here. Considerably more detail on the multimodular treatment of English complementation can be found in Kathman (to appear).

5. WEST GREENLANDIC REFLEXIVE REFERENCE

As a second example of how several individually simple phrase structure grammars linked by the lexicon can conspire to produce a very complex pattern, I will briefly discuss reflexive reference in West Greenlandic. Reflexive reference is signaled in this language by personal inflection on nouns and verbs, by certain categories of verbal mood, and by some stems. Here I will discuss only personal inflection, though with appropriate addenda, the treatment given will extend to the other mechanisms as well. A much more thorough discussion than it is possible for me to provide here can be found in Sadock (1994).

5.1 *Basic clause structure*

Clauses of West Greenlandic are either transitive or intransitive. Transitive clauses include both an ergative and an absolutive NP, while intransitive clauses contain only an absolutive. I will refer to the ergative of a transitive clause or the absolutive of an intransitive clause as the 'highest term' of the clause. The verb of an intransitive clause is inflected for the person and number of the absolutive term and the verb of a transitive clause is inflected for the person and number of both the absolutive and ergative terms.

5.2. *Possessive inflection*

Nouns are inflected for the person and number of the possessor (an ergative case NP). The personal category can be 1, 2, 3, or 3R, the reflexive. A reflexive possessor ordinarily refers to the highest term of the clause in which it is found. An important exception arises in the case of verbs derived with one of a small number of transitivizing suffixes. With such verbs, the reflexive can refer ambiguously to the ergative or the absolutive of a transitive clause (compare (5) with (6)).

(4)	Hansi	illuminit	aallarpoq.	
	Hans(ABS)	house-3RS-from	left-3S	
	"Hans$_i$ left from his$_i$ house."			

(5)	Hansip	Nuka	illuminit	suaarfigaa.
	Hans(ERG)	Nuka(ABS)	house-3RS-from	yelled.to-3S/3S
	"Hans$_i$ yelled to Nuka$_j$ from his$_i$ house."			

(6)	Hansip	Nuka	illuminit	aallartippaa.
	Hans(ERG)	Nuka(ABS)	house-3RS-from	made-leave3S/3S
	"Hans$_i$ made Nuka$_j$ leave from his$_{i/j}$ house."			

5.3. *Verbal inflection*

In the independent moods, which are used only for main clauses, there is no reflexive inflection at all. Neither the category that agrees with the ergative in a transitive verb nor the category that agrees with the absolutive can be 3R. In the subordinate moods reflexive inflection is possible for either the ergative or absolutive agreement categories, but not both at the same time. (Ergative agreement is the first of two personal categories listed in morpheme glosses; absolutive agreement is the second.) Any 3R inflection on a subordinate clause verb refers to the highest term of a higher clause.

(7)	Hansi	oqarpoq	aallarluni.	
	Hansi (ABS)	said	left-CONJ/3Ri	
	"Hans$_i$ said that he$_i$ had left."			

(8)	Hansip	Nuka	oqarfigaa	aallarluni.	
	Hansi (ERG)	Nukaj (ABS)	tell	left-CONJ/3RSi	
	"Hans$_i$ told Nuka$_j$ that he$_i$ had left."				

(9)	Hansi	qiavoq	Nukap	naveermani.
	Hans(ABS)	cried	Nuka(ERG)	scold-PSUB/3S/3RS
	"Hans$_i$ cried because Nuka$_j$ scolded him$_i$."			

(10)	Hansi	qiavoq	Nuka	naveeramiuk.
	Hans(ABS)	cried	Nuka(ABS)	scold-PSUB/3RS/3S
	"Hans$_i$ cried because he$_i$ scolded Nuka$_j$"			

5.4. *Possessive inflection in subordinate clauses*

A 3R nominal inflection on the highest term of a subordinate clause refers to the highest term of a higher clause.

(11)	Hansi	oqarpoq	ernini	ajortoq.
	H.(ABS)	say	son-ABS/3RS	sick-PART/3S
	"Hans$_i$ said that his$_i$ son was sick."			

A 3R possessor of anything but the highest term of a subordinate clause refers ambiguously to the highest term of its own clause or the highest term of a higher clause.

(12)	Hansi	oqarpoq	Piitap	ernini	asagaa.
	H(ABS)	say	P(ERG)	son-ABS/3RS	love-PART/3S/3S
	"Hans$_i$ said that Piitaq$_j$ loves his$_{i/j}$ son."				

5.5 *Analysis*

This complex and unusual pattern of reference can be shown to arise from the interaction of three individually simple and independently justifiable aspects of West Greenlandic grammar. A fuller and more formal treatment can be found in Sadock (1994). The crux of the analysis is the idea that syntactic representation, semantic representation, and the morphological structure can be partially at odds with each other.

5.6. *Syntax*

There is no evidence such as we find in English for a syntactic VP in West Greenlandic. I therefore conclude that West Greenlandic clauses have flat constituent structure with respect to the ergative and absolutive terms. The basic clause rules, then, are:

(13) S --> NP[ERG) NP[ABS] VP[+TRNS]
(14) S --> NP[ABS] VP[-TRNS]

NPs are structured by the following rule, where NP[ERG] is the possessor NP:

(15) NP --> NP[ERG) N

5.7. *Semantics*

The semantic structure of West Greenlandic, as opposed to the syntax, is configurational. There is a great deal of semantic evidence for a constituent For example, there is a stem *taamaalior-* 'to do as has just been described' that refers to semantic predicates:

(16) Hansi aallarpoq. Piitar-li taamaaliorumanngilaq.
Hans left. Piitaq-however not.want.to.do.so
"Hans left. But Piitaq didn't want to do so (leave)."

(17) Hansip neqi nerivaa. Piitar-li taamaaliorumanngilaq.
Hans meat eat. Piitaq-however not.want.to.do.so
"Hans ate the meat. But Piitaq didn't want to (eat the meat)."

Thus the PS rules for this much of semantic structure are the same as those for English, namely (2i) and (2ii) above. I will refer to the ARG that combines with an IV to form a PROP as the semantic subject, following Dowty (1982).

5.8. *Morphology*

Morphologically, it is necessary to distinguish between stems and words. Derivational affixes combine with stems to form new stems; inflections combine with stems to form words:

(18) STEM[a] --> STEM[b] AF (a, b = N or V)
(19) WORD[a] --> STEM[a] INF

5.9. *Lexicon*

With this much simple and cross-linguistically ordinary structure in three components, all that is needed is an appropriate lexicon to forge the connection between the independent modules. Ordinary intransitive and transitive verbs will be semantic IV and TV expressions, respectively.

(20) *aallar-* ('leave'):
syntax = V[-TRNS]
semantics = IV

(21) *suaarfig-* ('yell-to'):
syntax = V[+TRNS]
semantics = TV

It is the lexical properties of affixes that give West Greenlandic its special synthetic character. For one thing, the personal inflections on nouns and verbs sometimes count as both semantic arguments and syntactic terms. The possessive inflections, for example, count as ergative NPs (cf. rule (15)) and as arguments in the appropriate semantic structures of possessives (which I will not specify further here). Thus the reflexive possessor inflection in (11) and (12) will have a lexical representation like that in (22).

(22) *-ni* syntax = NP[ERG, 3Rs])
semantics = ARG(r)
morphology = INF (viz. N --> N[ABS, 3Rs])

The verbal inflections can likewise count as terms in syntactic structure and arguments in semantic structure. The contemporative mood inflection in (7) and (8), for example, adds an absolutive NP in syntax:

(23) *-luni* syntax = (NP[ABS, 3Rs])
semantics = ARG(r)
morphology = INF (viz. V --> V[CONT, 3Rs])

The last sort of affix that needs to be discussed is the verb-to-verb derivational suffix of the kind represented by example (6). Contrary to suggestions that have been made elsewhere, there is no need to represent these as being the analogs of complement-taking verbs in the syntax so long as we recognize that they are operators in the semantics. A sentence containing a complex verb like *aallartippaa* in (6) will thus be monoclausal in syntax, but bipropositional in semantic structure. The required lexical entry will be along the lines of (24).

(24) *-tit-* ('make, cause')
syntax = nil
semantics = TOP
morphology = AF (viz. V --> V[+TRNS])

5.10. *The meaning of the reflexive category*

The last piece in the puzzle is a statement about the actual meaning of the reflexive in West Greenlandic, that is to say, a statement concerning what may count as an antecedent of the reflexive variable that the 3R suffixes such as those in (22) and (23) introduce in the semantics. There are two such requirements, one referring to semantic structure, and one referring to the independent semantic structure in which the affix is found:

(25) The variable *r* refers to an antecedent which is:
a. syntactically an NP that C-commands the term with *r* in its meaning and not vice versa
b. semantically an argument that combines with an IV to form a proposition (i.e., a semantic subject)

5.11. *Accounting for the data*

The rather complex array of data discussed above is predicted by the tricomponential analysis just given. First, the fact that reflexives in general refer only to the highest term of a clause, the ergative of a transitive or the absolutive of an intransitive, comes from the semantic requirement in (25). Although both the terms of the clause meet the syntactic requirement of (25) in a sentence such as (5) or (8), only the ergative meets the semantic requirement. When there is a complex verb forming affix, however, the semantic structure will contain two propositions, each of which has a semantic subject. Thus in an example like (6), both terms meet both of the requirements in (25) and the sentence is ambiguous.

Next consider the fact that the independent moods do not allow inflection for the reflexive category. This follows from the assumption that the verbal inflections are the terms of the clause. Since the terms of a West Greenlandic clause c-command each other, neither can have the other as an antecedent, and since the independent moods do not occur embedded, there would be no possibility of a 3R inflection in one of them finding an antecedent in the other. In subordinate moods, the personal inflections also count as terms in the clause, so once again a reflexive in this position will not be able to refer to another term of the same clause. But since subordinate moods do occur embedded, their reflexive terms will be able to have antecedents in higher clauses.

Lastly, let us examine possessive inflections. In main clauses both the ergative and absolutive term asymmetrically c-command the inflection, which is syntactically a possessive NP within an NP. If one of these is also a semantic subject, then it may therefore count as an antecedent. Now let us consider subordinate clauses. If the possessor is on the highest term of a subordinate clause, then the antecedent will have to be in a higher clause, since there is either no other term in the same clause to c-command it, or there is another term, but it is not a semantic subject. In any other position in a subordinate clause, a possessive will be able to refer to a c-commanding NP that is a semantic subject either in the same clause or in a higher clause.

7. CONCLUSIONS

What I hope to have shown through the examples from English and West Greenlandic that I have discussed is that phrase structure and lexicon, the twin topics of this series of lectures, can together offer insightful descriptions of linguistic fact. To allow them to do so, however, it is crucial that we recognize not just one phrase structure grammar, but, as I have been arguing for quite some time now, several independent ones, each corresponding to a separate dimension of linguistic organization.

REFERENCES

Chomsky, Noam: 1957, *Syntactic Structures*, Mouton, The Hague.

———: 1981, *Lectures on Government and Binding*, Foris, Dordrecht.

Dowty, David R.: 1982, 'Grammatical Relations and Montague Grammar', in P. Jacobson and G. K. Pullum (eds.), *The Nature of Syntactic Representation*, D. Reidel, Dordrecht, pp. 79-130.

Dowty, David, Robert Wall and Stanley Peters: 1981, *Introduction to Montague Semantics*, D. Reidel, Dordrecht.

Gross, Maurice and André Lentin: 1970, *Introduction to Formal Grammars*, Springer-Verlag, New York.

Gazdar, Gerald, Ewan Klein, Geoffrey K. Pullum, and Ivan A. Sag: 1985, *Generalized Phrase Structure Grammar*, Blackwell, Oxford.

Kathman, David: to appear, 'Control in Autolexical Syntax', in Eric Schiller and Elisa Steinberg (eds.), *Autolexical Syntax: Ideas and Methods*, Mouton, the Hague.

Lakoff, George: 1970, *Irregularity in Syntax*, Holt, Rinehart and Winston, New York.

Latta, Michael John: 1993, *The Intersection of Context-Free Languages*, unpublished Ph.D. dissertation, University of Texas, Austin.

Partee, Barbara H., Alice ter Meulen, and Robert E. Wall (eds.): 1990, *Mathematical Methods in Linguistics*, Kluwer, Dordrecht.

Rosenbaum, Peter: 1967, *The Grammar of English Predicate Complement Constructions*, MIT Press, Cambridge, MA.

Sadock, Jerrold M.: 1985, 'Autolexical syntax: A theory of noun incorporation and similar phenomena', *Natural Language and Linguistic Theory* **3**, 379-440.

———: 1991, *Autolexical Syntax: A Theory of Parallel Grammatical Representations*, University of Chicago Press, Chicago.

———: 1994, 'Reflexive Reference in West Greenlandic', in J. Goldsmith, S. Mufwene, B. Need, and D. Testen (eds.), *Contemporary Linguistics* **1**, Department of Linguistics, University of Chicago, Chicago, pp. 137-160.

Scheinberg, Stephan: 1960, 'Notes on the Boolean Properties of Context Free Languages', *Information and Control* **3**, 372-375.

Schiller, Eric and Elisa Steinberg (eds.): to appear, *Autolexical Syntax: Ideas and Methods*, Mouton, the Hague.

NULL OBJECTS IN FUNCTIONAL PROJECTIONS*

Margaret Speas

0. INTRODUCTION

Virtually all recent studies of null pronouns follow Rizzi (1986) in assuming that null pronouns must meet a *licensing* condition and an *identification* condition. The majority of investigations of these two conditions have focused on null Subjects, for which elements of INFL are generally implicated in both licensing and identification.

When we look at the distribution of null objects, interesting problems arise with both the licensing and the identification conditions. The goal of this paper is to address some of these problems by looking primarily at data on the distribution of null Objects in Navajo. Navajo is an interesting case, because it does have object agreement morphology, and it does allow null objects, but null objects are allowed only if the subject is also null. Thus, it has looked like rich object agreement is not always sufficient to license null objects.

I will propose that an identification condition based upon a general principle of control, following Huang (1984, 1988), governs the distribution of Navajo null objects. This proposal raises two questions. First, with a Huang-style identification condition on *pro*, is a separate licensing condition necessary, and if so, what form should it take? Second, in what ways can the identification condition vary cross-linguistically?

This paper will be organized as follows: in Section 1, I will introduce the Navajo data, and will provide an account of the Navajo facts which adapts the Generalized Control Rule of Huang (1984). In Section 2, I will discuss the nature of licensing conditions on null arguments, and will argue that the licensing condition ought be stated not in terms of licensing by a designated head, but instead in terms of economy of projection. I will also briefly discuss the issue of possible parameterization of the relevant principles.

1. ON NULL OBJECTS IN NAVAJO

1.1. *Navajo Null Objects and the Generalized Control Rule*

Navajo has a fairly rigid SOV word order, with rich verbal morphology[1] and no Case morphemes on NPs, as illustrated in (1) and (2).

(1) a. At'ééd ashkii yidootsǫ́s
boy girl 3O-3S-will:kiss
"The boy will kiss the girl."

b. Yidoots'ǫ́s
"S/he will kiss him/her."

(2) Mósí tsís'ná yiishish
cat bee 3O-3S-stings
"The cat stings the bee." NOT "The bee stings the cat."

As (1b) shows, both Subject and Object may be null in Navajo. However, the interesting fact is illustrated by (3) and (4). Here, we see that if a transitive sentence has only one overt NP, that NP must be interpreted as the Object. Such a sentence cannot have an interpretation in which there is a null object and the overt NP is the subject, even if a somewhat anomalous interpretation results, as in (4).

(3) Ashkii yiyiiłtsą́ *pro* NP V
boy 3O-3sgS-saw
"He/she/it saw the boy."
NOT: "The boy saw him/her/it." *NP *pro* V

(4) Tsís'ná yiishish
bee 3O-3S-stings
"He/she/it stings the bee." NOT "The bee stings him/her/it."

As Platero (1978, 1982) pointed out, it appears that these sentences are subject to a constraint whereby a null third person argument cannot be preceded by an overt third person argument.

(5) *NP-PRO CONSTRAINT*:
If PRO immediately follows an overt noun phrase NP', it must be coreferential with NP'. (Platero 1982:288)

This constraint is essentially identical to the Generalized Control Rule proposed by Huang (1984, 1988) for Mandarin and Portuguese.

(6) *GENERALIZED CONTROL RULE*:
Coindex an empty pronominal with the closest nominal element.

Since the GCR is obligatory, it has the effect of creating a violation of Principle B of the Binding Theory whenever it applies to a null pronominal in object position. However, a crucial feature of the Navajo facts is that the constraint on null objects only holds if the subject NP is overt. Null objects are fine if the subject is also null.

This fact (among others) has led Jelinek (1984) and Willie (1991) to conclude that Navajo uses a set of string-dependent mapping principles to relate overt NPs to argument positions. As Willie states it, the person/number marking morphemes on the verb serve as pronominal arguments, and the NPs are adjuncts, which are related to the pronominal arguments by means of a set of mapping rules. The rule which accounts for the constraint on null objects is shown in (7).

(7) When a transitive sentence has only one adjunct, that adjunct is interpreted as coindexed with the object (patient) argument.
(Willie 1991:59)

In Willie's discussion of this rule, she presents a number of intriguing counterexamples, in which certain features of the verb appear to 'override' the word order convention. Her examples are given in (8).

(8) a. Ashkii yiyííbį́į́'
boy 3O-3S-picked:round:objects
"The boy picked them."

b. Ashkii yiyííłta'
boy 3O-3S-count:pl.:objects
"The boy counted them."

c. Ashkii yóldon
boy 3O-3S-shooting
"The boy is shooting at it."

These observations of Willie's led me to investigate the question of exactly what sorts of features allow the mapping principle to be overridden. It has generally been assumed in the literature that whatever principle is operating here functions to eliminate ambiguity, and so one might simply think that the mapping principle can be overridden whenever the verb gives enough information to avoid ambiguity. However, I will show some additional Navajo facts that suggest that the mapping strategy has more to do with syntactic agreement and less to do with avoidance of ambiguity than has previously been thought.[2]

1.2. *The Distribution of Null Objects in Navajo*

My investigation indicates that sentences in Navajo which allow null objects fall into three types. In the first type, pointed out by Platero (1978), the object agreement morpheme is other than neutral third person. In (9a), the object is first person singular, in (9b) the object is second person singular, and in (9c), and object is first or second person duoplural.

(9) a. Hastiin nashiłté
man 1sgO-3S-carry:around
"The man is carrying me around."

b. Hastiin nigháád
man 2sgO-3S-shaking
"The man is shaking you."

c. Hastiin nihigháád.
man 1/2plO-3S-shaking
"The man is shaking you(dpl)/us."

Into this group, I would also put the examples of what has been called the 'inverse' construction. Navajo has two different markers of third person object. The examples shown above have the marker *-yi*, and in these cases the word order is SOV. The other third person marker is *-bi*, and when the *bi* marker is used, the word order is OSV. I have argued in previous work that *bi* is an incorporated pronoun, so that object in a *bi* sentence is in a dislocated position, as represented in (11).

(10) a. Łį́į́' dzaanééz *yiztał*.
horse mule *yi*-kicked
"The horse kicked the mule."

b. Łį́į́' dzaanééz *biztał*.
horse mule *bi*-kicked
"The mule kicked the horse."[3]

(11) Łį́į́'$_i$ [$_S$ dzaanééz *bi*$_i$ - ztał]
horse mule *bi* - kicked
"The horse, the mule kicked it." (=the mule kicked the horse)

Platero shows that when the *bi*-construction features a single overt NP, it is interpreted as the subject:

(12) Dzaanééz *biztał*.
mule *bi*-kicked
"The mule kicked it." NOT "It kicked the mule."

Superficially, at least, sentences like (12) have the same structure as the sentences with one NP plus first or second person agreement: There is a null object, which is apparently licensed by the presence of the marker of object agreement.

(13) Dzaanééz e *biz*tał.

So, I suggest that one type of sentence which allows a null object is that in which the object agreement morpheme on the verb licenses the null object. These are illustrated in (14).

(14) a. Hastiin na*shi* łté
man 1sgO-3S-carry:around
"The man is carrying me around."

b. Dzaanééz *bi*iiłtsą́
mule 3O-3S-saw
"The mule saw him/her/it."

The second type of null object sentence occurs when the object is an indefinite or interrogative pronoun. In a transitive sentence with two overt NPs, if the first NP is indefinite or interrogative, the sentence is ambiguous, with the indefinite or interrogative being interpretable as either Subject or Object.

(15) a. Háísh Kii yizts'ǫ́s.
who Kii 3O-3S-kissed
"Who kissed Kii?"
OR "Who did Kii kiss?"

b. Kii háísh yizts'ǫ́s.
Kii who 3O-3S-kissed
"Who kissed Kii?"

(16) a. £a'da ashkii yidoots'ǫ́s.
somebody boy 3O-3S-will:kiss
"Somebody will kiss the boy." OR
"The boy will kiss somebody."

b. Ashkii ła'da yidoots'ǫ́s.
boy somebody 3O-3S-will:kiss
"The boy will kiss somebody."

I suggest that in sentences like (15a) and (16a), the indefinite or interrogative may either be in subject position, or may be interpreted as having been fronted to an A' position, leaving a variable in object position. Thus, in this second type of null object sentence, the object is an A' bound variable rather than a null pronoun. This type of sentence is an interesting counterexample to the hypothesis that null objects are allowed whenever the verb can somehow disambiguate the sentence. Null objects are allowed here even though the relevant sentences are ambiguous.

My hypothesis is that sentences (15a) and (16a) are ambiguous because they may involve a variable in object position, and not because of any other property of indefinites and interrogatives. This hypothesis predicts that if an indefinite or interrogative were the only overt NP in a transitive sentence, the sentence would be unambiguous. The indefinite or interrogative may occupy object position, or could bind a variable in object position, but cannot occur as Subject with a null pronominal as object, since there is no special property of the indefinite or interrogative that allows this. This prediction is right, as shown in (17).

(17) a. Háísh yizts'ǫ́s.
who 3O-3S-kissed
"Who did he/she kiss?"
NOT *"Who kissed him/her?"

b. £a'da yidoots'ǫ́s.
Somebody 3O-3S-will:kiss
"He/she will kiss somebody."
NOT "Somebody will kiss him/her."

A null object which is a variable also seems to be occurring for some speakers in contexts in which the object has been made heavily topical. For some speakers, a null object is possible in a question-answer pair like that in (18).

(18) S1: Háísh Kii yizts'ǫ́s.
who Kii 3O-3S-kissed
"Who kissed Kii?"

S2: Mary yizts'ǫ́s.
M 3O-3S-kissed
"Mary kissed him." (some speakers)

Here, I would follow Huang (1984)'s analysis of Mandarin, and suggest that the answer to the question contains a null topic, which binds a variable in object position.

(19) OP [Mary t yizts'ǫ́s]

The third type of null object sentence is represented by Willie's examples. In these, the agreement morpheme is the neutral third person *-yi*, yet apparently some other feature of the verb exceptionally allows a null object. Willie suggests that the relevant feature is that the subject is animate.

(20) a. Ashkii yiyíínbįį́'
boy 3O-3S-picked:round:objects
"The boy picked them."

b. Ashkii yiyííłta'
boy 3O-3S-count:pl.:objects
"The boy counted them."

However, further investigation indicates that animacy cannot be the crucial feature. In (21) and (22), the subject is necessarily animate, yet a null object is not possible. When asked about the well-formedness of (21b) and (22b), consultants say that it sounds like you are saying that someone is boiling the woman/someone is weaving the woman. The null object reading seems not to be available, and consultants say that these examples contrast with examples like (20), in which the null object reading is preferred.

(21) a. Asdzą́ą́ atoo' yiyiiłbéézh (not a handling stem)
woman stew 3-3-boiling
"The woman is boiling the stew."

b. Asdzą́ą́ yiyiiłbéézh
woman 3-3-boiling
"S/he is boiling the woman."
(???*"The woman is boiling it.")

(22) a. Asdzą́ą́ diyogi yitł 'ó.
woman rug 3O-3S-weaving
"The woman is weaving the rug."

b. Asdzą́ą́ yitł 'ó.
woman 3O-3S-weaving
"He/she is weaving the woman."
(???*"The woman is weaving it.")

(23) a. Ashiiké didzé ndayizhjaa'
boys berry PL-3O-3S-brought-rnd-Os
"The boys brought berries."

b. Ashiiké ndayizhjaa'
boys PL-3O-3S-brought-rnd-Os
"The boys brought them."
(or, "S/he brought the little round boys.")

I suggest that rather than animacy, the relevant factor is that the verb in the null object examples is one of the type called handling stems. These stems are for the verbs of motion and handling, and they classify the theme of the action according to size, shape, consistency and sometimes number. Some examples of these verbs are given in (24).

(24) a. *Slender stiff object*:
Nástáán ła' dzídzáátą́
log a 3O-fire-1sgS-handle:SSO
"I put a log into the fire."

Ashkii bee'ak'e'elchíhí ła' shaa yinítą́
boy pencil a me-to 3O-3sgS-handle:SSO
"The boy gave me a pencil."

b. *Flat flexible object*:
Naaltsoos dzídzááłtsooz
paper 3O-fire-1sgS-handle:FFO
"I put the paper into the fire."

Ashkii naaltsoos shaa yiníłtsooz
boy paper me-to 3O-3sgS-handle:FFO
The boy brought me the paper."

c. *Multiple small round objects:*
Yoo' níléidi shijaa'
beads over-there sitting:round:plO
"The beads are sitting over there."

Kii didzé yíjááh
Kii berry 3O-3S-carrying:round:pl:O
"Kii is carrying them (round objects)."

With this type of stem, the object apparently may always be null:

(25) a. Ashkii shaa yinítą́
boy me-to 3O-3sgS-handle:SSO
"The boy gave it/one to me."

b. Kii nistsóós
Kii 3O-3S-carrying:flat:flexible:O
"Kii is carrying it (flat flexible object, e.g.,. paper)."

c. Kii yíjááh
Kii 3O-3S-carrying:round:pl:O
"Kii is carrying them (round objects)."

I suggest that the handling stems manifest a kind of lexical agreement, which is distinct from the inflectional agreement system of Navajo. Thus, in the null object sentences with handling stems, lexical agreement features are either licensing or identifying the null object.

That Navajo does have two distinct systems of agreement can be seen by facts such as those in (26), where we can see the two systems operating independently. In (26a, b), the verb stem is one which classifies for singular actors. The stem in (26c) is one which classifies for plural actors. In (26d), the syntactic subject of the intransitive verb is first person singular, yet the stem for plural actors is used. This is because the understood number of people walking is plural.

(26) a. Shí yi-sh-áál
I prog-1sgS-sg:walk
"I am walking along."

b. Kii yi-0-gááł
Kii prog-3S-walk
"Kii is walking along."

c. Ashiiké yi-0-kah
boys prog-3S-pl:walk
"The boys are walking along."

d. Shí ashiiké bił yi-sh-kah
I boys with prog-1sgS-pl:walk
"I am walking with the boys."

Adapting an analysis by Hale (1975), I suggest that *shí ashiiké bił* ('I with the boys.') forms a constituent at D-Structure, and that this constituent is in the VP-internal subject position. The first person NP moves to the specifier of IP at S-Structure. Hence, at D-Structure, the verb undergoes VP-internal lexical agreement, with the plural actors, and then at S-structure the NP *shi* undergoes syntactic agreement with INFL. This is diagrammed in .

(27) Shí ashiiké bił yi-sh-kah
I boys with prog-1sgS-pl:walk
"I am walking with the boys."

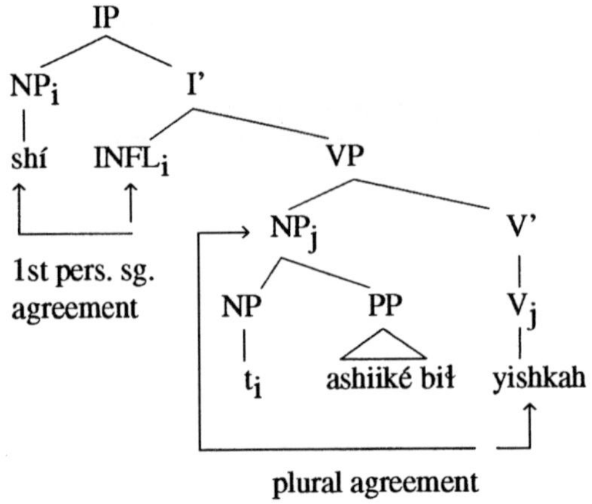

To summarize this section, null objects are allowed in Navajo in the three cases shown in (28).

(28) Possible Null Objects: t
e licensed by *shi, ni, nihi, bi*
e licensed by lexical agreement

What is not allowed is a null object with overt subject if the third person agreement morpheme is the neutral *yi*. This suggests that traces are licensed in object position when bound by a phrase in an A' position, and that the other two types of empty categories are null pronouns, possible whenever verbal or inflectional agreement is 'rich enough'. Under such an account, the neutral third person *yi* does not count as "rich enough". Let us explore now what might be lacking in the neutral third person *yi.*[4]

It seems clear that we cannot say that *yi* is not rich enough to be a designated head which licenses a null pronoun, since null objects occur with *yi* when the subject is also null.

(29) *pro pro yi*doots'ǫ́s
3O-3S-will:kiss
S/he will kiss him/her."

To capture the fact that Agreement seems to be correlated with the presence of null arguments yet is not a necessary or sufficient condition on them, Rizzi (1986) proposed the following principles, in which agreement participates in the identification of *pro*, but not in the licensing of *pro*:

(30) a. *pro* is formally licensed through Case assignment by a designated head.

(30) b. *pro* has the grammatical specification of the features of its licensing head coindexed with it.

Still, these two conditions do not suffice to account for the Navajo facts. If identification required only that the *pro* in Object position have the grammatical specification of the features of the Object Agreement on the verb, then either there should never be *pro* Objects (if *-yi* is not rich enough to identify *pro*) or there should be *pro* Objects even when the Subject is overt (if *-yi* is rich enough to identify *pro*).

I suggest rather that Huang's Generalized Control Rule is the identification condition operating here, and that Navajo differs from some other languages only in that the definition of what counts as a 'closest nominal element' includes morphological richness as a sub-part.

(31) GENERALIZED CONTROL RULE:
Coindex an empty pronominal with the closest nominal element.

CLOSEST NOMINAL ELEMENT:
Mandarin/English: Any NP or AGR
Navajo: Overt/rich NP or AGR

This accounts for the various types of sentences, shown in (32) as follows:

(32) a. NP *pro* {*sh/ni/bi*}-V
b. NP *pro* V[+handling stem]
c. *pro* *pro* *yi*-V
d. *NP *pro* *yi*-V

In (32a), the object agreement morphology on the verb is first or second person, or the 'rich' third person *bi*, and this morpheme will count as the closest nominal element, and the null pronoun in object position will be coindexed with it. In (32b), the stem of the verb is of the handling type, and this stem will include a type of agreement which is rich enough to count as a closest nominal element, and the null pronoun will be coindexed with it.[5] In (32c), there is no nominal element with which the null object must be coindexed. It is identified as third person by the morpheme *yi*, but this morpheme does not count as a nominal element, and so the GCR applies only vacuously and the sentence is grammatical. Finally, in (32d), the subject NP counts as the closest nominal element, and so the null object must be coindexed with it. This indexing results in the null pronoun being bound within its governing category, in violation of Binding Principle B. Therefore, the sentence is ungrammatical.

The GCR applies whenever there is a null pronoun, not just in the case of null objects. This predicts that dislocated NPs may not be construed with an object over a null subject. This prediction is true, both when the object is a variable and when the object is licensed by the third person *bi*. The sentences in

(33) are unambiguous, because they can only have the representations shown in (34) and they cannot have the representations shown in (35).

(33) a. Háísh *yizts'ǫ́s.*
who 3O-3S-kissed
"Who did he/she kiss?"
NOT "Who kissed him/her."

b. Dzaanééz *biiiłtsą́*
mule 3O-3S-saw
"The mule saw him/her/it."
NOT "S/he/it saw the mule."

(34) a. *pro* Háísh *yizts'ǫ́s.*
b. Dzanééz *pro biiiłtsą́*

(35) a. *Háísh$_i$ *pro* t$_i$ *yizts'ǫ́s.*
b. *Dzaanééz$_i$ *pro pro*$_i$ *biiiłtsą́*

In (35a, b), the GCR would automatically coindex the subject *pro* with the dislocated NP, causing all arguments to be coindexed. Thus, the representation is impossible.

In this section, I have argued that the contexts in which null objects are permitted in Navajo fall into three types. One type involves a variable, licensed by an NP in an A' position. The other two types, I have argued, involve a null pronoun licensed by rich agreement. When the agreement is not rich enough to count as a closest nominal element for the GCR, the null object is not permitted. Thus, there is a direct relationship between richness of agreement and the possibility of null pronominal objects. Notice however that the relation is not simply one of *pro* being licensed by rich agreement. Pro is licensed when the agreement is the neutral *yi*. However, the GCR does not require *pro* to be coindexed with *yi* as it does with the richer agreement. Hence, the GCR rules out cases of *pro* in object position when there is a closest overt NP in subject position.

1.3. *Some Residual Problems*

In this section I will discuss three problems that remain under my account. First, I have claimed that handling stems license null objects but that other stems do not. One of Willie's three examples seems to be a counterexample to this:

(36) Ashkii yóldon
boy 3O-3S-shooting
"The boy is shooting at it."

The stem *don* is not a handling stem. According to Young and Morgan (1988), it means roughly 'explodes' and occurs in various verbs of shooting with a gun. Two properties of this verb may be relevant. First, it does seem that the theme of this verb is incorporated, i.e., expressed in the stem, although this is not one of the handling stems. This verb cannot be used if the shooting involved arrows rather than a gun (cf. *'adisht'oh* 'I am shooting (arrows).'). Second, because the theme has been incorporated, the null object here is the goal. This is quite unusual in Navajo: it is very rare to find a direct object which is not a theme. Predicates which would in English involve a non-theme direct object (such as psych predicates) have no object in Navajo and instead have the experiencer in a postpositional phrase, as in (37).

(37) Kii bá háshchį́įh
Kii 3O-for 1S-cause:anger
"I am angering Kii." LIT: "I am causing anger for Kii."

A second problem, related to the first, is that objects of postpositional phrases seem to allow the object of the postposition to be null, and such sentences seem to allow even the direct object to be null. Willie (1991) gives the following sentence as grammatical:

(38) Asdzą́ą́ yii' yiyiiłéézh
woman 3-in 3-3-boiling
"The woman is boiling it in it."

This fact is not predicted by my theory.

Finally, although I have treated *bi* and *yi* both as object agreement morphemes, an important morphological fact about them remains unexplained. This is that they only appear if the subject is also third person. If the subject is first or second person, no morpheme at all appears in the verbal slot for object agreement:

(39) a. Ch'íníshteeh
ch'í+0+ni+sh+teeh
out+3O+perf+1S+carry
"I carried him out."

b. Nítł'ó
0+nitł'ó
3O+2S+weaving
"You are weaving it."

c. *Ch'íbíníshteeh
out+bi+perf+1S+carry
"I carried him out."

It seems that *yi* and *bi* in fact carry information about both subject and object. Rice and Saxon (1991) have analyzed *yi* as a subject agreement morpheme. Their insights may help explain why *yi* does not count as the closest nominal element to a null object.

2. LICENSING CONDITIONS ON *pro*

In the preceding section, I argued that a version of Huang's Generalized Control Rule is operating in Navajo. An interesting feature of Huang's theory is that he has no special licensing condition on *pro*. Rather, *pro* is in principle licensed in any position in every language, but its actual distribution is constrained by the operation of the Generalized Control Rule. The way in which Huang accounts for the various familiar cases is summarized in .

(40) a. English subject of finite clause:
GCR forces *pro* to be coindexed with AGR, and then AGR fails to be rich enough to identify *pro*.

b. Italian subject of finite clause:
GCR forces *pro* to be coindexed with AGR, and then AGR is rich enough to identify *pro*

c. Chinese subjects:
GCR forces *pro* to be coindexed with higher subject.

d. Chinese objects:
GCR forces object to be coindexed with subject, in violation of principle B. Null objects in Chinese are variables, not *pro*

e. Null object in language with rich object AGR (Pashto):
GCR forces *pro* to be coindexed with Object AGR, which is rich enough to identify *pro*.

Huang's theory thus does not have a special licensing condition on Pro. This is an attractive feature of his theory, since theories like Rizzi's which do have a licensing condition need to rely on an arbitrary stipulation of whether a given head is or is not a 'designated' head. The class of licensing heads in a given language may include INFL, and also may include other heads, as long as there is a way for *pro* to get phi features. For example, Rizzi argues that Italian has *pro* in object position licensed by V, and suggests that there is an independent rule that can assign arbitrary interpretation to a direct argument. Under this theory, the class of licensing heads seems to be completely arbitrary.

Further, there are important conceptual problems that arise in a theory with a licensing condition on *pro*. This condition has two unusual properties, both having to do with the special phonological status of *pro*. First, the condition necessitates that the Grammar allow some heads to be designated as licensers of a category with particular phonological properties (namely, the property of being unpronounced). There are no equivalent designations in other components of syntax involving other phonological properties. For example, there do not exist specific heads that license stressed NPs, specific heads that assign theta roles only to overt NPs, or specific heads that subcategorized for NPs with nasal consonants in them.

Second, it necessitates that a particular lexical entry, *pro*, is subject to a special requirement in virtue of its phonological status. Such a condition is especially surprising in that the intuitive content of the need for a special requirement on an unpronounced constituent is satisfied by the identification requirement, independent of an additional licensing condition: if a constituent is not pronounced, it must be recoverable. Intuition aside, there are no other lexical items whose phonological properties cause them to be subject to some special syntactic requirement. Even the Case filter, which states that all NPs must bear Case to be visible, applies to any NP chain, and in the view of some (e.g. Chomsky 1993) also to PRO, hence need not include reference to the phonological properties of the NP. If, as is generally assumed, *pro* is simply a pronoun which lacks phonetic realization, there is no reason to expect its phonetic properties to call for a special licensing requirement.

These two properties of the licensing condition are related, but are distinct in that we can imagine the grammar including elements which are subject to special requirements in virtue of their phonological properties but not including heads that are designated to license certain elements in virtue of the licensee's properties. Likewise, we can imagine the Grammar designating certain classes of heads to license elements with particular phonological properties without there being items that are subject to special conditions in virtue of their own properties. At issue here is the fact that the licensing condition is a syntactic condition that makes special reference to the phonological properties of the licensee.[6]

A theory in which no special licensing condition on null arguments is needed will be more in keeping with the working hypothesis of Principles and Parameters theory, that the modules of Grammar are separate and distinct.

Unfortunately, some problems with Huang's approach have been uncovered by researchers who have applied his criteria to other languages which lack agreement. Huang's theory makes the prediction that null objects can be *pro* only in a language which has rich object agreement. In a language like Chinese with no agreement, null objects must be variables. However, several authors who have applied Huang's tests to other languages lacking agreement have found that by Huang's tests, these languages have *pro* in object position. Two such languages are Korean, investigated by Yoon (1985), and Thai, investigated by Hoonchamlong (1991). A summary and discussion of these types of data can be found in Cole (1987). Here I will look only at one set of facts, which involves Huang's basic argument that Chinese null objects cannot be *pro*. As the example in (41) shows, an embedded null object in Chinese cannot be coreferential with the matrix subject. Huang proposed that this is because the object must be a variable, bound by a null topic. Coindexing this variable with the matrix subject results in a strong crossover violation (Condition C).

(41) Chinese:
a. Zhangsan$_i$ shuo Lisi kanjianle $0_{j/*i}$.
Z says L saw
"Zhangsan$_i$ says Lisi saw him$_{j/*i}$."

b. $OP_{j/*i}$ [Zhangsan$_i$ shuo [Lisi kanjianle $0_{j/*i}$]]
c. *Zhangsan shuo Lisi$_i$ kanjianle *pro*$_i$.

Yoon and Hoomchanlong showed that in Korean and Thai, embedded null objects can be coreferential with the matrix subject, behaving exactly like a pronoun.

(42) a. Korean: (Yoon 1985)
Chelswu$_i$-ka [Yenghi-ka *pro*$_i$ hyeppakha-ess-ta]-ko
C-NOM Y-NOM threaten-PAST-DECL-COMP
cwucangha-ess-ta
claim-PAST-DECL
"Chelswu$_i$ claims that Yenghi threatened him$_i$."

b. Thai: (Hoonchamlong 1991)
Nit$_i$ b))k waa Nuan hen *pro*$_i$
N speak say N see
"Nit$_i$ said that Nuan saw him$_i$."

To account for such facts in a parametric theory, Cole (1987) proposed that the Generalized Control Rule is parameterized: languages like Korean and Thai do not obey the GCR. The problem with this is that Huang's GCR was designed to be a simple extension of the principles of Control, and was intended to be subject to internal parameterization with respect to the possible minimal domain and possible controllers. However, it was not intended to apply only in some languages. Further, there is no clear independent evidence of the operation or lack of operation of the GCR in the relevant languages. If we have to stipulate whether a given language uses/does not use the GCR, as Cole suggested, then we might as well simply stipulate that the language does/does not allow null pronominal objects. Thus, as with the designated head theory, we are left with a stipulation that a given language either does or does not allow null pronominal objects.

To summarize, there are conceptual reasons to prefer a theory like Huang's with no specific licensing condition on *pro,* but the use of Control as the condition governing the distribution of *pro* does not work for languages like Korean and Thai, which have no agreement yet apparently allow *pro* in object position.[7]

In Speas (1994), I suggested that the principle which governs the distribution of *pro* is a simple economy principle. The focus of that paper was the relationship between rich agreement and the licensing of *pro*, and so the discussion was primarily of *pro* in subject position. However, some suggestions about the application of the theory to null objects were made. In this section I will sketch out briefly how an economy-based theory might apply to null objects.

The basic idea is that the distribution of null arguments follows directly from the way in which principles of economy constrain the projection of syntactic categories. The way in which economy principles restrict projection is stated in (43).

(43) Project XP only if XP has content.

I adopted the proposal of Rohrbacher (1993), who claims that in languages which have strong agreement, each agreement morpheme has its own lexical entry, while in languages that have weak agreement, the morphemes do not have independent lexical entries.[8] Rather, verbs in weak agreement languages are listed in the lexicon in verbal paradigms, and hence Agreement has no independent lexical entry in such languages.

(44) a. strong AGR: b. weak AGR:

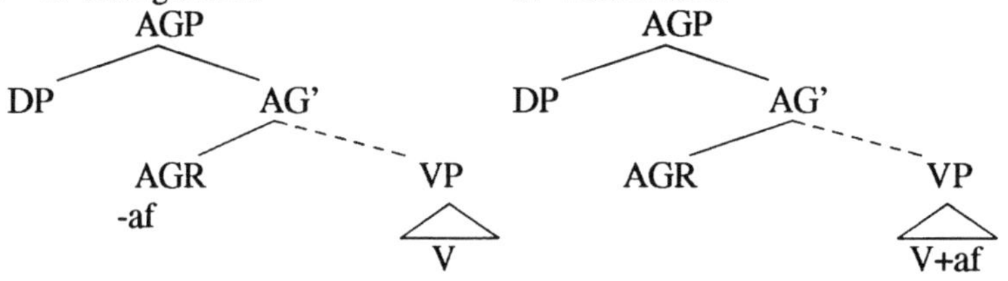

I claimed that null arguments are found in all and only those languages in which the specifier of AGR-P is not needed to satisfy any condition of the Grammar. In "weak agreement" languages, the specifier of AGRP must be filled prior to Spellout in order to fulfill conditions of economy of projection. In "strong agreement" languages, the specifier of AGRP may be empty, since the head of AGRP is filled. In a language with no agreement at all, there is no AGRP, and so the question of whether its specifier needs to be filled is moot.

In applying this theory to null objects, I suggested that null objects are licensed if an overt object is not needed in order to allow the projection of a VP shell in the sense of Hale and Keyser (1991) and Larson (1988).

Larson and Hale and Keyser propose that the internal structure of VP includes more than one maximal projection of the predicate. That is, they suggest that in addition to the immediate projection of the lexical head, there is an upper VP shell into which the verb moves. The direct object, in their theory, occupies the specifier of the internal VP, and the verb moves over it to reach its surface position.

(45) VP "shells" (Larson 1988, Hale and Keyser 1991)

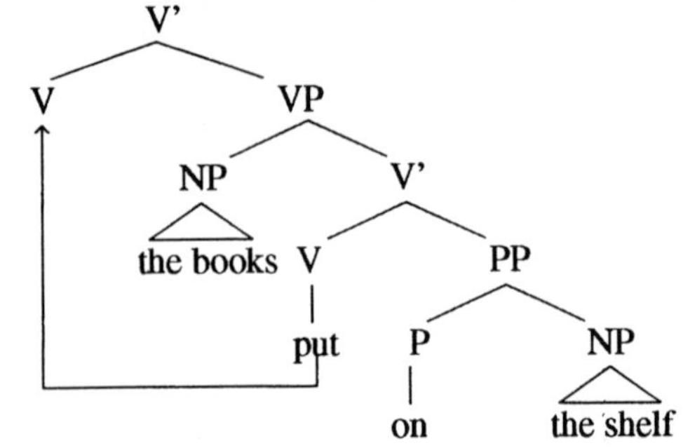

Actually, it is unclear whether the verb moves to its surface position, or is base-generated in the upper VP and controls the lower V position. Hale and Keyser use the movement account because they want to claim that a phrase like *shelve the books* is derived through movement from an underlying structure which is just like (45), and in which the N *shelf* moves through an empty P, an empty V, on up to the higher V. The problem with this (pointed out to me by Hagit Borer (p.c.)) is that for many such derivations, there is evidence that the resulting verb must be formed in the lexicon rather than in syntax. These problems might be avoided if a fully derived verb were inserted into the higher position, and controlled lower head positions, in a relation that we can call *H(ead)-Control*. For the simple verb phrase in (45), this results in a structure like (46), which is a control-type structure in the sense that the higher verb controls the base-generated empty head in the lower VP.

(46)

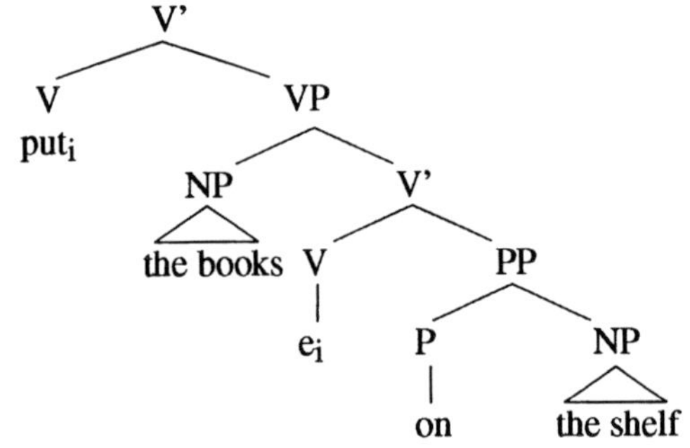

We may note that the operation of a general principle of economy such as the one that I made explicit above in (43) is implicit in Hale and Keyser's and Larson's work. In their theories, VP shells are allowed to be projected above the VP which projects from the verbal lexical entry. Presumably this process is restricted so that only XPs which will receive some sort of interpretation can be projected. It is interesting then, if we find empirical consequences supporting the presence of such a principle.

Suppose that (46) is the underlying structure for a ditransitive VP in English. The lower verbal head is empty. By the economy principles discussed above, we would expect that the specifier of this projection could then not be empty. If it were, both the head and the specifier would be empty and the lower VP projection would not be licensed. (*pro* does not count as a specifier with content, because it does not have phi features until they are filled in by agreement or control.)

(47) English:

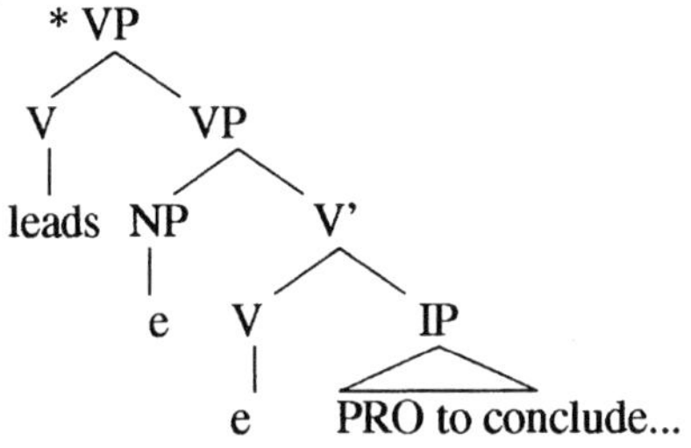

Thus, in a language that projects VPs in H-control configurations, we predict that *pro* will be impossible in object position. Object position (in a transitive) must be filled in order not to violate the economy principles.[9]

Now suppose, following Speas (1994), that languages like Italian, which allow null objects, use a raising-type structure like (45), as illustrated in (48).[10]

(48)

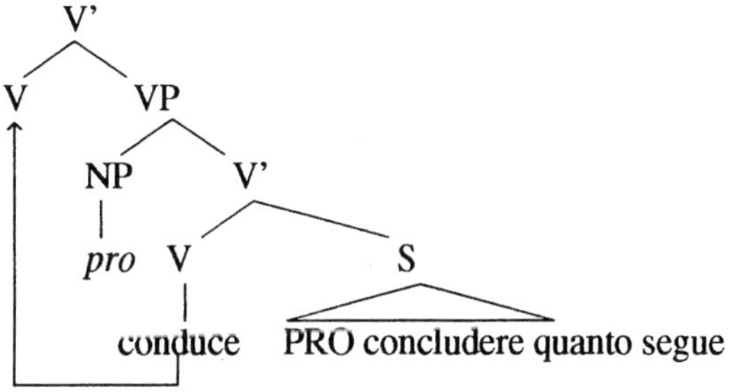

This structure is consistent with the fact that Verbs in Italian move out of VP to a higher Functional Category. In a language in which verbs begin in the lowest V-head within the VP shell, we would expect that it would be possible to leave the specifier of that lower VP empty (i.e., to generate *pro* there), since the principles of economy allow this lower VP to be projected without a filled specifier, since its head is filled.

These suggestions are tentative, but they illustrate how we might extend to null objects a theory which does away with the stipulative licensing and identification conditions in favor of general principles of economy.

What is needed now is independent evidence in favor of the suggested difference in underlying structures between Romance languages and English. There is one intriguing independent difference between English and various Romance languages with may result from this proposed underlying difference. This is the fact that certain verbs in English may be interpreted as involving 'conflation' (Talmy 1985) of the path with the verbal action, whereas this conflation is apparently not possible in Spanish or Italian. In English, a sentence like (49) is ambiguous. It means either that the boat was just floating under the bridge, or that the boat floated on a path which passed under the bridge. Talmy (1985) and Rapoport (1987) report that such sentences in Spanish are not ambiguous. Preliminary inquiries indicate that they are also not ambiguous in Italian.

(49) The boat floated under the bridge.

I suggest that this difference is due to the differences in the underlying structure of VP in the two languages. In English, transitive VPs have a structure in which the verb controls an empty head within the lower shell. In Italian, the verb starts out in the lower VP. This means that in English there must be a lower head, whereas in Italian, it is not clear that the upper verbal head serves any purpose. Let us suppose that Italian verbs move directly to some functional head. Now the English structures have an extra head. I suggest that the lower head may receive an interpretation, and that this interpretation corresponds to the path which is taken to be conflated with the meaning of the verb.[11]

(50)

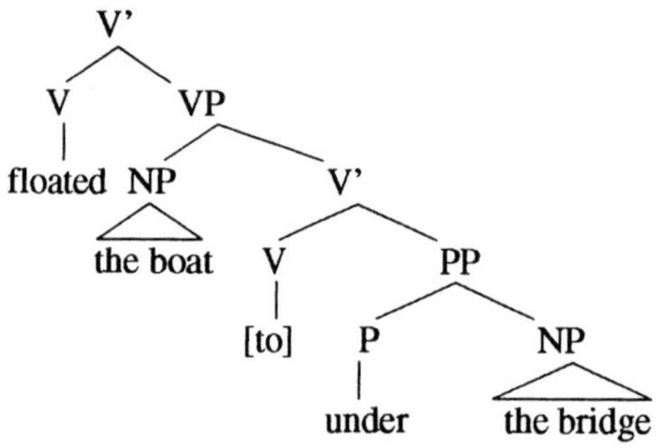

In Italian, since the lower head is not empty, it is not available to receive this additional interpretation, and so parallel sentences are not ambiguous.

This theory makes the prediction that there will be a correlation between the possibility of null objects in a language and the interpretation of these conflation type sentences. In languages like Thai and Korean that allow null objects, such sentences should be unambiguous. In languages like Chinese, such sentences should be ambiguous, as they are in English. According to Y. Hoonchamlong (personal communication), the data show mixed results.[12]

The word for 'float' in Thai in *l@@y1*. It can be used both as transitive and intransitive verb.

(51) Transitive: khaw4 l@@y1 rUa1
he float boat
"He is floating the boat."

When used as an intransitive, an additional word is used to indicate whether what is meant is a state of floating or the action of bobbing or floating.

(52) rUa1 l@@y1 yuu2 tay3 sa1phaan1
boat float "state" under bridge
"The boat is in the state of floating under the bridge."

(53) rUa1 kra1daat2 lam2 nan4 com1 lEEw4k@3 l@@y1 khUn3
boat paper CLF that sink then float/bob up
maa1 tay3 sa1phaan1
DIR under bridge
"That paper boat sank, then floated upward under the bridge

In both intransitive sentences above, the sentences are not ambiguous. This would be consistent with our prediction: since Thai allows *pro* in object position, we expect that it does not have the conflation type structures.

However, *l@@y1* 'float' can be ambiguous in a sentence like:

(54) rUa1 l@@y1 tay3 sa1phaan1
boat float under bridge
"The boat is floating under the bridge." (EITHER "toward a point under the bridge" OR "at a point under the bridge")

Still, Hoonchamlong reports that the preferred interpretation is the stative reading. The stative reading is in my analysis the one that corresponds to the Italian-type structure, in which the verb is base-generated in the lower VP, and so there is no understood path. Clearly more work needs to be done on the status of the preference for the stative reading in sentences like (54). If the sentence is ambiguous just as the equivalent English sentence is, then my prediction is wrong. If the nonstative reading is different from the path reading in English, then there is some evidence for a correlation between null objects and the lack of the conflation type structures.[13] If there turns out to be no correlation between conflation and null objects, then this means that this particular attempt to find independent evidence for the suggested structural difference between English and null object languages has failed, and we need to look elsewhere for independent evidence.

Another possible correlation may be between syntactic verb movement and the possibility of null objects. Italian has overt verb movement (Belletti 1990) and English does not. Perhaps the verb starts out in the lower verbal projection in all and only languages that have overt V movement to INFL. If this were true, then we would expect that languages like Chinese which do not allow *pro* objects must not have V movement, while languages like Thai do. I know of no conclusive evidence one way or another for these languages[14], and so I must leave this matter open.

What I have presented in this section is an attempt to apply a general principle of economy of projection to account for the distribution of null objects.

The account is very sketchy, but I hope to have demonstrated an alternative to either stipulating a class of licensing heads, or allowing the Generalized Control Rule to apply only in certain languages.

3. CONCLUSION

In this paper, I have argued that a version of Huang's Generalized Control Rule applies in Navajo, but that contrary to Huang's theory, it is not entirely possible to dispense with licensing conditions on *pro*. I have discussed some conceptual problems with the existing licensing conditions, and have suggested that the correct conditions follow from general principles of economy as they apply to the projection of phrase structure. Under this proposal, differences in the licensing of null objects follow from differences in the nature of the VP projection.

NOTES

* I am grateful for comments and criticism to the audience at Indiana University. I am also grateful to audiences at the University of Illinois and the 1993 WECOL conference. Thanks for comments and advice to Evangeline Parsons Yazzie and Emmon Bach. This research was supported during the summer of 1992 by a Faculty Research Grant from the University of Massachusetts.

1 I give a gloss of the relevant parts of the verbal morphology, but I do not attempt a morpheme by morpheme breakdown. Phonological processes obscure the morpheme by morpheme breakdown so much that it would only confuse matters if I tried to provide such a breakdown. Also, Navajo has between 10 and 14 prefix positions, and in some cases I am not certain what the exact breakdown is in such categories as aspect, mode and adverbial modification. Therefore, I gloss only the agreement morphemes and the stem.

2 The facts also suggest that Navajo NPs are in argument positions, contra Willie (1991) and Jelinek (1984), who have claimed that NPs in Navajo are always adjoined, and that what I have characterized as agreement morphemes are actually pronominal clitics that fill the argument positions. See Speas (1992) for discussion.

3 It is difficult to get an accurate translation of the *bi*-construction, since there is an implication that the patient somehow let him/herself have the action done to him/her. A more accurate translation might be 'The horse, he had the mule kick him'.

4 The morpheme *yi* is in other contexts found as a meaningless affix, added to a verb in order to fulfill a general requirement in Navajo that all verbs must be at least two syllables. Kari (1976) calls this a 'peg' morpheme. For example, in (i), the verb in intransitive, and the subject agreement morpheme is the first person singular *sh-*. Since *sh* is not syllabic, when it is added to the stem, an additional syllable is needed in order to ensure that the word will have two syllables. The syllable added in such cases is *yi*.

(i) yisháál
yi+sh+áál
peg+1sgS+walking:along
"I am walking along."

(ii) *sháál

5 If Jelinek (forthcoming) is correct in claiming that handling verbs involve some sort of abstract incorporation, then both handling stems and verbs with the 'rich' inflectional

agreement actually involve object incorporation rather than licensing of a null pronoun. In this case, the definition of 'closest nominal element' could be simplified to include only overt NPs.

6 What about the Empty Category Principle? Isn't this another case of a special condition on a category in virtue of its phonologically null status? As Rizzi (1986) has pointed out, the ECP apparently applies only to *nonpronominal* empty categories, in fact, to traces of movement. Traces of movement are crucially different from *pro* in that assuming a derivational view of the Grammar, traces occupy positions that have at some point in the derivation been occupied by a constituent with phonetic content.

The intermediate traces of empty operators would seem to be a counterexample to this, but the status of the chain involved here is not clear. Lasnik and Stowell (1991) and Cinque (1990) claim that the foot of the chain is something other than a WH-t (a pronominal variable for L&S and an epithet for Cinque). If null operators are in spec positions and head a garden variety A' chain, this presents a challenge to many of the claims in this paper. If the null operator is a semantically contentful operator that is adjoined to a maximal projection and enters into a binding relation with a pronominal variable, it may not be subject to the requirements that I will propose here. I leave this question open. Thus, although the ECP as currently phrased appears to be a special condition on categories which lack phonological content, it seem clear that it could be recast as a condition on either movement launching sites or on non-head links in an antecedent government chain. To do so brings up many interesting questions that are beyond the scope of this paper. The point I wish to make here is that the existence of the ECP should not be taken as evidence that syntactic principles referring to the phonological content of items are pervasive or desirable.

7 In Huang (1991), it is suggested that the classification of empty categories needs to be revised, and that under the appropriate revision what looked like a null pronoun in certain languages is actually a null epithet. If that proposal is correct, then Huang's original claim that *pro* is never possible in object position, due to the interaction between Control Theory and Principle B, could be maintained, and the null object in languages like Thai or Italian would be either a variable or an epithet. Such a result would render moot the discussion in this section of the distribution of null pronouns, and would be consistent with my prediction so far that the Economy principles allow *pro* in principle to be generated freely in object position, but that such representations are ruled out by the interaction of Control and Binding Principles.

8 Rohrbacher's claim correlates verb movement with lexical entries for AGR morphemes rather than associating *pro* drop with this property as I am doing. Rohrbacher's generalization is based upon his extensive examination of the Germanic languages in order to pin down the precise nature of the inflectional morphology of those languages which have verb movement vs. those which do not. For *pro*-drop, Rohrbacher suggests that some additional condition is needed, perhaps a condition on referentiality of AGR features.

9 This suggestion raises interesting questions about the status of pleonastics in object position.

10 It is not clear whether the higher head to which the verb moves in Italian is actually a higher verbal shell or the first available Functional projection that it lands in on its way up to AGR-S.

11 I have assumed that *boat* is the underlying direct object of *float*. Under the theory I am suggesting here, we might expect that path conflation will take place only with unaccusative verbs. This is not the case—it takes place I believe with any verb that can normally be assumed to have an inherent path:

(i) a. Mary walked under the bridge (ambiguous)
b. Mary slept under the bridge (unambiguous)
c. Mary arrived under the bridge (unambiguous)

Walk is unergative, yet path conflation is possible. *Slept* is unergative, and path conflation is not possible. *Arrived* is unaccusative, but path conflation is not possible. Perhaps the path endows the head with semantic content, allowing it to head a projection even with an unergative verb.

12 Numbers at the ends of words indicate the tone class. @ is low back unrounded vowel.

13 Another problematic case, brought to may attention by J. Rooryck, is the fact that Dutch apparently is like English in having both stative and dynamic interpretations of *float* (*De fles dreef onder de brug.* 'The bottle floated under the bridge.') but Dutch allows for empty objects controlling PRO in infinitives. Note however that coreference of this empty object with an anaphor is impossible. See Rooryck (1992) for details.

14 It has been argued by Huang (1988) that Chinese does have V-movement. However Cheng and Li (1991) and Ernst (to appear) argue against a V-movement analysis. I am grateful to Tom Ernst for providing me with these references.

REFERENCES

Belletti, Adriana: 1990, *Generalized Verb Movement*, Foris, Dordrecht.

Cheng, Lisa and Yafei Li: 1991, 'Double Negation in Chinese and Multi-Projections', paper presented at NACCL, Cornell University, Ithaca, NY.

Chomsky, Noam: 1993, 'A Minimalist Program for Linguistic Theory', in Hale, K. and S. J. Keyser (eds.), *The View from Building 20: A Festschrift for Sylvain Bromberger*, MIT Press, Cambridge MA, pp. 1-52.

Cinque, Guglielmo: 1990, *Types of A´-Dependencies*, MIT Press, Cambridge, MA.

Cole, Peter: 1987, 'Null Objects in Universal Grammar', *Linguistic Inquiry* **18**, 597-612.

Ernst, Thomas: to appear, 'Negation in Mandarin Chinese', to appear in *Natural Language and Linguistic Theory*.

Hale, Kenneth: 1975, 'Counterexamples and Explanations in Navajo Linguistics: Syntax', *Diné Bizaad Nánīl'įįh* 2.1.

Hale, Ken and S.J. Keyser: 1991, 'On the Syntax of Argument Structure', *Lexicon Project Working Papers No. 34*, Center for Cognitive Science, MIT, Cambridge, MA.

Hoonchamlong, Yuphaphann: 1991, *Some Issues in Thai Anaphora: A Government and Binding Approach*, unpublished Ph.D. dissertation, University of Wisconsin, Madison.

Huang, J.: 1991, 'Remarks on the Status of the Null Object', in Freiden, Robert (ed.), *Principles and Parameters in Comparative Grammar*, MIT Press, Cambridge, MA.

———: 1989, 'Pro-Drop in Chinese' in Jaeggli, Osvaldo and Kenneth Safir (eds.), *The Null Subject Parameter*, Kluwer Academic Publishers, Dordrecht.

———: 1988, '*Wo pao de kuai* and Chinese Phrase Structure', *Language* **64**.2, 274-311.

———: 1984, 'On the Distribution and Reference of Empty Pronouns', *Linguistic Inquiry* **15**, 531-574.

Jaeggli, Osvaldo and Kenneth Safir: 1989, *The Null Subject Parameter*, Kluwer Academic Publishers, Dordrecht.

Jelinek, Eloise: 1984, 'Empty Categories, Case and Configurationality', *Natural Language and Linguistic Theory* **1**.1, 39-76.

Jelinek, Eloise and Mary Willie: 1993, 'Pronoun Attachment to the Verb in Navajo', paper presented at the Athabaskan Linguistics Conference, Santa Fe, NM, July 1993.

Kari, James: 1976, *Navajo Verbal Prefix Phonology*, unpublished Ph.D. dissertation, University of New Mexico, Albuquerque.

Larson, Richard: 1988, 'On the Double Object Construction', *Linguistic Inquiry* **19**, 335-392.

Lasnik, Howard and Tim Stowell: 1991, 'Weakest Crossover', *Linguistic Inquiry* **22**.4, 687-770.

Platero, Paul: 1982, 'Missing Noun Phrases and Grammatical Relations in Navajo', *International Journal of American Linguistics*, **48**.2, 286-305.

——— 1978, *Missing Noun Phrases in Navajo*. unpublished Ph.D. dissertation, MIT, Cambridge, MA.

Rapoport, Tova: 1987, *Copular, Nominal and Small Clauses*, unpublished Ph.D. dissertation, MIT, Cambridge, MA.

Rice, Keren and Leslie Saxon: 1991, 'A Structural Analysis of **y* in Athapaskan', paper presented at the Athapaskan Linguistics Conference, University of California, Santa Cruz.

Rizzi, Luigi: 1986, 'Null Objects in Italian and the Theory of *pro*', *Linguistic Inquiry* **17**: 501-557.

Rohrbacher, Bernhard: 1993, *The Germanic VO Languages and the Full Paradigm: A Theory of V to I Raising*, unpublished Ph.D. dissertation, University of Massachusetts, Amherst.

Rooryck, Johan. 1992, 'On Control and Binding by Null Arguments', paper presented at Going Romance 1992: Exploiting and Enriching the Resources of Romania, University of Utrecht, Utrecht.

Speas, Margaret: 1994, 'Null Arguments in a Theory of Economy of Projection', in Benedicto, E. and J. Runner (eds.), *University of Massachusetts Occasional Papers in Linguistics* **17**, Amherst.

———: forthcoming, 'Projection and Pronominal Arguments', in Coopmans, Peter, Martin Everaert and Jane Grimshaw (eds.), *Lexical Specification and Insertion*, Lawrence Erlbaum, Hillsdale, NJ.

Talmy, Leonard: 1985, 'Lexicalization Patterns', in Shopen, T. (ed.) *Language Typology and Syntactic Description*, Cambridge University Press, Cambridge, pp. 57-149.

Willie, Mary Ann: 1991, *Navajo Pronouns and Obviation*, unpublished Ph.D. dissertation, University of Arizona, Tucson.

Yoon, J.: 1985, 'On the Treatment of Empty Categories in Topic Prominent Languages', unpublished, University of Illinois, Champaign-Urbana.

Young, Robert and W. Morgan: 1988, *The Navajo Language: A Grammar and Colloquial Dictionary*, University of New Mexico Press, Albuquerque.

CLITIC CONSTRUCTIONS*

Dominique Sportiche

0. ABSTRACT

An analysis of French and Romance clitic pronominal constructions in simple clauses is proposed, reconciling the two dominant approaches on this topic. This analysis treats them as involving both movement and base-generation and, as part of a larger research program, assimilates the syntax of clitics to that of other functional heads. Accordingly, a clitic is analyzed as heading its own projection and as licensing in its specifier a particular property of a designated argument agreeing with it in the relevant features (person, number, gender, Case, etc.). It is further argued that clitics subdivide in two types. The first type (such as French *en* or *le*) assimilates to such functional heads as [+wh] complementizers or [+negative] heads licensing certain operator-like properties (e.g., *wh* or negative quantifiers). We show that (some) Germanic Scrambling is fundamentally similar to these clitic constructions. This leads us to postulate that the operator-like property these clitics license is specificity in DPs as has often been proposed, but that *reciprocally* the specificity of some DPs must be licensed in similar clitic-like configurations. In essence, this comes down to assimilating pronouns to bare operators (like bare *wh*-phrases *who, what, why*), and specific DPs to non-bare operators with operator determiners (like *which book, what reason.*, etc.). The second type of clitics, such as French *lui*, are not linked to specificity. We suggest that these clitics should be analyzed as pure agreement, analogous to AGR_O or AGR_S, presumably responsible for Case assignment (here dative, i.e., AGR_{IO}).

1. INTRODUCTION

1.1. *Preamble*

The existence of pronominal clitics in languages like French and other (Romance) languages raises two questions, one of descriptive adequacy and one of explanatory adequacy. The question of descriptive adequacy asks what the correct structural analysis of constructions with these pronominal clitics is.

How to structurally analyze clitics has been the subject of very substantial discussion ever since the earliest studies of the late 1960s, and much disagreement remains. I want to suggest an analysis that reconciles two main, but conflicting, views on this problem.

The question of explanatory adequacy asks why language learners choose the analysis of pronominal clitics they do. This kind of question is the most central theoretical question generative linguists such as myself can ask about the analyses they propose; their field is defined by the fact that they ask these questions. It is unlikely that learners go through the kind of deductive reasoning that linguists go through; years of clever debate have not yet produced a consensus on the matter of clitics. How is it that learners reach such uniform conclusions on such complex systems on the basis of much more limited evidence than is available to linguists? It appears plausible to assume that the range of analyses that they can entertain at all is so restricted to start with that the choice is easy to make on the basis of the data available to them. In fact, in the extreme, it is conceivable that this range is a singleton. This most extreme position is the one I am going to suggest. Although I hope to substantiate this claim empirically, I independently believe that some such extreme narrowing of a priori possibilities is necessary; even the kind of extremely restrictive theories of syntactic structures proposed today allow so many possible syntactic analyses (possibly infinitely many) of any finite set of data as to make learning untractable (see Sportiche 1995).

At the most general level, I want to suggest that the kind of structural analysis that can be ascribed to clitic constructions is identical to those that can be ascribed to *wh*-constructions, negative quantifier constructions, focus constructions, and almost every other construction that can reasonably be argued to involve XP-movement (NP or DP movement constructions, lexical anaphor constructions, quantifier scope constructions, etc.), because there is only one kind of structural analysis available for these constructions in principle, namely movement demanded by specifier/head licensing. Substantiating this approach requires establishing its plausibility and accomplishments for each individual construction. This is what I will do for clitic constructions in this paper. The general theoretical approach this is a part of is discussed in more detail in Sportiche (1995) and some consequences for subject clitics are more specifically discussed in Sportiche (1993b).

1.2. *Boundary condition on analyses*

Every analysis of clitics must account for the fact that the items treated as clitics by French are treated as clitics by French. This is another side of the question of explanatory adequacy previously discussed. This very strongly suggests a fundamentally uniform analysis of clitics. For if universal grammar allows pronominal clitics to be analyzed in one of several ways, the question of converging on the right analysis for each individual case arises again, together with the problem of underdetermination of the theory by the evidence.

Although a uniform approach to the analysis of clitics is not forced, it is clearly more desirable a priori and I will adopt it as working hypothesis. As we will see, this seems largely justified a posteriori. As will be clear, I also take as point of departure the idea that this uniformity also holds true crosslinguistically, at least as far as the most analyzed Romance languages such as Italian and Spanish are concerned. Work on these languages has revealed enough similarity of functioning with each other and French clitic constructions to warrant this assumption. How uniform can these analyses be? Surely they cannot be uniform to the point of identity (since pronominal clitics do behave differently). Minimally, we may assume that clitics are uniformly analyzed up to lexical differences. One important consequence of this assumption is the following: it is reasonable to argue for or against particular proposals concerning the analyses of pronominal clitic constructions by bringing any pronominal clitic to bear on the question (again up to lexical differences).

1.3. *Outline of the central proposal*

There are strong arguments in favor of each of the two widely held, and apparently incompatible, types of analysis of Romance clitics found in the literature. Illustrating with a French accusative clitic, clitics are argued to be either base-generated in their surface position (Strozer 1976, Rivas 1977, Jaeggli 1982, Borer 1983, Sportiche 1983) or moved from the underlying XP* position (Kayne 1975, Kayne 1989a, Sportiche 1990):

(1) Marie les_i aura présentés XP_i* à Louis.
Marie them will-have introduced-AGR_i to Louis
"Marie will have introduced them to Louis."

Proponents of movement analyses have held that movement, but not base-generation, can explain the condition of locality holding between the clitic and XP* and reminiscent of conditions on A-movement (traditionally attributed to the Binding Theory). Base-generation has been argued to be unlike movement in being compatible with the lack of complementarity between clitic and a full XP* (Clitic Doubling constructions). Although I do not consider the argumentation based on this observation convincing, as I discuss below, I will offer some reasons to support its conclusions.

These properties suggest that both movement and base-generation are correct and this is what I will propose. Specifically: (i) All clitics are always base-generated in preexisting slots, namely as X^0 heading their own projection and (ii) clitic constructions may also involve movement. Illustrating the basic idea with (1), I suggest that the accusative clitic is a base-generated head, call it Acc, selecting as its specifier an accusative DP*. This selection must be satisfied by LF by moving DP* to SPEC, AccP = DP^, as an instance of Spec-head licensing:

(2) $[_{AccP}$ DP^ [$[_{Acc}$les] [. . . aura présentés DP^*_{+acc} . . .]]]

I will show how this approach reconciles the properties listed above and many others and can provide a unified analysis of clitics. This will lead to related proposals concerning Clitic Doubling, the treatment of participle agreement and the distribution of stranded quantifiers. I will also discuss why this approach is superior to recent alternatives such as Kayne's (1989a) (clitic movement as successive head movement) and supports a version of Sportiche's (1989) or (1990) approach (clitic movement as XP movement followed by incorporation of X). Finally, we will propose that overt clitic morphemes split in two classes. Members of the first class, which include accusative clitics, are similar to [+wh] complementizers or the head of NegP and characterize constructions resembling operator/variable configurations, which license parasitic gaps. We will propose that the presence of these clitics is a necessary and sufficient condition to license specificity in their associated argument phrase. We analyze accusative Scrambling (in Dutch - and that should extend to German) as an instance of a clitic construction as in (2) with XP^ filled and the head silent. Members of the second class, like dative clitics, behave like Agreement Phrases. The projection they head are thus AGR_{IO} responsible for dative Case, much in the same way that AGR_S and AGR_O are responsible for nominative and accusative Case properties.

2. SOME PRELIMINARIES ABOUT FRENCH CLITICS AND CLITICS IN GENERAL

French (representative of many Romance languages) has a rich system of preverbal clitics. Their surface distribution is summarized by the template below:

(3) French Clitic Template

Nom	Neg	1st/2nd/Refl	3rdAcc predicate	3rdDat	Loc	Gen
il	ne	me/te/se/nous	le/la/les	lui/leur	y	en

As Perlmutter (1972) describes it, for each column of the template, no more than one clitic is allowed (so for example, it is not possible to have a 1st person accusative object and a 2nd person dative object at the same time). Furthermore, the third and fifth column cannot be filled at the same time (e.g., * *Je me lui montre.* 'I show myself to him.'). Why there are these vertical cooccurence restrictions (only one clitic per slot), these horizontal cooccurence restrictions (not both third and fifth) and why the clitics are ordered this way is not understood, and I have no light to shed on these questions.

Syntactic clitics are so called because they are claimed not to constitute autonomous syntactic units. Rather, they seem to form a unit with some host. Kayne (1975) argues that pronominal clitics adjoin to V in French (a conclusion with substantial validity across Romance that Kayne 1991 refines by claiming that clitics adjoin to a functional category to which a verb may move). This is exemplified by the fact that they cannot be conjoined independently of their host nor can their host be conjoined independently of them:

(4) a. *Jean le et les connaît.
J. him and them know
"John knows him and them."

b. *Jean le connaît et/ou respecte.
J. him knows and/or respects
"John knows and/or respects him."

These properties are not true for all clitics. Subject clitics (except for *on, ce* 'one', 'it/that/this') alone allow the equivalent of (4b), and other clitics which in principle may tolerate conjunction (because there are several different instances occurring in the same clitic slot) allow disjunction:

(5) a. Il connaît et respecte Marie.
he knows and respects M.
"He knows and respects Marie."

b. Il ou elle connaît Marie.
he or she knows M.
"He or she knows Marie."

c. ?Pierre le ou les renverra.
Pierre him or them will-see
"Pierre will see him or her."

As Rizzi (1986b) points out, facts like (5a) as opposed to (4b) indicate that the cluster of clitics is not homogeneous (and unstructured), and that there is a break, which he places after the negative clitic *ne*. In particular, this seems to indicate that subject clitics do not have to be syntactic clitics at all (although they may become syntactic clitics under certain circumstances, such as in Complex Inversion constructions, cf. Sportiche 1993, and they look like phonological clitics, being devoid of possible stress). The significance of examples of the (5c) type in parallel with (4b) is less clear. We will continue assuming that non-subject pronominal clitics are syntactically cliticized, noting the potential problem raised by (5c) (that is discussed in Sportiche 1993).

In non-imperative clauses, the string of clitics immediately precedes the highest verb of its clause. In particular, it will always precede the highest auxiliary of its clause. This is illustrated below:

(6) a. Il le lui donnera.
he it to-him will-give
"He will give it to him."

b. Il le lui a donné.
he it to-him has given
"He gave it to him."

c. Ils lui ont été donnés.
they to-him have been given
"They were given to him."

d. Il ne le lui donnera pas.
he neg it to-him will-give not
"He will not give it to him."

e. Ils ne lui ont pas été donnés.
they neg to-him have not been given
"They were not given to him."

In infinitives, we find more evidence of the split in the clitic cluster noted by Rizzi (1986b) and mentioned above. The negative clitic may be separated from subsequent clitics and precede the negative marker *pas*, all other clitics will immediately precede the verb and follow *pas*.

(7) a. ne pas le lui donner /*ne le lui pas donner
neg not it to-him give_{INF}
"To not give it to him."

b. ne pas l' avoir donné/ ne l'avoir pas donné
neg not it have given
"To not have given it to him."

c. ne pas leur en avoir parlé/??ne leur en avoir pas parlé
neg not to-them of-it have talked
"To not have talked to them about it."

d. ne pas m' en avoir parlé
neg not to-me of-it have talked
"To not have talked about it to me."

3. TYPES OF PREVIOUS ANALYSES.

Previous analyses of the distribution of clitics can be broadly organized in two subclasses: lexical analyses and syntactic analyses. Lexical analyses in effect claim that a clitic is a derivational affix modifying the lexical entry of a predicate. To illustrate, the alternation between *lire un livre* 'to read a book' and *le lire* 'the book' would be one between a transitive verb *lire* and an intransitive *le+lire*. Initially, there is what appears to be a technical problem due to the fact that this derivational affix does not actually always show up on the verb that it intransitivizes (cf. section 2 above). In other words, a lexical analysis claims that adding a clitic in a clause is an operation on the lexical entry of some lexical item. However, since there are many cases in which a clitic appears on a verb to which it bears no lexical relation, this will lead to considerations strongly disfavoring this option. By the principle of uniformity of analysis discussed in section 1.2 above, this dismisses these analyses altogether. The examples below illustrate this point:

(8) a. Jean croit Pierre malade/ le croit malade.
Jean believes Pierre sick/ him believes sick
"Jean believes that Pierre/ he is sick."

b. Jean est semblable à sa mère/ lui est semblable.
Jean is similar to his mother/ to-her is similar
"Jean is similar to his mother/ her."

c. Jean croit Pierre friand de tout/en croit Pierre friand.
Jean believes Pierre fond of all/of-it believes Pierre fond
"Jean believes Pierre fond of everything/ it."

d. Jean veut manger la pomme/ la veut manger.
Jean wants to-eat the apple/ it wants to-eat
"Jean wants to eat the apple/ it."

e. Jean a peint la cheminée de l' usine/en a peint la cheminée.
Jean has painted the chimney of the factory
"John painted the chimney of the factory/its chimney."

In example (8a), the clitic stands for an argument DP subject of a small clause bearing no thematic relation, and hence no lexical relation, with the main verb. Although it is possible to devise theories in which a DP is subcategorized by a predicate without being theta-marked by it—hence bearing a lexical relation with it—such theories make it a mystery where subcategorization comes from and would require far stronger evidence that has ever been adduced in their favor to make them reasonable initial candidates. At any rate, none of the other examples could be so fixed. In the examples (8b,c), the clitic is an argument of the adjective and bears no lexical relationship to the main verbs. In (8d), the so-called RESTRUCTURING constructions (an example which is ungrammatical in standard French but well formed in middle French and its counterparts in many (all?) varieties of Italian or Spanish), the clitic bears no lexical relationship to the verb it is affixed to. Instead, if anything, it might be argued to be lexically related to the embedded verb. In (8e), the clitic stands for a dependent of the head of the object DP. All these cases duplicate the central observation made earlier regarding the basic distribution of clitics: clitics appear on the highest verb of their clause (with provisions made for Restructuring constructions). This essentially correct generalization is syntactic in nature and thus seems incompatible with a strictly lexical approach. At best, the detransitivization property would have to be coupled with a syntactic device ensuring that the clitic morpheme shows up in its proper place. Of course, this is not to deny that there may be a lexical component to the distribution of clitics, such as modification of Case properties of the affected predicate, but we must conclude that the CL+V sequence is not an intransitive verb.

In fact, turning now to syntactic analyses found in the literature, they all more or less have a lexical component to them. Syntactic analyses have typically assumed that the presence of a pronominal clitic, say CL, standing for some argument, say A, does not affect the thematic properties of the predicate Y taking A as argument. Consequently, by the Projection Principle, A is syntactically represented as some phrase XP* generated in its usual position. This conclusion seems warranted: a transitive verb as we just saw remains transitive even if there is a clitic 'standing for' its direct object. The question is to make explicit what 'stand for' means in structural terms and this is what the Projection Principle provides in part: clitic constructions obey the general schema (from now on, we will use XP* to refer to the argument position associated with a clitic):

(9) ....CL_i... [Y ... XP^*_i...] ...

For these syntactic analyses, the questions raised by clitic constructions have mostly concerned the nature of XP* and the properties of the relation between CL and XP*. Again, broadly speaking, past syntactic analyses can be grouped in two subsets: base-generation analyses and movement analyses. According to the base-generation analyses, the clitic is essentially base-generated in its surface position and XP* is to be analyzed as a *pro* or a PRO somehow related to the clitic. According to movement analyses, XP* is to be analyzed as a trace. The second position is usually correlated to the assumption that XP* is literally the trace of CL, a non-necessary assumption (as discussed in Sportiche 1990 and below). Let us survey these two proposals.

4. MOVEMENT AND BASE-GENERATION

The movement analysis is probably the oldest generative analysis and one that is adopted in Kayne (1975, 1989a) and Sportiche (1989, 1990). Base-generation analyses are probably most widely held today in one form or another. They are advocated by Strozer (1976), Rivas (1977), Jaeggli (1982), Borer (1983), Bouchard (1982), Burzio (1986) or Roberge (1990) (see Borer 1986 for a survey and references) for essentially the reasons discussed below in 4.1 and in Sportiche (1983) for somewhat different reasons not reviewed here.[1] We now briefly survey the motivations for each approach.

4.1. *Complementary Distribution*

One simple motivation for Kayne's (1975) movement analysis is the apparent complementary distribution between clitics and their associated XP* found in French illustrated below, where the (c) sentence contains one intonational phrase (i.e., no dislocation intonation, pause. etc.):

(10) a. Marie connaît Louis.
M. knows L.
"Marie knows Louis."

b. Marie le connaît
Marie him knows
"Marie knows him."

c. *Marie le connaît (à) Louis.
M. him knows to L.
"Marie him knows (to) Louis."

Kayne (1975) suggests that clitics are base-generated in the position XP* and are Chomsky-adjoined by a movement operation to an appropriate verb up the tree. Almost all the authors challenging Kayne's proposal have done so on the basis of the existence of Clitic Doubling constructions found in varieties of French (Roberge 1990), Spanish (Strozer 1976, Rivas 1977, Jaeggli 1982), Romanian, Hebrew, Arabic (Aoun 1981, Borer 1983) and exemplified below for Romanian and River Plate Spanish:

(11) a. L-am vazut pe Popescu
him-have-I seen OM Popescu
"I have seen Popescu."

b. Lo vimos a Juan
him saw-we to Juan
"We saw Juan."

In these constructions, both a clitic and a full phrase—the doubled phrase—seem to compete for the same grammatical function. In itself, this observation does not pose any particular challenge to Kayne's proposal. However, an analysis of these facts claiming that the doubled DP occupies XP* would appear fundamentally incompatible with a movement analysis. It is, however, quite difficult to conclusively establish this point. The position of the doubled XP* has been the subject of substantial debate, because of its assumed implications for the movement analysis. In general, however, these discussions have concentrated on the external distribution of the doubling element. In order to preserve the movement analysis, one may try to claim that the doubled element is not XP* but rather an adjunct related to XP*. For example, Hurtado (1984) defends the idea that the doubled XP in (11b) occupies the position of right dislocated phrases. Aoun (1981) defends a variant of this position. Jaeggli (1986) convincingly argues against these proposals, although he does not generally settle the wider question of whether or not the doubled XP is in an adjunct position (he only argues that they are not in dislocated position). However, as Pat Schneider (p.c.) remarks for Greek, doubled elements seem to occur in positions in which adjuncts are simply not tolerated, e.g., as subject of small clauses or ECM subjects:

(12) o Yiorghos tin-perimene [[tin Maria] na paraponiete]
the G. CL_{acc} expected the $Maria_{acc}$ subj complain
"George expected Maria to complain."

This evidence concurs with Jaeggli's conclusions that the doubled element is not an adjunct and in fact has the same external distribution as XP*. From this it is quite reasonable to conclude that the doubling element is indeed XP*. The fact that the doubled phrase has the same external distribution as the missing argument does not suffice, however, to establish the point. Indeed, it is conceivable that the doubled element may be in fact an adjunct as in (i) or an YP specifier as in (ii) to a silent X^0, head of XP* as illustrated below which would in effect further specify the intended content of the clitic element:

(13)
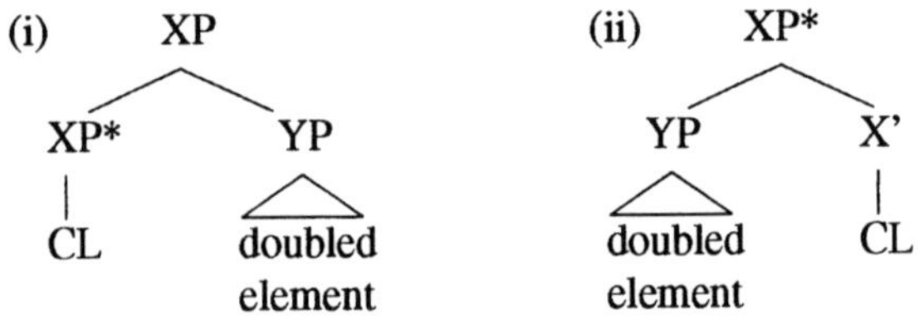

If this were the case, we would expect this doubled element to have the same external distribution as XP*. Until this question is settled (a non-trivial matter), the movement approach is not challenged by the existence of Clitic Doubling constructions. Nor is it particularly supported by the appearance of complementarity in some cases. Although complementarity of distribution between clitics and XP* might have provided an argument for a movement analysis, there may be other ways of handling this complementarity inspired by the treatment of Clitic Doubling constructions, particularly, as many authors have done, by capitalizing on 'Kayne's generalization'. Kayne observes that, in some languages and in some constructions at least, doubled elements must appear affixed by a morpheme (dative-looking in Spanish, the object marker *pe* in Romanian) that does not appear in the absence of the clitic. One idea pursued by the proponents of base-generation analyses attributes the presence of this morpheme on XP* to the fact that the Case which XP* would normally receive is lost ("to the clitic"). Requiring Case for clitics will yield complementarity effects in languages lacking these rescuing devices, such as insertion of a special morpheme.

4.2. *Movement properties*

There are however much stronger arguments adduced in favor of a movement analysis. The strongest such arguments are based on the observation that the clitic/XP* relation displays defining distance properties of movement. We document these properties below in non-doubled cases, strongly suggesting that movement is involved.

4.2.1. *Specified Subject Condition (SSC) effects*

One type of evidence Kayne (1975) used to corroborate his conclusions capitalized on the blocking effects of intervening subjects on (some type of) clitic placement (we will use *clitic placement* preanalytically, i.e., to refer to the surface distribution of a clitic, without taking a stand the mechanism responsible for it). One simple case is illustrated below:

(14) a. Jean a laissé Pierre parler à Marie.
J. has let P. to-speak to M.
"Jean let Pierre speak to Marie."

b. Jean l' a laissé lui parler.
J. him has let to-her to-speak
"Jean let him speak to her."

c. *Jean lui a laissé Pierre parler.
J. to-her has let P. to-speak
"Jean let him speak to her."

d. *Jean le lui a laissé parler
J. him to-her has let to-speak
"Jean let him speak to her."

Placement of the dative clitic cannot reach the main clause over the subject of the embedded clause, suggesting an SSC effect. Whether an SSC effect in turn is a diagnostic of movement is less clear. One construal of the binding theory (e.g., Chomsky's 1981) takes it as a condition on representations and not necessarily on movement relationships per se, so that it can straightforwardly extend to antecedent/lexical anaphor dependencies. Expanding on Lebeaux (1983), antecedent/lexical anaphor relations have also been treated in terms of movement (cf. Chomsky 1986b). If DP/trace or antecedent/anaphor anaphoric relations are indeed movement relations, then obeying Binding principle A is a diagnostic property of movement (although not necessarily an independent diagnostic property, as it might be, and very plausibly is, derived from the ECP antecedent government requirement).

4.2.2. *Condition on Extraction Domain (CED) and ECP effects*

Much more direct evidence in favor of a movement analysis comes from examining the kind of constituents out of which clitics can be extracted. Such data consistently suggest that movement is involved.

4.2.2.1 Extraction from PP

P-stranding under clear cases of movement is disallowed in French. For example, *wh*-movement of the object of the preposition is ill-formed (unless the P is pied-piped):

(15) a. Jean a voté pour Maastricht.
J. has voted for M.
"Jean voted for Maastricht."

b. *Quel traité Jean a-t- il voté pour t ?
which treaty J. has he voted for
"Which treaty did John vote for?"

c. Marie est partie avec la valise.
M. is left with the suitcase
"Marie left with the suitcase."

d. *Quelle valise est- elle partie avec t?
which suitcase is she left with
"Which suitcase did she leave with?"

The same observations hold for stranding under clitic placement ('sc' stands for silent category):

(16) a. Jean a voté pour lui/ *Jean lui a voté pour [sc]
J. has voted for him J. him has voted for
"Jean voted for him."

b. Marie est partie avec elle/ *Marie lui est partie avec [sc]
M. is left with it M. her is left with
"Marie left with it."

It is not true, however, that Ps cannot be stranded at all. As Zribi-Hertz (1984) discusses, the equivalents of (16) are perfectly well formed without the clitic:

(17) Jean a voté pour./ Marie est partie avec.
Jean has voted for/ Marie left with
"Jean voted in favor of it."/ Marie left with it/him/her."

In these cases, the missing object is interpreted as referring to some discourse-prominent entity, exactly as an overt pronoun object of the P is in (16b and d). In fact, Zribi-Hertz (1984) argues that this missing element is best analyzed as a silent pronoun *pro*. If the [sc] in (16) is a trace, the paradigm follows: (16) patterns like (15) and unlike (17) because the relevant part of the ECP only applies to traces.[2]

4.2.2.2. Extraction out of DP

Patterns of extractability out of DPs make the same point: clitic placement behaves exactly like a movement process. Extraction out of direct object DPs in French obeys a simple generalization (cf. Giorgi & Longobardi 1991, Sportiche 1989, Valois 1991, for recent discussion):

(18) Extractability Requirement
An XP may be extracted out of a DP in a given structure iff XP may otherwise appear as the possessor of this DP[3]

This generalization is illustrated by the paradigm below:

(19) a. Jean a vu une/la photo de qui?
J. has seen a/the picture of whom
"Jean saw a/the picture of whom?"

b. La personne dont$_j$ Jean a vu [une/la/*ma/*cette photo t_j]
the person of-whom J. has seen a/the/my/this picture
"The person of whom Jean saw a/the picture."

c. Jean a lu une dépêche de Paris.
J. has read a dispatch from Paris
"Jean read a dispatch from Paris."

d. *D' où$_j$ Jean a-t- il lu [une dépêche t_j]
from where J. has he read a dispatch
"From where did Jean read a dispatch?"

Only when the extracted phrase could otherwise be a possessor can it be extracted, though this is blocked by the presence of another possessor like *ma* or a demonstrative like *cette* as in (19b), or because only DPs and not locative PPs may be possessivized as in (19d). Sportiche (1990) and Valois (1991) propose that this pattern is explained by appealing to antecedent government, a property required of traces but not of silent categories: extraction of a postnominal XP must proceed through the SPEC, DP position guaranteeing antecedent government and deriving the generalization in (18). (20) illustrates this for the sentence in (19b):

(20) La personne dont$_j$ Jean a vu [$_{DP}$ t_j [la [$_{NP}$ photo t_j]]

The same pattern holds of clitic extraction:

(21) a. Jean a vu une/la photo de qui?
J. has seen a/the picture of whom
"Jean saw a/the picture of whom?"

b. Jean en$_j$ a vu [une/la/*ma/*cette photo t_j]
Jean of-him has seen a/the/*my/*this picture
"Jean saw a/the/my/this picture of him."

c. Jean a lu une dépêche de Paris.
J. has read a dispatch from Paris
"John read a dispatch from Paris."

d. *Jean en$_j$ a lu [une dépêche t_j]
Jean therefrom has read a dispatch
"Jean read a dispatch from there."

e. Jean vient de Paris/Jean en$_j$ vient t_j
J. comes from Paris/J. therefrom comes
"Jean comes from Paris." / "Jean comes from there."

Note in particular that cliticization of the locative of origin is disallowed in the sentence (21d), even though it may in principle be cliticized as *en* as in the sentence (21e). Note also that the sc following stranded prepositions is allowed in these contexts, further supporting the contention that we are dealing with different kinds of gaps:

(22) le/mon/ce vote pour (cela)/ mon départ avec (cela)
the/my/this vote for it my departure with it
"the/my/this vote for (it)/my leaving with (it)."

4.2.3. *Participle Agreement*

Participle agreement in French provides further reasons to adopt the movement analysis. A participle may (or must depending on the variety of French) agree with its accusative direct object when it precedes the participle. Agreement is excluded when the participle follows.

(23) a. Jean a peint(*e) la porte.
J. has painted(*FEM) the door
"Jean painted the door."

b. La porte$_i$ que Jean a peint(e) t$_i$
the door that J. has painted(FEM)
"The door that John painted."

c. Jean l' a peint(e) [sc]
John it has painted(FEM)
"John painted it."

(23b) illustrates this with a relativized object, (23c) with a cliticized object. Under a movement analysis, these data make sense if, as Kayne (1989b) suggests:

(i) There is only one way to get agreement: Participle/object agreement is similar to subject/tense agreement in being the reflex of a relation between a head and its specifier.
(ii) There is an intermediate specifier (of the participial morphology) through which the moved object may (or must) transit.

Of course, only assumption (ii) is linked to a movement analysis. Assumption (i) is just a particular (and quite convincing) construal of how agreement arises. As Sportiche's (1989) or (1990) extensive discussion shows, there is substantial independent evidence for the existence of this intermediate position in French. At any rate, this account would attribute to (23c) the following analysis:

(24) le$_j$ a [t$_j$ [peinte ...t$_j$]]

Under a base-generation analysis, i.e., one in which the [sc] in (23c) is *pro* or PRO, this configuration appears arbitrary. Assuming the object is *pro* is essentially saying the object remains postparticipial. Since the agreement in this case would have to be treated differently than in the subject/verb agreement case, there is no reason why the facts turn out this way rather than the other way around (i.e., agreement only with a postverbal (lexical) object).

Corroborating evidence for the movement plus Spec-head approach is found when a fuller picture of agreement is presented. As mentioned, in some varieties of French (like mine), participle agreement is optional with direct object clitics. Now, in all varieties of French, the participle agrees with the subject (instead of the object) if the verb uses the auxiliary *être* 'to be' (including in passive constructions), and this agreement is obligatory.

(25) La porte a été peint*(e).
the door(FEM) has been painted*(FEM)
"The door was painted."

Verbs using the auxiliary *être* are all constructions with derived subjects; in all these cases (which include passive and reflexive constructions (cf. Sportiche 1990 and Cortés 1992), the superficial subject is an underlying object. Now there are two observations to account for: (i) first, why does NP-movement pattern with clitics in being able to trigger agreement; (ii) secondly, why is NP-movement more restricted than clitics in that it must trigger participial agreement.

Both of these facts follow if clitic placement is analyzed as movement plus agreement under Spec-head. First, clitic placement and NP-movement both trigger agreement because they both involve movement (in fact XP-movement, as we will see later). Furthermore, it comes as no surprise either that *wh*-movement may (optionally) trigger agreement. Agreement on this account arises as a result of movement.

Secondly, a movement analysis of clitic placement can account for the second observation as follows. If both clitic placement and raising to subject involve movement, we expect that this movement may pass through the specifier position of the participial phrase. We may suggest that the intermediate step through the specifier of the participial phrase is optional in the case of clitic placement but not in the case of NP-movement: only in the course of the movement involved in clitic placement may this position be skipped. This is consistent with what we know of NP-movement, namely that it is the most restricted kind of movement and the one subject to the strictest locality conditions, i.e., quite possibly more restricted than clitic movement.[4] If any difference is found between NP movement and clitic movement, it is reasonable to expect more latitude for clitic movement. In particular, if movement through the participial specifier is available in principle for clitic movement and raising to subject (and it is, as agreement demonstrates), we expect skipping this position in the course of movement to be at least as available for clitic movement as it is for NP-movement and possibly more so. In other words, the French agreement pattern comes as no surprise. Note in particular that the opposite pattern is predicted impossible (requiring participle agreement with object clitics and allowing but not requiring participle agreement with derived subjects). This seems correct: no variety of French (or, as far as I know, of Romance, for that matter) patterns in the opposite way as the French just described. It is less clear how to get the same results in a base-generation approach. There is no good reason why NP-movement or *wh*-movement should pattern in any way like clitics in being able to trigger agreement.

We will now review reasons in favor of adopting a base-generation analysis. Basically they are either lack-of-source arguments (there is no possible source from which the clitic could have moved) or impossibility-of-movement arguments (the distance between the clitic and its source are not allowed by movement).

4.2.4. *Ethical datives and inherent clitics*

Two lack of source cases are illustrated by the ethical dative construction in (26a) and the inherent clitic construction in (26b):

(26) a. Je t'achèterais un cadeau à Pierre.
I you$_{CL}$-buy-would a present for Peter
"I tell ya, I would buy Peter a present."

b. Pierre en a bavé.
Peter of-it has drooled
"Peter suffered."

In the first, the clitic *te* (also possible with some other dative clitics but probably most natural with 2nd person singular) simply cannot be replaced by any full XP. In fact, the function of the clitic is not to link to any argument. This would seem to argue against a movement analysis for these clitic structures, and by uniformity, against movement analyses in general, for lack of a possible source. Example (26b) illustrates the same point. The clitic *en* does not correspond to any XP slot. It would seem to be in some way part of the lexical entry of the verb *en-baver* but nevertheless behaves positionally like a regular clitic in preceding the auxiliary verb *avoir*. By uniformity, we would then expect all clitics to be part of the lexical entries of their predicate. As we have discussed before, this is clearly an unacceptable conclusion, which might cast doubt on the requirement that clitics be uniformly analyzed.

However, as R. Kayne (p.c.) points out, the lack of source argument is seriously weakened by the existence of such English examples as *John perjured himself, John kicked the bucket*. In these examples, we have direct objects which, as part of an idiom, must somehow be listed as part of a lexical entry including the verb and at the same time be realized as independent DP objects, even though they do not seem to receive any 'real' theta role. If having a 'real' theta role is not a precondition for DPs to occur as objects, the lack of source argument disappears: French inherent clitic verbs could just as well list a theta-less clitic object, which would then be subject to the normal rules of clitic placement. Likewise, for ethical dative constructions, in which the clitic is not obviously related to the verb, we would have to allow the generation of a theta-less XP headed by the dative clitic which would then be subject to the normal rules of clitic placement.

Note finally that a base-generation analysis faces somewhat the same complication as a movement analysis. Since clitics usually are linked to an argument position, inherent clitics and ethical datives would constitute an exceptional class of clitics. However, the base-generation analysis does not entail the existence of an XP* corresponding to the clitic, and, in that, it appears slightly simpler than the movement analysis. In sum, we conclude that these constructions, although they pose a problem, do not really help to decide the issue and in particular do not invalidate a movement analysis.

4.2.5. *Stranded quantifiers in L-tous cases*

The distribution of stranded or floating quantifiers seems difficult to reconcile with a movement analysis of clitics. Stranded quantifiers are illustrated in the following examples:

(27) a. Les enfants ont *tous* mangé.
The children have all eaten
"The children all ate."

b. Je les ai vus *tous*.
I them have seen all
"I have seen them all."

Following Sportiche's (1988) proposal, we take it that the distribution of these quantifiers is determined in part by the position of intermediate traces of their antecedents: these quantifiers are in fact adjacent to a silent DP (trace, *pro* or PRO) bound by another (usually overt) DP they quantify over. Thus, in (27a), the presence of the quantifier *tous* reveals that the subject of the sentence has raised from a lower position (yielding the VP internal subject hypothesis). Koopman (1991) and Schlonsky (1990) have convincingly argued that the mechanism of Q-stranding under DP movement involves raising the DP through SPEC, QP as revealed by the fact that the Q agrees with the DP only under stranding in Hebrew (Schlonsky) and by the existence of phrases like *eux tous* 'them all' in French and *them all* in English (Koopman) (in effect, a modern version of Kayne's (1975) Q-post analysis).[5]

There are actually two distinct ways of implementing Sportiche's (1988) basic idea in a way consistent with Koopman's and Schlonsky's proposals. The first one is to assume, as did Sportiche (1988), that a strandable Q is always generated with a DP complement. Stranding under this view is always under syntactic movement of this DP through the specifier position of the QP. An alternative is to postulate that this kind of Q may be generated in a wider variety of environments, e.g., as a Q taking a VP complement, and is understood to quantify over some DP moving through its specifier position (and thereby triggering agreement): $[_{QP}\ DP_i\ [tous\ [_{VP}\ V...t_i]]]$. This last analysis of *tous* would be akin to that of other quantifiers appearing to be both determiners and adverbials (e.g., *Il a vu beaucoup d'enfants, il a beaucoup vu d'enfants* 'He saw a lot of children.'). Either approach straightforwardly extends to case (28a) but not to (28b-d):[6]

(28) a. Marie les a tous pris.
Marie them has all taken
"Marie took them all."

b. Marie a toutes voulu [les manger].
Marie has all wanted them eat_{INF}
"Marie wanted to eat them all."

c. Il a tous fallu [qu' ils parlent].
It has all necessitated that they speak
"It was necessary that they all speak."

d. Il a tous fallu [que Louis les lise].
It has all necessitated that Louis them read
"It was necessary that Louis read them all."

In the last three examples, which we shall call L-tous cases (from Kayne's 1975 Leftward-tous rule) the stranded Q is higher than the clitic it modifies. In fact, it is outside the clitic's clause altogether.[7] The fact that an intervening head, the complementizer *que*, does not block this construction indicates that, if the Q is placed by movement in its overt position, it does not move out of its clause by head movement but rather by XP movement. This movement is most plausibly of the A-bar type, given that NP-movement out of a tensed clause is strictly forbidden in French. Sportiche (1988) attributed the possibility of (28c,d) to the syntactic application of Quantifier Raising (QR).

Suppose we adopt both one of the analyses of floating quantifiers described above and a movement analysis of clitics. This might be more precisely construed as follows: (i) the clitic is the head of the DP modified by or quantified over by *tous*, (ii) the clitic itself moves to its surface position, (iii) *tous* quantifying over this DP is licensed by this DP moving through the specifier position of the Q. Consider now what this would mean for a sentence like (28d). The following configuration will need to be arrived at:

(29) $[_{QP}$ [tous V ... $[_{CP}$ ... $[_{D}les_i]$ ... $[_{DP}\ t_i$]]]]

The clitic, i.e., the D head of the object DP, has incorporated to some host. If the stranded Q gets to its surface position by movement, and gets stranded by movement of its complement DP (or the head D of such a DP) out of QP, the raised QP will contain the unbound trace of this D or this DP. If, alternatively, the stranded Q is base-generated in the top clause, its licensing will require the following scenario: by LF, this DP will have to raise to the position SPEC, QP even though it would contain a trace of the incorporated clitic.[8] This violates the requirement that traces be properly bound. This problem of course does not arise if the clitic is generated independently of the DP argument it is related to, a basic property of base-generation analyses.One potential way to remove this offending trace would require reconstruction of this DP into the lower clause at LF. It is clear however that these leftward moved Qs have matrix scope, not embedded scope. This is illustrated by the following pair:

(30) a. Il aurait tous fallu que tu ne les
it would-have all necessitated that you neg them
aies pas vus.
have not seen
"It would have been necessary that you see none of them."

b. Il aurait fallu que tu ne les
it would-have necessitated that you neg them
aies pas tous vus.
have not all seen
"It would have been necessary that you do not see all of them."

As the paraphrases indicate, in the first sentence the Q must have scope wider than the embedded negation. If reconstruction was required, we would expect at the very least the Q to be able to take narrower scope than the embedded negation as in the second sentence.

4.2.6. *Dative constructions and stranded quantifiers*

There is a second class of clitic constructions which superficially also seem to lack a plausible movement source for their clitics. The movement analysis makes the claim that the relation between the clitic and its associated XP* is a possible movement relation. The base-generation makes no such claim (although there is a need under the base-generation analysis, to elucidate the nature of the locality relation holding between the clitic and its associated XP*). The central paradigm I want to discuss, representative of all the constructions involving a dative clitic is illustrated below:[9]

(31) a. Je (*leur) ai offert un cadeau à tous les enfants.
I (to-them) have given a present to all the children
"I gave a present to all of these children."

b. Je (*à) leur ai (tous) offert un cadeau *(à) tous.
I to them have all given a present to all
"I gave them all a present."

(31) c. Ces garçons, *(à) qui j' ai (??tous) offert
These boys, to whom I have (all) given
un cadeau ((à) tous)...
a present (to all)
"These boys, all of whom I gave a present."

These examples show that a dative clitic may appear in conjunction with a stranded quantifier, but not with a full phrase. If this Q appears stranded by clitic placement in the normal dative position, this Q must be preceded by the preposition (or the dative marker) *à*. Otherwise, it must be bare. These dative Qs cannot be stranded under *wh*-movement however. They may be very marginally stranded as bare Qs in preparticiple position. This behavior is in marked contrast with that of accusative objects, which allow stranding of Q's both under clitic placement and under *wh*-movement *Je les ai tous lus*. 'I read them all.', *ces livres que j'ai tous lus*. "These books, which I have all read'.

These examples constitute a serious problem for a movement analysis of clitics in the dative case. The complementarity of the clitic and full DP suggests that the two positions are related by movement. But the difference between clitic placement and *wh*-movement with postverbal stranded Qs preceded by *à* suggests otherwise: if clitics actually moved, why should they pattern any differently from *wh*-phrases? One possibility is that they do not move as phrases—unlike *wh*-phrases—but rather as heads throughout, an option consistent with some of Kayne's recent proposals and also with Kayne's (1975) handling of this problem.[10] He suggests that dative *à* may be transformationally inserted on a dative DP. The derivation of (31c) would include the following steps: ... *offert* $[_{Dative}$ *[tous* $[_{DP}$ *qui]]]* —> DP-to-SPEC —> *offert* $[_{DativeQP}$ $[_{DP}$ *qui] [tous t]]*. At this point A-insertion on the DP *qui* (cf. *J'ai parle à eux tous*. 'I spoke to them all'.) and DP movement (*wh*-movement) may apply in either order. This forces *à* to be carried along with the moved phrase as desired. The problem is to force the opposite with clitic placement in (31b). From the structure ...*offert* $[_{DativeQP}$ $[_{DP}$ *leur] [tous t]]*, pied-piping of an inserted *à* or insertion of a moved *leur* must be prevented. This behavior is surprising, if clitic placement is DP movement, but would follow if *leur* moves as a D rather than as a DP, construing *à* as a property of the DP rather than of the D. If, however, we can show that clitic movement cannot be construed as head movement throughout, as we will in 5.3, it suggests that clitic placement in these structures is not the result of movement.

5. ANALYSIS

Throughout, we restrict ourselves to cases in which the clitic is associated with an argument XP*. Other cases, as discussed earlier, can be similarly treated.

5.1. *Clitic Voices*

The previous discussion suggests we have a contradiction. On the one hand, the search for explanatory adequacy strongly supports a uniform analysis of clitic constructions. On the other, different clitic constructions seem compatible with different analyses. As mentioned in section 1.3, this contradiction may be resolved. Movement analyses have typically assumed that movement is *movement of the clitic*. None of the arguments supporting a movement analysis actually shows this. The first proposal we make is to abandon the assumption made by movement theories, namely that the movement involved in clitic constructions is movement of the clitic. Base-generation analyses, on the other hand, seem to be faced with a fundamental problem. It is particularly striking that the movement properties holding of the relation between a clitic and its XP* hold regardless of whether or not XP* is silent: in Clitic Doubling constructions as well, the clitic and the doubled phrase are in a possible movement relationship, in fact the exact same as in non-doubled constructions. The second proposal we make is to abandon one assumption made by base-generation theories, namely that no movement is involved.

If the clitic is not the element moved from the position XP*, we need to account for the fact that the clitic agrees with XP*. Thus, if the missing argument XP* is understood to be what is denoted by a third person singular pronoun direct object, the clitic appearing in the structure is a third person singular accusative clitic. Furthermore, as we have discussed in section 2, clitics are so called because they do not form autonomous syntactic units. Rather, they seem to form a unit with some host. As Kayne (1989a) points out, there is a natural interpretation of this clitic property in contemporary syntactic theory: the clitics are heads whose close syntactic connection with a host can be analyzed as a case of head-to-head movement incorporating the clitic head to the host head (or vice versa).[11] This immediately suggests that the agreement between a clitic and its corresponding XP* be viewed as an instance of agreement between a phrasal constituent and a head, a kind of agreement naturally handled as a reflex of a relation between a head and its specifier and is consistent with the general idea that agreement is always a phrase/head relation between a specifier and a head.

In order to implement this agreement requirement as the result of a Spec-head relationship, we must provide a projection whose head is the clitic and whose specifier is a landing site for movement of the corresponding XP*. This is, of course, the proposal outlined in section 1. Without getting into much structural detail for the moment, remember that a typical clitic construction (such as the one exemplified in (1), repeated below) would receive the analysis indicated in (2) (repeated below), given that XP* is in this case a DP:[12]

(1)	Marie	les_i	aura	présentés XP_i*	à Louis
	M.	them	will-have	introduced-AGR_i	to Louis
	"Marie would have introduced them to Louis."				

(2) [$_{AccP}$ DP^ [[$_{Acc}$les] [... aura présentés DP*$_{[acc]}$ ...]]]

In order to achieve or sanction agreement, DP* will have to move to DP^ at some point. More generally, with each clitic slot of the clitic template given in (3), there is a corresponding projection available. Call these projections CLITIC VOICES, and individual instances of them Nominative Voice, Accusative Voice, Dative Voice, and so on.[13] Thus, a sentence such as (32a) will be associated with the structure in (32b) (linear order irrelevant at this point):

(32) a. Il le lui donnera.
He it to-him/her will-give
"He will give it to him/her."

b.

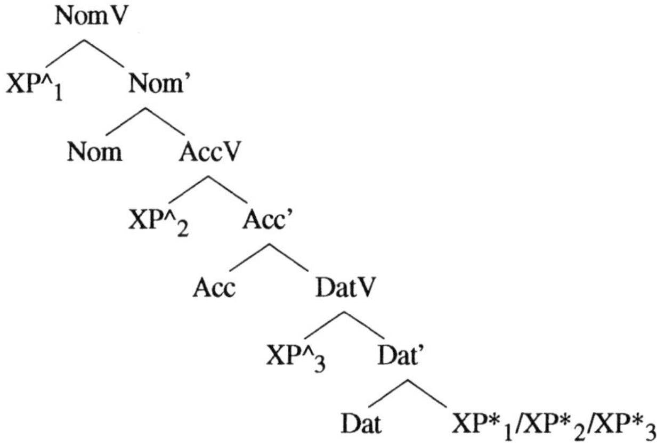

We must now answer the following questions:

(33) (i) How docs this analysis reconcile movement and base-generation
(ii) How is it compatible with the properties of individual clitic constructions.
(iii) What kind of movement is involved, what causes movement (linked to the question of the function of these clitic projections).
(iv) What is the nature of XP* (when it is silent)?
(v) What is the nature of the position XP^?
(vi) Where are these clitic projections located structurally?

Of these, (33iv) can be partially answered immediately. Reflexive (or rather *se* clitic constructions) behave differently from the others (see Sportiche 1990 and the references cited therein). In a non-reflexive clitic construction, a silent XP* is interpreted exactly as a pronoun would be. We therefore postulate that XP* is *pro* (as did Sportiche 1983) for exactly the same reason; see also Bouchard 1982). XP* moves to XP^ where it does not have to be bound (ignoring the possibility of further movement). PRO would not give rise to the right interpretation (of definite pronoun) in the absence of any antecedent (and none is necessary in clitic constructions).[14] As *pro*, XP* needs to be properly identified, which it is after movement to XP^, by the coindexed clitic head. In effect, we are treating non-reflexive clitic constructions (i.e., Accusative Voice, Dative Voice, Genitive Voice, Locative Voice and Nominative Voice) as *pro*-drop constructions, again very much along the lines of Sportiche (1983) (see also Roberge 1990, Bouchard 1982). Sportiche (1993) explores ways of extending this approach to pro-drop throughout, claiming in effect that subject agreement is not what licenses pro drop, but that Subject clitics are.

5.1.1. *The Clitic Criterion*

We may now give a preliminary answer to question (33iii) in relation to what causes movement. We have already noted the similar behavior of *wh*-movement and clitics with respect to agreement. Let us pursue the analogy with *wh*-movement one step further. We know that *wh*-phrases typically occur overtly only clause-initially in specific clauses bearing the property [+Q] or [+wh]. Rizzi (1990) captures this generalization by updating May's (1985) *wh*-Criterion and by taking into account Chomsky's (1986a) generalized X-bar proposal extending the X-bar schema to the complementizer system:

(34) *Wh*-criterion or Q-criterion:
 i. A *wh*- head must be in a Spec-head relationship with a *wh*- XP at LF
 ii. A *wh*- XP must be in a Spec-head relationship with a *wh*- head at LF

Satisfaction of this criterion will guarantee the proper distribution of *wh*-phrases at LF. We can treat clitics along similar lines. Assume that clitics license in XPs a particular property or feature [+F] (about which we will speculate in section 7; for concreteness' sake, consider it in French to be that of being a null pronoun). Assume further that this property may be licensed at LF only in an appropriate agreement relationship. By analogy with (34), we may state[15]

(35) Clitic Criterion
 i. A clitic must be in a Spec-head relationship with a [+F] XP at LF
 ii. A [+F] XP must be in a Spec-head relationship with a clitic at LF[16]

where the agreement reflex of the Spec-head relationship is expressed by Case, number, gender and person agreement (at least in French). Thus, if a clitic is related to an XP*, this XP* will have to move in order to satisfy the Clitic Criterion (35).

Looking at this analysis in full generality, we see that a clitic construction is a (non-local) movement relationship between two XP's, XP* and XP^ mediated by a (clitic) head H, such that XP^=SPEC, HP, so that XP* agrees with H. By LF, XP* must have moved to XP^. Some of the parameters of the constructions are then as follows:

(36) Clitic construction parameters[17]
 (i) Movement of XP* to XP^ occurs overtly or covertly
 (ii) H is overt or covert
 (iii) XP* is overt or covert

All clitic constructions (involving a Cl/XP* dependency), we claim, involve movement. The movement of XP* is to the specifier position of the projection headed by the clitic, where agreement between Cl and XP* is sanctioned. This approach treats clitics as complex agreement morphemes, deriving the agreement relation XP*/Cl as an instance of a Spec-head relation, and it determines the locality relation between the clitic and XP* as in effect being characterized by the necessary movement relation between XP^ = SPEC, ClP and XP*.[18] This provides a general way of handling true Clitic Doubling constructions, i.e., Clitic Doubling constructions not analyzable as in (13). Superficially, (true) Clitic Doubling constructions differ from non-doubled constructions in that XP* is overt in the first and covert in the second. So far, we have not specified whether movement should be overt or covert. When XP* is overtly realized in the XP* position, as might be the case in Spanish Clitic Doubling constructions, the analysis will postulate covert movement of XP* to XP^. This does not mean that movement of an overt XP* may not be overt as well. I suggest later that this happens in Dutch Scrambling constructions. Similarly, when XP* is covert, movement may a priori be overt or covert. Settling this question will require checking the properties of the XP^/XP* relation in individual constructions.

If the parameters given in (36) are independent, it is easy to see the kind of constructions each combination of the options in (36) will give rise to. A covert XP* moving overtly or covertly to XP^ with H overt gives rise to undoubled clitic constructions as in French or Italian or Dutch. An overt XP* moving covertly with an overt H gives rise to Clitic Doubling constructions as might be illustrated by Spanish or Romanian. An overt XP* moving overtly with H overt will give some object agreement constructions such as might be found in Lebanese Arabic. The Clitic Left-Dislocation construction of Cinque (1991) may also be such a case, or a case of overt movement of XP* to XP^ and then beyond, as is found in Romanian or Spanish *wh*-questions. An overt XP* moving overtly with a covert H will have the appearance of simple phrasal movement . We argue that Scrambling of Specific DPs in Dutch is such an instance.

5.1.2. *The Position of Clitic Voices*

We now briefly address question (33vi). It subdivides into two: (i) where are the clitic projections generated within the clause? (ii) how are the clitic projections ordered with respect to each other? I will limit myself to the first question here and leave the second entirely open, as its understanding requires resolving many issues about the internal structure of strings of clitics about which little is understood. Relevant to this determination are the Head Movement Constraint, which prohibits movement of heads to skip intermediate heads and Baker's Mirror Principle, which claims that morphological constituent structure reflects syntactic constituent structure. Here we are only concerned with non-nominative clitics which obey the basic generalization given in section 2:[19]

(37) Clitics occur adjoined to the highest verbal element of the clause containing XP*.

Consider again the sentences given in section 2:

(6) a. Il le lui donnera.
he it to-him will-give
"He will give it to him."

b. Il le lui a donné.
he it to-him has given
"He gave it to him."

c. Ils lui ont été donnés.
they to-him have been given
"They were given to him."

d. Il ne le lui donnera pas.
he neg it to-him will-give not
"He will not give it to him."

e. Ils ne lui ont pas été donnés.
they neg to-him have not been given
"They were not given to him."

(7) a. ne pas le lui donner / *ne le lui pas donner
neg not it to-him give$_{INF}$
"To not give it to him."

b. ne pas l' avoir donné/ ne l'avoir pas donné
neg not it have given
"To not have given it to him."

(7) c. ne pas leur en avoir parlé/??ne leur en avoir pas parlé
neg not to-them of-it have talked
"To not have talked to them about it."

d. ne pas m' en avoir parlé
neg not to-me of-it have talked
"To not have talked about it to me."

Pollock (1989) demonstrates, mostly on the basis of adverbial/verb ordering possibilities, the existence of two different head positions (which he takes to be T and AGR). He shows that French tensed verbs must raise from V to the highest of the two and French infinitival verbs optionally raise from V to the lowest of the two (except for auxiliaries which may marginally raise to the higher slot). Suppose initially the following construal of his results: INFL is split between AGR_S and T with AGR_S the higher head. The order of projections is thus AGR_S T, with short V movement (of infinitivals) being to T and long V-movement (obligatory for tensed verbs, optional for infinitival auxiliaries) being to AGR_S.[20] Generally, in clauses with one or two auxiliary verbs, we have the following relevant structures:

(38) a. *Tensed clauses*

(ne)	Cl	AUX1+Tense	(pas)	(AUX2)	Verb	XP*
ne	lui	aura	pas	été	rapporté	
Neg_1	to-him	will-have	Neg_2	been	brought-back	

"Will not have been brought back to him."

b. *Tenseless clauses*[21]

(ne)	(pas)	Cl	AUX1+Inf	(AUX2)	Verb	XP*
ne	pas	lui	avoir	été	rapporté	
Neg_1	Neg_2	to-him	to-have	been	brought-back	

"Not to have been brought back to him."

If there is no auxiliary verb, the position of AUX1 above is occupied by the main verb. Note the two negative particles *ne* (=Neg_1) and *pas* (= Neg_2.) Clearly, the fact that the highest verbal element is on different sides of Neg_2 is consistent with Pollock's conclusions and might indicate that we should have the order $Neg_1 > H_1 > Neg_2 > H_2$ with H_1=AGR_S and H_2=T.

How should clitic Projections be ordered with respect to these? Let us begin with tensed clauses (38a). Given the possibility of (5c) *?Pierre le ou les renverra* 'Peter will send him or them back.' and the imperative order of V + Tense + AGR_S + Cl (*renvoyons-les* 'let's send them back'), the morphological structure of the sequence Cl + V + Tense + AGR_S seems to be Cl + [V + Tense + AGR]. By the Mirror Principle, the corresponding projections should be ordered ClP>AGR_SP>TP>VP, with Aux raising to T, (then to AGR_S) then to Cl. Now, given the infinitive case, and in particular the fact that the whole verbal complex follows Neg_2, the order will have to be: $Neg_1 > H_1 > Neg_2 >$

ClP > AGR_SP > TP > VP. This shows that it is incorrect to identify H_1 with AGR_S and H_2 with T. Rather, it is more plausible to take H_1 to be an additional projection. Furthermore, given that clitics in standard French always end up on V, even in infinitives, we must assume that all verbs *eventually* raise at least to AGR_S.

If, following Chomsky's (1992) proposal of morphological checking, words are inserted in the syntax fully formed and morpheme properties and ordering are checked under successive head movement to the relevant projections, we may assume that a clitic is base-generated on its verbal host and we may construe Pollock 's split between tenseless verbs and tensed verbs as a failure for tenseless verbs to raise *overtly* to AGR_S. If we limit Chomsky's proposal to words (excluding clitics from being base-generated lower than the projection in which they are checked, and thus deriving the difference between clitics and inflectional bound morphemes), this split must be handled differently than we have assumed above, since raising to ClP, and hence to AGR_S, will have to be overt. We are led to assume that all verbs raise to AGR_S and to Cl. To handle Pollock's split, we must postulate that there is an additional head above ClP but below Neg_2, say H_2, to which tensed verbs obligatorily raise (and thus obligatorily preceding adverbs like *complètement* 'completely') and tenseless auxiliaries optionally raise but to which tenseless main verbs cannot. In other words, we are led to construe Pollock's observations as evidence for two projections, as he does, but to take these projections H_1 and H_2 to be *higher* than AGR_S. Taking morphemes to head their own projections (with PM = participial morphology), we will have the following template for French, with each verbal element raising to the next head (*pas* does not count as an intervening head for purposes of the Head Movement Constraint, just like other adverbials, cf. Pollock 1989):

(39) *ne* H_1 *pas* H_2 ClP AGR_S $T_{[+/- \text{ tense}]}$ (avoir PM_1) (être PM_2) V

In all cases, the highest verb raises to AGR_S and Cl if necessary.[22] Tenseless verbs may then raise to H_2. Tensed verbs must raise to H_1, presumably via H_2.

5.2. *A second look at the various arguments*

We now go back to each of the arguments for or against movement discussed earlier. Clearly, arguments for movement (i.e., those involving SSC, CED or ECP effects, as well as the pattern of participle agreement) pose no particular problems, since we adopt a movement analysis. Left to handle properly are questions of complementary distribution and Clitic Doubling in the case of L-tous Stranding of quantifiers or quantifier doubling in dative constructions.

5.2.1. *Clitic Doubling*

So far, we have concentrated mostly on Standard French. Standard French appears not to allow Clitic Doubling, except for the cases of Complex Inversion (cf. *Jean est-il malade?* 'Is John sick?') which Sportiche (1993) analyses as Clitic Doubling.[23] This is correct for object clitics, if it is understood as requiring the lexical head of XP* to be silent. However, some other varieties of French do allow true Clitic Climbing and many Romance languages (and in fact even non-Romance languages) do as well. Recall that Clitic Doubling is the cooccurence of a clitic and an overt XP*, and that we have analyzed it as postponement until LF of the necessary movement of XP* to XP^. In fact, there is nothing in the analysis presented so far that really bears on the overt/covert character of XP*: whether overt or covert, XP* will have to raise by LF to the right specifier so that the Clitic Criterion is met. Clitic doubling constructions and non-doubled clitic constructions are analyzed exactly the same way: the problem is not to account for the possibility of Clitic Doubling. This central dilemma faced by earlier accounts disappears. Rather, the problem is to account for the distribution of Clitic Doubling, and for the differences between Clitic Doubling and non-doubled clitics.

We may preanalytically subdivide the problem of distribution in two subproblems, whose exact boundaries are of course unknown as yet: necessary distributional properties and (apparently) accidental distributional properties. If Clitic Doubling exhibits necessary properties, they should follow from its analysis. One such necessary property seems to be the following:

(40) If Clitic Doubling is allowed, it is allowed with (stressed) pronouns.[24]

This gives us Clitic Doubling problem #1: why is (40) true?

In the second category, we find questions such as why does French disallow it while Spanish allows it? Why do different dialects of Spanish allow it in different circumstances, e.g., only with indirect objects, or only with indirect objects and pronominal direct objects? This is Clitic Doubling problem #2: What accounts for the inter- and intralinguistic distribution of Clitic Doubling?

Another kind of variable property is Kayne's generalization, already mentioned earlier (which does not appear to hold of all Clitic Doubling languages): it claims that bare objects may not be doubled, but must be affixed by a dummy marker (typically a preposition, often the one otherwise inducing dative Case). This is Clitic Doubling problem #3: What accounts for Kayne's generalization?

Unfortunately, apart from problem #1, I do not have good answers to provide to these problems. Past proposals can be incorporated within the present account, as I will do, but none of them is really satisfactory. Let us postpone the consideration of Problem #1 until the discussion of the function of clitic projections in section 7.2. There, we will suggest a possible answer to the first problem.

As for problems #2 and #3, I can suggest some speculations along the lines of similar problems arising in other constructions. We need to answer the following questions: (i) why do certain languages (or constructions) allow the cooccurrence of overt clitics and overt XP* and others do not; ii) why do certain languages (or constructions) allowing overt XP* disallow its overt raising to XP^ while others do not. Adapting the line that the proponents of base-generating clitics have proposed, we might rule Clitic Doubling out by appealing to Case theory. More specifically, we might argue that languages disallow realizing the same Case on two different nominal elements. Because Romance clitics are nominal and encode Case morphology, they cannot cooccur at the same time as a full Case-marked XP* (unless an extra option exists to Case-mark this XP* , cf. Kayne's generalization). One way of implementing this idea pursues the analogy with *wh*-movement entertained earlier. The output of syntactic *wh*-movement is subject to the doubly filled COMP filter. Suppose that just as the Clitic Criterion suggests a generalization of the *wh*-criterion to a more general principle of licensing (a general line pursued in Sportiche 1995), the doubly filled COMP filter generalizes in such a way that it covers clitic projections or voices as well. The general idea might be that functional heads such as certain Cs or certain clitics cannot be simultaneously filled as their specifier if they encode a property overtly realized on this specifier (here this might be Case). This would be a sort of principle of economy minimizing use of unnecessary morphophonological overtness (similar in a sense to the Avoid Pronoun principle):[25]

(41) Doubly filled Voice Filter
$* [_{HP}$ XP [H...]]
where H is a functional head and both XP and H overtly encode the same property P.

Clitic Doubling may arise in a language if the clitic encodes no (relevant) property that the doubling phrase expresses; this might be the case in languages such as Lebanese Arabic that have a morphologically poorer clitic system than Romance or in Spanish, where the insertion of a preposition embeds XP* under a P that makes the property expressed by XP* inaccessible to (41). Another possibility, which we will ultimately reject, would be to limit the scope of (41) to overt movement. XP* raising would behave in a way similar to what is assumed of LF *wh*-movement (possibly because (41) is not operative on LF or because its effects can be trivially voided by deleting a semantically empty C). Delaying XP* movement until LF would then provide a way of preventing a violation of (41) with an overt XP* in the presence of an overt clitic.

5.2.2. *Participle Agreement*

Let us now return to participle agreement within the approach of clitic constructions proposed here. The basic premise we adopt is that put forth in

Kayne (1989b): participle agreement (and agreement in general) is an XP/head relation that should be handled in a fashion similar to subject/tense agreement. Given that the latter is analyzed as a Spec-head relation, the former should be, too. Pursuing the analogy, given that the subject agrees with T and that this is analyzed as T raising to an agreement head, AGR_S, we postulate that participle agreement is triggered by the moving of a phrase through the specifier position, which we call $SPEC_{AGR\text{-}O}$, of an agreement head AGR_O to which the participle raises.[26]

(42)

agreement

... [$SPEC_{AGR\text{-}O}$ [[participle] ... YP]] ...

Here, we limit ourselves to agreement with accusative DPs. As mentioned earlier, such agreement may not take place if the accusative DP overtly follows the participle. When the DP precedes the participle, as in clitic constructions, agreement is possible, but not necessary, except in more formal registers. This is illustrated below:

(43) a. Jean a peint(*e) la porte.
J. has painted(*FEM) the door
"Jean painted the door."

b. Jean l' a peint(e).
John it has painted(FEM)
"John painted it."

This optionality is actually not an isolated fact of French participle agreement. The same is true of Catalan participle agreement in clitic constructions, as discussed in Cortés (1992). It is also true of Italian participle agreement in clitic constructions when the object clitic is not a 3rd person clitic.

(44) a. Giovanni la ha accusata/ *accusato.
Giovanni her has accused$_{FEM}$/ *accused$_{MASC}$)
"Giovanni has accused her."

b. Maria e Paola, vi ho visto/ viste
M. and P., you$_{FEM.PL}$ I-have seen$_{MASC.SG}$/ seen$_{FEM.PL}$
"Maria and Paola, I have seen you."

How should we handle this optionality? First, subject/tense agreement suggests that agreement is not optional. If the agreement configuration is met, agreement takes place. In movement theories moving the clitic from the position XP* (essentially) to its surface position, the only way to get the right result is to provide two possible movement paths, one of which may skip the position $SPEC_{AGR-O}$. This is the proposal put forth in Sportiche (1990) (and also in an earlier draft of the present article). Sportiche (1990) adopts Kayne's proposal that if a clitic moves, the movement must involve head movement at some point, since the clitic does end up incorporated to the verb as only a head may do. To reconcile this view of clitic movement as head movement with Kayne's analysis of agreement (which assumes XP movement) as well as with the Head Movement Constraint (Head movement from XP* to its surface position would violate this condition), Sportiche (1990) proposed that clitic movement is decomposed into two different steps. The first step is a phrasal movement up to a position from which the clitic may incorporate as a head to its hosts without violating the HMC. Now consider a case of an accusative clitic not triggering agreement:

(45) l'avoir $[_{AGRP}$ $SPEC_{AGR-O}$ $[_{AGR'}$ [construit] ...XP...

The clitic head of XP must move out of VP and skip $SPEC_{AGR-O}$ to a position from which it may incorporate to the auxiliary. Since incorporation cannot be done from within AGR', and there is no A-position available into which XP could move, we are led to assume that XP moves to some A-bar position XP', governed by the auxiliary where from the clitic may incorporate to *avoir*. That is, we are forced to assume that clitic movement involves A-bar movement when participle agreement fails. This predicts that accusative clitics should be able to license parasitic gaps from this position XP'. This consequence appears to contradict Chomsky's (1982) or Sportiche (1983) conclusions, according to which these clitics do not license parasitic gaps. We return to this problem in section 6.2.2.

Consider now the optionality problem within the framework of the analysis of clitics proposed here.

(46) $[_{ClP}$ XP^ [[le] ...$[_{AGRP}$ $SPEC_{AGR-O}$ $[_{AGR'}$ ...XP*...

The clitic does not move. Only its associated XP* does.[27] Under a skipping approach to agreement failure, we may claim that XP* moves to XP^ without moving through $SPEC_{AGR-O}$. We do not face the potential parasitic gap problem if XP^ is an A-position. If XP^ is an A-bar position, we do. We may also propose that agreement fails because movement of XP* does not occur early enough to feed the phonology, i.e., it is delayed until LF. In other words, agreement is triggered if XP* movement takes place overtly in the syntax. Agreement is not triggered if movement of XP* takes place covertly at LF.

Either option seems compatible with the function of $SPEC_{AGR-O}$, although the second one seems simpler: as mentioned, only accusatively Case-marked NPs have access to $SPEC_{AGR-O}$. This restriction can be explained if object agreement and accusative Case are two sides of the same coin. Adopting Chomsky's (1991) or Sportiche's (1990) views on the subject, we take $SPEC_{AGR-O}$ to be the position in which accusative Case is obligatorily sanctioned at LF: accusative NPs must in the end move to (or through) $SPEC_{AGR-O}$. If agreement is present, this means that XP* movement to XP^ through $SPEC_{AGR-O}$ takes place overtly. If agreement is absent, the delaying view assumes that this exact same movement is delayed until LF. The skipping view is forced to assume that XP* moves to XP^ skipping $SPEC_{AGR-O}$, but accusative checking later needs to incorporate $SPEC_{AGR-O}$ in the movement chain (e.g., by moving the trace of XP* to $SPEC_{AGR-O}$).

The delaying approach (movement of XP* to XP^ is LF movement—in Chomsky's (1992) terms, movement is *procrastinated*) seems more straightforward than the skipping approach and I will tentatively adopt it, at least for accusatives, for two reasons: (i) there are good grounds for believing that XP^ should count as an A-bar position (see section 7 on Dutch Scrambling), and (ii) accusative clitics do not license parasitic gaps (see section 6.3). There are however a number of problems requiring mention. First, *wh*-movement may also optionally trigger participle agreement in a clause containing an accusative *wh*-trace.[28]

(47) Quelle maison as-tu construit(e?
which$_{FEM}$ house have-you built(FEM)
"Which house did you build?"

In this case, movement is obviously overt. The delaying approach is thus not an option. Only the skipping option is. If the skipping option must be appealed to for *wh*-movement, it comes as no cost for clitic constructions. Secondly, if XP* movement to XP^ may be delayed until LF, we might expect Clitic Doubling to be allowed if the Doubly Filled Voice filter is an S-structure filter. Consequently, Clitic Doubling should surface in all French dialects allowing optional participial agreement with accusative clitics, a prediction contrary to what is observed. This indicates, in a way consistent with Chomsky's (1992) Minimalist assumptions, that this filter is specifically not an S-structure filter but rather an LF filter, and this is what I will assume.

Thirdly, we have seen in section 4.2.2 that *lui* object of prepositions displays CED effects. This used to be taken as a diagnostic property of overt syntactic movement. Again, to be consistent, we must deny the validity of this conclusion, which raises very general problems about the apparent lack of CED effects for covert movement. We leave this general problem, which also arises as a consequence of Chomsky's (1992) proposals, unaddressed here.

5.2.3. *Stranded Quantifiers*

We can now return to the properties of stranded quantifiers discussed earlier in sections 4.3.2 and 4.3.3. One type of problem was illustrated in (28), repeated here:

(28) a. Marie les a tous pris.
Marie them has all taken
"Marie took them all."

b. Marie a toutes voulu [les manger].
Marie has all wanted them eat_{INF}
"Marie wanted to eat them all."

c. Il a tous fallu [qu' ils parlent].
It has all necessitated that they speak
"It was necessary that they all speak."

d. Il a tous fallu [que Louis les lise].
It has all necessitated that Louis them read
"It was necessary that Louis read them all."

The analysis of clitics we propose allows a simple treatment of these facts: in all cases, XP* will be analyzed as moving to the specifier position of the Q *tous*. If *tous* is actually moved to its surface position, we may analyze XP* as [pro_i [*tous* [$_{DP}$ t_i]]. This QP raises to XP^, whence it moves to its surface position by A-bar movement:[29]

(48) [$_{QP}$ *pro* [tous [$_{DP}$ t]]$_j$] fallu [que Louis [t_j les lise t_j]]

This approach to (28b-d) extends straightforwardly to the sentences below, which do not involve clitics modified by Qs but bare Q DPs:

(49) a. Marie a tout voulu manger.
Marie has all wanted eat_{INF}
"Marie wanted to eat everything."

b. Il a tout/rien fallu [que Louis lise t]
it has all/nothing necessitated that Louis read
"It was necessary that Louis read everything/nothing."
(= "There is nothing that it was necessary for Louis to read.")

Alternatively, we may generate *tous* in the matrix clause and raise a *pro* XP* to its specifier (be it overtly or covertly, with different predictions concerning agreement, parasitic gaps, etc.).

A similar approach extends to the problematic cases of (31) (repeated here):

(31) b. Je (*à) leur ai (tous) offert un cadeau *(à) tous.
I to them have all given a present to all
"I gave them all a present."

c. Ces garçons, *(à) qui j' ai (??tous) offert
These boys, to whom I have (all) given
un cadeau ((à) tous)...
a present (to all)
"These boys, all of whom I gave a present."

The obligatory vs. impossible pied-piping of the dative marker can now be attributed to a difference between overt and covert movement: *wh*-movement of the DP [*à qui*] must pied-pipe the dative case marker. In the clitic case, we may claim that overt movement is prevented by the insertion of the dative marker *à*. The structure would include *leur...XP** with an unmoved XP* of the form [à+[$_{DP}$ *pro*] [*tous* t]].

5.3. *Head movement and Clitic Placement*

Our analysis of clitics imposes boundary conditions on the analysis of Clitic Climbing (and of Restructuring constructions). In what follows, we explore this issue within the context of a proposal made in Kayne (1989a) as to the treatment of clitic movement and of its critique.

Clitic movement is typically clause bound, a property we have not yet discussed. In the short generative tradition, this property has most often been taken to follow from assimilating clitic placement to some kind of NP movement. This was always a problem; the locality of NP-movement used to be handled by assimilating NP-traces to anaphors, a reasonable assumption if the trace of the clitic is phrasal. However, the movement analyses typically assume that clitic placement was movement of the clitic itself, which seemed to share no other property with NP-movement than locality (which led Sportiche 1983 to conclude that clitic placement did not involve movement).

Theories reducing locality constraints of NP-movement rules to the ECP, such as Chomsky (1986a, 1986b) and, more precisely, to antecedent government do not face this problem. The apparent similarity between NP-movement and clitic placement can be derived even if clitic placement is not phrasal movement. In particular, if clitic placement is head movement, locality effects will be found, too, since traces of heads are subject to antecedent government as well. This is in fact the view taken in Kayne (1989a). He proposes to treat clitic movement as head movement throughout: in our terms, the head of XP* moves as a head from its base position to adjoin to its host head. This view is at odds with what we are suggesting. We do treat clitics as heads. As such, they may move as heads do, and in fact they do.[30] But we claim the fundamental relation between Cl and XP* is not one of head movement. Kayne's (1989a) analysis of clitic placement as head movement throughout seems to contradict Kayne's (1989b) proposal about participle agreement that we have adopted here. If clitic placement is head movement, agreement of the object with the participle can no longer be seen as an XP/Y^0 specifier/head relation. Furthermore, Kayne's proposal makes it surprising that participle agreement may be triggered by clitic placement, NP-movement (as in passives, etc.) and *wh*-movement, the last two being clear cases of phrasal movement (cf. section 4.2.3).

5.3.1. *Restructuring and Clitic Climbing*

Kayne wants to correlate the possibility for a clitic to leave its VP, the possibility of Clitic Climbing in Restructuring constructions (see below) and the licensing of null subjects (*pro*-drop) and trace them all to the same property, namely whether or not INFL is strong enough to make a VP boundary transparent to movement. What actually matters for Kayne's analysis is not so much that clitic movement is head movement from XP* on. Most of his proposals can be preserved if a clitic can escape its minimal VP only by head movement. What happens inside the VP is not really relevant.

Our position and his can be reconciled by altering Kayne's (1989a) proposal along the lines of Sportiche (1990): as previously discussed: clitic movement could be XP movement VP-internally or more precisely within AGR_OP - triggering agreement - followed by head movement.[31] Although this would preserve most of Kayne's (1989a) analysis, it appears incompatible with the data discussed below in (54). The main type of evidence Kayne (1989a) presents to independently support the idea that clitic movement is head movement involves showing that intervening heads intercept clitic movement, an expected Minimality effect. Below, we discuss one such case. The others could be discussed in a similar way.

There are apparent violations of the clause boundedness effect on clitic placement in Restructuring constructions, present in earlier stages of French and in contemporary Italian and Spanish, among others.

(50) a. Pierre le voulait [lire XP*] (*in Modern French)
Pierre it wanted to-read
"Pierre wanted to read it."

b. Gianni li vuole vedere. (Italian)
Gianni them wants to-see
"Gianni wants to see them."

c. Lo quiero ver. (Spanish)
him/it I-want to-see
"I want to see him/ it."

These constructions raise many more questions than we can answer here. Here we ask what the process is by which the clitic appears in the matrix clause. The most common view is that the process of clitic placement in these Restructuring constructions is identical to that found in simple clauses. The appearance of Clitic Climbing derives from the prior application of another process. This Restructuring process affects the syntactic structure in such a way that normal application of clitic placement will have the Clitic Climbing effect. Since this scenario is independent of the precise characterization of Clitic Climbing, it is perfectly compatible with our analysis.[32]

Kayne (1989a) suggests a different view illustrated in the diagram below:

(51)

INFL .... [..cl+INFL .... t ....]

He suggests that clitic placement in Restructuring constructions is different from normal clitic placement: Clitic Climbing arises because these constructions involve raising of a lower INFL to a higher INFL. The clitics climb because, being adjoined to the lower INFL, they get a ride up to the higher INFL, so to speak. The central data Kayne cites supporting this proposal are due to Rizzi (1982). They shows that, in a Restructuring construction of colloquial Italian, an intervening head in C blocks Clitic Climbing, while an intervening XP in SPEC, CP does not, strongly suggesting a Head Movement Constraint effect of some sort.[33] In this variety of Italian, we find Clitic Climbing out of infinitival indirect questions:

(52) a. ?Mario, non lo$_j$ saprei [a chi affidare t$_j$]
Mario not him I-would-know to whom entrust$_{INF}$
"Mario, I would not know to whom to entrust him."

b. *Su questo problema, non lo$_j$ saprei [se consigliare t$_j$]
On this problem, not him I-would-know whether advise
"On this problem, I would not know whether to advise him."

The significant observation is this: the complementizer *se* blocks Clitic Climbing while the *wh*-phrase *a chi* does not.[34] This is a clear indication that head movement is somehow involved, and is interfered with by the intervening head *se*.

For us, these data might appear at first unexpected, if we always fundamentally treat clitic placement as a case of phrasal movement rather than as head movement. We would expect an intervening phrase to block clitic placement and an intervening head not to interfere. As heads, object clitics can incorporate to some head, say INFL. Thus we may in principle adopt Kayne's treatment of Restructuring constructions. It would be extremely suspicious however, if the surface distribution of clitics in a restructured clause were identical to that found in a comparable simple clause even though the processes involved are fundamentally different.

Further data provide interesting clues. First of all, Rizzi (1982) reports that the data in (52) with climbed clitics are mirrored by Object Preposing (see Burzio 1986, Rizzi 1978 for discussion and description of Object Preposing):

(53) a. ?Certe riposte non si sanno mai come dare.
Certain answers not si know never how give$_{INF}$
"One never knows how to give certain answers."

b. *Certe riposte non si sanno mai se dare.
Certain answers not si know never whether give$_{INF}$
"One never knows whether to give certain answers."

Object Preposing of this sort behaves like clitic placement: it is usually clause bound, except in Clitic Climbing contexts. In Restructuring contexts allowing a clitic to climb out of its clause, an object may also be preposed out of its clause. Following Burzio (1986), call this Long Object Preposing (LOP). This preposing is an instance of movement to subject position of the main clause (that may occur in the presence of the clitic *si*), as evidenced by the agreement reflex on the matrix verb. Since object preposing is clearly a case of phrasal (DP) movement, why is it blocked by an intervening head and not by an intervening phrase?

From the earliest approaches to Restructuring (such as Evers 1975 for Dutch, or Rizzi 1978 for Italian) to recent ones (such as Kayne 1989a), Restructuring has been postulated to involve incorporation of some head from the lower clause (V, or INFL) to a head in the higher clause (V or INFL). We expect that process to be sensitive to intervening heads, and thus to be blocked by a C but not by a SPEC, CP. Taking the possibility of LOP to be contingent on Restructuring being available predicts the data: in (53b), *se* blocks Restructuring. The context for LOP is not met.

The same line of explanation can now be applied to the cases of Clitic climbing in (52). Clitic climbing itself is not blocked by *se*, but it may not apply if Restructuring cannot. There is no need to suppose that clitic placement itself is head movement. Furthermore our analysis can straightforwardly capture the coextensiveness of Clitic Climbing and LOP, since both are phrasal movement. In this connection, the facts of (53) might appear surprising from the point of view of Kayne's proposal, or from the point of ours since we see that the intervening *wh*-phrase does not block phrasal movement over it. Since LOP is an instance of A-movement, this is less surprising. In the spirit of minimality effects, we would not expect an intervening A-bar position such as SPEC, CP to interfere with A-movement.[35]

5.3.2. *Agreement and Restructuring*

Not only is there no need to take clitic placement to be head movement, but there is also some evidence directly supporting the idea that clitic placement must involve some phrasal movement beyond the smallest VP containing XP*. Our reinterpretation of Rizzi's data, together with the analysis of Clitic Climbing as another instance of XP* movement, predicts the clustering of clitic, *wh*, or NP movement constructions with respect to participle agreement.

Furthermore, it predicts that participle agreement should be available on either main clause or embedded clause participle in Restructuring constructions, which is correct:

(54) a. Li$_j$ vorrei [aver gia [e$_j$]$_{XP*}$ letti/*letto [e$_j$]$_{XP*}$]
them I-would-want have$_{INF}$ already read$_{PL}$/read$_{SG}$
"I would want to have already read them."

b. Li$_j$ ho [e$_j$]$_{XP*}$ voluti/ *voluto leggere [e$_j$]$_{XP*}$
them I-have wanted$_{PL}$/ wanted$_{SG}$ read$_{INF}$
"I have wanted to read them."

c. Non li$_j$ avrei [e$_j$]$_{XP*}$?saputi/ *saputo a chi dare [e$_j$]$_{XP*}$
Not them I-would-have known$_{PL}$/known$_{SG}$ to whom give$_{INF}$
"I would not have known to whom to give them."

In all these cases, the participle must agree with the preposed clitic (remember that participle agreement is obligatory in standard Italian with 3rd person clitics), thereby demonstrating the presence of a phrasal element related to the clitic, namely XP*, in the bottom clause of a Restructuring construction as in (54a), or in the top clause, be it a regular Restructuring construction as in (54b), or an exceptional *wh*-island Restructuring construction as in (54c). This last case is particularly significant since we are clearly dealing with a biclausal structure. This means that clitic placement must involve moving an XP* out of a clause and a fortiori out of a VP.

6. CLITICS, BINDING, PARASITIC GAPS, AND THE NATURE OF XP^

We now turn to a discussion of the properties of individual clitics in French. We essentially limit ourselves to some Cased clitics, i.e., genitives, accusatives, datives, ignoring the clitic *se* and predicate *le*. Nominative clitics are discussed in Sportiche (1995).[36]

6.1. *Clitics and Binding Theory*

In this section we explore how clitics interact referentially with other nominals. Nonreflexive clitics have often been treated as pronominal elements of some sort. The main reason, which has led us to analyze XP* as *pro*, is that they are understood the way pronouns would be. Another, more directly relevant reason is based on their behavior with respect to coreference or binding with other nominals. Just like a pronoun, a clitic must be disjoint in reference from a nominal c-commanding it in its clause or its governing category, but may be coreferential or bound by a more remote nominal:

(55) a. Marie l' a vue.
M. her has seen
"Marie saw her."

b. Marie dit que le lion l' a vue.
M. says that the lion her has seen
"Marie$_j$ says that the lion saw her$_{j\text{ or }k}$"

c. Personne ne dit que le lion l' a vue.
no-one neg says that the lion her has seen
"No one$_j$ says that the lion saw her$_{j\text{ or }k}$"

These data do not establish whether it is the clitic itself that counts for the interaction. It may be the position of the clitic itself, it may be the position of XP*, or it may be the position XP^ (or it may be some other, presumably intermediate, position, a possibility we will not consider here). Only the present approach postulates the existence of XP^. If it turned out that it is XP^, it would strongly support our approach.

First of all, note that the c-command domain of the clitic and that of XP^ are (almost) identical. If it turns out that it is one of the two that is relevant for Binding effects, we will not be able to determine on empirical grounds which one is actually relevant. However, simplicity considerations favor XP^: referential dependencies are minimally found between potentially denoting elements, i.e., DPs. If the clitic itself mattered, we would have to extend this to include heads. If, on the other hand, it is DP^, nothing further needs to be added.

Secondly, to distinguish between XP^ and XP*, we need to find one of two configurations (given that XP^ or the clitic must c-command XP*): either a DP c-commanding XP* but not XP^, or a DP that XP^, but not XP*, c-commands. It is difficult to find convincing cases of the first configuration. The second one however can be constructed in French:

(56) a. Jean a présenté l' auteur de ce livre$_j$ à l'
J. has introduced the author of this book to the
éditeur de ce livre$_j$.
editor of this book
"John introduced the author of this book to the publisher of this book."

b. Jean a présenté son$_j$ auteur à l' éditeur de ce livre$_j$.
J. has introduced its author to the editor of this book
John introduced its author to the publisher of this book."

c. *Jean en$_j$ a présenté l' auteur à l' éditeur de ce livre$_j$.
J. of-it has introduced the author to the editor of this book
"John introduced its author to the publisher of this book."

Coreference between the two DPs *ce livre* is possible in (the admittedly awkward) (56a), even if the first one is pronominalized to *son* (presumably a D coindexed with a *pro* in SPEC, DP), as in (56b)). Cliticizing this first DP yields an unacceptable form. Superficially, it is the clitic that matters. We conclude that it is the position XP^ that matters for Binding effects.[37] This has to do with the status of the position XP^ associated with the clitic *en*. Movement to XP^ from XP* is from within a DP and thus must be A-bar movement (see Sportiche 1990 or Valois 1991 for discussion). Binding principle C must therefore be formulated so as to require names to be A-free as well as A-bar free. The conclusion that SPEC, *en* is an A-bar position in these cases is strengthened by the inability of XP^ to provide a possible binder for an anaphoric element, since they require A-binders:

(56) d. Jean_j a présenté [le frère de $[\text{Pierre}]_k]_l$ à
J. has introduced the brother of P. to
$[\text{son propre}]_{j,*k,l}$ père.
his own father
"Jean introduced the brother of Pierre to his own father."

e. Jean_j en_k a présenté [le $\text{frère}]_l$
J. of-him has introduced the brother
à $[\text{son propre}]_{j,*k,l}$ père.
to his own father
"Jean introduced the brother of Pierre to his own father".

To show that we are not merely dealing with a linearity effect, we should be able to reverse the judgment of (56c) by removing the offending DP from the c-command domain of the clitic, while keeping the same relative ordering of the two, despite the right branching structure of French. The following paradigm illustrates this possibility:

(57) a. Jean n' a pas critiqué l' auteur de ce livre
J. neg has not criticized the author of this book
[à cause de ce livre].
because of this book
"Jean did not criticize the author of this book because of this book."

b. *Jean n' en_j a pas critiqué l' auteur
Jean neg of-it_j has not criticized the author
[à cause de ce livre_j]
because of this book_j
"Jean did not criticize the author of it because of this book."

In (57a), coreference between the two DPs *ce livre* is possible. The sentence is ambiguous as to whether the causal adjunct is in the scope of the negation or not. We get the two readings: (i) It is not because of this book that John criticized its author, (ii) It is because of this book that John did not criticize its author. In (57b), with the first DP cliticized as *en*, the first reading becomes more difficult, if at all available, but the second remains. We may interpret this state of affairs as follows. Under the second reading, the causal adjunct is outside the scope of negation, hence outside the c-command domain of *en* (or its associated XP^). Under the first one, the causal adjunct is within the c-command domain of *en*, hence within the scope of the negation, but the corresponding reading is excluded as a Principle C effect.

This line of reasoning, based on French, does not depend on the level at which the Binding theory applies since movement of XP* to XP^ is overt in French. However, there are theoretical and empirical reasons to want the Binding theory to hold at LF. The empirical reasons are well known (reconstruction effects, etc.). The theoretical reasons are twofold. First, Binding theory deals with matters of (possible) referential interpretation. It should therefore operate on and only operate on the level(s) relevant for referential interpretation, namely LF. Secondly, as Chomsky (1992) discusses, there are reasons to doubt the existence of a well defined level of S-structure. Since the Binding theory cannot be assumed to hold exclusively at D-structure, there are only two options: Binding theory holds everywhere, hence at LF, or it only holds at LF. So it holds at LF. What this means for prohibition principles such as principles B or C, as opposed to prescriptive principles such as principle A, is that the prohibition must either be met at LF, or everywhere, hence at LF. In particular, the conclusion we reached for French should also hold in cases of Clitic Doubling, where raising of XP* to XP^ is delayed until LF. That this is the case is shown in Varela (1988).

6.2. *Clitics and Parasitic Gaps*

6.2.1. *Genitive en*

We mentioned earlier a conclusion reached in Chomsky (1982) based on Italian examples and discussed in Sportiche (1983), to the effect that clitics do not license parasitic gaps. Descriptively, parasitic gaps are licensed in S-structure configurations like (58) (linear order irrelevant),

(58) .... A-bar binder .... RG .....[... PG ... $]_K$

where the A-bar binder binds both gaps, and there is no c-command between the real gap (RG) and the parasitic gap (PG). If K is the most inclusive constituent containing PG but not RG, overt movement from the position PG must be possible to a position immediately dominated by K (See Aoun and Clark's 1985 A-bar anaphor treatment, or Chomsky's 1986a 0-subjacency treatment for discussion). This last condition was not recognized at the time of Chomsky

(1982). Some clitics do license parasitic gaps. Using again the genitive clitic *en*, we have grammatical forms such as in (59):

(59) a. Marie en_j a présenté [le frère e_j] à [la sœur e_j].
M. of-him has introduced the brother to the sister
"Marie introduced his brother to the sister."

b. *Marie en_j a présenté [le frère e_j] à [cette sœur e_j]
M. of-him has introduced the brother to this sister
"Marie introduced his brother to this sister."

c. La personne $dont_j$ Marie a présenté [le frère e_j]
the person of-whom M. has introduced the brother
à [la sœur e_j].
to the sister
"The person of whom Marie introduced the brother to the sister."

In (59a), *en* is interpreted as linked both to the argument of *frère* and the argument of *soeur*. The second gap is inaccessible to movement of *en*, being in a PP. But movement within the PP must be unimpeded, as exemplified by the unacceptability of (59b) under the relevant reading, in which the demonstrative *cette* blocks DP internal movement (see previous discussion in 4.2.2). This kind of sentence is very closely reminiscent of sentences of the type (59c) with *wh*-movement, extensively studied in Tellier (1991), and convincingly analyzed there as involving parasitic gaps. They essentially behave in identical ways, apart from the differences due to the position of the A-bar binder, i.e., *wh-* in SPEC, CP vs. *en*.

A number of important conclusions follow from these observations. First, just as in the case of the binding theoretic argument of the previous section, we may simply attribute this licensing of parasitic gaps to the presence of the appropriate A-bar binder XP^. Alternatively, we may envision extending the theory of parasitic gaps licensers to include (certain kinds of) heads. But again, this last move appears otherwise unmotivated. We conclude that the existence of parasitic gaps with *en* shows that: (i) *en* clitic placement is actually phrasal movement, and (ii) [SPEC, *en*] is an A-bar position. Because of uniformity we certainly want to extend these two conclusions to all clitics. Extending the first is what we have been proposing here. Extending the second raises some difficulties concerning parasitic gaps with accusative clitics which we now discuss.

6.2.2. *Accusatives and Parasitic Gaps*

For uniformity, we would like to treat all SPEC, ClP as A-bar positions, not A-positions. This conclusion is probably incorrect for clitics not linked to Case such as Reflexive *se*, which we will ignore here. As for Cased clitics, they do not seem to license parasitic gaps, except, of course, *en*. With respect to 3rd person datives, we will conclude that XP^ is an A-position. At any rate, the question only arises for accusatives, because, for various reasons, the relevant configurations are difficult or impossible to construct with other clitics.[38]

An illustration of this failure for accusatives to license parasitic gaps is found in Chomsky (1982), based on some Italian data of Luigi Rizzi's given below (RG=t, PG=e), and is equally applicable for French:

(60) a. I libri che li dobbiamo far mettere *t* nello
the books that him we-must make put on-the
scaffale [invece di lasciare *e* sul tavolo].
shelf instead of leave on-the table
"The books that we must make him put on the shelf instead of leaving on the table."

b. *Glieli dobbiamo far mettere *t* nello scaffale
them-him we-must make put on-the shelf
[invece di lasciare *e* sul tavolo]
instead of leave on-the table
"We must make him put them on the shelf instead of leaving them on the table."

(60a) is acceptable, (60b) is not. In its essentials, the relevant structure is (61):

(61)

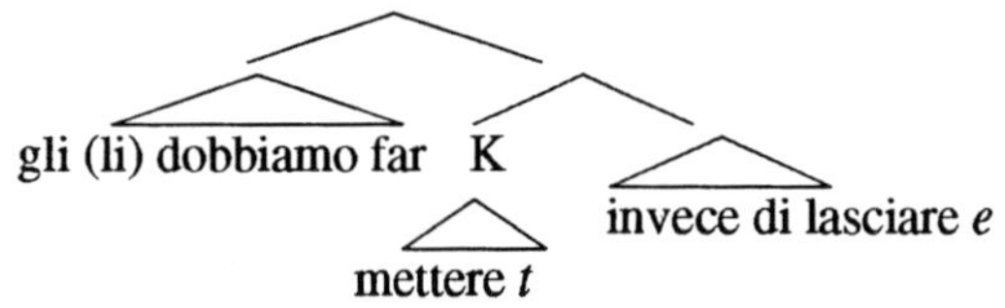

In (60a), *t* is bound by the relative operator, which also c-commands *e*. Neither *e* nor *t* c-commands the other, and *e* is free to move up within K.[39] Let us consider the clausal structure more carefully. Four positions are relevant: XP^, XP*, PG and SPEC, AGR_OP.

(62)

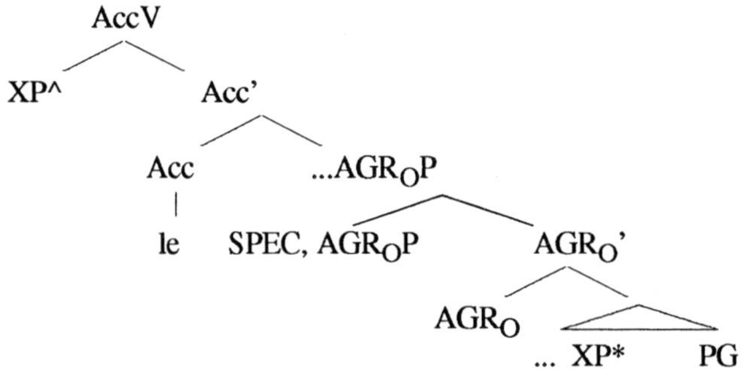

We know that SPEC, AGR_OP is an A-position (as it may be an intermediate landing site for raising to subject). At LF, we must have a chain (XP^, SPEC, AGR_OP, XP*) to license both accusative Case and the clitic. If movement of XP* to XP^ is overt and if XP^ is an A-bar position, we should expect parasitic gaps to be licensed, even in simple clauses, contrary to fact, viz. **Louis les a offensé(s) en insultant* 'Louis offended them by insulting (them)'.
In order to circumvent this problem, we may try either to argue that XP^ is not an A-bar position or that raising of XP* to XP^ must be delayed until LF. As mentioned earlier, I will argue that the accusative XP^ must be an A-bar position; I thus suggest adopting the second option. That raising of an accusative XP* may be delayed until LF is independently motivated by the optionality of participle agreement. However we must now argue that raising of XP* to XP^ must be delayed until LF in French (otherwise PG should be licensed when movement is overt) even when participle agreement obtains. This is because participle agreement does not seem to interfere with PG licensing: parasitic gaps may be licensed whether agreement obtains or not, viz. *wh*-movement of a direct object XP* to SPEC, CP as in *?Quelles maisons as-tu construit(es) sans habiter?* 'Which houses have you built(FEM) without inhabiting'. This means that (i) movement of XP* to SPEC, AGR_OP may take place overtly, (ii) it does not license parasitic gaps (this is consistent with its A-position status), and (iii) it does not force movement to XP^.

In sum, French (or Italian) accusative clitics do not license PGs because they involve LF raising to XP^. This means that there is no principled bar against accusative clitics licensing PGs. They should do so in a language or in a construction where overt movement of XP* to XP^ is possible. This is, for example, the case of French genitive clitics. It is also the case with accusative Scrambling in Dutch which we later argue can be viewed as overt movement of XP* to XP^=SPEC, AccP (via SPEC, AGR_OP), where XP^ is the specifier of a silent clitic head. The relevant fact here is that accusative Scrambling does license PGs, i.e., XP^ is an A-bar position.

6.3. *The nature of XP^*

We may now turn to question (33v). Let us therefore first list a number of properties distinguishing A and A-bar positions, as in (63):

(63) i. Movement to an A-position obeys the SSC, not movement to an A-bar position.
ii. Movement to an A-position must be from an A-position, movement to an A-bar position may be from either kind.
iii. Movement to an A-position must be from a Caseless position, movement to an A-bar position can be from a Case position (and must be, if it is from an A-position).
iv. An A-position can be a Case position, an A-bar position cannot.

(63) v. Movement to an A-bar position but not to an A-position licenses parasitic gaps.

vi. Movement to an A-position does not create Weak Crossover effects, movement to an A-bar position may, (if the moved element is not "referential").[40]

vii. A-positions qualify as binders for lexical anaphors, A-bar positions may not.

6.3.1. *Genitives*

The conclusion that $XP^\wedge_{en}$ = SPEC, *en* is an A-bar position and only an A-bar position is consistent with all these properties. Corresponding to the list in (63), we find:

i. It does not obey the SSC (*Marie en$_i$ croit [Louis capable t]$_i$* 'Marie believes Louis capable of it.')
ii. Movement to it is from an A-bar position: extraction out of DP must be through SPEC, DP, an A-bar position (cf. Sportiche 1990, Valois 1991).
iii. Genitive Case is assigned DP-internally: movement to $XP^\wedge_{en}$ is from a DP-internal Case position.
iv. same as above
v. parasitic gaps: as discussed above
vi. irrelevant: XP^ is *pro*, hence referential.
vii. movement to $XP^\wedge_{en}$ does not provide an antecedent for lexical anaphors, as noted in (56d, e) above.

6.3.2. *Accusatives*

The behavior of accusative clitics suggests this conclusion should be extended to them. Accusative Case is assigned independently of and lower than the specifier of its clitic voices. Movement to these specifiers is thus movement from (or through) Cased positions, indicating that these specifiers are A-bar positions. It is at best difficult to construct relevant examples to test criterion (vii).[41] With respect to criterion (v), we have already discussed parasitic gaps, which provide evidence for accusative clitics only. For criterion (vi), Weak Cross Over is irrelevant as in the case of *en*. The only criterion that might favor the idea that the specifier of these clitics is an A-position is (i). We may distinguish between violations of the SSC and intervention effects of INFL or T. The SSC cases discussed in section 4.2.1 do not distinguish between the two since the INFL of the embedded clause might be rich enough to block clitic placement, since an intervening INFL system (e.g., the presence of T or similar elements) seems to block all clitic movement. Given the other criteria, we conclude that XP^ of accusatives is an A-bar position.

6.3.3. *Locatives*

The case of locatives would seem to lead to the same conclusion, if the question makes sense. There is no principled reason why the specifiers of clitic voices should be DPs or should be allowed to contain DPs, but the properties of all other clitics we have so far discussed do suggest that XP^ in these cases are DPs. If locatives are also DPs, the specifier of locative *y* would seem to be best analyzed as an A-bar position, since *y* placement violates the SSC. Examples similar to those for *en* which violate the SSC can be constructed for the clitic *y*, with the locative extracted from inside the small clause:

(63) i'. Louis croit [Marie fidèle à ses idées].
L. believes M. faithful to her ideas
'Louis believes Marie faithful to her ideas."

Louis y croit [Marie fidèle].
L. to-them believes M. faithful
"Louis believes Marie faithful to them."

6.3.4. *Datives*

Turning now to datives, a different picture emerges. The dative object of an adjective can cliticize in certain cases:

(64) a. Marie$_j$ lui est [t$_j$ toute dévouée].
M. to-3S is all devoted
"Marie is entirely devoted to him/her."

b. Marie *lui/*me croit [Louis tout dévoué].
M. to-3S/me believes L. all devoted
"Marie believes Louis entirely devoted to him/me."

c. A qui Marie croit- elle [Louis tout dévoué]
to whom Marie believe she Louis all devoted
"Who does Marie think Louis is entirely devoted to?"

The unacceptability of (64b) suggests that dative clitics are subject to the SSC. The minimal contrast of dative clitics in (64b) with datives *wh*-phrases (64c) further supports singling out dative clitic placement as A-movement, since it demonstrably diverges from *wh*-movement with respect to SSC configurations.[42] Although this might seem inconsistent with the facts of (64a), where a dative clitic has moved over (the trace of) a subject, Rizzi (1986a) has argued that these are Restructuring constructions, thus resolving the inconsistency (cf. also Stowell, T. 1991). Taking the other criteria in (63) seriously, we have to conclude that movement of a dative XP* to SPEC, *lui* must be from a Caseless position. To accommodate this consequence, I suggest treating the Dative Voice not as a clitic voice but rather as the dative equivalent of AGR_O or AGR_S, i.e., as the locus of assignment (or checking) of dative Case; in effect, then, it is AGR_{IO} (Indirect object agreement).[43]

6.3.5. *Summary*

Overall, we have the following picture in French: different clitics differ as to the A/A-bar status of the specifier of their Voice, and whether or not they allow (or require) overt raising of their associated XP* to their XP^. Both genitive and accusative clitic voices (as well as nominative, if Sportiche 1993 is correct) have A-bar specifiers, while datives have A-specifiers. Furthermore, movement of a genitive XP* to the specifier of *en* may (must?) take place overtly, while movement is necessarily covert for accusative XP*. In the case of datives, we have seen some evidence in 5.2.3 that movement may be delayed until LF. As we will see, the discussion of the function of clitic voices provides independent reasons to treat the specifiers under discussion as A-bar positions, as does the analysis of Scrambling in Dutch (section 7), since Scrambling does license PGs.

Two issues remain unresolved that have much larger implications than the analysis of clitics proper. First, the issue of the locality of clitic placement to an A-bar XP^, sensitive to what we have called intervening INFL material remains unsettled. It should be noted that the very same question arises for other processes, most notably here for the locality of Scrambling in Dutch, but in general for some cases of long distance anaphora (cf. Koster and Reuland 1991) and such dependencies as that between the negative head *ne* and negative quantifiers like *personne* 'no one'. Second, the treatment of apparent differences in properties between overt and covert movement, be they their sensitivity to the CED, licensing of parasitic gaps, etc., is left open.

7. SCRAMBLING IN DUTCH, THE CLITIC CRITERION, AND SPECIFICITY

7.1. *Dutch Scrambling*

In this section, we briefly discuss Dutch Scrambling, and show why it can be analyzed exactly like clitic constructions in French (possibly all the same conclusions would hold of German, given Moltmann 1990). Let us begin by summarizing the findings of Koopman (1988) on direct objects which provides a crucial basis for the following discussion.

7.1.1. *Accusative Scrambling*

Throughout this section, we limit the discussion to direct objects. Dutch has clitic objects. Specific full DP objects, non-specific objects and clitic objects (pronominal and specific) all have a different distribution. Non-clitic specific objects must occur higher than the negative marker *niet* and may occur lower or higher than adverbs such as *waarschijnlijk* 'probably'. Clitics must occur higher than all of these different elements. We illustrate these observations now (All examples in this section are drawn from Koopman 1988):[44]

(65) a. Hij heeft 't waarschijnlijk (*'t) niet (*'t) gezien.
He has it probably not seen
"He probably has not seen it."

b. Hij heeft Jan waarschijnlijk (Jan) niet (*Jan) gezien
He has Jan probably (Jan) not (Jan) seen
"He probably has not seen Jan."

Nonspecific objects must occur essentially in what appears to be VP initial position. Furthermore, they must follow VP external particles, such as *niet, waarschijnlijk* or particles such as *maar* 'but', *toch, nu* 'yet', *al* 'already', *eens* 'once'.

(66) a. Pak 't maar / *maar 't
Take it but / but it
"Go ahead and take it."

b. Pak dat boekje maar/?*maar dat boekje
Take that book but/ but that book
"Go ahead and take that book."

c. Pak maar een boekje/*een boekje maar.
Take but a book/ a book but
"Go ahead and take a book."

Koopman concludes that besides the base position for objects, three positions are needed: one VP initially (for case assignment reasons, she claims) where non-specific objects occur, one for specific objects (which she claims is high enough to be governed by a—sometimes covert—inflectional head) and one for the clitics (which she claims are incorporated to this inflectional head).[45] Compare Koopman's analysis for Dutch (67a) with our analysis for French (67b):

(67) a. $[_{IP}$ $[_{I'}$ [CL+$[_{I}$] *specifics* maar niet $[_{VP}$ *non-specifics*
b. F CL avoir pas AGR_O PM Verb

The analysis of Romance clitics we have pursued so far, as well as the structural analysis of the middle field of a French clause, provides an interpretation of the data consistent with Koopman's conclusions. The VP initial position to which non-specific DPs raise from their VP internal base positions can be taken to be SPEC, AGR_OP, where accusative Case is assigned/sanctioned (Dutch differs in that respect from French in requiring S-structure movement to this position). The position of specifics is nothing else but XP^=SPEC, *het*, i.e., the specifier of the Accusative Voice. In Dutch, as in French, the Doubly Filled Voice Filter is operative, preventing simultaneous appearance of the clitic and the accusative specific object. If the object is null, the clitic head of the Accusative Voice reappears, but just like in French, it must incorporate to a higher functional projection. The fact that the adverb *waarschijnlijk* may either precede or follow XP^ simply indicates that it does not interfere with the government by this Functional head of the clitic voice and its head.

Note finally that this clitic voice in Dutch must appear quite high in the structure, and in particular higher than the position of the negative *niet*. If Sportiche (1995) is correct in analyzing *niet* as a negative adverb corresponding to French *pas* and not to French *ne*, we have some justification for taking the position of the clitic voices in French to be where we assumed they were in 5.1.2.

7.1.2. *Dative Scrambling*

Dutch has dative clitic pronouns appearing in the same position as other clitics, as shown in (68a).[46] Datives can also scramble, much like accusatives. When they are specific, they must move out of the VP to a position adjacent to that hosting scrambled accusatives. Datives exhibit a number of differences from accusatives. First, datives must move in front of such particles as *maar* even if they are not specific, and they must always precede the direct object, if there is one. In particular, if a specific direct object has been scrambled, the indirect object, whether specific or not must precede it. These observations are illustrated in (68b,c). Finally, datives do not license parasitic gaps, whether scrambled or not.

(68) a. Hij heeft 'm waarschijnlijk (*'m) deze brief
He has to-him probably (to-him) this letter
niet (*'m) geschreven.
not (to-him) written
"He probably has not written this letter to him."

b. Hij heeft Jan deze brief waarschijnlijk niet geschreven.
Hij heeft Jan waarschijnlijk deze brief niet geschreven.
?*Hij heeft deze brief waarschijnlijk Jan niet geschreven.
?*Hij heeft waarschijnlijk deze brief Jan niet geschreven.
"He probably has not written this letter to Jan."

(68) c. Verzoek iemand maar om uit te stappen.
?*Verzoek maar iemand om uit te stappen.
Ask someone but/ to out to step
but someone
"Just ask someone to get off."

Aide from the failure to license parasitic gaps (which cannot be made much of in the present context since datives seem to fail to license PGs quite generally), these facts can get a straightforward interpretation within the system of assumptions we have developed here. We analyze scrambling of datives as movement to the specifier XP^ of the Dative Voice, headed by a (covert) dative clitic. Suppose, as we have discussed for French, that the dative clitic is in fact heading AGR_{IO}. We expect the dative object, when non-specific, to move overtly to SPEC, $AGR_{IO}P$. Indeed the fact that such direct objects must occur VP initially (in fact in SPEC, AGR_O as discussed above) indicates that Case licensing in Dutch must be satisfied at S-structure. If the AGR_{IO} projection is higher than the Accusative Voice in Dutch, an indirect object will have to scramble out of VP to a position preceding that of specific direct objects.

7.1.3. *Scrambling, Parasitic Gaps and Locality*

If accusative Scrambling is nothing else than movement to XP^, the fact that it licenses parasitic gaps, as noted by Bennis and Hoekstra (1984), supports the conclusion that XP^ may be an A-bar position:

(69) dat ik deze boeken [zonder t in te kijken] aan Jan doorverkoop.
that I these books [without in to look] to Jan sell
"That I sold these books without looking into (them)."

Furthermore, the fact that Scrambling is local despite being movement to an A-bar position, and the fact that it is local in the same way as clitic placement makes our conclusions concerning the locality of clitic placement and the need to appeal to some additional locality principle more plausible (although unfortunately not explained).[47]

7.2. *The Clitic Criterion and the Function of Clitic Projections*

7.2.1. *Licensing Specificity*

So far, we have only assumed clause (i) of the Clitic Criterion:

(35) Clitic Criterion
i. A clitic must be in a Spec-head relationship with a [+F] XP at LF

(35) ii. A [+F] XP must be in a Spec-head relationship with a clitic at LF

There is one property of Dutch Scrambling that we have left unaccounted for, namely the fact that accusative or dative specific DPs must raise to XP^. I suggest that we derive this property by enforcing clause (ii) of the Clitic Criterion above, choosing the property [+F] to be specificity. This means that at LF, specific DPs will have to raise to their corresponding XP^.[48] In other words, as Sportiche (1995) proposes, some clitics (in French, those with structural Case—nominative, accusative, genitive) license specificity in DPs. In this respect, clitics are like [+wh] Cs, which license *wh*-phrases, [+neg] heads, which license negative quantifiers and polarity items, and [+focus] heads, which license focalized items and are overtly realized as particles (cf. Chinese *shi* (Chiu 1992), or phonologically realized in intonational contours (English or French). This provides an answer to question (33iii).

If this approach is on the right track, we need to reformulate the Clitic Criterion somewhat. In Dutch, specificity is licensed within particular projections the heads of which are not necessarily clitics. They may in fact be silent. Upon reflection, it is clear that the fact that the heads of these projections are clitics in French is accidental. Anticipating on Sportiche (1995), we replace (35) with (70). There is a set of properties $P_1...P_n$, that phrasal categories may have or lack (such as Specificity, *Wh*, Neg, Focus, Scope, etc.) which we denote by assigning these categories the features $[+/-F_1],...,[+/-F_n]$. We can then further generalize the Clitic Criterion:

(70) Generalized Licensing Criterion
i. A [+F] head must be in a Spec-head relationship with a [+F] XP at LF
ii. A [+F] XP must be in a Spec-head relationship with a [+F] head at LF

If [+F] denotes specificity, the corresponding heads in French will either be clitics or possibly silent (see below in next section). In Dutch, the corresponding heads will be clitics in case the specific element is *pro*. If the specific phrase to be licensed is lexical, the corresponding head is silent. From this perspective, we can return to Clitic Doubling problem # 1 from section 5.2.1. Since pronouns are quintessentially specific DPs, we expect that if anything is doubled (i.e., singled out as specific by a clitic marking specificity), it will at least include the archetype of specific DPs, i.e., pronouns.

Generalizing the Clitic Criterion so that it and Rizzi's *wh*-criterion (and Haegeman and Zanuttini's 1991 Neg Criterion, etc.) are special cases of a more general licensing requirement fits well with our conclusions that XP^ is an A-bar position. All the other cases involve operators of some sort which, because of the respective criteria, will have to be in a Spec-head relationship with their licensing head. As operators, we expect them to end up at LF in an A-bar position (as is certainly the case for both *wh*-phrases and negative quantifiers).

If the analogy is indeed to be complete, we expect XP^ to be an A-bar position.[49]

7.2..2. *Datives, Clitics and Agreement*

Not all elements classified as object clitics license specificity. Although all object clitics in French do, this is not telling since the only doubled elements are (silent) pronouns anyway.[50] Across Romance, the data consistently suggest that dative clitics, as opposed to others, are not bijectively linked to specificity (see Suñer 1988, 1992 for Spanish or Dobrovie-Sorin 1990 for Romanian). This suggests that we should extend to other Romance languages the conclusion we reached for French (and Dutch), that is, that a dative clitic is not like other clitics, which head specificity licensing projections with A-bar specifiers. Rather a dative clitic is the head of an agreement projection devoid of interpretive consequences, and assigning or licensing dative Case in its A-position specifier.[51]

Of course, this does not exclude the existence of a projection licensing specificity in datives. In fact, because of the GLC (70), such a projection is required. This means that in the functional system of a clause, two systems of projections coexist: Case-licensing projections and Specificity-licensing projections. This considerably complicates the question of explanatory adequacy raised in the introduction. Limiting ourselves to nominatives, accusatives and datives, we have as many as six functional projections. This raises a number of new questions which we will not address here: Which ones overtly occur? On what basis does the language learner decide the answer to the previous question? Why is specificity licensing Case driven?

From a broader perspective, it is the question of the synchronic and diachronic relationship between agreement and clitics that is raised. Fundamentally, our answer is that they are identical, both being heads agreeing with phrasal specifiers. They also differ. Agreement, as is clear from French subject/verb agreement or participial agreement, imposes no particular interpretative requirement on the agreeing DP, while some clitics obviously do, namely specificity. Another related aspect is that clitic voices have A-bar specifiers, while AGRPs have A-specifiers. Finally, a clitic linked to a DP is typically unique, while a same DP can trigger agreement on several different categories (as e.g., passivized objects trigger agreement on both T and on participles).[52] This is consistent with the many traditional proposals treating agreement as weakened pronouns.

8. CONCLUDING REMARKS

8.1. *On Related Questions and Proposals*

The ideas presented here concerning clitic constructions have consequences or suggest research directions for a number of open questions which we will not pursue in detail here.[53] Three of the most lively research question relating to clitic constructions not d are the interaction of Clitic Doubling with Weak Crossover discussed for example in Suñer (1988, 1992) and Dobrovie-Sorin (1990), the Clitic Left-Dislocation constructions (discussed by Cinque 1990) which we have briefly alluded to, and the general problem of Scrambling crosslinguistically.

8.1.1. *Clitic Left-Dislocation*

From the present perspective, it is tempting to take Clitic Left-Dislocation (in Italian or Greek) to be similar to the kind of Clitic Doubling found in French with Quantifiers to the left of the clitic, i.e., as obligatory movement of the doubled element to or beyond the specifier of the clitic it is associated with, because 'true' Clitic Doubling is not allowed. The specifier of the clitic voice would provide the position postulated by Iatridou (1990) from which the dislocated constituent is moved in her analysis of this construction in Greek.

8.1.2. *Weak Crossover (WCO)*

It should be clear how the present proposals affect WCO. Clitics may have either free A-positions or specific A-bar positions as specifiers and are quite high in the structure of the clause: depending on what kind of specifiers a particular clitic has, the effects of the existence of this position on Weak Crossover will be radically different. Roughly, we expect specificity inducing clitics to remove WCO effects entirely, probably because the doubled element simply does not qualify as a WCO inducer (see Dobrovie-Sorin 1990 or Lasnik and Stowell 1991 for discussion). This is what is reported to take place by Suñer (1988), and the same is true of Romanian accusative doubling:[54]

(71) a. ¿[A cuales de ellos]$_j$ no los aguanta ni su$_j$ madre?
to which of them not them stand not-even their mother
"Which ones of them can't even their mother stand?"

b. ¿[A cuales de ellos]$_j$ dijo su$_j$ madre que no los aguanta?
to which of them said their mother that not them stand
"Which ones of them did their mother say that she can't stand?"

On the other hand, we expect non-specificity inducing Clitic Doubling such as dative doubling in Spanish to possibly remove WCO within its clause but not beyond (much as discussed in Mahajan 1990 in a slightly different setting). This appears to be found in Spanish and (for some speakers of) Romanian, though the example (72b) is less acceptable than the example (72a):

(72) a. ¿A quién$_j$ le$_j$ habló su$_j$ madre?
to whom$_j$ to-him$_j$ spoke his$_j$ mother
"To whom did his mother speak?"

b. ¿A quién$_j$ dice su$_j$ madre que le$_j$ dieron un premio?
to whom$_j$ says his$_j$ mother that to-him$_j$ they-gave a prize
"To whom did his mother say that they gave (him) a prize?

The straightforward interpretation is that the pronoun *su* in (72a) is bound from an A-position, namely the specifier of the dative clitic voice. No WCO effect arises. In the sentence (72b), there is no such available A-position (the relevant specifier is in the embedded clause), and the WCO effect reappears.

8.1.3. *Scrambling and Agreement*

It should be apparent that some of the ideas that we have presented here have been anticipated in different forms. Approaches to Clitic (Doubling) emphasizing the agreement relation between the clitic and the doubled element (Strozer 1976, Rivas 1977, Sportiche 1983 or Suñer 1988 would naturally lead to our proposal, if the contemporary construal of agreement is taken seriously.

On the question of the analysis of Scrambling, the work of Koopman (1988) on the internal structure of VP in Dutch or that of Mahajan (1990) on Scrambling and Case assignment in Hindi are prominent precursors. Expressed in our terms, Mahajan's analysis of Hindi assimilates AGR_OP and Accusative Voice, leading to the view that accusative Case is assigned differently to specific DPs and nonspecific DPs. If we are correct, this view is inadequate for Romance languages, as there is no longer a specificity requirement for accusative objects triggering object agreement (see Sportiche 1990 for examples) than there is a specificity requirement for nominative subjects triggering agreement on verbs. More generally, we want to keep accusative Case assignment and Accusative Voice separate. Given the existence in Hindi of participial agreement similar to that found in Romance, we will want to take AGR_O to materialize as participial agreement in Hindi, in the same way as in French. We then might reinterpret Mahajan's work as providing substantial and independent support for the existence of an Accusative Voice. Mahajan (1990) also postulates a relationship between the landing site of Scrambling (his Argument Shift) and some agreement projection (his AGR_O which is a conflation of our AGR_O and clitic), and suggests a typology of Scrambling roughly distinguishing between clausebound Scrambling (his Argument Shift) and nonclausebound scrambling (his adjunction-to XP-Scrambling). As Dutch illustrates, there seem to be two types of (clausebound) Scrambling: one for Case-assignment purposes, to an AGR projection, and one for specificity reasons, to a clitic voice. It is tempting to recast the results of recent work on Scrambling in the Germanic languages and the dichotomy found there (see Vikner 1990) in terms of whether movement is to an Agreement Projection (A-movement) or to a Voice projection (A-bar movement), and to distinguish both from the kind of unbounded Scrambling more akin to English Topicalization.

8.1.4. *Summary and Problems*

First of all, we analyze clitics as agreement heads or morphemes. Each clitic heads its own projection, which we call a clitic voice, and agrees with its specifier in a way similar to the general treatment of agreement between a head and a phrase. This specifier is in turn linked by a movement dependency with the argument position the clitic agrees with.

Beyond this fundamental uniformity, clitics split in two classes depending on whether they have interpretive import or not. When they do not (datives in Romance), we observe a number of correlated properties. Their associated argument (XP*) is not required to display any particular interpretive property. Their specifier (XP^) is an A-position. The XP^/XP* relation is subject to the SSC. The movement from XP* to XP^ does not license parasitic gaps and may relieve weak crossover effects only in restricted configurations. When they do (have interpretive import, cf. accusatives in Romance), their associated argument is required to be specific. Their specifier (XP^) is an A-bar position. The XP^/XP* relation is not subject to the SSC (although it is not unbounded). The movement from XP* to XP^ licenses parasitic gaps and relieves weak crossover effects throughout.

We leave a number of questions open and some observations unaccounted for. We offer no reason as to why there is such a remarkable uniformity across the Romance languages in treating datives as agreement and accusatives as a specificity licenser. This is particularly striking given that, for example, doubling of direct objects in Rio de la Plata Spanish starts behaving like doubling of indirect objects if the doubling clitic is dative like (the so-called *leismo*). Similarly, we claim that specificity of DPs is always licensed through movement to the specifier of an appropriate head. This was partly motivated by the obligatoriness of Scrambling in Dutch. Yet not all specific DPs overtly (must) scramble. We have no account of this disparity (although here an analogy with *wh*-movement with or without pied piping is obviously promising).

8.2. *Conclusion: Modularity and Uniformity of Licensing*

Beyond the particular problem of clitics, this proposal instantiates the general approach presented in Sportiche (1995) according to which all dependencies which are not strictly local are of the same structural type. Taking phrases (such as DPs) to be a matrix of properties, some lexical and some "scopal" in a general sense, the fundamental idea can be formulated as requiring that every single scopal property of every phrase must be satisfied in a Spec-head relationship with an appropriate head whose unique function is the licensing of this particular property, very much in the way *wh*-movement is thought of. The centerpiece of this conception is the Generalized Licensing Criterion given in (70), which is motivated by a fundamentally uniform approach to property licensing. At the same time, this conception yields a highly modular view of constituent structure in which the organization of a clause can be seen as made of a succession of groups of projections, each meant to license a particular property type. Thus for French, we have roughly the following clausal organization:

In this representation, the projections for operator-like property licensing are the highest, and projections licensing thematic properties the lowest.

NOTES

* This is in part a written version of work presented at various universities in the USA and Europe. I would like to thank their audiences for their input and Hilda Koopman and Guglielmo Cinque for very useful discussion. This work was supported in part by a UCLA Academic Senate Grant.

1 Note that Sportiche alone, it seems, has argued for both positions, so some burden is on him to reconcile the two positions.

2 The base generation analysis could be salvaged if the [sc] in (16) were a PRO: it could be ruled out by the PRO Theorem. Because Ps are governors (if not proper governors), this appears dubious, unless as Jaeggli (1982) has argued, a clitic may absorb the government property of the predicate selecting XP*, here of the P. This view is criticized in Sportiche (1983) on the grounds that government is a configurational property, not a lexical property. Furthermore, the evidence Jaeggli bases his case on is inconclusive, as shown by Suñer (1988) (cf. also Borer 1983).

3 More precisely, if the XP could bind SPEC, DP.

4 We have not yet discussed what kind of movement clitic movement could be. See section 6.3.

5 This proposal might find direct support even in French as non-stranded Qs are pronounced *tous* [tu] 'all-masc.', *toutes* [tut] 'all-fem.', but stranded Qs are *tous* [tus], *toutes* [tut]. The difference in form for the masculine form can be taken to indicate that number agreement between the Q and the DP only occurs under stranding, in a way

reminiscent of the Hebrew data. Note that gender agreement seems to obtain regardless of stranding, a surprising fact under this view but not unlike subject verb agreement in standard Arabic in the SV and VS orders (cf. Aoun, Benmamoun and Sportiche 1994 for discussion).

6 The distinction corresponds to the distinction made in Kayne (1984, chapter 4) between Qs as anaphors and Qs as quantifiers. Our discussion in this section can be seen as an update of this distinction in the framework of Sportiche (1988).

7 The examples (28c,d) are perfectly acceptable for me. They are sometimes judged as ?. Movement out of a clause is only possible from infinitivals or subjunctives.

8 At the latest. If the analysis of the [tu]/[tus] alternation is correct, this configuration will have to have been reached by S-structure.

9 I report my own judgments here, in the standard register. As far as I can tell, they hold for all cases involving dative clitics e.g., indirect objects, affected objects of locative prepositions (*Je leur ai tiré dessus.* 'I shot at them'), and inalienable possession constructions (*Les livres lui sont tombés des mains.* 'The books fell from his hands.'; see Vergnaud and Zubizaretta 1991). In that, I differ from what is reported in Kayne (1975) (e.g., he gives *cela leur est tous arrivé.* 'That happened to all of them.' as deviant, while this sentence is fine for me). This suggests a much more complicated and much more dialectally detailed situation.

10 We update his proposals, essentially in the way we construe his Q-post.

11 Kayne also proposes that the clitic/XP* relation is head movement, a view to which we return below in section 5.3.1

12 This analysis is a contemporary instantiation of Sportiche's (1983) analysis, which argues that (i) the clitic is a morpheme not occupying a phrasal position (i.e., a head, in contemporary terms) and (ii) its relation with its associated argument is one of agreement (which is now instantiated as Spec-head). Sportiche's (1983) analysis of clitics conformed almost exactly to the schema adopted here, in a way reminiscent of Kayne's (1972) analysis of French subject clitic constructions.

13 By extending a usage adopted in some French traditional grammars for reflexive clitics and in some Spanish traditional grammars for accusative clitics as well (cf. the references in Suñer 1988). There is also a theoretical rationale to lump together active, passive, reflexive and other clitic voices discussed in Sportiche (1993a).

14 This is the part that does not necessarily apply to *se* constructions. .

15 Sportiche (1993a) argues that this analogy is far from accidental and extends to all other type of non-local head/phrase or phrase/phrase relations.

16 We add this second clause for symmetry at this point. It will be discussed in section 7.

17 I use 'overt movement' to mean syntactic movement, i.e., feeding the phonology, as opposed to LF movement, which doesn't, even if the moved category is covert.

18 But not identical to agreement morphemes: clitics possess properties other than regular subject or object agreement morphemes that make them akin to pronouns.

19 Given the discussions of Kayne (1975, 1990) and Rizzi (1986), it seems that nominative clitics are not syntactic clitics (except the indefinite *on* or in certain constructions like Complex Inversion). Their distribution is discussed in Sportiche (1993b).

20 Thus I assume that AGR_O is not involved at all, based on the fact that it must be available for participle agreement.

21 The order (ne)-Cl+AUX_1+Inf-(pas)-(AUX_2)-Verb is also marginally possible (cf. Pollock 1989a), as noted in the text.

22 Marginally, a tenseless verb only raises to AGR_S and the clitics cliticize to a higher host, viz. *n'en pas parler* 'not to speak about it', where the head of NegP *ne*. See Sportiche (1993a) for arguments to the effect that *ne*, the head of NegP, is higher than AGR_S.

23 This standard description is somewhat incorrect if it is taken to mean that the XP* must be null, as is shown by doubling of clitics by stranded quantifiers.

24 Another property, which seems true of Romance and is related to problem #2 below in the text, appears to be the following: if Clitic Doubling is allowed of accusatives, it is allowed of datives (but not vice versa).

25 The idea that XP*/XP^ coexists with a clitic and that only one of them may surface is not unlike Kayne's (1972) analysis of French subject clitic constructions. A similar idea with *wh*-movement is developed in Cheng (1991). At this point the formulation in (41) is tentative in particular concerning the set of relevant properties that (41) is sensitive to.

26 This view is essentially Kayne's (1989b). Many questions relating to object agreement will not be addressed here. A detailed look at this proposal and its implications is found in Sportiche (1990). There and in Chomsky (1991) (see also Mahajan 1990, for closely related although somewhat different views), it is argued that participle agreement with Case marked DPs is limited to accusative DPs, the two properties being different reflexes of the same underlying configuration. Detailed discussions of many complex case are also examined there.

27 Let us note that this analysis of clitic placement is consistent with that of Sportiche (1989, 1990). The present analysis specifies that the position XP' of the text about (45) is XP^, or is reached after movement through XP^. We conclude later that it is indeed XP^.

28 Though there exists an agreement asymmetry between *wh*-movement and clitic placement. We use the fact that skipping is necessary for *wh*-movement to reinforce the plausiblity of this approach for the optionality of agreement under clitic placement. The facts are more complex: agreement with *wh*-movement, when it takes place, belongs to a more formal register than agreement with clitic placement (Burzio 1986 reports the same observation for Italian). Furthermore, as Kayne (1989b) discusses, there are varieties of Romance which have agreement with clitics and lack agreement with *wh*-phrases (as standard Italian). The reverse situation is not found.

29 See Kayne (1984) for a discussion of the differences and similarities with *wh*-movement as far as the ECP, etc. is concerned.

30 Rightward incorporation of the subject clitic *il* in Complex Inversion constructions or Subject Clitic inversion are such instances *(Louis) est-il fatigué/?* 'Is Louis/he tired?'. See Sportiche (1993b) for further discussion.

31 This is not the only option. Another option is to revise the theory of agreement to make all species of agreement related to head movement, as attempted in a talk given by Taraldsen at the 1992 GLOW conference.

32 Kayne expresses doubts as to the correctness of a Restructuring approach to Clitic Climbing. The general issue here is one of domain extension: clitic placement or Object preposing (see below (53)) can operate over a larger domain (two clauses) than otherwise possible. The earlier approaches made Restructuring collapse two clauses into one, by incorporating the bottom verb into the top one. These approaches are no longer compatible with basic theoretical principles but their effect can be mimicked by head movement of some head in the lower clause to the main clause with a concomitant domain extension —see Sportiche (1990). Kayne in fact adopts such an approach as we see below: his Restructuring is raising of the bottom INFL to the top one.

33 This (somewhat marginal) case of Restructuring requires the higher verb to be in a subjunctive mood. Apparently, the same facts hold of Catalan.

34 See Kayne (1991) for arguments that *se* is a complementizer.

35 We conclude later that clitic placement is also A-bar movement of a different sort than *wh*-movement. Clitic Climbing over a *wh*-phrase is nevertheless allowed, either because of this difference (reflected in the fact that SPEC, CP is not a possible intermediate site for XP*) or because Italian allows *wh*-island violations.

36 Throughout this section *en* is meant to be the genitive complement of nominals and adjectives and not the *en* of quantity, unless otherwise indicated.

37 One significant consequence that we elaborate on later in section 6.3.

38 Dative or locative XPs do not license PGs, quite generally and for poorly understood reasons. In the case of datives, it might be related to the specifier of Dative Voice being an A-position, especially if Mahajan's (1991) approach concerning the analysis of parasitic gaps is correct. Only structurally Case-marked NPs appear to license parasitic gaps, i.e., nominatives, accusatives and genitives. Relevant configurations cannot be constructed for nominative clitics.

39 The reason why Rizzi uses complex causative constructions to illustrate his point is that, in a simple clause, it is difficult to guarantee that XP* in our terms does not c-command the PG while the clitic does (especially given that at the time, the clitic was thought to be more or less inside VP). Sentences like (60b) circumvent this problem.

40 See Sportiche (1983) and Lasnik and Stowell (1991) for a more comprehensive discussion.

41 Since *Marie* is a possible antecedent for *propre* in

(i) Louis a cru [Marie$_j$ fière de ses propres$_j$ idées].
L. has believed M. proud of her own ideas
"Louis believed Marie proud of her own ideas."

a possible example might be the following, if the indicated structure is correct

(ii) *Louis l$_j$' a fait [[croire t$_j$ épuisé] à son propre$_j$ auteur].
L. him has made to-believe run-out to its own author
"Louis made its own author believe it out of print."

42 See Kayne's (1975) detailed discussions, and also Sportiche (1990).

43 Given that dative clitics have an A-position XP^, they should never license PGs. We expect that dative Scrambling in Dutch should not license PGs, as appears to be the case.

44 In embedded clauses, we would get:

(i) Omdat hij 't waarschijnlijk (*'t) niet (*'t) gezien heeft.
because he it probably not seen has
"Because he probably has not seen it."

(ii) Omdat hij Jan waarschijnlijk (Jan) niet (*Jan) gezien heeft.
because he J. probably not seen has
"Because he probably has not seen Jan ."

Koopman notes that care should be taken to avoid contrastive or focal stress on the objects.

45 Koopman offers many other arguments not reproduced here; e.g., pied-piping of non-specific DPs is obligatory under VP-preposing, but not for specific DPs. In addition, clitics exhibit Clitic Climbing.

46 One potential difference with Romance clitics is whether the order of clitics is fixed or not. Dutch or German may substandardly allow for alternative clitic orderings.

47 In other words, it is apparently blocked by a certain type of INFL material—accusative Scrambling may violate the SSC but may not violate the Tensed S Condition.

48 In particular, the reasoning we appealed to in section 6.3

49 We intend the analogy with *wh*-movement to be pushed as far as possible. Thus, Specific DPs in PPs or complements to Ns, adjectives, etc., will be licensed under movement to the specifier of a specificity-licensing head (situated in the structure

presumably where Romance clitics are) very much in the way *wh*-phrases in situ are licensed in the framework of the *Wh*-Criterion, i.e., by covert movement, pied-piping, etc.

50 Sportiche (1993b) shows that this conclusion for objects extends to French nominatives as well ,except for the indefinite *on* 'one'. Just as in the object cases, there might be crosslinguistic variation here: Trentino subject clitics have been argued not to license specificity and thus constitute a nominative counterpart to our analysis of datives.

51 We will not elaborate on this last proposal here but I would conjecture that a number of facts can be linked to this proposal: (i) the obligatory presence of the dative clitic *le* in dialects of Spanish in *wh*-extraction of an indirect object (e.g., *A quién *(le) regalaron un auto?* 'Who did they give a car to', (ii) participle agreement with superficial subject in indirect object reflexive constructions with nonclitic direct objects (e.g., *Maria si è comprata/??comprati libri /Maria se li è *comprata/comprati.* 'Maria bought books/them for herself', and similar (dialectal) facts in French, e.g., *Marie s'est construit(e) un abri.* 'Marie built a shelter for herself'.

52 I would conjecture that the cases of doubled clitics such as *Je le veux le voir.* 'I want to see him.' found in certain Romance dialects or in child speech reflect a stage or a grammar in which the clitic *le* is treated as a pure agreement marker.

53 Some phenomena we do not discuss here at all are the so-called accusative Case markers in languages like Hebrew or Turkish. Given that they are linked to specificity, they should be viewed as the analog of Clitic Doubling particles rather than Case-markers.

54 Thanks to A. Comorovski, C. Dobrovie Sorin, D. Steriade, M. Suñer and M-L. Zubizarreta for their help with the judgments of Romanian and Spanish in this section.

REFERENCES

Aoun, Joseph: 1981, *The Formal Nature of Anaphoric Relations*, unpublished Ph.D. dissertation, MIT.

Aoun, Joseph and Robin Clark: 1985, 'On Non-Overt Operators', *Southern California Occasional Papers in Linguistics* **10**, University of Southern California.

Aoun, Joseph, Elabbas Benmamoun and Dominique Sportiche: 1994, 'Agreement, Word Order and Conjunction in Several Varieties of Arabic', *Linguistic Inquiry* **25**, 195-221.

Bennis, Hans and Teun Hockstra: 1984, 'Gaps and Parasitic Gaps', *The Linguistic Review* **4**, 29-87.

Borer, Hagit: 1983, *Parametric Syntax*, Foris, Dordrecht.

———: 1986, *The Syntax of Pronominal Clitics*, Syntax and Semantics 19, Academic Press, Orlando.

Bouchard, Denis: 1982, *On the Content of Empty Categories*, unpublished Ph.D. dissertation, MIT.

Burzio, Luigi: 1986, *Italian Syntax*, D. Reidel, Dordrecht.

Chiu, Bonnie: 1992, *The Syntax of Functional Words in Chinese*, unpublished Ph.D. dissertation, University of California, Los Angeles.

Cheng, Lisa: 1991, *On the Typology of Wh-Questions*, unpublished Ph.D. dissertation, MIT.

Chomsky, Noam: 1981, *Lectures on Government and Binding*, Foris, Dordrecht.

———: 1982, *Some Concepts and Consequences of the Theory of Government and Binding*, MIT Press, Cambridge, MA.

———: 1986a, *Barriers*, MIT Press, Cambridge, MA.

———: 1986b, *Knowledge of Language: Its Nature, Origin, and Use*, Praeger, New York.

———: 1991, 'Some Notes on Economy of Derivation and Representation', in Robert Freidin (ed.), *Principles and Parameters in Comparative Grammar*, MIT Press, pp. 417-454.

——— 1992, 'A Minimalist Program for Linguistic Theory', *MIT Occasional Papers in Linguistics* **1**, Cambridge, MA.

Cinque, Guglielmo: 1991, *Types of A-bar Dependencies*, MIT Press, Cambridge, MA.

Cortés, Corinne: 1992, *Issues in Catalan Syntax*, unpublished Ph.D. dissertation, University of California, Los Angles.

Dobrovie-Sorin, Carmen: 1990, 'Clitic Doubling, *Wh*- Movement, and Quantification in Romanian', *Linguistic Inquiry* **21**, 351-397.

Enç, Murvet: 1991, 'The Semantics of Specificity', *Linguistic Inquiry* **22**, 1-27.

Evers, Arnold: 1975, *The Transformational Cycle in Dutch*, unpublished Ph.D. dissertation, University of Utrecht.

Giorgi Alessandra and Giuseppe Longobardi: 1991, *The Syntax of Noun Phrases: Configurations, Parameters and Empty Categories*, Cambridge University Press, Cambridge.

Haegeman, Liliane and Rafaella Zanuttini: 1991, 'Negative Heads and the Neg-criterion', *The Linguistic Review* **8**, 233-251.

Hurtado, Alfredo: 1984, 'On the Properties of LF', *Cornell Working Papers in Linguistics* **5**, Ithaca, NY.

Iatridou, Sabine: 1990, 'Clitics and Island Effects', unpublished, MIT.

Jaeggli, Oswaldo: 1982, *Topics in Romance Syntax*, Foris, Dordrecht.

———: 1986, 'Three Issues in the Theory of Clitics', in H. Borer (ed.), *The Syntax of Pronominal Clitics*, New York, Academic Press, Orlando, pp. 15-42.

Kayne, Richard: 1972, 'Subject Inversion in French Interrogatives', in J. Casagrande and B. Saciuk (eds.), *Generative Studies in Romance Languages*, Newbury House, Rowley, MA., pp. 70-126.

———: 1975, *French Syntax: The Transformational Cycle*, MIT Press, Cambridge, MA.

———: 1984, *Connectedness and Binary Branching*, Foris, Dordrecht.

———: 1988, 'Romance *se/si*', paper presented at the GLOW conference, Budapest, *GLOW Newsletter* **20**.

———: 1989a, 'Null Subjects and Clitic Climbing', in O. Jaeggli and K. Safir (eds.), *The Null Subject Parameter*, Kluwer, Dordrecht, pp. 239-261.

———: 1989b, 'Facets of Romance Past Participle Agreement', in P. Beninca (ed.), *Dialect Variation and the Theory of Grammar*, Foris, Dordrecht, pp. 85-103.

———: 1991a, 'Romance Clitics, Verb Movement and PRO', *Linguistic Inquiry* **22**, 647-686.

———: 1991b, 'Italian Negative Infinitival Imperatives and Clitic Climbing', unpublished, CUNY.

Koopman, Hilda: 1988, 'The Internal Structure of Dutch VPs', Notes to lectures given at Université de Genève, Tilburg Katholieke Universiteit and MIT.

———: 1991, 'The Verb Particle Construction and the Syntax of PPs', unpublished, University of California, Los Angeles.

———: 1993, 'Licensing Heads', in N. Hornstein and D. Lightfoot (eds.), *Verb Movement*, Cambridge University Press, Cambridge, pp. 261-297.

Koopman, Hilda and Dominique Sportiche: 1991, 'The Position of Subjects', *Lingua* **85**, 211-285.

Koster, Jan and Eric Reuland: 1991, *Long Distance Anaphora*, Cambridge University Press, Cambridge.

Lasnik, Howard and Tim Stowell: 1991, 'Weakest Crossover', *Linguistic Inquiry* **22**, 687-720.

Lebeaux, David: 1983, 'A Distributional Difference Between Reciprocals and Reflexives', *Linguistic Inquiry* **14**, 723-730.

Mahajan, Anoop: 1990, *The A/A-bar Distinction and Movement Theory*, unpublished Ph.D. dissertation, MIT.

——— 1991, 'Operator Movement, Agreement and Referentiality', *MIT Working Papers* **15**, Cambridge, MA..

May, Robert: 1985, *Logical Form*, MIT Press, Cambridge, MA.

Moltmann, Friederike: 1990, 'Scrambling in German and the Definiteness/ Specificity Effect', unpublished, MIT.

Noonan, Maire: 1992, *Case and Syntactic Geometry*, unpublished Ph.D. dissertation, McGill University.

Perlmutter, David: 1972, *Deep and Surface Structure Constraints in Syntax*, Holt, Rinehart and Winston, New York.

Pollock, Jean-Yves: 1989, 'Verb Movement, Universal Grammar and the Structure of IP', *Linguistic Inquiry* **20**, 365-424.

Rivas, A: 1977, *A Theory of Clitics*, unpublished Ph.D. dissertation, MIT.

Rizzi, Luigi: 1978, 'A Restructuring Rule in Italian Syntax', in S.J. Keyser (ed.), *Recent Transformational Studies in European Languages*, MIT Press, Cambridge, MA., pp. 113-159.

———: 1982, *Issues in Italian Syntax*, Foris, Dordrecht.

——— 1986a, 'On Chain Formation', in H. Borer (ed.),*The Syntax of Pronominal Clitics*, Academic Press, Orlando, pp. 15-42.

———: 1986b, 'On the Status of Subject Clitics in Romance', in O. Jaeggli and C. Silva Corvalán (eds.), *Studies in Romance Linguistics*, Foris, Dordrecht, pp. 391-421.

———: 1990, *Relativized Minimality*, MIT Press, Cambridge, MA..

Rizzi, Luigi and Ian Roberts: 1989, 'Complex Inversion in French', *Probus* **1**, 1-30.

Roberge, Yves: 1990, *The Syntactic Recoverability of Null Arguments*, McGill-Queen's University Press, Montreal.

Ruwet, Nicolas: 1972, *Théorie syntaxique et syntaxe du français*, Le Seuil, Paris.

———: 1969, 'A propos des prépositions de lieu en français', in C. Hyart (ed.), *Mélanges Fohalle*, Université de Liège, pp. 115-137.

Schlonsky, Ur: 1990, 'Quantifiers as Heads: a Study of Quantifier Float in Hebrew', unpublished, Haifa University.

Sportiche, Dominique: 1983, *Structural Invariance and Symmetry in Syntax*, unpublished Ph.D. dissertation, MIT, distributed by *MIT Working Papers in Linguistics*.

———: 1988, 'A Theory of Floating Quantifiers and its Corollaries for Constituent Structure', *Linguistic Inquiry* **19**, 425-449.

———: 1989, 'Le mouvement syntaxique: contraintes et paramètres', *Langages* **95**, 35-80.

———: 1990, 'Movement, Agreement and Case', unpublished, University of California, Los Angeles.

———: 1995, 'Sketch of a Reductionist Approach to Syntactic Variation and Dependencies', in H. Campos and P. Kempchinsky (eds.), *Evolution and Revolution in Romance Syntax*, Georgetown University Press, Washington, D.C.

———: 1993, 'Subject Clitics in French and Romance, Complex Inversion and Clitic Doubling', unpublished, University of California, Los Angeles.

Stowell, Tim: 1991, 'Small Clause Restructuring', in R. Freidin (ed.), *Principles and Parameters in Comparative Grammar*, MIT Press, Cambridge, MA..

Strozer, Judith: 1976, *Clitics in Spanish*, unpublished Ph.D. dissertation, University of California, Los Angeles.

Suñer, Margareta: 1988, 'The Role of Agreement in Clitic Doubled Constructions' *Natural Language & Linguistic Theory* **6**, 391-434.

———: 1992, 'Two Properties of Clitics in Clitic Doubled Constructions', in J. Huang and R. May (eds.), *Logical Structure and Linguistic Structure: Cross Linguistic Perspectives*, D. Reidel, Dordrecht, pp. 233-253.

Tellier, Christine: 1991, *Licensing Theory and French Parasitic Gaps*, Kluwer, Dordrecht.

Valois, Daniel: 1991, *The Internal Syntax of DP*, unpublished Ph.D. dissertation, University of California, Los Angeles.

Varela, Anna: 1988, *Binding in Spanish: A Theoretical and Experimental Study*, unpublished Ph.D. dissertation, University of Connecticut.

Vikner, Sten: 1990, *Verb Movement and the Licensing of NP-Positions*, unpublished Ph.D. dissertation, University of Geneva.

Vergnaud, Jean-Roger and Maria-Luisa Zubizaretta: 1991, 'The Definite Determiner and the Inalienable Construction in English and French', unpublished, University of Southern California.

Zribi-Hertz, Anne: 1984, 'Prépositions orphelines and pronoms nuls', *Recherches Linguistiques* **12**, 46-91.

THE PHRASE STRUCTURE OF TENSE

Tim Stowell

0. INTRODUCTION

In this article I present an outline of a theory of phrase structure that incorporates a series of functional projections forming the basis for the interpretation of tense. Most previous theories of tense have relied on an idiosyncratic set of semantic rules to account for the distribution and interpretation of particular tense forms. The theory that I develop here seeks to derive most of the semantics of tense from independently motivated principles of syntactic theory. To this end, I introduce a minimum of new theoretical machinery, though a more complex syntactic structure is required, involving an additional functional projection dominating the verb phrase and various phonetically null elements. In this respect, the theory is in the spirit of work in the Principles and Parameters framework associated with the interpretation of argument structure, thematic roles, and pronominal reference.

Temporal interpretation is a complex affair; tense morphemes can be construed in seemingly quite different ways, depending on the interaction of several factors, including scope relations with other tenses, verbal aspectual class (stative vs. eventive), grammatical aspect (progressive vs. perfective), verbal epistemological class (intensional vs. extensional), and clause type (complement clause vs. relative clause, and finite clause vs. infinitive). Needless to say, I cannot discuss all of these issues here. I will concentrate on the phrase structure associated with the English morphemes *present* and *past* and the elements forming the perfect construction (*have* plus past participle). In addition, I will be concerned with the semantic interpretation of constructions containing these elements. For a fuller discussion of these and related matters, I refer the reader to Stowell (1993, 1995, to appear).

As a point of departure, I would like to consider the past perfect (pluperfect) construction illustrated in (1), mainly as a vehicle for clarifying some points of terminology.

(1) The thieves had (already) escaped when the police arrived.

There are some general points of agreement about the interpretation and morphosyntactic composition of this construction. From a morpho-syntactic perspective, the past perfect is composed of the preterite (simple past) form of the aspectual auxiliary verb *have* (*had*), followed by the past participle form of another verb. From a semantic perspective, the past perfect is used to locate an event or situation in the remote past. In the familiar rendition offered by Reichenbach (1947), the time of the event or situation associated with the thematic verb (the EVENT TIME, E) is located prior to some other time (the REFERENCE TIME, R), which is itself located prior to the time at which the full sentence is uttered (the SPEECH TIME, S).

In Reichenbach's treatment, as in many traditional descriptions of English grammar, the past perfect construction is referred to as a TENSE, one of a number of tenses in English. (Other Reichenbachian tenses include the simple present, the simple past, the future perfect, and so on.) Within the research tradition of generative grammar, however, the term TENSE has generally been used to refer specifically to the tense inflection of the finite verb form, which in English takes one of two forms: *present* or *past* (preterite). From this perspective, the perfect is not a true tense *per se*; it is a complex syntactic construction that contains Tense as one of its component parts.

Although my terminology adheres in spirit to this latter usage, I draw a further distinction between the morphological tense features (or affixes) that show up on the inflected finite verb and the abstract syntactic X-bar category TENSE (T) introduced by Pollock (1989), which plays a role in theory of phrase structure.1 I use the italicized lower-case terms *tense*, *present*, and *past* to refer to the morphological tense affixes, and the uppercase terms TENSE, PAST, and PRESENT to refer to Pollock's X-bar phrase structure heads. When referring to tenses and times in an informal way, I use regular lower-case orthography. Thus PAST is an instantiation of TENSE (T), the X-bar theoretic head of TP, while *past* is simply a morphological affix. This distinction (*past* vs. PAST, etc.) is motivated by my account of the interpretation of various constructions containing *present* and *past*, which I will touch on only very briefly here.[2]

1. THE TENSE PREDICATE AND ITS ARGUMENTS

Let us now consider the syntactic status of TENSE and its relation to the English morphological *tense* affixes. As the null hypothesis, I will assume that English *present* and *past* originate as affixes on V, and that they must be licensed by virtue of occurring syntactically in the T^0 position at some point in the mapping to Logical Form (LF), presumably by means of head-to-head verb movement. Thus, either *tense* occurs in T^0 at LF, or it occurs in some higher position at LF, and binds a chain-internal trace in the T^0 position. For my purposes, it doesn't matter precisely how *tense* and TENSE are connected in mechanical terms; the central empirical assumption is that *tense* uses the T^0 position as its 'base of operations' in the syntax of LF representations. I must emphasize that I am adopting this standard assumption only as a point of departure.

Of course, this does not tell us what the semantic content of TENSE is. Semantic analyses of Tense are diverse; it has been analyzed (a) as a sentential operator designating the time at which the truth of a sentence is to be evaluated; (b) as a referential expression denoting the Event Time or Reference Time (or some related notion); and (c) as a temporal predicate analogous to a verb. In the theory developed here, the traditional category *Tense* is broken down syntactically into its component semantic parts, roughly along the lines suggested by Zagona (1990). Tenses are dyadic predicates of temporal ordering, and as such do not refer; however, they take two time-denoting phrases as their arguments, and it is in these categories that the referential properties associated with tenses reside.

Zagona's treatment is concerned primarily with tenses in main clauses. Simplifying somewhat, she posits a tense predicate located in the head position of a functional category F^0; I will translate this into the terms of Pollock's (1989) theory of inflection, by equating her F^0 with Pollock's TENSE (T^0). Zagona's TENSE predicate selects two arguments; its internal argument (i.e. its complement) is VP, which denotes the Event Time E (according to her). The external argument of TENSE originates in the Spec of TP position and denotes the evaluation time, which for her is equivalent to the Speech Time S. The notions of Event Time and Speech Time are treated by Zagona as theta-roles assigned by the tense predicate, an idea that I will adopt here in a modified form.[3]

In Zagona's theory, the TENSE head has no intrinsic semantic content, apart from whatever theta-roles or features it assigns to its arguments. For her, the distinction between present and past tense is encoded as a feature assigned to the internal VP argument of T. If VP is assigned [+PAST], it is interpreted as bearing "a [+PAST] relation to the time of speaking". Although she states that "the ordering of times is semantic rather than syntactic in nature", she does not give a precise characterization of what that semantics is. In her view, the sole contribution of the syntax to tense interpretation is in the domain of Binding Theory, in terms of the coreference relations among temporal arguments that it allows or prohibits. For instance, a [+PAST] VP (the complement of a past tense) has the binding properties of Chomsky's (1981) R-expressions: it must be disjoint in reference to the external argument of T (the Speech Time, S). On the other hand, a [-PAST] VP (the complement of a present tense) can be bound by the external argument of T, though it need not be.

The theory that I wish to defend here adopts certain features of Zagona's account, while rejecting others. Like her, I assume that TENSE is a predicate head, taking two time-denoting arguments, and that the internal argument denotes the Event Time (E). I will also adopt her idea that the time-denoting arguments of TENSE are subject to Binding Theory, just like other types of referential expressions (pronouns, definite and indefinite descriptions, names, anaphors, etc.). However, my theory differs from hers in a number of other ways. First, I assume that temporal ordering relations are reflected in the syntax, in the form of the inherent predicative content of the TENSE predicate. Just as the inherent content of the preposition *after* specifies a temporal ordering relation holding between its two event-denoting arguments in a sentence such as *The party is after the class*, so the inherent predicative content of PAST establishes an analogous temporal ordering relation between its two arguments (S and E) in *John hit the ball*. Thus, the primary semantic function of TENSE is to temporally locate the denotation of E in relation to the denotation of its external argument. This makes it unnecessary to assume that T assigns a [+PAST] feature to its internal argument; the notion of 'past' resides in T itself, in the form of PAST (roughly synonymous with *after*).

A second difference between my theory and Zagona's is that I posit an additional functional category ZP (ZEIT-PHRASE) intervening between TP and VP; it is this ZP category that serves as the time-denoting internal argument of T, denoting the Event Time E. ZP is a referential category analogous to DP (cf. Abney (1987), Szabolcsi (1987), Stowell (1989)). Loosely speaking, ZP bears a structural relation to VP that is analogous to the relation that DP bears to NP. For the sake of concreteness, I assume that ZP denotes a time, and that some element at the ZP-level (for concreteness, an operator residing in the Spec of ZP) binds a temporal variable within VP, corresponding to Kratzer's (1988) external event argument.

Concerning the status of the external (subject) argument of T, I assume, following Zagona, that it originates in the Subject position of TP, where it is assigned a temporal theta-role by T. However, I assume no necessary connection between the temporal theta-role assigned to this position and the denotation of Speech Time (S). I will refer to this external temporal theta-role assigned by T as the Reference Time argument (R). My use of the term 'Reference Time' differs in an important way from the traditional sense of the term originating with Reichenbach (1947); I will compare these two usages further below. For present purposes, it is sufficient to think of the Reference Time argument in the following terms: like the internal ZP argument, it denotes a time, so presumably it too has the categorial status of ZP. Like the internal ZP argument, it has no fixed indexical denotation; it simply refers to a time relative to which the Event Time ZP is ordered. In a main clause, it so happens that the Reference Time ZP denotes the Speech Time S, but in subordinate clauses, it typically denotes the Event Time E of the immediately higher clause. I will discuss the mechanics of how this works later on.

Thus the sentence *John hit the ball* would have the structure in (2):

(2)

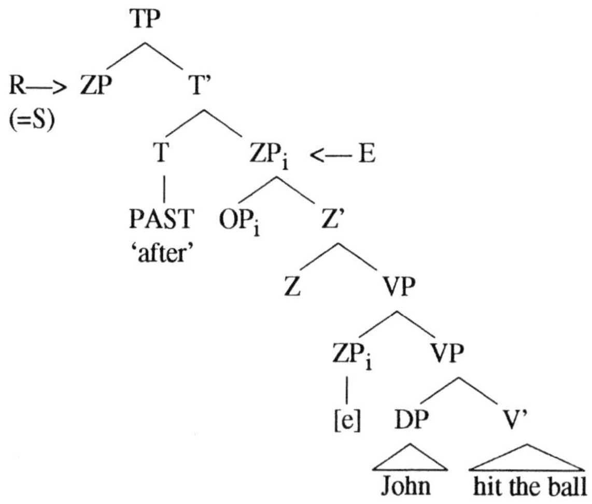

In (2), the external ZP argument of PAST is the Reference Time (here, this ZP denotes the Speech Time S); the internal ZP argument denotes the Event Time; and PAST itself establishes an ordering between these two times. The structure translates as: 'The Speech Time is after a time ZP$_i$ at which John hit the ball.'

By breaking down Tense in this way into its three component parts (TENSE, the event-time ZP, and the reference-time ZP), we can integrate each part into the theory of syntax somewhat independently of the others. This integration makes it possible to account for the complexities of tense interpretation in terms of the interaction of various familiar principles from established modules of grammar. The semantics of TENSE itself is straightforward; PAST means 'after'; *will* means (at least) 'before', and PRESENT (if it exists as a true TENSE) means 'simultaneous with' or 'overlaps'. The semantics of the Event Time ZP, the internal argument of TENSE, is analogous to that of a definite or indefinite DP. With a stative predicate, the Event Time ZP is generally understood to have definite reference; in other words, it is typically understood as referring to a time already mentioned. With an eventive predicate, the Event Time ZP can have either definite or indefinite reference: it can either refer to a time already mentioned, or it can introduce a new time.

The denotation of the Reference Time argument is fixed by Control Theory. Just as the overt complement of Tense (the Event Time ZP) is a temporal analog of a definite or indefinite DP, so the null external argument of Tense (the Reference Time ZP) is a temporal analog of PRO. When PAST occurs in a main clause, as in (2), its external Reference Time time argument is a PRO-ZP lacking any c-commanding ZP to serve as its controller; in this case, the PRO-ZP behaves like an indexical; it denotes the Speech Time S, and PAST orders the Event Time E in relation to S. When PAST occurs in a complement clause, as in (3),

(3) John said [that Bill hit the ball]

its Reference Time argument behaves like control PRO; the PRO-ZP is controlled by the closest c-commanding ZP--the temporal argument of the matrix verb (i.e. the variable bound by the head Z of the matrix Event Time ZP), as in (4).

(4)

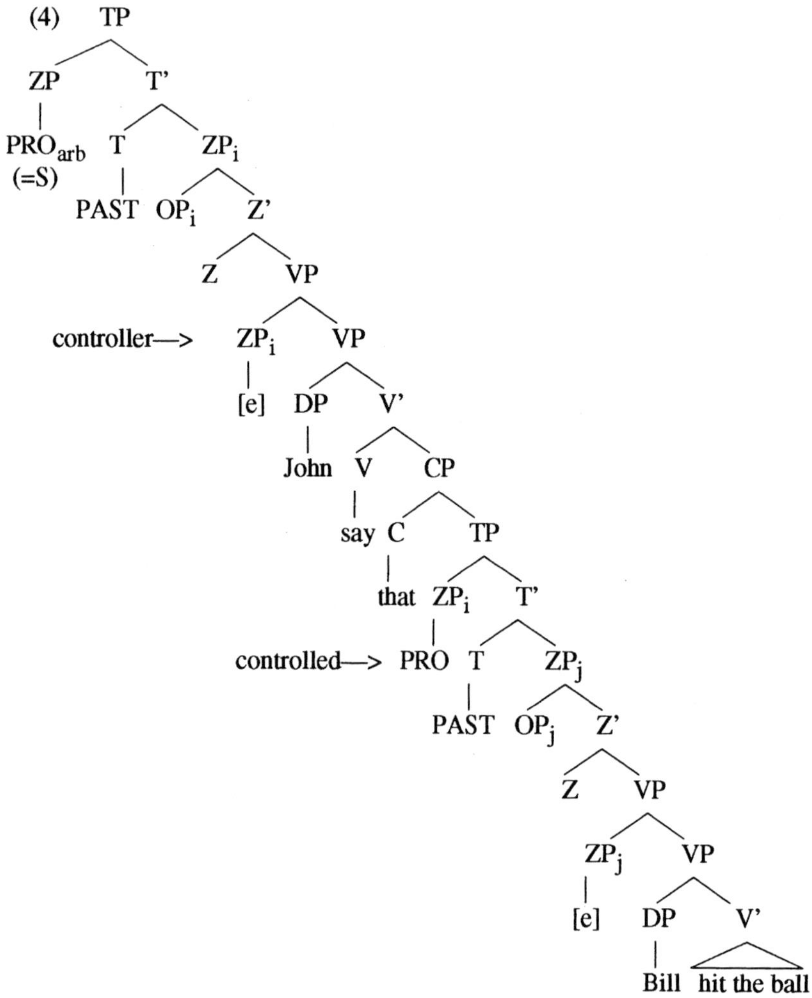

This gives rise to shifted tense construals, where the complement clause Event Time is fixed in relation to the matrix clause Event Time; the structure translates as: 'The Speech Time is after a time ZP_i at which John say that ZP_i is after a time ZP_j at which Bill hit the ball.'

In both (2) and (4), I locate the traditional subject DP within a projection of VP at D-structure. I have omitted from (2) and (4) the traditional Spec position in TP to which (or through which) the subject DP raises. This is purely for the sake of simplifying the visual presentation of the tense structure; strictly speaking, these trees are incomplete. I assume that TP contains both a thematic subject position for its external ZP argument and a nonthematic Spec position for the traditional subject DP. Subject raising is clearly insensitive to the presence of the external temporal argument of TP, just as control of PRO-ZP is insensitive to intervening DP arguments in the matrix VP. Presumably ZP control relations and DP chains can interweave through the structure because minimality conditions on binding relations are relativized in the sense of Rizzi (1990).

2. REFERENCE TIMES AND THE PERFECT CONSTRUCTION

An important feature of Zagona's thematic argument structure for tense, adopted here, is that it specifies a relation holding between just two times. This is a significant departure from Reichenbach's (1947) view, according to which tenses involve a set of relations holding between three time coordinates on a time-line diagram. Although Reichenbach's system has been largely abandoned in recent accounts of tense in the formal semantics literature, it has been widely adopted (in modified form) within the formal syntax literature, especially within the Principles and Parameters framework (see, for instance, Hornstein 1977, 1990, Bouchard 1984, Vikner 1985, and Giorgi and Pianesi 1991).

As noted above, Reichenbach's account of the English tenses provides a set of ordering relations holding among three primitive time coordinates, including not only the Event Time (E) and the Speech Time (S), but also the Reference Time (R). These time coordinates can be either simultaneous (overlapping) or discrete and temporally ordered relative to each other. Thus, the past perfect is analyzed as E-R-S (E before R; R before S); the present perfect is E-RS (E before R and S; R and S simultaneous); the simple past is supposed to be ER-S (E and R simultaneous; both before S). Reichenbach held that the semantics of every tense involves a similar scheme, arranging E, R, and S in various ways. Rephrased in terms of temporal argument structure, this is a claim that all tenses are three-place (complex) predicates of temporal ordering.

Various objections to specific analytical details of Reichenbach's treatment have been raised in the literature, mostly stemming from his lack of concern with the relationship between the morphosyntactic composition of the various tense constructions and their semantic interpretation. (Reichenbach assumed the morphosyntactic makeup of the various tenses as a given, and did not seek to provide a true syntactic analysis in the modern sense.) Bouchard (1984) and Vikner (1985) point out that one cannot provide a uniform one-to-one semantic translation for individual morphosyntactic elements in English and other languages, given Reichenbach's particular analyses of various tense constructions; they suggest a number of analytical revisions to make such a translation possible.

Comrie (1985), Vikner (1985), and Hornstein (1990) argue that Reichenbach's three-place relation involving S, R, and E draws distinctions that no natural language actually makes use of. In some cases, several Reichenbachian tenses correspond to a single natural language tense construction, as with the simple future and future perfect. These authors conclude that Reichenbach was wrong in assuming that E and S are directly ordered relative to each other, and suggest that his three-place relation should be replaced by a pair of binary relations, between S and R on the one hand, and between R and E on the other. These proposals maintain Reichenbach's notion of Reference Time more or less in the form that he proposed; they also accept his claim that all tenses involve three time-coordinates (i.e., three temporal arguments). Translated into the framework of temporal predicate argument structure adopted here, Vikner and Hornstein view each tense as a complex predicate, composed of one predicate that orders R relative to S, and another predicate that orders E relative to R.[4]

Reichenbach's Reference Time (R) provides a formalization, for the purposes of tense interpretation, of the traditional notion of point of view. This has considerable intuitive appeal, but mainly in the case of the perfect tense constructions. In the past perfect (E-R-S),the location of R between E and S captures an intuition that the event is viewed from the perspective of a past time subsequent to it. In the present perfect (E-RS),the alignment of R with S captures an intuition that the Event is being viewed from the perspective of the Speech Time. For Reichenbach, the future perfect is a conflation of three different tenses involving various relations between S and E (E-S-R, SE-R, and S-E-R), but Comrie (1985), Vikner (1985), and Hornstein (1990) all argue persuasively that there is just one future perfect tense construction, with S and E simply unordered with respect to each other.

Although there is an intuitive basis for Reichenbach's use of R in the perfect tense constructions, this is far from clear elsewhere. In the simple past (Reichenbach's ER-S), there is no intuitive sense that the event is necessarily being viewed from the perspective of the time at which it occurs, except perhaps in strings of narrative text, where other explanations for the effect are possible.[5] The same is true of the future modal *will*, which lacks any particular sense of a distinctive temporal point of view. Although the simple present tense certainly has the Speech Time as its point of view, we don't need Reichenbach's R to account for this. The bottom line seems to be that Reichenbach's R is needed only in the perfect constructions[6].

Although Reichenbach's formalism succeeds in distinguishing the simple past from the present and past perfect, one could capture the same distinctions by eliminating R from the semantic representation of the simple past, treating it simply as E-S. Similar remarks hold for the simple present, which could be characterized as ES (i.e. as a predicate indicating simultaneity of E and S). In fact some authors, notably Enç (1990), have suggested that the present tense need not be thought of as a tense at all, since it induces no temporal shift of the evaluation time away from its starting point (the Speech Time, in a main clause).

This alternative treatment of the simple present and past tenses is in keeping with the dyadic structure for tenses proposed above. Although my variation on Zagona's structure makes use of a Reference Time argument, this is not Reichenbach's notion of R. In his theory, S and R have an independent status alongside E in the argument structure of every tense. In contrast, the system proposed here does not treat the Speech Time (S) as a theta-role *per se*; the Speech Time is simply one of the possible denotations of the Reference Time argument, as in (2). Consequently, no single tense can have both S and R as independent arguments, so there is no way to represent the semantics of the past perfect or future perfect as a single tense.

On the other hand, it is relatively simple to represent the perfect tenses as complex temporal constructions, composed of two elementary tense predicates, as Vikner (1985), Zagona (1990), and many others, have recognized. This assumption allows us to derive the temporal argument structure of these constructions from their morphosyntactic structure in an obvious way. Suppose that the past participle contains a past tense predicate synonymous with PAST, so that the past, present, and future perfect tense constructions are each composed of two tenses; in this limited sense, the perfective constructions are biclausal. Suppose, further, that the perfect auxiliary *have* denotes a result state, with an Event Time argument like any other stative verb. Then the higher tense (PAST, PRESENT, or *will*) provides its usual temporal argument structure, locating the time of the result state (the time of 'having') in relation to a Reference Time (i.e. the Speech Time, in a main clause). The past participle provides an additional PAST tense, which orders the thematic verb's Event Time in relation to that of the result state. The D-structure of the past perfect in (5) emerges as (6).

(5) John had telephoned

The PrtP in (6) has a status analogous to that of the embedded clause TP in (4); its external argument PRO-ZP is controlled by the temporal argument of the minimal VP dominating it. Thus (6) translates as: 'The Speech Time is after a 'having' time ZP_i, which is after a time ZP_j, at which John telephone'. The 'having time' ZP_i in this translation of (6) corresponds to the intuitive intermediate past-time perspective point from which the main Event Time is viewed. Reichenbach's system characterizes this intermediate time simply as R; but in (6), ZP_i is both the Event Time of the higher tense predicate PAST, and the Reference Time of the perfective tense predicate *-en* PAST.

(6)

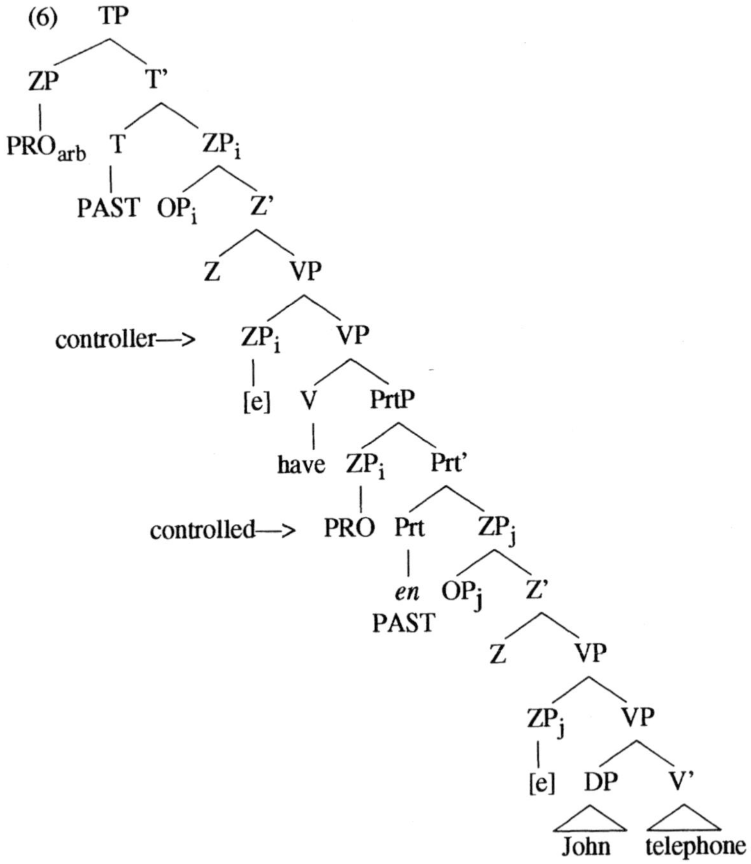

3. TEMPORAL ADVERBIALS

So far I have not discussed the status of temporal adverbial phrases. These are usually described in the literature as adjuncts, but from the perspective of the theory of temporal argument structure explored here, this notion requires some rethinking. Temporal adverbials are usually thought to denote the time of the event associated with the VP in which they occur. In terms of the structure for tense given above, this implies that temporal adverbials are associated syntactically either with the ZP complement of TENSE (its internal argument) or with the VP-internal variable (the position theta-marked by the verb as its temporal argument). It is tempting to think of the temporal adverbial as being the verb's temporal argument, replacing the VP-internal ZP variable in (2) and (4). But the variable is needed for the proper interpretation of the ZP structure, so it is more likely that temporal adverbials are adjunct modifiers, either of the VP-internal variable or of the full ZP dominating VP. (This is consistent with the adjunct-like behavior of temporal adverbials with respect to extraction.) For concreteness, I will assume that a temporal adverbial is a restricting modifier for the VP-internal variable (the verb's temporal argument). Whether or not this adverbial modifier is actually adjoined to the variable need not concern us here.

The discussion thus far has treated all temporal adverbials alike. Actually, it is well known that they are a diverse lot. Some denote intervals (*for five minutes*), and are incompatible with Vendler's (1967) achievement verbs, while others denote instantaneous points (*at ten past six*), and are incompatible with his accomplishment verbs. Some are clausal (*when Bill left the room*), while others are not (*then*). Some are indexical (*yesterday, now*), others are anaphoric (*then*) or relational (*the day before*); while others are referential (*at six o'clock*). I will not attempt to give a precise account of any of these distinctions here, but a few brief remarks are in order.

The distinctive properties exhibited by Vendler's aspectual verb classes, with respect to the kinds of adverbials that they are compatible with, clearly reveals that (at least from a semantic perspective) the notion of Event Time has a fine substructure that distinguishes among states, activities, achievements, and accomplishments. Campbell (1989) captures these distinctions in terms of thematic role assignment, by allowing the verb's argument structure to include not only the temporal interval or point corresponding to the duration of the event, but also the event's onset time and completion time. One might also conceive of Vendler's distinctions in terms of traditional S-selection, in the sense of Pesetsky (1982); just as a verb can select an animate DP argument, so it can select an interval-denoting ZP argument. The structure that I have proposed here does not provide any syntactic means for expressing Vendler's aspectual class distinctions in structural terms, and perhaps it should be enriched in order to do so. However, the differences among Vendler's event-classes (achievements, activities, and accomplishments) seem to have little effect on tense construal, apart from the well-known effects on temporal adverbial selection. On the other hand, the distinction between stative and eventive verbs is quite clearly relevant for tense construal, as virtually all studies of the syntax and semantics of tense recognize. For instance, only stative verbs can be used with the simple *present* in English, unless a generic/habitual reading is intended. Perhaps this indicates a fundamental difference between stative and eventive verbs with respect to the syntactic status of their temporal arguments, but I will not pursue this here; see Stowell (1995) for discussion.

Clausal temporal adverbials also raise interesting issues, but these mainly concern the internal structure of these clauses (e.g., concerning the application of *wh*-movement of *when* or its phonetically null twin in *after the police arrived*). One curious property of these clauses, which is surely relevant for the theory of tense, is that they must bear the same *tense*:

(7) a. John arrived when/after/before the police were (*are) here.
b. John will arrive when/after/before the police are (*were) here.

This fact probably tells us something significant about the structure of these clauses and about the logic of English *tense* morphology, but I will not speculate about these matters here. Regardless of their internal structure, these clauses behave externally like other adverbials; they denote times and function as adjunct modifiers of the Event Time variable in a similar way.

4. MORPHOLOGICAL TENSE VERSUS SYNTACTIC TENSE

I would now like to return to the question of how English *tense* relates to the syntactic category TENSE. So far, I have built a theory of tense interpretation around the idea that the head of TP, TENSE, is a temporal ordering predicate, and I have given no reason to doubt that *tense* is simply the phonological form of TENSE; in other words, *past* is the spellout of PAST. Every occurrence of *past* has been accompanied by the semantics of PAST, so it is reasonable to equate them. However, the interpretation of the subordinate clause *past* in (8) poses a problem:

(8) John said that Bill was sick

The subordinate *past* can be interpreted in two ways. First, it can refer to a time T' that is prior to John's saying time; this corresponds to the past shifted reading in (4). This past shifted reading seems to be possible with stative verbs only if T' is already under discussion,[7] suggesting that the VP-internal variable here may be bound by a null Topic ZP denoting T'.

In any event, a more serious problem concerns another reading of (8), where the Event Time of the subordinate clause (i.e. the time of Bill's state of sickness) is interpreted as being simultaneous with the main clause Event Time (the time at which John spoke). This illustrates the phenomenon of sequence of tense, where a past tense in indirect discourse corresponds to a present tense in direct quotation. The theory of tense construal advocated above incorrectly excludes this reading, if *past* means PAST, since the matrix verb's temporal argument obligatorily controls the Reference Time argument of the subordinate clause PAST, and PAST orders this time after (rather than simultaneous with) the subordinate clause Event Time. Therefore some aspect of the analysis must be revised. It would be inappropriate to abandon the control analysis of the PRO-ZP Reference Time argument, since this yields the correct result for eventive verbs. Rather, it seems that we must allow for the possibility that *past* (sometimes, at least) does not really mean PAST.

The decomposed temporal argument structure developed here suggests a possible revision to accommodate this simultaneous reading. Suppose that English *past* is really an instantiation of the head Z of the time-denoting category ZP, rather than an instantiation of T, the head of the predicative category TP. (In a sense, this represents a partial return to Enç's (1987) view that tenses are referential expressions.) Thus Z is overt (alternating between *past* and *present*) while T itself is nonovert (null), at least when it is headed by PAST or PRESENT. (Obviously the future modal *will* is overt, and this must be treated as a true tense predicate, since it never yields a simultaneous construal.) This being the case, we are free to assume that the subordinate clause in (8) contains no occurrence of PAST, so that the subordinate clause Event Time need not be ordered prior to any other time. Instead, we are free to assume that the subordinate clause contains either a null PRESENT, or perhaps no TENSE at all, in the spirit of Enç (1990). Suppose, for concreteness, that the null T in the subordinate clause is free to assume the value of either PAST or PRESENT. In the former case, the structure will yield the past shifted reading; in the latter case, it will yield the simultaneous construal.

An obvious question arises immediately, however. If *past* does not mean PAST, and does not even require the presence of PAST in the same clause, then why is it that whenever *past* occurs on a verb in a simple sentence, the Event Time is always understood as being ordered prior to the Speech Time? The idea that *present* and *past* are both instantiations of Z (rather than of T) obviously does not explain the difference between them. My answer to this question, first proposed in Stowell (1992), is developed further in Stowell (1993, to appear); I will present a synopsis of the solution here.

Recall that I have suggested that the Event Time ZP is normally interpreted in a way similar to a definite or indefinite noun phrase, with Z having a status analogous to that of a determiner. Suppose that we now draw a more articulated analogy between Z and D, by comparing *present* and *past* with the quantificational determiners *some* and *any*. It is well known that *some* and *any* can be analyzed as existential quantifiers, distinguished from each other chiefly in terms of their scopal properties; *any* must appear at LF under the scope of Negation or another downward-entailing polarity-inducing element, while *some* must appear outside the scope domain of any such element (cf. Ladusaw (1979).) Suppose that *past* is also a kind of polarity item, with an LF scope position fixed under PAST; in other words, *past* is a PAST Polarity Item (PPI). When *past* occurs as the head of the Event Time ZP in a simple clause, that clause must contain PAST in T, or else the PPI *past* would not be licensed. On the other hand, when *past* occurs in a subordinate clause, as in (8), its polarity requirements can be satisfied by virtue of its appearing at LF under the c-command domain of the matrix PAST, whose presence is forced independently by the polarity requirements of the matrix PPI *past*. Hence the subordinate clause can freely contain either (null) PAST or (null) PRESENT in its T position, providing the desired ambiguity between the past shifted and simultaneous construals in (8). On the other hand, *present* is an 'anti-PPI'; just as *some* may not occur under the scope of Negation, so *present* may not occur under the scope of PAST; for this reason, a clause containing *present* tense morphology on the finite verb must be understood to contain (null) PRESENT rather than (null) PAST in T.

This is, of course, only a sketch of an analysis; for a more thorough justification of the claim that English tense morphology encodes polarity relations, the reader is referred to Stowell (1993, to appear), where more complex structures (involving 'independent' and 'double-access' tense construals) are analyzed in these terms. However, I hope to have conveyed the basic idea of how this theory can be applied to account for the familiar phenomenon of sequence of tense, without appealing either to a sequence of tense rule or to a nonunified treatment of the semantics of *past*. It is perhaps worth observing, in this context, that the analysis of *past* as a PPI can be applied to imperfect tenses in many European languages, more or less directly. It can also be applied to the use of *past* in conditional clauses in English, which exhibits a similar polarity behavior, unrelated to any past tense meaning. On the other hand, this analysis cannot be applied either to the English perfect (which never yields a simultaneous construal) or to the perfective tenses of other languages; these must be regarded as containing a true PAST temporal ordering predicate, always resulting in a past shifted construal.

5. CONCLUSION

I have proposed a phrase structure for tense, based on the idea that TENSE is a dyadic temporal ordering predicate, taking two time-denoting phrases as its arguments, in the spirit of Zagona (1990). I have also proposed a new functional category ZP, a referential (time-denoting) category modeled on DP. In English, T is null, but Z can be instantiated overtly by either *present* or *past*, at least in a finite clause; the choice between these elements is determined by the scope of their ZP in relation to PAST at LF. The internal argument of T has the referential properties of a definite or indefinite referring expression. The external argument has the referential properties of PRO; when it occurs in a subordinate clause, its denotation is fixed by Control Theory. Finally, I have argued that it is possible to account for the semantics of tense strictly within the bounds of a dyadic argument structure, without appealing to a Reichenbachian Reference Time R distinct from the Speech Time S. The desired effects of Reichenbach's R are captured here by assuming that the perfective tense constructions contain two dyadic temporal ordering predicates, together with a verb denoting a result state.

NOTES

1 This distinction is implicit in Pollock (1989) and most other generative accounts. Nevertheless these studies generally assume that a given occurrence of morphological tense affix originates in (or must be licensed by) the X-bar head T. The theory of English tense morphology developed in Stowell (1992, 1993, to appear) explicitly rejects this assumption, in a way that will be made clear further below.

2 For fuller discussion, see Stowell (1993).

3 In addition, she suggests that this predicate sometimes assigns a theta role Reference Time, more or less in the spirit of Reichenbach's (1947) theory (see below.)

4 Actually, Vikner proposes an additional complexity that I will ignore here.

5 For instance, suppose that narrative requires a temporal ordering of events in a chronological sequence. One way to encode this formally is to suppose that the Event Time of a given sentence S will serve as the antecedent for a null Topic time-denoting phrase binding an Event Time variable in the VP of the clause immediately following S.

6 Bertinetto (1982) and Kamp and Reyle (1993) have also proposed to refine Reichenbach's notion of Reference Time, distinguishing between the notion relevant to the semantics of the perfect construction and a distinct notion relevant to temporal ordering in texts.

7 I am grateful to R. Boogaart for drawing this fact to my attention. See also fn. 5.

REFERENCES

Abney, Steven: 1987, *The English Noun Phrase in Its Sentential Aspect*, unpublished Ph.D. dissertation, MIT, Cambridge, MA.

Bertinetto, Pier Marco: 1982, 'Intrinsic and extrinsic temporal reference. On restricting the notion of 'reference time'', *Journal of Italian Linguistics*, 71-108.

Bouchard, Denis: 1984, 'Having a Tense Time in Grammar', *Cahiers Linguistiques d'Ottawa* **12**, 89-113.

Campbell, Richard: 1989, *The Grammatical Structure of Verbal Predicates*, unpublished Ph.D. dissertation, University of California, Los Angeles.

Chomsky, Noam: 1981, *Lectures on Government and Binding*, Foris, Dordrecht. Comrie, Bernard: 1985, *Tense*, Cambridge University Press, Cambridge.

Enç, Mürvet: 1987, 'Anchoring Conditions for Tense', *Linguistic Inquiry* **18**, 633-657.

———: 1990, 'On the Absence of the Present Tense Morpheme in English', unpublished, University of Wisconsin, Madison.

Giorgi, Alessandra, and Fabio Pianesi: 1991, 'Toward a Syntax of Temporal Representations', *Probus* **2**, 187-213.

Hornstein, Norbert: 1977, 'Towards a Theory of Tense', *Linguistic Inquiry* **8**, 521 57.

———: 1990, *As Time Goes By*, MIT Press, Cambridge, MA.

Kamp, Hans and Uwe Reyle: 1993, *From Discourse to Logic*, Kluwer, Dordrecht.

Kratzer, Angelika: 1988, 'Stage Level and Individual Level Predicates', in M. Krifka, (ed.), *Genericity in Natural Language*., Universität Tübingen, Tübingen.

Ladusaw, William: 1979, *Polarity Sensitivity as Inherent Scope Relations*, unpublished Ph.D. dissertation, University of Texas, Austin.

Pesetsky, David: 1982, *Paths and Categories*, unpublished Ph.D. dissertation, MIT, Cambridge, MA.

Pollock, Jean-Yves: 1989, 'Verb Movement, Universal Grammar, and the Structure of IP', *Linguistic Inquiry* **20**, 365-424.

Reichenbach, Hans: 1947, *Elements of Symbolic Logic*, MacMillan, New York.

Rizzi, Luigi: 1990, *Relativized Minimality*, MIT Press, Cambridge, MA.

Stowell, Tim: 1989, 'Subjects, Specifiers, and X-bar Theory', in M. Baltin and A. Kroch (eds.), *Alternative Conceptions of Phrase Structure*, University of Chicago Press, Chicago.

———: 1992, 'Past Polarity', paper presented at the 1992 NELS meeting, University of Ottawa, Ottawa.

———: 1993, 'Syntax of Tense', unpublished, University of California, Los Angeles.

———: 1995, 'Times, States, and Events', unpublished, University of California, Los Angeles.

———: to appear, 'What do the Present and Past Tenses Mean?', in P.M. Bertinetto, V. Bianchi, J. Higginbotham, and M. Sqartini (eds.), *Temporal Reference, Aspect and Actionality, Vol. 1: Semantic and Syntactic Perspectives*, Rosenberg & Sellier, Torino.

Szabolcsi, Anna: 1987, 'Functional Categories in the Noun Phrase', in I. Kenesei (ed.), *Approaches to Hungarian* **2**, University of Szeged.

Vendler, Zeno: 1967, *Linguistics in Philosophy*, Cornell University Press, Ithaca, New York.

Vikner, Sten: 1985, 'Reichenbach Revisited: One, Two, or Three Temporal Relations?', *Acta Linguistica Hafniensia* **19**, 81-98.

Zagona, Karen: 1990, 'Times as Temporal Argument Structure', unpublished, University of Washington, Seattle.

INDEX

Studies in Natural Language and Linguistic Theory

Managing Editors

Publications

1. L. Burzio: *Italian Syntax.* A Government-binding Approach. 1986.
ISBN Hb 90-277-2014-2; Pb 90-277-2015-0
2. W.D. Davies: *Choctaw Verb Agreement and Universal Grammar.* 1986.
ISBN Hb 90-277-2065-7; Pb 90-277-2142-4
3. K. É. Kiss: *Configurationality in Hungarian.* 1987.
ISBN Hb 90-277-1907-1; Pb 90-277-2456-3
4. D. Pulleyblank: *Tone in Lexical Phonology.* 1986.
ISBN Hb 90-277-2123-8; Pb 90-277-2124-6
5. L. Hellan and K. K. Christensen: *Topics in Scandinavian Syntax.* 1986.
ISBN Hb 90-277-2166-1; Pb 90-277-2167-X
6. K. P. Mohanan: *The Theory of Lexical Phonology.* 1986.
ISBN Hb 90-277-2226-9; Pb 90-277-2227-7
7. J. L. Aissen: *Tzotzil Clause Structure.* 1987.
ISBN Hb 90-277-2365-6; Pb 90-277-2441-5
8. T. Gunji: *Japanese Phrase Structure Grammar.* A Unification-based Approach. 1987. ISBN 1-55608-020-4
9. W. U. Wurzel: *Inflectional Morphology and Naturalness.* 1989
ISBN Hb 1-55608-025-5; Pb 1-55608-026-3
10. C. Neidle: *The Role of Case in Russian Syntax.* 1988 ISBN 1-55608-042-5
11. C. Lefebvre and P. Muysken: *Mixed Categories.* Nominalizations in Quechua. 1988. ISBN Hb 1-55608-050-6; Pb 1-55608-051-4
12. K. Michelson: *A Comparative Study of Lake-Iroquoian Accent.* 1988
ISBN 1-55608-054-9
13. K. Zagona: *Verb Phrase Syntax.* A Parametric Study of English and Spanish. 1988 ISBN Hb 1-55608-064-6; Pb 1-55608-065-4
14. R. Hendrick: *Anaphora in Celtic and Universal Grammar.* 1988
ISBN 1-55608-066-2
15. O. Jaeggli and K.J. Safir (eds.): *The Null Subject Parameter.* 1989
ISBN Hb 1-55608-086-7; Pb 1-55608-087-5
16. H. Lasnik: *Essays on Anaphora.* 1989
ISBN Hb 1-55608-090-5; Pb 1-55608-091-3
17. S. Steele: *Agreement and Anti-Agreement.* A Syntax of Luiseño. 1990
ISBN 0-7923-0260-5

Studies in Natural Language and Linguistic Theory

18. E. Pearce: *Parameters in Old French Syntax.* Infinitival Complements. 1990
ISBN Hb 0-7923-0432-2; Pb 0-7923-0433-0
19. Y.A. Li: *Order and Constituency in Mandarin Chinese.* 1990
ISBN 0-7923-0500-0
20. H. Lasnik: *Essays on Restrictiveness and Learnability.* 1990
ISBN 0-7923-0628-7; Pb 0-7923-0629-5
21. M.J. Speas: *Phrase Structure in Natural Language.* 1990
ISBN 0-7923-0755-0; Pb 0-7923-0866-2
22. H. Haider and K. Netter (eds.): *Representation and Derivation in the Theory of Grammar.* 1991
ISBN 0-7923-1150-7
23. J. Simpson: *Warlpiri Morpho-Syntax.* A Lexicalist Approach. 1991
ISBN 0-7923-1292-9
24. C. Georgopoulos: *Syntactic Variables.* Resumptive Pronouns and A' Binding in Palauan. 1991
ISBN 0-7923-1293-7
25. K. Leffel and D. Bouchard (eds.): *Views on Phrase Structure.* 1991
ISBN 0-7923-1295-3
26. C. Tellier: *Licensing Theory and French Parasitic Gaps.* 1991
ISBN 0-7923-1311-9; Pb 0-7923-1323-2
27. S.-Y. Kuroda: *Japanese Syntax and Semantics.* Collected Papers. 1992
ISBN 0-7923-1390-9; Pb 0-7923-1391-7
28. I. Roberts: *Verbs and Diachronic Syntax.* A Comparative History of English and French. 1992
ISBN 0-7923-1705-X
29. A. Fassi Fehri: *Issues in the Structure of Arabic Clauses and Words.* 1993
ISBN 0-7923-2082-4
30. M. Bittner: *Case, Scope, and Binding.* 1994
ISBN 0-7923-2649-0
31. H. Haider, S. Olsen and S. Vikner (eds.): *Studies in Comparative Germanic Syntax.* 1995
ISBN 0-7923-3280-6
32. N. Duffield: *Particles and Projections in Irish Syntax.* 1995
ISBN 0-7923-3550-3; Pb 0-7923-3674-7
33. J. Rooryck and L. Zaring (eds.): *Phrase Structure and the Lexicon.* 1996
ISBN 0-7923-3745-X
34. J. Bayer: *Directionality and Logical Form.* On the Scope of Focusing Particles and Wh-in-situ. 1996
ISBN 0-7923-3752-2

Kluwer Academic Publishers – Dordrecht / Boston / London